# the collected plays of mart crowley

# the collected plays of mart crowley

ALYSON books

The Collected Plays of Mart Crowley

© 2009 Mart Crowley

*The Boys in the Band* copyright © 1968, 1996, 2008, 2009 by Mart Crowley
*Remote Asylum* copyright © 2009 by Mart Crowley
*A Breeze From the Gulf* copyright © 1974, 1996, 2009 by Leo Productions Ltd.
*Avec Scmaltz* copyright © 2009 by Mart Crowley
*For Reasons That Remain Unclear* copyright © 1994, 1996, 2009 by Mart Crowley
*The Men from the Boys* copyright © 2003, 2009 by Mart Crowley
Introduction copyright © 2009 by Donald Spoto

*The Boys in the Band* was first published by Farrar, Straus, & Giroux: 1968

Published by Alyson Books
245 West 17th Street, Suite 1200, New York, NY 10011
www.alyson.com

**ALYSON**books

First Alyson Books edition: November 2009

Library of Congress Cataloging-in-Publication data are on file.

ISBN-10: 1-59350-146-3
ISBN-13: 978-1-59350-146-4

10   9   8   7   6   5   4   3   2   1

Cover design by Scott Idleman
Book interior by Neuwirth & Associates, Inc.

Printed in the United States of America
Distributed by Consortium Book Sales and Distribution
Distribution in the United Kingdom by Turnaround Publisher Services Ltd

This collection is for Buddy Thomas

# Contents

# Introduction

## DONALD SPOTO

It began in darkness.

In his early thirties, Mart Crowley was pitched into a fearful depression caused, as he later said with characteristic candor, by the unsettling circumstances of prolonged unemployment. A graduate of the highly esteemed drama department at the Catholic University of America, Crowley had worked on a few movies, traveled widely and had been production assistant to no less a theatrical hierarch than Elia Kazan. But with the mid-1960s came times that were frighteningly lean and, he thought, quite devoid of prospects. "I was forced to sublet my small apartment in Los Angeles, and I wondered where I was going to live, where I was going to work and how I would just survive." Then a friend telephoned, asking if he could look after her home in Beverly Hills for six weeks while she traveled. "There I was, house-sitting in all that luxury—but with nothing to do." Almost immobilized with despair, he picked up a yellow pad and started to write. The result, by the time the traveling friend returned home, was close to the finished version of *The Boys in the Band*.

But the road to the historic New York stage production of the play was neither easy nor immediate. Crowley's agent warned him that no respectable producer would back a frank, outspoken work about homosexuals in contemporary urban society. Yes, the humor was rich, but it was also uncompromisingly bawdy. And yes, the characters were sharply drawn, but they were also unusually blunt about their sexual orientation. Yes, too, the play was impatient with cant, cruelty and hypocrisy and was noteworthy for its unsentimental compassion. But up to this time, the American theater had never presented so direct a treatment about the alienation of gays in society as in *The Boys in the Band*. Gay men were not negligible, minor comic characters here, nor were they apologetic about a damned thing.

Crowley countered that the agent ought to send the play to Richard Barr, who had, a few years earlier, produced Edward Albee's *Who's Afraid of Virginia Woolf?* With that, things began to happen quickly—thanks to a chain of happy coincidences and the unwavering support of Crowley's close friend Natalie Wood, who became a kind of godmother to the play, making important professional connections on its behalf.

In early 1968, a modest workshop production of *The Boys in the Band* was staged in downtown Manhattan. Enthusiastic actors like Laurence Luckinbill and Peter White, who had read the play, recognized its considerable merit and wanted very much to participate in it—despite their agents' warnings that such a step would forthwith end their careers. They took that chance, and of course precisely the opposite occurred—as it did for players like Kenneth Nelson, Cliff Gorman and Leonard Frey. Patrons filled the few dozen seats at the Vandam Theatre every night that winter of 1968, and very quickly word got round Manhattan that *The Boys in the Band* was something not to be missed.

I saw the play several times during its subsequent midtown run of 1001 performances at Theatre Four. After the premiere there on April 4, it was notoriously difficult to obtain tickets, and the appreciative audiences regularly included the most fervent and sophisticated New Yorkers. [I remember seeing Marlene Dietrich at one performance and Jacqueline Onassis at another.] Before the clock struck 1970, Crowley's play had also become a rousing success in London, and very soon it sped into other major cities worldwide.

*   *   *

*The Boys in the Band* was drawing capacity crowds for more than a year in New York when a crowd of gay men failed to yield to a platoon of surly, abusive policemen at a pub called the Stonewall Inn, in Greenwich Village, on June 28, 1969. That event and that date were important in what came to be called Gay Liberation, and Mart Crowley's play became forever associated with a brave and sometimes bitter movement. Nothing was achieved in a day.

At the time, it was almost unimaginable for a play to present homosexuals who struggled with the accumulated hatred of ingrained, inherited prejudice and its effect on their own benighted spirits; more to the point, they were not gay characters who, at the final curtain, committed suicide, were murdered, succumbed to an addiction or were dismissed into irrelevance.

Reading the text of the play or attending a production in the post-Stonewall era, one is struck by the gallantry of Crowley's wit and by the pointed poignancy of his observations. Scenes develop organically, but the play never becomes a thesis. It certainly has a social conscience, and there is a strong subtext [here as in all his plays] that homosexuality is not merely to be tacitly accepted, or only tolerated. But *Boys* lacks that all too familiar tone of the polemic or of agitprop theatre. Two years after the premiere, Crowley said that Albee's *Virginia Woolf* "influenced me a lot, as did Hitchcock's [1948 movie] *Rope*, which gave me the idea of using confined quarters as a dramatic device."

But of course there were many "influences," and in fact, the entire Crowley corpus of plays has not so much in common with thesis-playwrights like Clifford Odets and Sidney Kingsley as with Richard Brinsley Sheridan [1751-1816; think of his classic comedies *The Rivals* and *The School for Scandal*]. Oscar Wilde [1854-1900] also comes to mind—perhaps especially *Lady Windermere's Fan* and *The Importance of Being Earnest*. Closer to our own time, Philip Barry [1896-1949] is also a literary forebear; Crowley has admitted to an enormous admiration for Barry's *Holiday* and *Hotel Universe*.

As with these literary ancestors, the agile humor of Crowley's pen is never forced; the points about [for example] bigotry and hypocrisy are never declaimed. The nine men gathered here for a birthday party are sometimes flamboyant and often uncertain about their futures, but that is what makes them, their histories and viewpoints, their issues, dilemmas and desires so recognizable and comprehensible. They have no time for subtleties, nor for the facile snobberies of modern class distinctions: they are WASPS, Catholics, Jewish and unaffiliated; they are Caucasian and African-American; well educated and uneducated. That they also elicit our uncondescending sympathy is a credit to the playwright's overarching humanity.

Carefully observing all the classical unities, *The Boys in the Band* is securely in the tradition of the well-made play; it is also wrenchingly cathartic. After an evening that is rather like a modern auto-da-fé, each character has reason for renewed hope as well as a deeper connection to someone. Michael may have a long way to go, for, after all [as Crowley said in 1970], "he's conflicted and doesn't know what he wants. But some of the other characters are well adjusted. Hank has made a very serious commitment in leaving his wife for Larry. And Harold is very well adjusted to his homosexuality: he knows his neuroses and lives with them. I'm not saying that Harold's way is the healthiest way of life, but at least he's not in the dark about himself."

These men, for the most part, reach across their misunderstandings toward a new patience with one another. Bernard and Emory, more deeply disenfranchised by the accident of race and personality than the others, limp away as supportive friends, tending one another's physical and emotional bruises. Alan, certainly in crisis over something in his marriage, returns to his wife—but not, it seems, to anything like marital bliss. Harold, whose laser insight cannot alleviate his own psychic pain, brutally diagnoses the source of Michael's habitual self-torture—and yet he promises the long arm of ongoing friendship.

Crowley's most moving scene, however, is reserved for the finale, in which he recapitulates and renews the bond between the self-loathing Michael and the loyal Donald. No one is destroyed during this dark night of the spirit; to the contrary, each is illumined, and there is the distinct impression that healing is possible—perhaps even likely.

Of course, *Boys* is a play of its time—what significant work of dramatic art is not? So is Lorraine Hansberry's classic *A Raisin in the Sun*, which deals with what is now called low self-esteem among poor black people. So is *Hamlet*, about an emotional block in the heart of a confused young Danish prince who doesn't much like his family. It is not mere reductionism to say that these plays are, among other things, cautionary tales.

In this regard, American society once held it as a self-evident truth that gays and blacks ought indeed to be full of self-loathing: "If only we could just learn not to hate ourselves so very much," as Michael says in *Boys*; for all his faux sophistication, he thus reveals himself as the most victimized character of the lot—we do not all hate ourselves so very much, dear. Battles can be won with characters like Michael, but skirmishes erupt within and around him from time to time.

\* \* \*

In the autumn of 2002, I was in the San Francisco audience for the world premiere of *The Men From the Boys*, one of the few successful sequel plays in American theater history.

Except for Cowboy, Alan and Larry, all the original characters from *The Boys in the Band* are here—in important ways, they've been chastened by time and age, by chance and choice. They don't seem to have quite the cunning and guile of their youth, and the earlier edge of contempt that flashed so blithely has been mercifully softened. But there is still the healthy reaction against double standards, and an awareness that cruelty gets you nowhere—there is nothing like Michael's telephone game in *Boys*, nothing like his verbal attack on Alan. The men haven't become wisdom-figures or exemplars for younger gays: Crowley is too savvy about human nature for that, and besides, young men rarely want role models.

One of the new boys is alert enough to recognize the significance of enduring camaraderie among the elders: "How could anybody's younger friends stand up next to you guys . . . for longevity of friendship?" In a crucial way, of course, friendship is at the emotional core of both plays. "Before there were marches, there was a band," says Emory, now sixty-two, campy and valiant as ever. He and the boys once led that band; as men, they still do, but now the music is muted.

*Boys* was set at a birthday party; it's noteworthy that *Men* occurs at a "celebration of life" for one of them, recently deceased. The clan gathers, six old friends and three arrivistes. Of course there's an undertaste of melancholy beneath the awkward festivity, and we see what raw, tested courage has attended the maturation of these older men, now leaning from both sides against the fulcrum of age sixty. "Getting old is the greatest sin in America," observes Harold, his sharpness unblunted by the years. For the most part, the men who were once boys seem to have accepted aging with admirable grace, not just steely stoicism. They sin boldly, and they revel in the prerogatives of age.

Among Crowley's remarkable achievements in *Men*—as in *Remote Asylum* and *A Breeze from the Gulf*, is a kind of Chekhovian wistfulness, a calm meditation on life's fundamental fragility and a refusal to luxuriate in anger. In *Men*, for example, Michael speaks not only for himself when he tells young Scott, "I don't know how I survived . . . I met people who were smarter and wiser than I was, and I learned from them—like I've tried to pass on things to you. Like believing in yourself. Your self: the thing that you feel when you go through a revolving door—that post, that center, that something unshakeable around which everything else spins."

At the end, there is the certainty of fresh challenge and inevitable heartbreak—realities that will, however, be leavened by the kind of deep solidarity that only true friendship effects. "Call you tomorrow!" was Harold's exit line to Michael in *Boys*—just as it is in *Men*, and just as it will be as they face a future of darkness, diminishment and the sort of devotion that has nothing to do with Eros.

\*    \*    \*

*Remote Asylum*, which opened at the Ahmanson, Los Angeles, in December 1970, is surely Crowley's most poetically allusive work, demanding a great deal from a gifted cast and no less from an attentive audience. The dialogue leaps and changes color, spinning a kind of gossamer web to bind and then set free characters who would really prefer not to have come together in this apparently idyllic setting. The play was in good hands with the likes of actors William Shatner, Anne Francis and Nancy Kelly.

*Asylum* presents a group of bruised souls—wanderers all, forced to deal with their fears of loneliness and mortality and to open past emotional wounds not yet healed. At first, they seem to be on the perfect holiday—"a little bit of heaven," as one of them says. But this odyssey has not brought them to paradise: the summer heat in fact becomes a suffocating inferno until [as in all Crowley's plays] there is the purgatorial breakthrough in a strong, painful recognition scene that is classical in its force and resonance. The emotional temperature rises. Tempers flare. As I read this play, I sometimes think of it as a hallucinatory movie—the sort of thing Ingmar Bergman or Federico Fellini might have transposed had they come to America. Like them, Crowley is too honest to suggest an easy transfer from the purgatorio right on to empyrean bliss.

In this regard, the conversations in *Remote Asylum* suggest the orchestration of a dramatic tone poem. "We all need a rest," as Tom says. "We need to get away. We're tired. It's the end of the tour." In staccato speech like this, which is typical of the play, tennis pro Tom speaks of recent sports events, but of course there's another timbre in the words, as there is in much of *Asylum*'s double-edged language—spare, lean, sometimes terrifying, always provocative. The "tour" suggests a play as much as an athletic enterprise—a sense not lost on the other characters.

Crowley took an enormous risk here, and his courage paid off: the crucial character of Ray [played by the venerable Arthur O'Connell] never utters a word right up to the moment of his on-stage death. He is, however, more present to himself than he is to the others, for all their self-absorbed chatter— virtually a silent, gently accusatory wisdom-figure. "In the end, it's simply easier to tell the truth," says Michael, who seems once again [and will be yet once more, in *A Breeze from the Gulf*] the playwright's alter ego, with appropriate emendations. The kind of truth-telling that Michael enjoins is very much the honorable achievement of the Crowley catalogue.

In this regard, it's interesting to recall that, the year after *Remote Asylum*, Edward Albee's *All Over* also explored the theme of death without trans-figuration, and when you read Crowley's play you may think of Albee's— and perhaps, too, of a lesser work than these, Tennessee Williams's *The Milk Train Doesn't Stop Here Anymore*, which twice had a sad fate on Broadway, in 1963 and 1964. Williams, Albee and Crowley were frequently absorbed by the notion of death as it haunts the privileged classes. This is not a theme guaranteed to please audiences, but Mart Crowley does it without homiletics, and always with gentle compassion.

\* \* \*

*A Breeze from the Gulf*, which opened Off-Broadway in October 1973, is a kind of dream-like memory piece covering ten years in the life of three characters. The play is a series of fluid scenes that bend backward and forward in time, as the fearful yet feisty Michael [a role created by Robert Drivas] and his parents Teddy and Loraine [Scott McKay and Ruth Ford] feint and parry. Irresistibly moving, *Breeze* seems to me in the tradition of Williams's *The Glass Menagerie* and O'Neill's *A Long Day's Journey into Night*. But the voice and tone are Crowley's own. Michael, whom we follow from boyhood to young adulthood, has to deal with a mother addicted to drugs and a father dependent on liquor. There's a grim humor that prevents the play from being only a dark exorcism of past ghosts, and there is the distinct impression that Michael will be haunted in the future by the specter of being gay in a hostile culture.

*Breeze* is a grave and intense drama, not a gauzy memoir with a neat and comforting resolution. The terrified mother, clinging desperately to her "baby" even when he's in his twenties, slips into a tragic psychosis; the father succumbs to a heart attack, whispering, as he dies in his son's arms, the words recalled by other characters in other Crowley plays: "I don't understand any of it. I never did." The prevailing mood of *Breeze* is one of profound compassion, which is not just a word but also an ideal: "I'm glad that you are patient and understanding," says Teddy. "It's a mark of compassion—how I love that word. A great and happy virtue. One that if cultivated can be your source of future great joy."

\* \* \*

*Avec Schmaltz* seems, at first, a straightforward play about marital grumblings—but in this playwright's hands, you can count on it that there will be all sorts of surprising complexities. Originally performed at the Williamstown Theatre Festival in 1984 as *The Spirit of It All*, the play concerns a perilously smug, comfortable family on the brink of dissolution. Again, people unwittingly embark on a kind of odyssey—this time in the two acts that move from Christmas in Connecticut to New Year's Eve in California. The marriage of Kit and Manny [roles created by Marsha Mason and James Naughton] has produced two precocious, sassy children; if I read the play correctly, this is a sterile family in every other way. Lovers and would-be lovers enter and exit, and there is no facile resolution for characters steeping in self-pity but still very much alive and clinging to what relational lifeboats they may be tossed. [The cast also included twenty-five-year-old Kevin Spacey, who had one Broadway credit but was then unknown to movie audiences.]

Crowley's acute observations puncture the characters' pretenses: "Everybody named Wendy has jewelry," says Kit, who, at the finale speaks the grave, graceful point of the play:

"There ought to be some little something that just naturally comes from loving someone—some gentle, effortless benefit—something that innately, ineffably enriches—that is graciously given on its own. It shouldn't have to be such hard work all the time. So relentlessly uphill. So patently unrewarding. Something must be shared—a thought, a laugh, half the weary load . . . "

For me, the quiet center of *Avec Schmaltz* is a relationship we never see but are asked to trust—that of Jim, who has died, and Colin, his survivor. "Jim and I were real, true friends," Colin tells his old friend Manny. "Not just lovers—best friends. It happens when you hang in with each other long enough, surviving what life has in store for you. And the night he died is the night I needed another friend—and I thought it was you." I won't spoil the surprises and the great reading pleasure to be had as you turn the pages of *Avec Schmaltz* for the first time. Watch out for Colin's dashed and dreadful hopes, and Manny's astonished heart . . .

*   *   *

"There's something very poignant," as Patrick says in *For Reasons That Remain Unclear*, "about the frailty of a group of vulnerable human beings, struggling valiantly against their darker instincts." I attended the first performance of that remarkable play, too—at the venerable Olney Theatre, in November 1993. Patrick's words are a fair summary of the playwright's wise, witty, grave and astonishingly affirmative vision of human possibility in all his works. *Reasons*, whose narrative and dramatic fulcrum is a long past incident of clerical sexual abuse acted out against a boy, is a theme ripe for easy exploitation—but Mart Crowley has too much respect for human complexity to opt for lurid, facile analysis. This two-character play [first performed by Philip Anglim and Ken Ruta] is a constant wonder, not least of all because it deals directly with the nature of forgiveness, which seems not to have much currency in today's contemporary literature and drama.

We are fortunate to have these six plays in a single volume at last. Families in crisis, lonely souls battering at the gate of heaven: in many ways, they are all fearful adolescents. Mart Crowley pushed back the frontiers of what was possible for gay playwrights and characters. Sometimes he accomplished this wittily, sometimes with calm, insistent rue. Always, he remains more than a "gay playwright" writing "gay plays." He seems to have had no such self-restricting agenda, and so he can limn portraits of recognizable antagonists in a variety of situations. He gets under their skin—and so under ours, too. Holding the mirror up to nature, he diagnoses—with unflinching empathy, uncanny insight and leavening humor—much of the spiritual sickness of our time. This he achieves without the alienating rage, the facile negativity or the easy smugness of lesser writers. In the last fifty years, few dramatists have developed his unerring instinct for stagecraft—and few have found so distinctive a voice on behalf an important, marginalized group in American society. We owe him an enormous debt of gratitude for his singular benevolent voice.

May 2009

**DONALD SPOTO** earned his Ph.D. degree from Fordham University. He is the author of twenty-five books published in many languages—among them internationally best-selling biographies of Alfred Hitchcock, Tennessee Williams, Laurence Olivier, Ingrid Bergman, Audrey Hepburn and Grace Kelly. He is married to the Danish academic administrator and artist Ole Flemming Larsen; they live in a quiet village, an hour's drive from Copenhagen.

# The Boys in the Band

For
Howard Jeffrey
and
Douglas Murray

*The Boys in the Band* was first performed in January 1968 at the Playwrights Unit, Vandam Theatre, Charles Gnys, managing director.

*The Boys in the Band* was first produced on the New York stage by Richard Barr and Charles Woodward Jr. at Theatre Four on April 14, 1968. The play was designed by Peter Harvey and directed by Robert Moore.

The original cast was:

| | |
|---|---|
| MICHAEL | *Kenneth Nelson* |
| DONALD | *Frederick Combs* |
| EMORY | *Cliff Gorman* |
| LARRY | *Keith Prentice* |
| HANK | *Laurence Luckinbill* |
| BERNARD | *Reuben Greene* |
| COWBOY | *Robert La Tourneaux* |
| HAROLD | *Leonard Frey* |
| ALAN | *Peter White* |

The play is divided into two acts. The action is continuous and occurs one evening within the time necessary to perform the script.

Characters:

| | |
|---|---|
| MICHAEL | Thirty, average face, smartly groomed |
| DONALD | Twenty-eight, medium-blond, wholesome American good looks |
| EMORY | Thirty-three, small, frail, very plain |
| LARRY | Twenty-nine, extremely handsome |
| HANK | Thirty-two, tall, solid, athletic, attractive |
| BERNARD | Twenty-eight, Negro, nice-looking |
| COWBOY | Twenty-two, light-blond, muscle-bound, |
| HAROLD | Thirty-two, dark, lean, strong limbs, unusual Semetic face |
| ALAN | Thirty, aristocratic, Anglo-Saxon features |

# Act I

*A smartly appointed duplex apartment in the East Fifties, New York, consisting of a living room and, on a higher level, a bedroom. Bossa nova music blasts from a phonograph.*

*MICHAEL, wearing a robe, enters from the kitchen, carrying some liquor bottles. He crosses to set them on a bar, looks to see if the room is in order, moves toward the stairs to the bedroom level, doing a few improvised dance steps en route. In the bedroom, he crosses before a mirror, studies his hair—sighs. He picks up comb and a hair dryer, goes to work.*

*The downstairs front door buzzer sounds. A beat. MICHAEL stops, listens, turns off the dryer. More buzzing. Michael quickly goes to the living room, turns off the music, opens the door to reveal DONALD, dressed in khakis and a Lacoste shirt, carrying an airline zipper bag.*

MICHAEL: Donald! You're about a day and a half early!

DONALD: [*Enters*] The doctor canceled!

MICHAEL: Canceled! How'd you get inside?

Donald: The street door was open.

MICHAEL: You wanna drink?

DONALD: [*Going to bedroom to deposit his bag*] Not until I've had my shower. I want something to work out today—I want to try to relax and enjoy *something.*

MICHAEL: You in a blue funk because of the doctor?

DONALD: [*Returning*] Christ, no. I was depressed long before I got *there.*

MICHAEL: Why'd the prick cancel?

DONALD: A virus or something. He looked awful.

MICHAEL: [*Holding up a shopping bag*] Well, this'll pick you up. I went shopping today and bought all kinds of goodies. Sandalwood soap . . .

DONALD: [*Removing his socks and shoes*] I feel better already.

MICHAEL: [*Producing articles*] . . . Your very own toothbrush because I'm sick to death of your using mine.

DONALD: How do you think *I* feel.

MICHAEL: You've had worse things in your mouth. [*Holds up a cylindrical can*] And, also for you . . . something called "Control." Notice nowhere is it called hair spray—just simply "Control." And the words "For Men" are written about thirty-seven times all over the goddamn can!

DONALD: It's called Butch Assurance.

MICHAEL: Well, it's *still* hair spray—no matter if they call it "*Balls*"! [*Donald laughs*] It's all going on your very own shelf, which is to be labeled: Donald's Saturday Night Douche Kit. By the way, are you spending the night?

DONALD: Nope. I'm driving back. I still get very itchy when I'm in this town too long. I'm not that well yet.

MICHAEL: That's what you say every weekend.

DONALD: Maybe after about ten more years of analysis I'll be able to stay one night.

MICHAEL: Maybe after about ten more years of analysis you'll be able to move back to town permanently.

DONALD: If I live that long.

MICHAEL: You will. If you don't kill yourself on the Long Island Express-way some early Sunday morning. I'll never know how you can tank up on martinis and make it back to the Hamptons in one piece.

DONALD: Believe me, it's easier than getting here. Ever had an anxiety attack at sixty miles an hour? Well, tonight I was beside myself to get to the doctor—and just as I finally make it, rush in, throw myself on the couch, and vomit out how depressed I am, he says, "Donald, I have to cancel tonight—I'm just too sick."

MICHAEL: Why didn't you tell him you're sicker than he is?

DONALD: He already knows *that*.

[*Donald goes to the bedroom, drops his shoes and socks. Michael follows*]

MICHAEL: Why didn't the prick call you and cancel? Suppose you'd driven all this way for nothing?

DONALD: [*Removing his shirt*] Why do you keep calling him a prick?

MICHAEL: Whoever heard of an analyst having a session with a patient for two hours on Saturday evening?

DONALD: He simply prefers to take Mondays off.

MICHAEL: Works late on Saturday and takes Monday off—what is he, a psychiatrist or a hairdresser?

DONALD: Actually, he's both. He shrinks my head and combs me out. [*Lies on the bed*] Besides, I had to come in town to a birthday party anyway. Right?

MICHAEL: You had to remind me. If there's one thing I'm not ready for, it's five screaming queens singing "Happy Birthday."

DONALD: Who's coming?

MICHAEL: They're really all Harold's friends. It's *his* birthday and I want everything to be just the way he'd want it. I don't want to have to listen to him kvetch about how nobody ever does anything for anybody but themselves.

DONALD: Himself.

MICHAEL: Himself. I think you know everybody anyway—they're the same old tired fairies you've seen around since the day one. Actually, there'll be seven, counting Harold and you and me.

DONALD: Are you calling me a screaming queen or a tired fairy?

MICHAEL: Oh, I beg your pardon—six tired screaming fairy queens and one anxious queer.

DONALD: You don't think Harold'll mind my being here, do you? Technically, I'm *your* friend, not his.

MICHAEL: If she doesn't like it, she can twirl on it. Listen, I'll be out of your way in just a second. I've only got one more thing to do.

DONALD: Surgery, so early in the evening?

MICHAEL: Sunt! That's French, with a cedilla. [*Gives him a crooked third finger, goes to mirror*] I've just got to comb my hair for the thirty-seventh time. MICHAEL (CONT'D): Hair—that's singular. My hair, without exaggeration, is clearly falling on the floor. And *fast,* baby!

DONALD: You're totally paranoid. You've got plenty of hair.

MICHAEL: What you see before you is a masterpiece of deception. My hairline starts about here. [*Indicates his crown*] All this is just tortured forward.

DONALD: Well, I hope, for your sake, no strong wind comes up.

MICHAEL: If one does, I'll be in terrible trouble. I will then have a bald head and shoulder-length fringe. [*Runs his fingers through his hair, holds it away from his scalp, dips the top of his head so that Donald can see. Donald is silent*] Not good, huh?

DONALD: Not the best.

MICHAEL: It's called, "getting old." Ah, life is such a grand design—spring, summer, fall, winter, death. Who*ever* could have thought it up?

DONALD: No one *we* know, that's for sure.

MICHAEL: [*Turns to study himself in the mirror, sighs*] Well, one thing you can say for masturbation . . . you certainly don't have to look your best. [*Slips out of the robe, flings it at Donald. Donald, laughs, takes the robe, exits to the bath. Michael takes a sweater out of a chest, pulls it on*] What are you so depressed about? I mean, other than the usual *everything*.

[*A beat*]

DONALD: [*Reluctantly*] I really don't want to get into it.

MICHAEL: Well, if you're not going to tell me, how can we have a conversation *in depth*—a warm, rewarding, meaningful friendship?

DONALD: Up yours!

MICHAEL: [*Southern accent*] Why, Cap'n Butler, how you talk!

[*Pause. Donald appears in the doorway holding a glass of water and a small bottle of pills. Michael looks up*]

DONALD: It's just that today I finally realized that I was *raised* to be a failure. I was *groomed* for it. [*A beat*]

MICHAEL: You know, there was a time when you could have said that to me and I wouldn't have known what the hell you were talking about.

DONALD: [*Takes some pills*] Naturally, it all goes back to Evelyn and Walt.

MICHAEL: Naturally. When doesn't it go back to Mom and Pop? Unfortunately, we all had an Evelyn and a Walt. The crumbs! Don't you love that word—crumb? Oh, I love it! It's a real Barbara Stanwyck word. [*A la Stanwyck's frozen-lipped Brooklyn accent*] "Cau'll me a keab, you kr-rumm."

DONALD: Well, I see all vestiges of sanity for this evening are now officially shot to hell.

MICHAEL: Oh, Donald, you're so serious tonight! You're fun-starved, baby, and I'm eating for two! [*Sings*] "Forget your troubles, c'mon, get happy! You better chase all your blues away. Shout Hallelujah! C'mon get happy . . ." [*Sees Donald isn't buying it*] —what's more boring than a queen doing a Judy Garland imitation?

DONALD: A queen doing a Bette Davis imitation.

MICHAEL: Meanwhile—back at the Evelyn and Walt Syndrome.

DONALD: America's Square Peg and America's Round Hole.

MICHAEL: Christ, how sick analysts must get of hearing how mommy and daddy made their darlin' into a fairy.

DONALD: It's beyond just that now. Today I finally began to see how some of the other pieces of the puzzle relate to them. Like why I never finished anything I started in my life . . . my neurotic compulsion to not succeed. I've realized it was always when I failed that Evelyn loved me the most—because it displeased Walt, who wanted perfection. And when I fell short of the mark she was only too happy to make up for it with her love. So I began to identify failing with winning my mother's love. And I began to fail on purpose to get it. I didn't finish Cornell—I couldn't keep a job in this town. I simply retreated to a room over a garage and scrubbing floors in order to keep alive. Failure is the only thing with which I feel at home. Because it is what I was taught at home.

MICHAEL: Killer whales is what they are. Killer whales. How many whales could a killer whale kill . . .

DONALD: A lot, especially if they get them when they were babies.

[*Pause. Michael suddenly tears off his sweater, throws it in the air, letting it land where it may, whips out another, pulls it on as he starts down the stairs for the living room. Donald follows*]

Hey! Where're you going?

MICHAEL: To make drinks! I think we need about thirty-seven!

DONALD: Where'd you get *that* sweater?

MICHAEL: This clever little shop on the right bank called Hermès.

DONALD: I work my ass off for forty-five lousy dollars a week *scrubbing* floors and you waltz around throwing cashmere sweaters on them.

MICHAEL: The one on the floor in the bedroom is vicuña.

DONALD: I *beg* your pardon.

MICHAEL: You could get a job doing something else. Nobody holds a gun to your head to be a charwoman. That is, how you say, your neurosis.

DONALD: Gee, and I thought it's why I was born.

MICHAEL: Besides, just because I *wear* expensive clothes doesn't necessarily mean they're paid for.

DONALD: That is, how you say, *your* neurosis.

MICHAEL: I'm a spoiled brat, so what do I know about being mature? The only thing mature means to me is *Victor* Mature, who was in all those pictures with Betty Grable. [*Sings à la Grable*] "I can't begin to tell you, how much you mean to me . . ." Betty sang that in 1945. '45? —'43. No, '43 was *Coney Island,* which was remade in '50 as *Wabash Avenue.* Yes, *Dolly Sisters* was in '45.

DONALD: How did I manage to miss these momentous events in the American cinema? I can understand people having an affinity for the stage— but movies are such garbage, who can take them seriously?

MICHAEL: Well, I'm sorry if your sense of art is offended. Odd as it may seem, there wasn't any Shubert Theatre in Hot Coffee, Mississippi!

DONALD: However—thanks to the silver screen, your neurosis has got style. It takes a certain flair to squander one's unemployment check at Pavillion.

MICHAEL: What's so snappy about being head over heels in debt? The only thing smart about it is the ingenious ways I dodge the bill collectors.

DONALD: Yeah. Come to think of it, you're the type that gives faggots a bad name.

MICHAEL: And you, Donald, *you* are a credit to the homosexual. A reliable, hardworking, floor-scrubbing, bill-paying fag who don't owe nothin' to nobody.

DONALD: *I* am a model fairy.

[*Michael has taken some ribbon and paper and begun to wrap Harold's birthday gift*]

MICHAEL: You think it's just nifty how I've always flitted from Beverly Hills to Rome to Acapulco to Amsterdam, picking up a lot of one-night stands and a lot of custom-made duds along the trail, but I'm here to tell you that the only place in all those miles—the only place I've ever been *happy*—was on the goddamn plane. [*Puffs up the bow on the package, continues*] Bored with Scandinavia, try Greece. Fed up with dark meat, try light. Hate tequila, what about Slivovitz? Tired of boys, what about girls—or how about boys and girls mixed and in what combination? And if you're sick of people, what about poppers? Or pot or pills or the hard stuff. And can you think of anything else the bad baby would like to indulge his spoiled-rotten, stupid, empty, boring, selfish, self-centered self in? Is that what you think has style, Donald? Huh? Is that what you think you've missed out on—my hysterical escapes from country to country, party to party, bar to bar, bed to bed, hangover to hangover, and all of it, hand to mouth! [*A beat*] Run, charge, run, buy, borrow, make, spend, run, squander, beg, run, run, run, waste, waste, *waste!* [*A beat*] And why? And why?

DONALD: Why, Michael? Why?

MICHAEL: I really don't want to get into it.

DONALD: Then how can we have a conversation in depth?

MICHAEL: Oh, you know it all by heart anyway. Same song, second verse. Because my Evelyn refused to let me grow up. She was determined to keep me a child forever and she did one helluva job of it. And my Walt stood by and let her do it. [*A beat*] What you see before you is a thirty-year-old infant. And it was all done in the name of love—what *she* labeled love and probably sincerely believed to be love, when what she was really doing was feeding her own need—satisfying her own loneliness. [*A beat*] She made me into a girlfriend dash lover. [*A beat*] We went to all those goddamn cornball movies together. I picked out her clothes for her and told her what to wear and she'd take me to the beauty parlor with her and we'd both get our hair bleached and a permanent and a manicure. [*A beat*] *And Walt let this happen.* [*A beat*] And she convinced me that I was a sickly child who couldn't run and play and sweat and get knocked around—oh, no! I was frail and pale and, to hear her tell it, practically female. I can't tell you the thousands of times she said to me, "I declare, Michael, you should have been a girl." And I guess I should have—I was frail and pale and bleached and curled and bedded down with hot-water bottles and my dolls and my paper dolls, and my doll clothes and my dollhouses! [*Quick beat*] *And Walt bought them for me!* [*Beat. With increasing speed*] And she nursed me and put Vicks salve on my chest and cold cream on my face and told me what beautiful eyes I had and what pretty lips I had. She bathed me in the same tub with her until I grew too big for the two of us to fit. She made me sleep in the same bed with her until I was fourteen years old—until I finally flatly refused to spend one more night there. She didn't want to prepare me for life or how to be out in the world on my own, or I might have left her. But I left anyway. This goddamn cripple finally wrenched free and limped away. And here I am—unequipped, undisciplined, untrained, unprepared, and unable to live! [*A beat*] And do you know until this day she still says, "I don't care if you're seventy years old, you'll always be my baby." And can I tell you how that drives me mad! Will that bitch never understand that what I'll always *be* is her son—but that I haven't been her baby for twenty-five years! [*A beat*] And don't get me wrong. I know it's easy to cop out and blame Evelyn and Walt and say it was *their* fault. That we were simply the helpless put-upon victims. But in the end, we are responsible for ourselves. And I guess—I'm not sure—but I want to believe it—that in their own pathetic, *dangerous* way, they just loved us too much. [*A beat*] Finis. Applause. [*Donald hesitates, walks over to Michael, puts his arms around him, and holds him. It is a totally warm and caring gesture*] There's nothing quite as good as feeling sorry for yourself, is there?

DONALD: Nothing.

MICHAEL: [*A la Bette Davis*] I adore cheap sentiment. [*Breaks away*] OK, I'm taking orders for drinks. What'll it be?

DONALD: An extra-dry-Beefeater-martini-on-the-rocks-with-a-twist.

MICHAEL: Coming up.

[*Donald exits up the stairs into the bath; Michael into the kitchen. Momentarily, Michael returns, carrying an ice bucket in one hand and a silver tray of cracked crab in the other, singing "Acapulco" or "Down Argentine Way " or some other forgotten Grable tune. The telephone rings*]

MICHAEL: [*Answering it*] Backstage, *New Moon.* [*A beat*] Alan? My God, I don't believe it. How *are* you? *Where* are you? In town! Great! When'd you get in? Is Fran with you? Oh. What? No. No, I'm tied up tonight. No, tonight's no good for me. You mean, *now?* Well, Alan, ole boy, it's a friend's birthday and I'm having a few people. No, you wouldn't exactly call it a birthday party—well, yes, actually I guess you would. I mean, what else would you call it? A *wake,* maybe. I'm sorry I can't ask you to join us—but—well, kiddo, it just wouldn't work out. No, it's not place cards or anything. It's just that—well, I'd hate to just see you for ten minutes and . . . Alan? Alan? What's the matter? Are you—are you crying? Oh, Alan, what's wrong? Alan, listen, come on over. No, no, it's perfectly all right. Well, just hurry up. I mean, come on by and have a drink, OK? Alan . . . are you all right? OK. Yeah. Same old address. Yeah. Bye.

[*Slowly hangs up, stares blankly into space. Donald appears, bathed and changed. He strikes a pose*]

DONALD: Well. Am I stunning?

[*Michael looks up*]

MICHAEL: [*Tonelessly*] You're absolutely stunning. You *look* like shit, but I'm absolutely stunned.

DONALD: [*Crestfallen*] Your grapes are, how you say, sour.

MICHAEL: Listen, you won't believe what just happened.

DONALD: Where's my drink?

MICHAEL: I didn't make it—I've been on the phone.

[*Donald goes to the bar, makes himself a martini*]

My old roommate from Georgetown just called.

DONALD: Alan what's-his-name?

MICHAEL: McCarthy. He's up here from Washington on business or something and he's on his way over here.

DONALD: Well, I hope he knows the lyrics to "Happy Birthday."

MICHAEL: Listen, asshole, what am I going to do? He's *straight*. And *Square City!* [*"Top Drawer" accent through clenched teeth*] I mean, he's rally vury proper. Auffully good family.

DONALD: [*Same accent*] That's *so* important.

MICHAEL: [*Regular speech*] I mean, they look down on people in the *theater*— so whatta you think he'll feel about this *freak show* I've got booked for dinner?

DONALD: [*Sipping his drink*] Christ, is that good.

MICHAEL: Want some cracked crab?

DONALD: Not just yet. Why'd you invite him over?

MICHAEL: He invited himself. He said he had to see me tonight. *Immediately.* He absolutely lost his spring on the phone—started crying.

DONALD: Maybe he's feeling sorry for himself too.

MICHAEL: Great heaves and sobs. Really boo-hoo-hoo-time—and that's not his style at all. I mean, he's so pulled-together he wouldn't show any emotion if he were in a plane crash. What am I going to do?

DONALD: What the hell do you care what he thinks?

MICHAEL: Well, I don't really, but . . .

DONALD: Or are you suddenly ashamed of your friends?

MICHAEL: Donald, *you* are the only person I know of whom I am truly ashamed. Some people *do* have different standards from yours and mine, you know. And if we don't acknowledge them, we're just as narrow-minded and backward as we think they are.

DONALD: You know what you are, Michael? You're a *real* person.

MICHAEL: Thank you and fuck you. [*Michael crosses to take a piece of crab and nibble on it*] Want some?

DONALD: No, thanks. How could you ever have been friends with a bore like that?

MICHAEL: Believe it or not, there was a time in my life when I didn't go around *announcing* that I was a faggot.

DONALD: That must have been before speech replaced sign language.

MICHAEL: Don't give me any static on that score. I didn't come out until I left college.

DONALD: It seems to me that the first time we tricked we met in a gay bar on Third Avenue during your *junior* year.

MICHAEL: Cunt.

DONALD: I thought you'd never say it.

MICHAEL: Sure you don't want any cracked crab?

DONALD: *Not yet! If you don't mind!*

MICHAEL: Well, it can only be getting colder. What time is it?

DONALD: I don't know. Early.

MICHAEL: Where the hell is Alan?

DONALD: Do you want some more club soda?

MICHAEL: What?

DONALD: There's nothing but club soda in that glass. It's not gin—like mine. You want some more?

MICHAEL: No.

DONALD: I've been watching you for several Saturdays now. You've actually stopped drinking, haven't you?

MICHAEL: And smoking too.

DONALD: And smoking too. How long's it been?

MICHAEL: Five weeks.

DONALD: That's amazing.

MICHAEL: I've found God.

DONALD: It *is* amazing—for you.

MICHAEL: Or is God dead?

DONALD: Yes, thank God. And don't get panicky just because I'm paying you a compliment. I can tell the difference.

MICHAEL: You always said that I held my liquor better than anybody you ever saw.

DONALD: I could always tell when you were getting high—one way.

MICHAEL: I'd get hostile.

DONALD: You seem happier or something now—and that shows.

MICHAEL: [*Quietly*] Thanks.

DONALD: What made you stop—the analyst?

MICHAEL: He certainly had a lot to do with it. Mainly, I just didn't think I could survive another hangover, that's all. I don't think I could get through that morning-after ick attack.

DONALD: Morning-after what?

MICHAEL: Icks! Anxiety! Guilt! Unfathomable guilt—either real or imagined—from that split second your eyes pop open and you say, "Oh, my God, what did I do last night!" and ZAP, total recall!

DONALD: Tell me about it!

MICHAEL: Then, the coffee, aspirin, Alka-Seltzer, Darvon, Daprisal, and a quick call to I.A.—Icks Anonymous.

DONALD: "Good morning, I.A."

MICHAEL: "Hi! Was I too bad last night? Did I do anything wrong? I didn't do anything terrible, did I?"

DONALD: [*Laughing*] How many times! How many times!

MICHAEL: And from then on, that struggle to live till lunch, when you have a double Bloody Mary—that is, if you've *waited* until lunch—and then you're half pissed again and useless for the rest of the afternoon. And the only sure cure is to go to bed for about thirty-seven hours, but who ever does that? Instead, you hang on till cocktail time, and by then you're ready for what the night holds—which hopefully is another party, where the whole goddamn cycle starts over! [*A beat*] Well, I've been on that merry-go-round long enough and I either had to get off or die of centrifugal force.

DONALD: And just how does a clear head stack up with the dull fog of alcohol?

MICHAEL: Well, all those things you've always heard are true. Nothing can compare with the experience of one's faculties functioning at their maximum natural capacity. The only thing is . . . I'd *kill* for a drink.

[*The wall-panel buzzer sounds*]

DONALD: Joe College has finally arrived.

MICHAEL: Suddenly, I have such an ick! [*Presses the wall-panel button*] Now listen, Donald . . .

DONALD: [*Quick*] Michael, don't insult me by giving me any lecture on acceptable social behavior. I promise to sit with my legs spread apart and keep my voice in a deep register.

MICHAEL: Donald, you are a real *card-carrying cunt.*

[*The apartment door buzzes several times. Michael goes to it, pauses briefly before it, tears it open to reveal EMORY, LARRY, and HANK. Emory is in Bermuda shorts and a sweater. Larry has on a turtleneck and sandals. Hank is in a dark Ivy League suit with a vest and has on cordovan shoes. Larry and Hank carry birthday gifts. Emory carries a large covered dish*]

EMORY: [*Bursting in*] ALL RIGHT THIS IS A RAID! EVERYBODY'S UNDER ARREST!

[*This entrance is followed by a loud raucous laugh as Emory throws his arms around Michael and gives him a big kiss on the cheek*]

EMORY: [*Referring to dish*] Hello, darlin! Connie Casserole. Oh, Mary, don't ask.

MICHAEL: [*Weary already*] Hello, Emory. Put it in the kitchen.

[*Emory spots Donald*]

EMORY: Who is this exotic woman over here?

MICHAEL: Hi, Hank. Larry.

[*They say, "Hi," shake hands, enter. Michael looks out in the hall, comes back into the room, closes the door*]

DONALD: Hi, Emory.

EMORY: My dear, I thought you had perished! Where have you been hiding your classically chiseled features?

DONALD: [*To Emory*] I don't live in the city anymore.

MICHAEL: [*To Larry and Hank, referring to the gifts*] Here, I'll take those. Where's yours, Emory?

EMORY: It's arriving later.

[*Emory exits to the kitchen. Larry and Donald's eyes have met. Hank has handed Michael his gift—Larry is too preoccupied*]

HANK: Larry! Larry!

LARRY: What!

HANK: Give Michael the gift!

LARRY: Oh. Here.[*To Hank*] Louder. So my mother in Philadelphia can hear you.

HANK: Well, you were just standing there in a trance.

MICHAEL: [*To Larry and Hank as Emory reenters*] You both know Donald, don't you?

DONALD: Sure. Nice to see you. [*To Hank*] Hi.

HANK: [*Shaking hands*] Nice to meet you.

MICHAEL: Oh, I thought you'd met.

DONALD: Well . . .

LARRY: We haven't exactly me but we've . . . Hi.

DONALD: Hi.

HANK: But you've what?

LARRY: . . . *Seen* . . . each other before.

MICHAEL: Well, *that* sounds murky.

HANK: You've never met but you've seen each other.

LARRY: What was wrong with the way *I* said it?

HANK: Where?

EMORY: [*Loud aside to Michael*] I think they're going to have their first fight.

LARRY: The first one since we got out of the taxi.

MICHAEL: [*Referring to Emory*] Where'd you find this trash?

LARRY: Downstairs leaning against a lamppost.

EMORY: With an orchid behind my ear and big wet lips painted over the lipline.

MICHAEL: Just like Maria Montez.

DONALD: Oh, *please!*

EMORY: [*To Donald*] What have you got against Maria—she was a good woman.

MICHAEL: Listen, everybody, this old college friend of mine is in town and he's stopping by for a fast drink on his way to dinner somewhere. But, listen, he's *straight,* so . . .

LARRY: *Straight!* If it's the one I met, he's about as straight as the Yellow Brick Road.

MICHAEL: No, you met Justin Stuart.

HANK: I don't remember anybody named Justin Stuart.

LARRY: Of course you don't, dope. *I* met him.

MICHAEL: Well, this is someone else.

DONALD: Alan McCarthy. A very close total stranger.

MICHAEL: It's not that I care what he would think of me, really—it's just that *he's* not ready for it. And he never will be. You understand that, don't you, Hank?

HANK: Oh, sure.

LARRY: You honestly think he doesn't know about you?

MICHAEL: If there's the slightest suspicion, he's never let on one bit.

EMORY: What's he had, a lobotomy? [*He exits up the stairs into the bath*]

MICHAEL: I was super-careful when I was in college and I still am whenever I see him. I don't know why, but I am.

DONALD: Tilt.

MICHAEL: You may think it was a crock of shit, Donald, but to him I'm sure we were close friends. The closest. To pop that balloon now just wouldn't be fair to him. Isn't that right?

LARRY: Whatever's fair.

MICHAEL: Well, of course. And if that's phony of me, Donald, then that's phony of me and make something of it.

DONALD: I pass.

MICHAEL: Well, even you have to admit it's much simpler to deal with the world according to its rules and then go right ahead and do what you damn well please. You do understand *that,* don't you?

DONALD: Now that you've put it in layman's terms.

MICHAEL: I was just like Alan when I was in college. Very large in the dating department. Wore nothing but those constipated Ivy League clothes and those ten-pound cordovan shoes. [*To Hank*] No offense.

HANK: Quite all right.

MICHAEL: I butched it up quite a bit. And I didn't think I was lying to myself. I really thought I was straight.

EMORY: [*Coming downstairs tucking a Kleenex into his sleeve*] Who do you have to fuck to get a drink around here?

MICHAEL: Will you *light* somewhere? [*Emory sits on steps*] Or I thought I thought I was straight. I know I didn't come out till after I'd graduated.

DONALD: What about all those weekends up from school?

MICHAEL: I still wasn't out. I was still in the "Christ-was-I-drunk-last-night syndrome."

LARRY: The *what?*

MICHAEL: The Christ-was-I-drunk-last-night syndrome. You know, when you made it with some guy in school, and the next day when you had to face each other there was always a lot of shit-kicking crap about, "Man, was I drunk last night! Christ, I don't remember a thing!"

[*Everyone laughs*]

DONALD: You were just guilty because you were Catholic, that's all.

MICHAEL: That's not true. The Christ-was-I-drunk-last-night syndrome knows no religion. It has to do with immaturity. Although I will admit there's a high percentage of it among Mormons.

EMORY: Trollop.

MICHAEL: We all somehow managed to justify our actions in those days. I later found out that even Justin Stuart, my closest friend . . .

DONALD: Other than Alan McCarthy.

MICHAEL: [*A look to Donald*] . . . was doing the same thing. Only Justin was going to Boston on weekends.

[*Emory and Larry laugh*]

LARRY: [*To Hank*] Sound familiar?

MICHAEL: Yes, long before Justin and I or God only knows how many others *came out,* we used to get drunk and "horse around" a bit. You see, in the Christ-was-I-drunk-last-night syndrome, you really *are* drunk. That part of it is true. It's just that you also *do remember everything.*

[*General laughter*]

Oh, God, I used to have to get loaded to go in a gay bar!

DONALD: Well, times certainly have changed.

MICHAEL: They *have.* Lately I've gotten to despise the bars. Everybody just standing around and standing around—it's like one eternal intermission.

HANK: [*To Larry*] Sound familiar?

EMORY: I can't stand the bars either. All that cat-and-mouse business— you hang around *staring* at each other all night and wind up going home alone.

MICHAEL: And pissed.

LARRY: A lot of guys have to get loaded to have sex. [*Quick look to Hank, who is unamused*] So I've been told.

MICHAEL: If you remember, Donald, the first time we made it I was so drunk I could hardly stand up.

DONALD: You were so drunk you could hardly *get* it up.

MICHAEL: [*Mock innocence*] Christ, I was so drunk I don't remember.

DONALD: Bullshit, you remember.

MICHAEL: [*Sings to Donald*] "Just friends, lovers no more . . ."

EMORY: You may as well be. Everybody thinks you are anyway.

DONALD: We never *were—really.*

MICHAEL: We didn't have time to be—we got to know each other too fast.

[*Door buzzer sounds*]

Oh, Jesus, it's Alan! Now, please, everybody, do me a favor and cool it for the few minutes he's here.

EMORY: Anything for a sis, Mary.

MICHAEL: That's *exactly* what I'm talking about, Emory. *No camping!*

EMORY: Sorry. [*Deep, deep voice to Donald*] Think the Giants are gonna win the pennant this year?

DONALD: [*Deep, deep voice*] Fuckin' A, Mac.

[*Michael goes to the door, opens it to reveal BERNARD, dressed in a shirt and tie and sport jacket. He carries a birthday gift and two bottles of red wine*]

EMORY: [*Big scream*] Oh, it's only another queen!

BERNARD: And it ain't the red one, either.

EMORY: It's the queen of spades!

[*Bernard enters. Michael looks out in the hall*]

MICHAEL: Bernard, is the downstairs door open?

BERNARD: It was, but I closed it.

MICHAEL: Good.

[*Bernard starts to put wine on bar*]

MICHAEL: [*Referring to the two bottles of red wine*] I'll take those. You can put your present with the others.

[*Michael closes the door. Bernard hands him the gift. The phone rings*]

BERNARD: Hi, Larry. Hi, Hank.

MICHAEL: *Christ of the Andes!* Donald, will you bartend, please?

[*Michael gives Donald the wine bottles, goes to the phone*]

BERNARD: [*Extending his hand to Donald*] Hello, Donald. Good to see you.

DONALD: Bernard.

MICHAEL: [*Answers phone*] Hello? Alan?

EMORY: Hi, Bernardette. Anybody ever tell you you'd look divine in a hammock, surrounded by louvres and ceiling fans and lots and lots of lush tropical ferns?

BERNARD: [*To Emory*] You're *such* a fag. You take the cake.

EMORY: Oh, what *about* the cake—whose job was that?

LARRY: Mine. I ordered one to be delivered.

EMORY: How many candles did you say put on it—eighty?

MICHAEL: . . . What? Wait a minute. There's too much noise. Let me go to another phone. [*Presses the hold button, hangs up, dashes toward stairs*]

LARRY: Michael, did the cake come?

MICHAEL: No.

DONALD: [*To Michael as he passes*] What's up?

MICHAEL: Do *I* know?

LARRY: Jesus, I'd better call. OK if I use the private line?

MICHAEL: [*Going upstairs*] Sure. [*Stops dead on stairs, turns*] Listen, everybody, there's some cracked crab there. Help yourselves.

[*Donald shakes his head. Michael continues up the stairs to the bedroom. Larry crosses to the phone, presses the free-line button, picks up receiver, dials information*]

DONALD: Is everybody ready for a drink?

[*Hank and Bernard say, "Yeah"*]

EMORY: [*Flipping up his sweater*] *Ready!* I'll be your topless cocktail waitress.

BERNARD: Please spare us the sight of your sagging tits.

EMORY: [*To Hank, Larry*] What're you having, kids?

MICHAEL: [*Having picked up the bedside phone*] . . . Yes, Alan . . .

LARRY: Vodka and tonic. [*Into phone*] Could I have the number for the Marseilles Bakery in Manhattan?

EMORY: A vod and ton and a . . .

HANK: Is there any beer?

EMORY: Beer! Who drinks beer before dinner?

BERNARD: Beer drinkers.

DONALD: That's telling him.

MICHAEL: . . . No, Alan, don't be silly. What's there to apologize for?

EMORY: Truck drivers do. Or . . . or wallpaperers. Not schoolteachers. They have sherry.

HANK: This one has beer.

THE BOYS IN THE BAND 23

EMORY: Well, maybe schoolteachers in *public* schools. [*To Larry*] How can a sensitive artist like you live with an insensitive bull like that?

LARRY: [*Hanging up the phone and redialing*] I can't.

BERNARD: Emory, you'd live with Hank in a minute, if he'd ask you. In fifty-eight seconds. Lord knows, you're *sss*ensitive.

EMORY: Why don't you have a piece of watermelon and hush up!

MICHAEL: . . . Alan, don't be ridiculous.

DONALD: Here you go, Hank.

HANK: Thanks.

LARRY: Shit. They don't answer.

DONALD: What're you having, Emory?

BERNARD: A Pink Lady.

EMORY: A vodka martini on the rocks, please.

LARRY: [*Hangs up*] Well, let's just hope.

[*Donald hands Larry his drink—their eyes meet again. A faint smile crosses Larry's lips. Donald returns to the bar to make Emory's drink*]

MICHAEL: Lunch tomorrow will be great. One o'clock—the Oak Room at the Plaza, OK? Fine.

BERNARD: [*To Donald*] Donald, read any new libraries lately?

DONALD: One or three. I did the complete works of Doris Lessing this week. I've been depressed.

MICHAEL: Alan, forget it, will you? Right. Bye.

[*Hangs up, starts to leave the room—stops. Quickly pulls off the sweater he is wearing, takes out another, crosses to the stairs*]

DONALD: You must not work in Circulation anymore.

BERNARD: Oh, I'm still there—every day.

DONALD: Well, since I moved, I only come in on Saturday evenings. [*Moves his stack of books off the bar*]

HANK: Looks like you stock up for the week.

[*Michael rises and crosses to steps landing*]

BERNARD: Are you kidding?—that'll last him two days.

EMORY: It would last *me* two years. I still haven't finished *Atlas Shrugged,* which I started in 1912.

MICHAEL: [*To Donald*] Well, he's not coming.

DONALD: It's just as well now.

BERNARD: Some people eat, some people drink, some take dope . . .

DONALD: I read.

MICHAEL: And read and read and read. It's a wonder your eyes don't turn back in your head at the sight of a dust jacket.

HANK: Well, at least he's a constructive escapist.

MICHAEL: Yeah, what do I do?—take planes. No, I don't do that anymore. Because I don't have the *money* to do that anymore. I go to the baths. That's about it.

EMORY: I'm about to do both. I'm flying to the West Coast—

BERNARD: You still have that act with a donkey in Tijuana?

EMORY: I'm going to *San Francisco* on a well-earned vacation.

LARRY: No shopping?

EMORY: Oh, I'll look for a few things for a couple of clients, but I've been so busy lately I really couldn't care less if I never saw another piece of fabric or another stick of furniture as long as I live. I'm going to the Club Baths and I'm not out till they announce the departure of TWA one week later.

BERNARD: [*To Emory*] You'll never learn to stay out of the baths, will you? The last time Emily was taking the vapors, this big hairy number strolled in. Emory said, "I'm just resting," and the big hairy number said, "I'm just *arresting*!" It was the vice!

[*Everybody laughs*]

EMORY: You have to tell everything, don't you!

[*Donald crosses to give Emory his drink*]

EMORY: Thanks, sonny. You live with your parents?

DONALD: Yeah. But it's all right—they're gay.

[*Emory roars, slaps Hank on the knee. Hank gets up, moves away. Donald turns to Michael*]

What happened to Alan?

MICHAEL: He suddenly got terrible icks about having broken down on the phone. Kept apologizing over and over. Did a big about-face and reverted to the old Alan right before my very eyes.

DONALD: Ears.

MICHAEL: Ears. Well, the cracked crab obviously did not work out. [*Starts to take away the tray*]

EMORY: Just put that down if you don't want your hand slapped. I'm about to have some.

MICHAEL: It's really very good. [*Gives Donald a look*] I don't know why everyone has such an aversion to it.

DONALD: Sometimes you remind me of the Chinese water torture. I take that back. Sometimes you remind me of the *relentless* Chinese water torture.

MICHAEL: Bitch.

[*Hank has put on some music*]

BERNARD: Yeah, baby, let's hear that sound.

EMORY: A drumbeat and their eyes sparkle like Cartier's.

[*Bernard starts to snap his fingers and move in time with the music. Michael joins in*]

HANK: I wonder where Harold is.

EMORY: Yeah, where *is* the frozen fruit?

MICHAEL: [*To Donald*] Emory refers to Harold as the frozen fruit because of his former profession as an ice skater.

EMORY: She used to be the Vera Hruba Ralston of the Borscht Circuit.

[*Michael and Bernard are now dancing freely*]

BERNARD: [*To Michael*] If your mother could see you now, she'd have a stroke.

MICHAEL: Got a camera on you?

[*The door panel buzzes. Emory lets out a yelp*]

EMORY: Oh, my God, it's Lily Law! Everybody three feet apart!

[*Michael goes to the panel, presses the button. Hank turns down the music. Michael opens the door a short way, pokes his head out*]

BERNARD: It's probably Harold now.

[*Michael leans back in the room*]

MICHAEL: No, it's the delivery boy from the bakery.

LARRY: Thank God.

[*Michael goes out into the hall, pulling the door almost closed behind him*]

EMORY: [*Loudly*] Ask him if he's got any hot cross buns!

HANK: Come on, Emory, knock it off.

BERNARD: You can take her anywhere but out.

EMORY: [*To Hank*] You remind me of an old-maid schoolteacher.

HANK: You remind me of a chicken wing.

EMORY: I'm sure you meant that as a compliment.

[*Hank turns the music back up*]

MICHAEL: [*In hall*] Thank you. Good night.

[*Michael returns with a cake box, closes the door, and takes it into the kitchen*]

LARRY: Hey, Bernard, you remember that thing we used to do on Fire Island?

[*Larry starts to do a kind of Madison*]

BERNARD: That was "in" so far back I think I've forgotten.

EMORY: *I* remember.

[*Pops up—starts doing the steps. Larry and Bernard start to follow*]

LARRY: Yeah. That's it.

[*Michael enters from the kitchen, falls in line with them*]

MICHAEL: Well, if it isn't the Geriatrics Rockettes.

[*Now they all are doing practically a precision routine. Donald comes to sit on the arm of a chair, sip his drink, and watch in fascination. Hank goes to the bar to get another beer. The door buzzer sounds. No one seems to hear it. It buzzes again. Hank turns toward the door, hesitates. Looks toward Michael, who is now deeply involved in the intricacies of the dance. No one, it seems, has heard the buzzer but Hank, who goes to the door, opens it wide to reveal ALAN. He is dressed in black tie. The dancers continue, turning and slapping their knees and heels and laughing with abandon. Suddenly Michael looks up, stops dead. Donald sees this and turns to see what Michael has seen. Slowly he stands up. Michael goes to the record player, turns it off abruptly. Emory, Larry, and Bernard come to out-of-step halts, look to see what's happened]*

MICHAEL: I thought you said you weren't coming.

ALAN: I . . . well, I'm sorry . . .

MICHAEL: [*Forced lightly*] We were just—acting silly . . .

ALAN: Actually, when I called I was in a phone booth around the corner. My dinner party is not far from here. And . . .

MICHAEL: Emory was just showing us this . . . silly dance.

ALAN: Well, then I walked past and your downstairs door was open and . . .

MICHAEL: This is Emory.

[*Emory curtsies. Michael glares at him*]

Everybody, this is Alan McCarthy. Counterclockwise, Alan: Larry, Emory, Bernard, Donald, and Hank.

[*They all mumble "Hello" "Hi"*]

MICHAEL: Would you like a drink?

ALAN: Thanks, no. I . . . I can't stay . . . long . . . really.

MICHAEL: Well, you're here now, so stay. What would you like?

ALAN: Do you have any rye?

MICHAEL: I'm afraid I don't drink it anymore. You'll have to settle for gin or Scotch or vodka.

DONALD: Or beer.

ALAN: Scotch, please.

[*Michael starts for bar*]

DONALD: I'll get it. [*Goes to bar*]

HANK: [*Forced laugh*] Guess I'm the only beer drinker.

ALAN: [*Looking around group*] Whose . . . birthday . . . is it?

LARRY: Harold's.

ALAN: [*Looking from face to face*] Harold?

BERNARD: He's not here yet.

EMORY: She's never been on time . . .

[*Michael shoots Emory a withering glance*]

*He's* never been on time in *his* . . .

MICHAEL: Alan's from Washington. We went to college together. George-town.

[*A beat. Silence*]

EMORY: Well, isn't that fascinating.

[*Donald hands Alan his drink*]

DONALD: If that's too strong, I'll put some water in it.

ALAN: [*Takes a quick gulp*] It's fine. Thanks. Fine.

HANK: Are you in the government?

ALAN: No. I'm a lawyer. What . . . what do you do?

HANK: I teach school.

ALAN: Oh. I would have taken you for an athlete of some sort. You look like you might play sports . . . of some sort.

HANK: Well, I'm no professional but I was on the basketball team in college and I play quite a bit of tennis.

ALAN: I play tennis too.

HANK: Great game.

ALAN: Yes. Great. [*A beat. Silence*] What . . . do you teach?

HANK: Math.

ALAN: Math?

HANK: Yes.

ALAN: Math. Well.

EMORY: Kinda makes you want to rush out and buy a slide rule, doesn't it?

MICHAEL: Emory. I'm going to need some help with dinner and you're elected. Come on!

EMORY: I'm *always* elected.

BERNARD: You're a natural-born domestic.

EMORY: Said the African queen! You come on too—you can fan me while I make the salad dressing.

MICHAEL: [*Glaring. Phony smile*] RIGHT THIS WAY, Emory!

[*Michael pushes the swinging door aside for Emory and Bernard to enter. They do and he follows. The door swings closed, and the muffled sound of Michael's voice can be heard. Offstage*]

You son of a bitch!

EMORY: [*Offstage*] What the hell do you want from me?

HANK: Why don't we all sit down?

ALAN: . . . Sure.

[*Hank and Alan sit on the couch. Larry crosses to the bar, refills his drink. Donald comes over to refill his*]

LARRY: Hi.

DONALD: . . . Hi.

ALAN: I really feel terrible—barging in on you fellows this way.

LARRY: [*To Donald*] How've you been?

DONALD: Fine, thanks.

HANK: [*To Alan*] . . . Oh, that's OK.

DONALD: [*To Larry*] . . . And you?

LARRY: Oh . . . just fine.

ALAN: [*To Hank*] You're married?

[*Larry hears this, turns to look in the direction of the couch. Michael enters from the kitchen*]

HANK: [*Watching Larry and Donald*] What?

ALAN: I see you're married. [*Points to Hank's wedding band*]

HANK: Oh.

MICHAEL: [*Glaring at Donald*] Yes. Hank's married.

ALAN: You have any kids?

HANK: Yes. Two. A boy, nine, and a girl, seven. You should see my boy play tennis—really puts his dad to shame.

DONALD: [*Avoiding Michael's eyes*] I better get some ice. [*Exits to the kitchen*]

ALAN: [*To Hank*] I have two kids too. Both girls.

HANK: Great.

MICHAEL: How *are* the girls, Alan?

ALAN: Oh, just sensational. [*Shakes his head*] They're something, those kids. God, I'm nuts about them.

HANK: How long have you been married?

ALAN: Nine years. Can you believe it, Mickey?

MICHAEL: No.

ALAN: Mickey used to go with my wife when we were all in school.

MICHAEL: Can you believe that?

ALAN: [*To Hank*] You live in the city?

LARRY: Yes, we do. [*Larry comes over to couch next to Hank*]

ALAN: Oh.

HANK: I'm in the process of getting a divorce. Larry and I are—roommates.

MICHAEL: Yes.

ALAN: Oh. I'm sorry. Oh, I mean . . .

HANK: I understand.

ALAN: [*Gets up*] I . . . I . . . I think I'd like another drink . . . if I may.

MICHAEL: Of course. What was it?

ALAN: I'll do it . . . if I may. [*Gets up, starts for the bar. Suddenly there is a loud crash offstage. Alan jumps, looks toward swinging door*] What was that?

[*Donald enters with the ice bucket*]

MICHAEL: Excuse me. Testy temperament out in the kitch!

[*Michael exits through the swinging door. Alan continues to the bar—starts nervously picking up and putting down bottles, searching for the Scotch*]

HANK: [*To Larry*] Larry, where do you know that guy from?

LARRY: What guy?

HANK: *That* guy.

LARRY: I don't know. Around. The bars.

DONALD: Can I help you, Alan?

ALAN: I . . . I can't seem to find the Scotch.

DONALD: You've got it in your hand.

ALAN: Oh. Of course. How . . . stupid of me.

DONALD: [*Donald watches Alan fumble with the Scotch bottle and glass*] Why don't you let me do that?

ALAN: [*Gratefully hands him both*] Thanks.

DONALD: Was it water or soda?

ALAN: Just make it straight—over ice.

[*Michael enters*]

MICHAEL: You see, Alan, I told you it wasn't a good time to talk. But we . . .

ALAN: It doesn't matter. I'll just finish this and go . . . [*Takes a long swallow*]

LARRY: Where can Harold be?

MICHAEL: Oh, he's always late. You know how neurotic he is about going out in public. It takes him hours to get ready.

LARRY: Why *is* that?

[*Emory breezes in with an apron tied around his waist, carrying a stack of plates, which he places on a drop-leaf table. Michael does an eye roll*]

EMORY: Why is what?

LARRY: Why does Harold spend hours getting ready before he can go out?

EMORY: Because she's a sick lady, that's why. [*Exits to the kitchen. Alan finishes his drink*]

MICHAEL: Alan, as I was about to say, we can go in the bedroom and talk.

ALAN: It really doesn't matter.

MICHAEL: Come on. Bring your drink.

ALAN: I . . . I've finished it.

MICHAEL: Well, make another and bring it upstairs.

[*Donald picks up the Scotch bottle and pours into the glass Alan has in his hand. Michael has started for the stairs*]

ALAN: [*To Donald*] Thanks.

DONALD: Don't mention it.

ALAN: [*To Hank*] Excuse me. We'll be down in a minute.

LARRY: He'll still be here.

[*A beat*]

MICHAEL: [*On the stairs*] Go ahead, Alan. I'll be right there.

[*Alan turns awkwardly, exits to the bedroom. Michael goes into the kitchen. A beat*]

HANK: [*To Larry*] What was *that* supposed to mean?

LARRY: What was what supposed to mean?

HANK: You know.

LARRY: You want another beer?

HANK: No. You're jealous, aren't you?

[*Hank starts to laugh. Larry doesn't like it*]

LARRY: I'm Larry. *You're* jealous. [*Crosses to Donald*] Hey, Donald, where've you been hanging out these days? I haven't seen you in a long time . . .

[*Michael enters to witness this disapprovingly. He turns, goes up the stairs. In the bedroom Alan is sitting on the edge of the bed. Michael enters, pauses at the mirror to adjust his hair. Downstairs, Hank gets up, exits into the kitchen. Donald and Larry move to a corner of the room, sit facing upstage, and talk quietly*]

ALAN: [*To Michael*] This is a marvelous apartment.

MICHAEL: It's too expensive. I work to pay rent.

ALAN: What are you doing these days?

MICHAEL: Nothing.

ALAN: Aren't you writing anymore?

MICHAEL: I haven't looked at a typewriter since I sold the very, very wonderful, very, very marvelous *screenplay*, which never got produced.

ALAN: That's right. The last time I saw you, you were on your way to California. Or was it Europe?

MICHAEL: Hollywood. Which is not in Europe, nor does it have anything whatsoever to do with California.

ALAN: I've never been there, but I would imagine it's awful. Everyone must be terribly cheap.

MICHAEL: No, not everyone.

[*Alan laughs. A beat. Michael sits on the bed*]

Alan, I want to try to explain this evening . . .

ALAN: What's there to explain? Sometimes you just can't invite everybody to every party and some people take it personally. But I'm not one of them. I should apologize for inviting myself.

MICHAEL: That's not exactly what I meant.

ALAN: Your friends all seem like very nice guys. That Hank is really a very attractive fellow.

MICHAEL: . . . Yes. He is.

ALAN: We have a lot in common. What's his roommate's name?

MICHAEL: Larry.

ALAN: What does *he* do?

MICHAEL: He's a commercial artist.

ALAN: I liked Donald too. The only one I didn't care too much for was— what's his name—Emory?

MICHAEL: Yes. Emory.

ALAN: I just can't stand that kind of talk. It just grates on me.

MICHAEL: What kind of talk, Alan?

ALAN: Oh, you know. His brand of humor, I guess.

MICHAEL: He can be really quite funny sometimes.

ALAN: I suppose so. If you find that sort of thing amusing. He just seems like such a goddamn little pansy. [*Silence. A pause*] I'm sorry I said that. I didn't mean to say that. That's such an awful thing to say about *anyone*. But you know what I mean, Michael—you have to admit he *is* effeminate.

MICHAEL: He is a bit.

ALAN: A bit! He's like a . . . a butterfly in heat! I mean, there's no wonder he was trying to teach you all a dance. He *probably* wanted to dance *with* you! [*Pause*] Oh, come on, man, you know me—you know how I feel—your private life is your own affair.

MICHAEL: [*Icy*] No. I *don't* know that about you.

ALAN: I couldn't care less what people do—as long as they don't do it in public—or—or try to force their ways on the whole damned world.

MICHAEL: Alan, what was it you were crying about on the telephone?

ALAN: Oh, I feel like such a fool about that. I could shoot myself for letting myself act that way. I'm so embarrassed I could die.

MICHAEL: But, Alan, if you were genuinely upset—that's nothing to be embarrassed about.

ALAN: All I can say is—please accept my apology for making such an ass of myself.

MICHAEL: You must have been upset, or you wouldn't have said you were and that you wanted to see me—*had* to see me and had to talk to me.

ALAN: Can you forget it? Just pretend it never happened. I know *I* have. OK?

MICHAEL: Is something wrong between you and Fran?

ALAN: Listen, I've really got to go.

MICHAEL: Why are you in New York?

ALAN: I'm dreadfully late for dinner.

MICHAEL: *Whose* dinner? Where are you going?

ALAN: Is this the loo?

MICHAEL: Yes.

ALAN: Excuse me.

[*Quickly goes into the bathroom, closes the door. Michael remains silent—sits on the bed, stares into space. Downstairs, Emory pops in from the kitchen to discover Donald and Larry in quiet, intimate conversation*]

EMORY: What's-going-on-in-here-oh-Mary-don't-ask!

[*Puts a salt cellar and pepper mill on the table. Hank enters, carrying a bottle of red wine and a corkscrew. Looks toward Larry and Donald. Donald sees him, stands up*]

DONALD: Hank, why don't you come and join us?

HANK: That's an interesting suggestion. Whose idea is that?

DONALD: Mine.

LARRY: [*To Hank*] He means in a conversation.

[*Bernard enters from the kitchen, carrying four wine glasses*]

EMORY: [*To Bernard*] Where're the rest of the wine glasses?

BERNARD: Ahz workin' as fas' as ah can!

EMORY: They have to be told everything. Can't let 'em out of your sight.

[*Breezes out to the kitchen. Donald leaves Larry's side and goes to the coffee table, helps himself to the cracked crab. Hank opens the wine, puts it on the table. Michael gets up from the bed and goes down the stairs. Downstairs, Hank crosses to Larry*]

HANK: I thought maybe you were abiding by the agreement.

LARRY: We have no agreement.

HANK: We *did*.

LARRY: *You* did. I never agreed to anything!

[*Donald looks up to see Michael, raises a crab claw toward him*]

DONALD: To your health.

MICHAEL: Up yours.

DONALD: Up my health?

BERNARD: Where's the gent?

MICHAEL: In the gent's room. If you can all hang on five more minutes, he's about to leave.

[*The door buzzes. Michael crosses to it*]

LARRY: Well, at last!

[*Michael opens the door to reveal a muscle-bound young man wearing boots, tight Levi's, a calico neckerchief, and a cowboy hat. Around his wrist there is a large card tied with a ribbon*]

COWBOY: [*Singing fast*]
"Happy birthday to you,
Happy birthday to you,
Happy birthday, dear Harold.
Happy birthday to you."

[*And with that, he throws his arms around Michael and gives him a big kiss on the lips. Everyone stands in stunned silence*]

MICHAEL: Who the hell are you?

[*Emory swings in from the kitchen*]

EMORY: She's Harold's present from me and she's *early!* [*Quick, to Cowboy*] And that's not even Harold, you *idiot!*

COWBOY: You said whoever answered the door.

EMORY: But *not until midnight!* [*Quickly, to group*] He's supposed to be a *midnight cowboy!*

DONALD: He *is* a midnight cowboy.

MICHAEL: He looks right out of a William Inge play to me.

EMORY: [*To Cowboy*] . . . Not until midnight and you're supposed to sing to the right person, for Chrissake! I *told* you Harold has very, very tight, tight, black curly hair. [*Referring to Michael*] This number's practically bald!

MICHAEL: Thank you and fuck you.

BERNARD: It's a good thing *I* didn't open the door.

EMORY: Not that tight and not that black.

COWBOY: I forgot. Besides, I wanted to get to the bars by midnight.

MICHAEL: He's a class act all the way around.

EMORY: What do you mean—get to the bars! Sweetie, I paid you for the whole night, remember?

COWBOY: I hurt my back doing my exercises and I wanted to get to bed early tonight.

BERNARD: Are you ready for this one?

LARRY: [*To Cowboy*] That's too bad, what happened?

COWBOY: I lost my grip doing my chin-ups and I fell on my heels and twisted my back.

EMORY: You shouldn't *wear* heels when you do chin-ups.

COWBOY: [*Oblivious*] I shouldn't do chin-ups—I got a weak grip to begin with.

EMORY: A weak grip. In my day it used to be called a limp wrist.

BERNARD: Who can remember that far back?

MICHAEL: Who was it that always used to say, "You show me Oscar Wilde in a cowboy suit, and I'll show you a gay caballero."

DONALD: I don't know. Who *was* it who always used to say that?

MICHAEL: [*Katharine Hepburn voice*] I don't know. Somebody.

LARRY: [*To Cowboy*] What does your card say?

COWBOY: [*Holds up his wrist*] Here. Read it.

LARRY: [*Reading card*] "Dear Harold, bang, bang, you're alive. But roll over and play dead. Happy birthday, Emory."

BERNARD: Ah, sheer poetry, Emmy.

LARRY: And in your usual good taste.

MICHAEL: Yes, so conservative of you to resist a sign in Times Square.

EMORY: [*Glancing toward stairs*] Cheese it! Here comes the socialite nun.

MICHAEL: Goddamn it, Emory!

[*Alan comes down the stairs into the room. Everybody quiets*]

ALAN: Well, I'm off . . . Thanks, Michael, for the drink.

MICHAEL: You're entirely welcome, Alan. See you tomorrow?

ALAN: . . . No. No, I think I'm going to be awfully busy. I may even go back to Washington.

EMORY: Got a heavy date in Lafayette Square?

ALAN: What?

HANK: Emory.

EMORY: Forget it.

ALAN: [*Sees Cowboy*] Are you . . . Harold?

EMORY: No, he's not Harold. He's *for* Harold.

[*Silence. Alan lets it pass. Turns to Hank*]

ALAN: Goodbye, Hank. It was nice to meet you.

HANK: Same here.

[*They shake hands*]

ALAN: If . . . if you're ever in Washington—I'd like for you to meet my wife.

LARRY: That'd be fun, wouldn't it, Hank?

EMORY: Yeah, they'd love to meet him—*her*. I have such a problem with pronouns.

ALAN: [*Quick, to Emory*] How many esses are there in the word pronoun?

EMORY: How'd you like to kiss my ass—that's got two or more *essessss* in it!

ALAN: How'd you like to blow me!

EMORY: What's the matter with your *wife,* she got lockjaw?

ALAN: [*Lashes out*] Faggot, fairy, pansy . . . [*Lunges at Emory*] . . . queer, cocksucker! I'll kill you, you goddamn little mincing swish! You goddamn freak! FREAK! FREAK!

[*Pandemonium. Alan beats Emory to the floor before anyone recovers from surprise and reacts*]

EMORY: Oh, my God, somebody help me! Bernard! He's killing me!

[*Bernard and Hank rush forward. Emory is screaming. Blood gushes from his nose*]

HANK: Alan! ALAN! ALAN!

EMORY: Get him off me! Get him off me! Oh, my God, he's broken my nose! I'm BLEEDING TO DEATH!

[*Larry has gone to shut the door. With one great, athletic move, Hank forcefully tears Alan off Emory and drags him backward across the room. Bernard bends over Emory, puts his arm around him, and lifts him*]

BERNARD: Somebody get some ice! And a cloth!

[*Larry runs to the bar, grabs the bar towel and the ice bucket, rushes to put it on the floor beside Bernard and Emory. Bernard quickly wraps some ice in the towel, holds it to Emory's mouth*]

EMORY: Oh, my face!

BERNARD: He busted your lip, that's all. It'll be all right.

[*Hank has gotten Alan down on the floor on the opposite side of the room. Alan relinquishes the struggle, collapses against Hank, moaning and beating his fists rhythmically against Hank's chest. Michael is still standing in the same spot in the center of the room, immobile. Donald crosses past the cowboy*]

DONALD: [*To Cowboy*] Would you mind waiting over there with the gifts?

[*Cowboy moves over to where the gift-wrapped packages have been put. Donald continues past to observe the mayhem, turns up his glass, takes a long swallow. The door buzzes, Donald turns toward Michael, waits. Michael doesn't move. Donald goes to the door, opens it to reveal HAROLD*]

DONALD: Well, Harold! Happy birthday. You're just in time for the floor show, which, as you see, is on the floor. [*To Cowboy*] Hey, you, *this* is Harold!

[*Harold looks blankly toward Michael. Michael looks back blankly*]

COWBOY: [*Crossing to Harold*]
  "*Happy birthday to you,*
  *Happy birthday to you,*
  *Happy birthday, dear Harold.*
  *Happy birthday to you.*"

[*Throws his arms around Harold and gives him a big kiss. Donald looks toward Michael, who observes this stoically. Harold breaks away from Cowboy, reads the card, begins to laugh. Michael turns to survey the room. Donald watches him. Slowly Michael begins to move. Walks over to the bar, pours a glass of gin, raises it to his lips, downs it all. Donald watches silently as Harold laughs and laughs and laughs*]


CURTAIN

END OF ACT I

# Act II

*A moment later. HAROLD is still laughing. MICHAEL, still at the bar, lowers his glass, turns to HAROLD.*

MICHAEL: What's so fucking funny?

HAROLD: [*Unintimidated. Quick hand to hip*] Life. Life is a goddamn laff-riot. You remember life.

LARRY: Happy birthday, Harold.

MICHAEL: [*To Harold*] You're stoned and you're late! You were supposed to arrive at this location at approximately eight-thirty dash nine o'clock!

HAROLD: What I *am*, Michael, is a thirty-two-year-old, ugly, pockmarked Jew fairy—and if it takes me a while to pull myself together and if I smoke a little grass before I can get up the nerve to show this face to the world, it's nobody's goddamn business but my own. [*Instant switch to chatty tone*] And how are *you* this evening?

[*Hank lifts Alan to the couch. Michael turns away from Harold, pours himself another drink. Donald watches. Harold sweeps past Michael over to where Bernard is helping Emory up off the floor. Larry returns the bucket to the bar. Michael puts some ice in his drink*]

EMORY: Happy birthday, Hallie.

HAROLD: What happened to *you*?

EMORY: [*Groans*] Don't ask!

HAROLD: Your lips are turning blue; you look like you been rimming a snowman.

EMORY: That piss-elegant kooze hit me!

[*Indicates Alan. Harold looks toward the couch. Alan has slumped his head forward into his own lap*]

MICHAEL: Careful, Emory, that kind of talk just makes him s'nervous.

[*Alan covers his ears with his hands*]

HAROLD: Who is she? Who was she? Who does she hope to be?

EMORY: Who knows, who cares!

HANK: His name is Alan McCarthy.

MICHAEL: Do forgive me for not formally introducing you.

HAROLD: [*Sarcastically, to Michael*] Not the famous college *chum*.

MICHAEL: [*Takes an ice cube out of his glass, throws it at Harold*] Do a figure eight on that.

HAROLD: Well, well, well. I finally get to meet dear ole Alan after all these years. And in black tie too. Is this my surprise from you, Michael?

LARRY: I think Alan is the one who got the surprise.

DONALD: And, if you'll notice, he's absolutely speechless.

EMORY: I *hope* she's in *shock!* She's a beast!

COWBOY: [*Indicating Alan*] Is it his birthday too?

EMORY: [*Indicates Cowboy to Harold*] *That's* your surprise.

LARRY: Speaking of beasts.

EMORY: From me to you, darlin'. How do you like it?

HAROLD: Oh, I suppose he has an interesting face and body—but it turns me right off because he can't talk intelligently about art.

EMORY: Yeah, ain't it a shame.

HAROLD: I could never *love* anyone like that.

EMORY: Never. *Who could?*

HAROLD: *I* could and *you* could, that's who could! Oh, Mary, she's *gorgeous!*

EMORY: She may be dumb, but she's all yours!

HAROLD: In affairs of the heart, there are no rules! Where'd you ever find him?

EMORY: Rae knew where.

MICHAEL: [*To Donald*] Rae is Rae Clark. That's R-A-E. She's Emory's dyke friend who sings at a place in the Village. She wears pinstriped suits and bills herself "Miss Rae Clark—Songs Tailored to Your Taste."

EMORY: Miss Rae Clark. Songs tailored to your taste!

MICHAEL: Have you ever heard of anything so crummy in your life?

EMORY: Rae's a fabulous chanteuse. I adore the way she does "Down in the Depths on the Ninetieth Floor."

MICHAEL: The faggot national anthem. [*Exits to the kitchen singing "Down in the Depths" in a butch baritone*]

HAROLD: [*To Emory*] All I can say is thank God for Miss Rae Clark. I think my present is a super-surprise. I'm so thrilled to get it I'd kiss you, but I don't want to get blood all over me.

EMORY: Ohhh, look at my sweater!

HAROLD: Wait'll you see your face.

BERNARD: Come on, Emory, let's clean you up. Happy birthday, Harold.

HAROLD: [*Smiles*] Thanks, love.

EMORY: My sweater is ruined!

MICHAEL: [*From the kitchen*] Take one of mine in the bedroom.

DONALD: The one on the floor is vicuña.

BERNARD: [*To Emory*] You'll feel better after I bathe your face.

EMORY: Cheer-up-things-could-get-worse-I-did-and-they-did.

[*Bernard leads Emory up the stairs*]

HAROLD: Just another birthday party with the folks.

[*Michael returns with a wine bottle and a green-crystal white-wine glass, pouring en route*]

MICHAEL: Here's a cold bottle of Pouilly-Fuissé I bought especially for you, kiddo.

HAROLD: Pussycat, all is forgiven. You can stay. No. You can stay, but not all is forgiven. Cheers.

MICHAEL: I didn't want it this way, Hallie.

HAROLD: [*Indicating Alan*] Who asked Mr. Right to celebrate my birthday?

DONALD: There are no accidents.

HAROLD: [*Referring to Donald*] And who asked *him?*

MICHAEL: *Guilty again.* When I make problems for myself, I go the whole route.

HAROLD: Always got to have your crutch, haven't you?

DONALD: I'm *not* leaving. [*Goes to the bar, makes himself another martini*]

HAROLD: Nobody ever thinks completely of somebody else. They always please themselves; they always cheat, if only a little bit.

LARRY: [*Referring to Alan*] Why is he sitting there with his hands over his ears?

DONALD: I think he has an ick.

[*Donald looks at Michael. Michael returns the look, steely*]

HANK: [*To Alan*] Can I get you a drink?

LARRY: How can he hear you, dummy, with his hands over his ears?

HAROLD: He can hear every word. In fact, he wouldn't miss a word if it killed him.

[*Alan removes his hands from his ears*]

HAROLD: What'd I tell you?

ALAN: I . . . I . . . feel sick. I think . . . I'm going to . . . throw up.

HAROLD: Say that again and I won't have to take my appetite depressant.

[*Alan looks desperately toward Hank*]

HANK: Hang on. [*Hank pulls Alan's arm around his neck, lifts him up, takes him up the stairs*]

HAROLD: Easy does it. One step at a time.

[*Bernard and Emory come out of the bath*]

BERNARD: There. Feel better?

EMORY: Oh, Mary, what would I do without you? [*Emory looks at himself in the mirror*] I am not ready for my close-up, Mr. De Mille. Nor will I be for the next two weeks.

[*Bernard picks up Michael's sweater off the floor. Hank and Alan are midway up the stairs*]

ALAN: I'm going to throw up! Let me go! Let me go!

[*Tears loose of Hank, bolts up the remainder of the stairs. He and Emory meet head-on. Emory screams*]

EMORY: Oh, my God, he's after me again!

[*Emory recoils as Alan whizzes past into the bathroom, slamming the door behind him. Hank has reached the bedroom*]

HANK: He's sick.

BERNARD: Yeah, sick in the head. Here, Emory, put this on.

EMORY: Oh, Mary, take me home. My nerves can't stand any more of this tonight.

[*Emory takes the vicuña sweater from Bernard, starts to put it on. Downstairs, Harold flamboyantly takes out a cigarette, takes a kitchen match from a striker, steps up on the seat of the couch, and sits on the back of it*]

HAROLD: TURNING ON! [*With that, he strikes the match on the sole of his shoe and lights up. Through a strained throat*] Anybody care to join me? [*Waves the cigarette in a slow pass*]

MICHAEL: Many thanks, no.

[*Harold passes it to Larry, who nods negatively*]

DONALD: No, thank you.

HAROLD: [*To Cowboy*] How about you, Tex?

COWBOY: Yeah. [*Cowboy takes the cigarette, makes some audible inhalations through his teeth*]

MICHAEL: I find the sound of the ritual alone utterly humiliating. [*Turns away, goes to the bar, makes another drink*]

LARRY: I hate the smell poppers leave on your fingers.

HAROLD: Why don't you get up and wash your hands?

[*Emory and Bernard come down the stairs*]

EMORY: Michael, I left the casserole in the oven. You can take it out anytime.

MICHAEL: You're not going.

EMORY: I couldn't eat now anyway.

HAROLD: Well, *I'm* absolutely ravenous. I'm going to eat until I have a fat attack.

MICHAEL: [*To Emory*] I said, you're *not going.*

HAROLD: [*To Michael*] Having a cocktail this evening, are we? In my honor?

EMORY: It's your favorite dinner, Hallie. I made it myself.

BERNARD: *Who* fixed the casserole?

EMORY: Well, *I* made the sauce!

BERNARD: Well, *I* made the salad!

LARRY: Girls, please.

MICHAEL: Please *what!*

HAROLD: Beware the hostile fag. When he's sober, he's dangerous. When he drinks, he's lethal.

MICHAEL: [*Referring to Harold*] Attention must *not* be paid.

HAROLD: I'm starved, Em, I'm ready for some of your Alice B. Toklas's opium-baked lasagna.

EMORY: Are you really? Oh, that makes me so pleased, maybe I'll just serve it before I leave.

MICHAEL: *You're not leaving.*

BERNARD: I'll help.

LARRY: I better help too. We don't need a nosebleed in the lasagna.

BERNARD: When the sauce is on it, you wouldn't be able to tell the difference anyway.

[*Emory, Bernard, and Larry exit to the kitchen*]

MICHAEL: [*Proclamation*] Nobody's going anywhere!

HAROLD: You are going to have schmertz tomorrow you wouldn't believe.

MICHAEL: May I kiss the hem of your schmata, Doctor Freud?

COWBOY: What are you two talking about? I don't understand.

DONALD: He's working through his Oedipus complex, sugar. With a machete.

COWBOY: Huh?

[*Hank comes down the stairs*]

HANK: Michael, is there any air spray?

HAROLD: Hair spray! You're supposed to be holding his head, not doing his hair.

HANK: *Air* spray, not *hair* spray.

MICHAEL: There's a can of floral spray right on top of the john.

HANK: Thanks. [*Hank goes back upstairs*]

HAROLD: Aren't you going to say "If it was a snake, it would have bitten you"?

MICHAEL: [*Indicating Cowboy*] That is something only your friend would say.

HAROLD: [*To Michael*] I am turning on and you are just turning. [*To Donald*] I keep my grass in the medicine cabinet. In a Band-Aid box. Somebody told me it's the safest place. If the cops arrive, you can always lock yourself in the bathroom and flush it down the john.

DONALD: *Very cagey.*

HAROLD: It makes more sense than where I *was* keeping it—in an oregano jar in the spice rack. I kept forgetting and accidentally turning my hateful mother on with the salad. [*A beat*] But I think she liked it. No matter what meal she comes over for—even if it's breakfast—she says, "Let's have a salad!"

COWBOY: [*To Michael*] Why do you say I would say "If it was a snake, it would have bitten you"? I think that's what I *would* have said.

MICHAEL: Of course you would have, baby. That's the kind of remark your pint-size brain thinks of. You are definitely the type who still moves his lips when he reads and who sits in a steam room and says things like "Hot enough for you?"

COWBOY: I never use the steam room when I go to the gym. It's bad after a workout. It flattens you down.

MICHAEL: Just after you've broken your back to blow yourself up like a poisoned dog.

COWBOY: Yeah.

MICHAEL: You're right, Harold. Not only can he not talk intelligently about art, he can't even follow from one sentence to the next.

HAROLD: *But he's beautiful.* He has *unnatural* natural beauty. [*Quick palm upheld*] Not that that means anything.

MICHAEL: It doesn't mean *everything.*

HAROLD: Keep telling yourself that as your hair drops out in handfuls. [*Quick palm upheld*] Not that it's not *natural* for one's hair to recede as one reaches seniority. Not that those wonderful lines that have begun creasing our countenances don't make all the difference in the world because they add so much *character.*

MICHAEL: Faggots are worse than women about their age. They think their lives are over at thirty. Physical beauty is not that goddamned important!

HAROLD: Of course not. How could it be—it's only in the eye of the beholder.

MICHAEL: And it's only skin deep—don't forget that one.

HAROLD: Oh, no, I haven't forgotten that one at all. It's only skin-deep and it's *transitory* too. It's *terribly* transitory. I mean, how long does it last—thirty or forty or fifty years at the most—depending on how well you take care of yourself. And not counting, of course, that you might die before it runs out anyway. Yes, it's too bad about this poor boy's face. It's tragic. He's absolutely cursed! [*Takes Cowboy's face in his hands*] How can *his* beauty ever compare with *my* soul? And although I have never seen my soul, I understand from my mother's rabbi that it's a knockout. I, however, cannot seem to locate it for a gander. And if I could, I'd sell it in a flash for some skin-deep, transitory, meaningless beauty!

[*Alan walks weakly into the bedroom and sits on the bed. Downstairs, Larry enters from the kitchen with salad plates. Hank comes into the bedroom and turns out the lamps. Alan lies down. Now only the light from the bathroom and the stairwell illuminate the room*]

MICHAEL: [*Makes sign of the cross with his drink in hand*] Forgive him, Father, for he knows not what he do.

[*Hank stands still in the half darkness*]

HAROLD: Michael, you kill me. You don't know what side of the fence you're on. If somebody says something pro-religion, you're against them. If somebody denies God, you're against *them.* One might say that you have some problem in that area. You can't live with it and you can't live without it.

[*Emory barges through the swinging door, carrying the casserole*]

EMORY: Hot stuff! Comin' through!

MICHAEL: [*To Emory*] One could murder you with very little effort.

HAROLD: [*To Michael*] You hang on to that great insurance policy called The Church.

MICHAEL: That's right. I believe in God, and if it turns out that there really isn't one, OK. Nothing lost. But if it turns out that there *is*—I'm covered.

[*Bernard enters, carrying a huge salad bowl. He puts it down, lights table candles*]

EMORY: [*To Michael*] Harriet Hypocrite, that's who you are.

MICHAEL: Right. I'm one of those truly rotten Catholics who gets drunk, sins all night and goes to Mass the next morning.

EMORY: Gilda Guilt. It depends on what you think sin is.

MICHAEL: Would you just shut up your goddamn minty mouth and get back to the goddamn kitchen!

EMORY: Say anything you want—*just don't hit me!* [*Exits. A beat*]

MICHAEL: Actually, I suppose Emory has a point—I only go to confession before I get on a plane.

BERNARD: Do you think God's power only exists at thirty thousand feet?

MICHAEL: It must. On the ground, I *am* God. In the air, I'm just one more scared son of a bitch.

[*A beat*]

BERNARD: I'm scared on the ground.

COWBOY: Me too. [*A beat*] That is, when I'm not high on pot or up on acid.

[*Hank comes down the stairs*]

LARRY: [*To Hank*] Well, is it bigger than a breadstick?

HANK: [*Ignores last remark. To Michael*] He's lying down for a minute.

HAROLD: How does the bathroom smell?

HANK: Better.

MICHAEL: Before it smelled like somebody puked. Now it smells like somebody puked in a gardenia patch.

LARRY: And how does the big hero feel?

HANK: Lay off, will you?

[*Emory enters with a basket of napkin-covered rolls, deposits them on the table*]

EMORY: *Dinner is served!*

[*Harold comes to the buffet table*]

HAROLD: Emory, it looks absolutely fabulous.

EMORY: I'd make somebody a good wife.

[*Emory serves pasta. Bernard serves the salad, pours wine. Michael goes to the bar, makes another drink*]

I could cook and do an apartment and entertain . . . [*Grabs a long-stem rose from an arrangement on the table, clenches it between his teeth, snaps his fingers and strikes a pose*] Kiss me quick, I'm Carmen!

[*Harold just looks at him blankly, passes on. Emory takes the flower out of his mouth*]

One really needs castanets for that sort of thing.

MICHAEL: And a getaway car.

[*Hank comes up to the table*]

EMORY: What would you like, big boy?

LARRY: Alan McCarthy, and don't hold the mayo.

EMORY: I can't keep up with you two—[*Indicating Hank, then Larry*]—I thought you were mad at him—now he's bitchin' you. What gives?

LARRY: Never mind.

[*Cowboy comes over to the table. Emory gives him a plate of food. Bernard gives him salad and a glass of wine. Hank moves to the couch, sits, and puts his plate and glass on the coffee table. Harold moves to sit on the stairs and eat*]

COWBOY: What is it?

LARRY: Lasagna.

COWBOY: It looks like spaghetti and meatballs sorta flattened out.

DONALD: It's been in the steam room.

COWBOY: It has?

MICHAEL: [*Contemptuously*] It looks like spaghetti and meatballs sorta flattened out. Ah, yes, Harold—truly enviable.

HAROLD: As opposed to you, who knows so much about *haute cuisine*. [*A beat*] Raconteur, gourmet, troll.

[*Larry takes a plate of food, goes to sit on the back of the couch from behind it*]

COWBOY: It's good.

HAROLD: [*Quick*] You like it, eat it.

MICHAEL: Stuff your mouth so that you can't say anything.

[*Donald takes a plate*]

HAROLD: Turning.

BERNARD: [*To Donald*] Wine?

DONALD: No, thanks.

MICHAEL: Aw, go on, kiddo, force yourself. Have a little *vin ordinaire* to wash down all that depressed pasta.

HAROLD: Sommelier, connoisseur, pig.

[*Donald takes the glass of wine, moves up by the bar, puts the glass of wine on it, leans against the wall, eats his food. Emory hands Bernard a plate*]

BERNARD: [*To Emory*] Aren't you going to have any?

EMORY: No. My lip hurts too much to eat.

MICHAEL: [*Crosses to table, picks up knife*] I hear if you puts a knife under de bed it cuts de pain.

HAROLD: [*To Michael*] I hear if you put a knife under your chin it cuts your throat.

EMORY: Anybody going to take a plate up to Alan?

MICHAEL: The punching bag has now dissolved into Flo Nightingale.

LARRY: Hank?

HANK: I don't think he'd have any appetite.

[*Alan, as if he's heard his name, gets up from the bed, moves slowly to the top of the stairwell. Bernard takes his plate, moves near the stairs, sits on the floor. Michael raps the knife on an empty wine glass*]

MICHAEL: Ladies and gentlemen. Correction: Ladies and ladies, I would like to announce that you have just eaten Sebastian Venable.

COWBOY: Just eaten *what?*

MICHAEL: Not *what,* stupid. *Who.* A character in a play. A fairy who was eaten alive. I mean the chop-chop variety.

COWBOY: Jesus.

HANK: Did Edward Albee write that play?

MICHAEL: No. Tennessee Williams.

HANK: Oh, yeah.

MICHAEL: Albee wrote *Who's Afraid of Virginia Woolf?*

LARRY: Dummy.

HANK: I know that. I just thought maybe he wrote that other one too.

LARRY: Well, you made a mistake.

HANK: So I made a mistake.

LARRY: That's right, you made a mistake.

HANK: What's the difference? You can't add.

COWBOY: Edward who?

MICHAEL: [*To Emory*] How much did you pay for him?

EMORY: He was a steal.

MICHAEL: He's a ham sandwich—fifty cents anytime of the day or night.

HAROLD: King of the Pig People.

[*Michael gives him a look. Donald returns his plate to the table*]

EMORY: [*To Donald*] Would you like some more?

DONALD: No, thank you, Emory. It was very good.

EMORY: Did you like it?

COWBOY: I'm not a steal. I cost twenty dollars.

[*Bernard returns his plate*]

EMORY: More?

BERNARD: [*Nods negatively*] It was delicious—even if I did make it myself.

EMORY: Isn't anybody having seconds?

HAROLD: I'm having seconds and thirds and maybe even fifths. [*Gets up off the stairs, comes toward the table*] I'm absolutely desperate to keep the weight up.

[*Bernard bends to whisper something in Emory's ear. Emory nods affirmatively and Bernard crosses to Cowboy and whispers in his ear. A beat. Cowboy returns his plate to the buffet and follows Emory and Bernard into the kitchen*]

MICHAEL: [*Parodying Harold*] You're *absolutely* paranoid about *absolutely* everything.

HAROLD: Oh, yeah, well, why don't you *not* tell me about it.

MICHAEL: You starve yourself all day, living on coffee and cottage cheese so that you can gorge yourself at one meal. Then you feel guilty and moan and groan about how fat you are and how ugly you are when the truth is you're no fatter or thinner than you ever are.

EMORY: Polly Paranoia. [*Emory moves to the coffee table to take Hank's empty plate*]

HANK: Just great, Emory.

EMORY: Connie Casserole, no-trouble-at-all-oh-Mary, D.A.

MICHAEL: [*To Harold*] . . . And this pathological lateness. It's downright *crazy*.

HAROLD: Turning.

MICHAEL: Standing before a bathroom mirror for hours and hours before you can walk out on the street. And looking no different after Christ knows how many applications of Christ knows how many ointments and salves and creams and masks.

HAROLD: I've got bad skin, what can I tell you.

MICHAEL: Who wouldn't after they deliberately take a pair of tweezers and *deliberately* mutilate their pores—no wonder you've got holes in your face after the hack job you've done on yourself year in and year out!

HAROLD: [*Coolly but definitely*] You hateful sow.

MICHAEL: Yes, you've got scars on your face—but they're not that bad and if you'd leave yourself alone you wouldn't have any more than you've already awarded yourself.

HAROLD: You'd really like me to compliment you now for being so honest, wouldn't you? For being my best friend who will tell me what even my best friends won't tell me. Swine.

MICHAEL: And the pills! [*Announcement to group*] Harold has been gathering, saving, and storing up barbiturates for the last year like a goddamn squirrel. Hundreds of Nembutals, hundreds of Seconals. All in preparation for and anticipation of the long winter of his death. [*Silence*] But I tell you right now, Hallie. When the time comes, you'll never have the guts. It's not always like it happens in plays, not all faggots bump themselves off at the end of the story.

HAROLD: What you say may be true. Time will undoubtedly tell. But, in the meantime, you've left out one detail—the cosmetics and astringents are *paid* for, the bathroom is *paid* for, the tweezers are *paid* for, and the pills *are paid for!*

[*Emory darts in and over to the light switch, plunges the room into darkness except for the light from the tapers on the buffet table, and begins to sing "Happy Birthday." Immediately Bernard pushes the swinging door open and Cowboy enters carrying a cake ablaze with candles. Everyone has now joined in with "Happy birthday, dear Harold, happy birthday to you." This is followed by a round of applause. Michael turns, goes to the bar, makes another drink*]

EMORY: Blow out your candles, Mary, and make a wish!

MICHAEL: [*To himself*] Blow out your candles, *Laura.*

[*Cowboy has brought cake over in front of Harold. He thinks a minute, blows out the candles. More applause*]

EMORY: Awwww, she's thirty-two years young!

HAROLD: [*Groans, holds his head*] Ohh, my God!

[*Bernard has brought in cake plates and forks. The room remains lit only by candlelight from the buffet table. Cowboy returns the cake to the table and Bernard begins to cut it and put the pieces on the plates*]

HANK: Now you have to open your gifts.

HAROLD: Do I have to open them here?

EMORY: Of course you've got to open them here. [*Hands Harold a gift. Harold begins to rip the paper off*]

HAROLD: Where's the card?

EMORY: Here.

HAROLD: Oh. From Larry. [*Finishes tearing off the paper*] It's *heaven!* Oh, I just love it, Larry. [*Harold holds up a graphic design—a large-scale deed to Boardwalk, like those used in a Monopoly game*]

COWBOY: What is it?

HAROLD: It's the deed to Boardwalk.

EMORY: Oh, gay pop art!

DONALD: [*To Larry*] It's sensational. Did you do it?

LARRY: Yes.

HAROLD: Oh, it's super, Larry. It goes up the minute I get home.

[*Harold gives Larry a peck on the cheek*]

COWBOY: [*To Harold*] I don't get it—you cruise Atlantic City or something?

MICHAEL: Will somebody get him out of here!

[*Harold has torn open another gift, takes the card from inside*]

HAROLD: Oh, what a nifty sweater! Thank you, Hank.

HANK: You can take it back and pick out another one if you want to.

HAROLD: I think this one is just nifty.

[*Donald goes to the bar, makes himself a brandy and soda*]

BERNARD: Who wants cake?

EMORY: Everybody?

DONALD: None for me.

MICHAEL: I'd just like to sleep on mine, thank you.

[*Hank comes over to the table. Bernard gives him a plate of cake, passes another one to Cowboy and a third to Larry. Harold has torn the paper off another gift. Suddenly laughs aloud*]

HAROLD: Oh, Bernard! How divine! Look, everybody! Bejeweled knee pads! [*Holds up a pair of basketball knee pads with sequin initials*]

BERNARD: Monogrammed!

EMORY: Bernard, you're a camp!

MICHAEL: Y'all heard of Gloria DeHaven and Billy De Wolfe, well, dis here is Rosemary De Camp!

BERNARD: Who?

EMORY: I never miss a Rosemary De Camp picture.

HANK: I've never heard of her.

COWBOY: Me neither.

HANK: Not all of us spent their childhood in a movie house, Michael. Some of us played baseball.

DONALD: And mowed the lawn.

EMORY: Well, *I* know who Rosemary De Camp is.

MICHAEL: You would. It's a cinch you wouldn't recognize a baseball or a lawn mower.

[*Harold has unwrapped his last gift. He is silent. Pause*]

HAROLD: Thank you, Michael.

MICHAEL: What? [*Turns to see the gift*] Oh. [*A beat*] You're welcome. [*Michael finishes off his drink, returns to the bar*]

LARRY: What is it, Harold?

[*A beat*]

HAROLD: It's a photograph of him in a silver frame. And there's an inscription engraved and the date.

BERNARD: What's it say?

HAROLD: Just . . . something personal.

[*Michael spins round from the bar*]

MICHAEL: Hey, Bernard, what do you say we have a little music to liven things up!

BERNARD: OK.

EMORY: Yeah, I feel like dancing.

MICHAEL: How about something good and ethnic, Emory—one of your specialties, like a military toe tap with sparklers.

EMORY: I don't do that at birthdays—only on the Fourth of July.

[*Bernard puts on a romantic record. Emory goes to Bernard. They start to dance slowly*]

LARRY: Come on, Michael.

MICHAEL: I only lead.

LARRY: I can follow.

[*They start to dance*]

HAROLD: Come on, Tex, you're on.

[*Cowboy gets to his feet but is a washout as a dancing partner. Harold gives up, takes out another cigarette, strikes a match. As he does, he catches sight of someone over by the stairs, walks over to Alan. Blows out match*]

Wanna dance?

EMORY: [*Sees Alan*] Uh-oh. Yvonne the Terrible is back.

MICHAEL: Oh, hello, Alan. Feel better? This is where you came in, isn't it?

[*Alan starts to cross directly to the door. Michael breaks away*]

Excuse me, Larry . . .

[*Alan has reached the door and has started to open it as Michael intercepts, slams the door with one hand, and leans against it, crossing his legs*]

As they say in the Deep South, don't rush off in the heat of the day.

HAROLD: Revolution complete.

[*Michael slowly takes Alan by the arm, walks him slowly back into the room*]

MICHAEL: . . . You missed the cake—and you missed the opening of the gifts—but you're still in luck. You're just in time for a party game.

[*They have reached the phonograph. Michael rejects the record. The music stops, the dancing stops. Michael releases Alan, claps his hands*]

. . . Hey, everybody! Game time!

[*Alan starts to move. Michael catches him gently by the sleeve*]

HAROLD: Why don't you just let him go, Michael?

MICHAEL: He can go if he wants to—but not before we play a little game.

EMORY: What's it going to be—movie-star gin?

MICHAEL: That's too faggy for Alan to play—he wouldn't be any good at it.

BERNARD: What about Likes and Dislikes?

[*Michael lets go of Alan, takes a pencil and pad from the desk*]

MICHAEL: It's too much trouble to find enough pencils, and besides, Emory always puts down the same thing. He dislikes artificial fruit and flowers and coffee grinders made into lamps—and he likes Mabel Mercer, poodles, and *All About Eve*—the screenplay of which he will then recite *verbatim*.

EMORY: I put down other things sometimes.

MICHAEL: Like a tan out of season?

EMORY: I just always put down little "Chi-Chi" because I adore her so much.

MICHAEL: If one is of the masculine gender, a poodle is the *insignia* of one's deviation.

BERNARD: You know why old ladies like poodles—because they go down on them.

EMORY: *They do not!*

LARRY: We could play B for Botticelli.

MICHAEL: We *could* play *Spin* the Botticelli, but we're not going to.

[*A beat*]

HAROLD: What would you like to play, Michael—the Truth Game?

[*Michael chuckles to himself*]

MICHAEL: Cute, Hallie.

HAROLD: Or do you want to play Murder? You all remember that one, don't you?

MICHAEL: [*To Harold*] Very, very cute.

DONALD: As I recall, they're quite similar. The rules are the same in both— you kill somebody.

MICHAEL: In affairs of the heart, there are no rules. Isn't that right, Harold?

HAROLD: That's what I always say.

MICHAEL: Well, that's the name of the game. The Affairs of the Heart.

COWBOY: I've never heard of that one.

MICHAEL: Of course you've never heard of it—I just made it up, baby doll. Affairs of the Heart is a combination of both the Truth Game and Murder—with a new twist.

HAROLD: I can hardly wait to find out what that is.

ALAN: Mickey, I'm leaving. [*Starts to move*]

MICHAEL: [*Firmly, flatly*] Stay where you are.

HAROLD: Michael, let him go.

MICHAEL: He really doesn't *want* to. If he did, he'd have left a long time ago—or he wouldn't have come here in the first place.

ALAN: [*Holding his forehead*] . . . Mickey, I don't *feel* well!

MICHAEL: [*Low tone, but distinctly articulate*] My name is Michael. I am called Michael. You must never call anyone called Michael Mickey. Those of us who are named Michael get very nervous about it. If you don't believe it—try it.

ALAN: I'm sorry. I can't think.

MICHAEL: You can think. What you can't do—is leave. It's like watching an accident on the highway—you can't look at it and you can't look away.

ALAN: I . . . feel . . . weak . . .

MICHAEL: You are weak. Much weaker than I think you realize. [*Takes Alan by the arm, leads him to a chair. Slowly, deliberately, pushes him down into it*] Now! Who's going to play with Alan and me? Everyone?

HAROLD: I have no intention of playing.

DONALD: Nor do I.

MICHAEL: Well, not everyone is a participant in *life*. There are always those who stand on the sidelines and watch.

LARRY: What's the game?

MICHAEL: Simply this: We all have to call on the telephone the *one person* we truly believe we have loved.

HANK: I'm not playing.

LARRY: Oh, yes, you are.

HANK: You'd like for me to play, wouldn't you?

LARRY: You bet I would. I'd like to know who you'd call after all the fancy speeches I've heard lately. Who would you call? Would you call me?

MICHAEL: [*To Bernard*] Sounds like there's, how you say, trouble in paradise.

HAROLD: If there isn't, I think you'll be able to stir up some.

HANK: And who would *you* call? Don't think I think for one minute it would be me. Or that one call would do it. You'd have to make several, wouldn't you? About three long-distance and God only knows how many locals.

COWBOY: I'm glad I don't have to pay the bill.

MICHAEL: Quiet!

HAROLD: [*Loud whisper to Cowboy*] Oh, don't worry, Michael won't pay it either.

MICHAEL: Now, here's how it works.

LARRY: I thought you said there were no rules.

MICHAEL: That's right. In Affairs of the Heart, there are no rules. This is the goddamn point system! [*No response from anyone. A beat*] If you make the call, you get one point. If the person you are calling answers, you get two more points. If somebody else answers, you get only one. If there's no answer at all, you're screwed.

DONALD: You're screwed if you make the call.

HAROLD: You're a *fool*—if you screw yourself.

MICHAEL: When you get the person whom you are calling on the line—if you tell them who you are, you get two points. And then—if you tell them that you *love* them—you get a bonus of five more points!

HAROLD: Hateful.

MICHAEL: Therefore you can get as many as ten points and as few as one.

HAROLD: You can get as few as none—if you know how to work it.

MICHAEL: The one with the highest score wins.

ALAN: Hank. Let's get out of here.

EMORY: Well, now. Did you hear that!

MICHAEL: Just the two of you together. The pals . . . the guys . . . the buddy-buddies . . . the he-men.

EMORY: I think Larry might have something to say about that.

BERNARD: Emory.

MICHAEL: The duenna speaks. [*Crosses to take the telephone from the desk, brings it to the group*] So who's playing? Not including Cowboy, who, as a gift, is neuter. And, of course, le voyeur. [*A beat*] Emory: ? Bernard?

BERNARD: I don't think I want to play.

MICHAEL: Why, Bernard! Where's your fun-loving spirit?

BERNARD: I don't think this game is fun.

HAROLD: It's absolutely hateful.

ALAN: Hank, leave with me.

HANK: You don't understand, Alan. I can't. You can . . . but I can't.

ALAN: Why, Hank? Why can't you?

LARRY: [*To Hank*] If he doesn't understand, why don't you explain it to him?

MICHAEL: *I'll* explain it.

HAROLD: I had a feeling you might.

MICHAEL: Although I doubt that it'll make any difference. That type refuses to understand that which they do not wish to accept. They reject certain facts. And Alan is decidedly from The Ostrich School of Reality. [*A beat*] Alan. . . Larry and Hank are lovers. Not just roommates, *bed*mates. *Lovers.*

ALAN: Michael!

MICHAEL: No man's still got a *roommate* when he's over thirty years old. If they're not lovers, they're sisters.

LARRY: Hank is the one who's over thirty.

MICHAEL: Well, you're pushing it!

ALAN: . . . Hank?

[*A beat*]

HANK: Yes, Alan. Larry is my lover.

ALAN: But . . . but . . . you're married.

[*Michael, Larry, Emory, and Cowboy are sent into instant gales of laughter*]

HAROLD: I think you said the wrong thing.

MICHAEL: Don't you love that quaint little idea—if a man is married, then he is automatically heterosexual. [*A beat*] Alan—Hank swings both ways—with a definite preference. [*A beat*] Now. Who makes the first call? Emory?

EMORY: You go, Bernard.

BERNARD: I don't want to.

EMORY: I don't want to either. I don't want to at all.

DONALD: [*To himself*] There are no accidents.

MICHAEL: Then, may I say, on your way home I hope you *will* yourself over an embankment.

EMORY: [*To Bernard*] Go on. Call up Peter Dahlbeck. That's who you'd like to call, isn't it?

MICHAEL: Who is Peter Dahlbeck?

EMORY: The boy in Detroit whose family Bernard's mother has been a laundress for since he was a pickaninny.

BERNARD: I worked for them too—after school and every summer.

EMORY: It's always been a large order of Hero Worship.

BERNARD: I think I've loved him all my life. But he never knew I was alive. Besides, he's straight.

COWBOY: So nothing ever happened between you?

EMORY: Oh, they finally made it—in the pool house one night after a drunken swimming party.

LARRY: With the right wine and the right music there're damn few that aren't curious.

MICHAEL: Sounds like there's a lot of Lady Chatterley in Mr. Dahlbeck, wouldn't you say, Donald?

DONALD: I've never been an O'Hara fan myself.

BERNARD: . . . And afterwards we went swimming in the nude in the dark with only the moon reflecting on the water.

DONALD: Nor Thomas Merton.

BERNARD: It was beautiful.

MICHAEL: How romantic. And then the next morning you took him his coffee and Alka-Seltzer on a tray.

BERNARD: It was in the afternoon. I remember I was worried sick all morning about having to face him. But he pretended like nothing at all had happened.

MICHAEL: Christ, he must have been so drunk he didn't remember a thing.

BERNARD: Yeah. I was sure relieved.

MICHAEL: Odd how that works. And now, for ten points, get that liar on the phone.

[*A beat. Bernard picks up the phone, dials*]

LARRY: You *know* the number?

BERNARD: Sure. He's back in Grosse Pointe, living at home. He just got separated from his third wife.

[*All watch Bernard as he puts the receiver to his ear, waits. A beat. He hangs up quickly*]

EMORY: D.A. or B.Y.?

MICHAEL: He didn't even give it time to find out. [*Coaxing*] Go ahead, Bernard. Pick up the phone and dial. You'll think of something. You know you want to call him. You know that, don't you? Well, go ahead. Your curiosity has got the best of you now. So . . . go on, call him.

[*A beat. Bernard picks up the receiver, dials again. Lets it ring this time*]

HAROLD: Hateful.

COWBOY: What's D.A. or B.Y.?

EMORY: That's operator lingo. It means—"Doesn't Answer" or "Busy."

BERNARD: . . . Hello?

MICHAEL: One point. [*Efficiently takes note on the pad*]

BERNARD: Who's speaking? Oh . . . Mrs. Dahlbeck.

MICHAEL: [*Taking note*] One point.

BERNARD: . . . It's Bernard—Francine's boy.

EMORY: *Son,* not *boy.*

BERNARD: . . . How are you? Good. Good. Oh, just fine, thank you. Mrs. Dahlbeck . . . is . . . Peter . . . at home? Oh. Oh, I see.

MICHAEL: [*Shakes his head*] Shhhhiiii . . .

BERNARD: . . . Oh, no. No, it's nothing important. I just wanted to . . . to tell him . . . that . . . to tell him I . . . I . . .

MICHAEL: [*Prompting flatly*] I love him. That I've always loved him.

BERNARD: . . . that I was sorry to hear about him and his wife.

MICHAEL: No points!

BERNARD: . . . My mother wrote me. Yes. It is. It really is. Well. Would you just tell him I called and said . . . that I was . . . just . . . very, very sorry to hear and I . . . hope . . . they can get everything straightened out. Yes. Yes. Well, good night. Goodbye.

[*Hangs up slowly. Michael draws a definite line across his pad, makes a definite period*]

MICHAEL: Two points total. Terrible. Next!

[*Michael whisks the phone out of Bernard's hands, gives it to Emory*]

EMORY: Are you all right, Bernard?

BERNARD: [*Almost to himself*] Why did I call? Why did I do that?

LARRY: [*To Bernard*] Where was he?

BERNARD: Out on a date.

MICHAEL: Come on, Emory. Punch in.

[*Emory picks up the phone, dials information. A beat*]

EMORY: Could I have the number, please—in the Bronx—for a Delbert Botts.

LARRY: *A* Delbert Botts! How many can there be!

BERNARD: Oh, I wish I hadn't called now.

EMORY: . . . No, the residence number, please. [*Waves his hand at Michael, signaling for the pencil. Michael hands it to him. He writes on the white plastic phone case*] . . . Thank you. [*A beat. And he indignantly slams down the receiver*] I do wish information would stop calling me "Ma'am"!

MICHAEL: By all means, scribble all over the telephone. [*Snatches the pencil from Emory's hands*]

EMORY: It comes off with a little spit.

MICHAEL: Like a lot of things.

LARRY: Who the hell is Delbert Botts?

EMORY: The one person I have always loved. [*To Michael*] That's who you said call, isn't it?

MICHAEL: That's right, Emory Board.

LARRY: How could you love anybody with a name like that?

MICHAEL: Yes, Emory, you couldn't love anybody with a name like that. It wouldn't look good on a place card. Isn't that right, Alan? [*Michael slaps Alan on the shoulder. Alan is silent. Michael snickers*]

EMORY: I admit his name is not so good—but he is absolutely beautiful. At least, he was when I was in high school. Of course, I haven't seen him since and he was about seven years older than I even then.

MICHAEL: Christ, you better call him quick before he dies.

EMORY: I've loved him ever since the first day I laid eyes on him, which was when I was in the fifth grade and he was a senior. Then, he went away to college and by the time he got out *I* was in high school, and he had become a dentist.

MICHAEL: [*With incredulous disgust*] A dentist!

EMORY: Yes. Delbert Botts, D.D.S. And he opened his office in a bank building.

HAROLD: And you went and had every tooth in your head pulled out, right?

EMORY: No. I just had my teeth cleaned, that's all.

[*Donald turns from the bar with two drinks in his hands*]

BERNARD: [*To himself*] Oh, I shouldn't have called.

MICHAEL: Will you shut up, Bernard! And take your boring, sleep-making icks somewhere else. *Go!*

[*Michael extends a pointed finger toward the steps. Bernard takes the wine bottle and his glass and moves toward the stairs, pouring himself another drink on the way*]

I remember I looked right into his eyes the whole time and I kept wanting to bite his fingers.

HAROLD: Well, it's absolutely mind-boggling.

MICHAEL: Phyllis Phallic.

HAROLD: It absolutely boggles the mind.

[*Donald brings one of the drinks to Alan. Alan takes it, drinks it down*]

MICHAEL: [*Referring to Donald*] Sara Samaritan.

EMORY: . . . I told him I was having my teeth cleaned for the Junior-Senior Prom, for which I was in charge of decorations. I told him it was a celestial theme and I was cutting stars out of tinfoil and making clouds out of chicken wire and angel's hair. [*A beat*] He couldn't have been less impressed.

COWBOY: I got angel's hair down my shirt once at Christmastime. Gosh, did it itch!

EMORY: . . . I told him I was going to burn incense in pots so that white fog would hover over the dance floor and it would look like heaven—just like I'd seen it in a Rita Hayworth movie. I can't remember the title.

MICHAEL: The picture was called *Down to Earth*. Any *kid* knows that.

COWBOY: . . . And it made little tiny cuts in the creases of my fingers. Man, did they sting! It would be terrible if you got that stuff in your . . .

[*Michael circles slowly toward him*]

I'll be quiet.

EMORY: He was engaged to this stupid-ass girl named Loraine whose mother was truly Supercunt.

MICHAEL: Don't digress.

EMORY: Well, anyway, I was a wreck. I mean a total mess. I couldn't eat, sleep, stand up, sit down, *nothing*. I could hardly cut out silver stars or finish the clouds for the prom. So I called him on the telephone and asked if I could see him alone.

HAROLD: Clearly not the coolest of moves.

[*Donald looks at Alan. Alan looks away*]

EMORY: He said OK and told me to come by his house. I was so nervous my hands were shaking and my voice was unsteady. I couldn't look at him this time—I just stared straight in space and blurted out why I'd come. I told him . . . I wanted him to be my friend. I said that I had never had a friend who I could talk to and tell everything and trust. I asked him if he would be my friend.

COWBOY: You poor bastard.

MICHAEL: SHHHHHH!

BERNARD: What'd he say?

EMORY: He said he would be glad to be my friend. And anytime I ever wanted to see him or call him—to just call him and he'd see me. And he shook my trembling wet hand and I left on a cloud.

MICHAEL: One of the ones you made yourself.

EMORY: And the next day I went and bought him a gold-plated cigarette lighter and had his initials monogrammed on it and wrote a card that said "From your friend, Emory."

HAROLD: Seventeen years old and already big with the gifts.

COWBOY: Yeah. And cards too.

EMORY: . . . And then the night of the prom I found out.

BERNARD: Found out what?

EMORY: I heard two girls I knew giggling together. They were standing behind some goddamn corrugated-cardboard Greek columns I had borrowed from a department store and had draped with yards and yards of goddamn cheesecloth. Oh, Mary, it takes a fairy to make something pretty.

MICHAEL: *Don't digress.*

EMORY: This girl who was telling the story said she had heard it from her mother—and her mother had heard it from Loraine's mother. [*To Michael*] You see, Loraine and her mother were not beside the point. [*Back to the group*] Obviously, Del had told Loraine about my calling and about the gift. [*A beat*] Pretty soon everybody at the dance had heard about it and they were laughing and making jokes. Everybody knew I had a crush on Doctor Delbert Botts and that I had asked him to be my friend. [*A beat*]What they didn't know was that I *loved* him. And that I would go on loving him years after they had all forgotten my funny secret.

[*Pause*]

HAROLD: Well, I for one need an insulin injection.

MICHAEL: *Call him.*

BERNARD: Don't, Emory.

MICHAEL: Since when are you telling him what to do!

EMORY: [*To Bernard*] What do I care—I'm pissed! I'll do anything. Three times.

BERNARD: Don't. *Please!*

MICHAEL: I said call him.

BERNARD: Don't! You'll be sorry. Take my word for it.

EMORY: What have I got to lose?

BERNARD: Your dignity. That's what you've got to lose.

MICHAEL: Well, *that's* a knee-slapper! I love *your* telling *him* about dignity when you allow him to degrade you constantly by Uncle Tom-ing you to death.

BERNARD: *He* can do it, Michael. *I* can do it. But *you can't* do it.

MICHAEL: Isn't that discrimination?

BERNARD: I don't like it from him and I don't like it from me—but I do it to myself and I let him do it. I let him do it because it's the only thing that, to him, makes him my equal. We both got the short end of the stick—but I got a hell of a lot more than he did and he knows it. I let him Uncle Tom me just so he can tell himself he's not a complete loser.

MICHAEL: How very considerate.

BERNARD: It's his defense. You have your defense, Michael. But it's indescribable.

[*Emory quietly licks his finger and begins to rub the number off the telephone case*]

MICHAEL: [*To Bernard*] Y'all want to hear a little polite parlor jest from the liberal Deep South? Do you know why *Nigras* have such big lips? Because they're always going "P-p-p-p-a-a-a-h!"

[*The labial noise is exasperating with lazy disgust as he shuffles about the room*]

DONALD: Christ, Michael!

MICHAEL: [*Unsuccessfully tries to tear the phone away from Emory*] I can do without your goddamn spit all over my telephone, you nellie coward.

EMORY: I may be nellie, but I'm no coward. [*Starts to dial*] Bernard, forgive me. I'm sorry. I won't ever say those things to you again.

[*Michael watches triumphant. Bernard pours another glass of wine. A beat*]

B.Y.

MICHAEL: It's busy?

EMORY: [*Nods*] Loraine is probably talking to her mother. Oh, yes. Delbert married Loraine.

MICHAEL: I'm sorry, you'll have to forfeit your turn. We can't wait.

[*Takes the phone, hands it to Larry, who starts to dial*]

HAROLD: [*To Larry*] Well, you're not wasting any time.

HANK: Who are you calling?

LARRY: Charlie.

[*Emory gets up, jerks the phone out of Larry's hands*]

EMORY: I refuse to forfeit my turn! It's *my turn,* and I'm taking it!

MICHAEL: That's the spirit, Emory! *Hit that iceberg—don't miss it! Hit it! Goddamn it!* I want a smash of a finale!

EMORY: Oh, God, I'm drunk.

MICHAEL: A falling-down-drunk-nellie-queen.

HAROLD: Well, that's the pot calling the kettle beige!

MICHAEL: [*Snapping. To Harold*] *I am not drunk!* You cannot tell that I am drunk! Donald! I'm not drunk! Am I!

DONALD: *I'm* drunk.

EMORY: So am I. I am a *major drunk.*

MICHAEL: [*To Emory*] Shut up and dial!

EMORY: [*Dialing*] I am a major drunk of this or any other season.

DONALD: [*To Michael*] Don't you mean "shut up and deal"?

EMORY: . . . It's ringing. It is no longer B.Y. Hello?

MICHAEL: [*Taking note*] One point.

EMORY: . . . Who's speaking? Who? . . . Doctor Delbert Botts?

MICHAEL: Two points.

EMORY: Oh, Del, is this really you? Oh, nobody. You don't know me. You wouldn't remember me. I'm . . . just a friend. A falling-down drunken friend. Hello? Hello? Hello? [*Lowers the receiver*] He hung up. [*Emory hangs up the telephone*]

MICHAEL: Three points total. You're winning.

EMORY: He said I must have the wrong party.

[*Bernard gets up, goes into the kitchen*]

HAROLD: He's right. We have the wrong party. We should be somewhere else.

EMORY: It's your party, Hallie. Aren't you having a good time?

HAROLD: Simply fabulous. And what about you? Are you having a good time, Emory? Are you having as good a time as you thought you would?

[*Larry takes the phone*]

MICHAEL: If you're bored, Harold, we could sing "Happy Birthday" again—to the tune of "Havah Nageelah."

[*Harold takes out another joint*]

HAROLD: Not for all the tea in Mexico. [*Lights up*]

HANK: My turn now.

LARRY: It's my turn to call Charlie.

HANK: No. Let me.

LARRY: Are *you* going to call Charlie?

MICHAEL: The score is three to two. Emory's favor.

ALAN: Don't, Hank. Don't you see—Bernard was right.

HANK: [*Firmly, to Alan*] I want to. [*A beat. Holds out his hand for the phone*] Larry?

[*A beat*]

LARRY: [*Gives him the phone*] Be my eager guest.

COWBOY: [*To Larry*] Is he going to call Charlie for you?

[*Larry breaks into laughter. Hank starts to dial*]

LARRY: Charlie is all the people I cheat on Hank with.

DONALD: With whom I cheat on Hank.

MICHAEL: The butcher, the baker, the candlestick maker.

LARRY: Right! I love 'em all. And what he refuses to understand—is that I've got to *have* 'em all. I am *not* the marrying kind, and I never will be.

HAROLD: Gypsy feet.

LARRY: Who are you calling?

MICHAEL: Jealous?

LARRY: Curious as hell!

MICHAEL: And a little jealous too.

LARRY: Who are you calling?

MICHAEL: Did it ever occur to you that Hank might be doing the same thing behind your back that you do behind his?

LARRY: I wish to Christ he would. It'd make life a hell of a lot easier. Who are you calling?

HAROLD: Whoever it is, they're not sitting on top of the telephone.

HANK: Hello?

COWBOY: They must have been in the tub.

MICHAEL: [*Snaps at Cowboy*] Eighty-six!

[*Cowboy goes over to a far corner, sits down. Bernard enters, uncorking another bottle of wine. Taking note*]

MICHAEL: One point.

HANK: . . . I'd like to leave a message.

MICHAEL: Not in. One point.

HANK: Would you say that Hank called? Yes, it is. Oh, good evening. How are you?

LARRY: Who the hell *is* that?

HANK: Yes, that's right—the message is for my roommate, Larry. Just say that I called and . . .

LARRY: It's our answering service!

HANK: . . . and said . . . I love you.

MICHAEL: *Five points!* You said it! You get five goddamn points for saying it!

ALAN: Hank! Hank! . . . Are you crazy?

HANK: . . . No. You didn't hear me incorrectly. That's what I said. The message is for Larry and it's from me, Hank, and it is just as I said: *I . . . love . . . you.* Thanks. [*Hangs up*]

MICHAEL: Seven points total! Hank, you're ahead, baby. You're way, way ahead of everybody!

ALAN: Why? . . . Oh, Hank, why? Why did you do that?

HANK: Because I do love him. And I don't care who knows it.

ALAN: Don't say that.

HANK: Why not? It's the truth.

ALAN: I can't believe you.

HANK: [*Directly to Alan*] I left my wife and family for Larry.

ALAN: I'm really not interested in hearing about it.

MICHAEL: Sure you are. Go ahead, Hankola, tell him all about it.

ALAN: No! I don't want to hear it. It's disgusting!

[*A beat*]

HANK: Some men do it for another woman.

ALAN: Well, I could understand *that*. That's *normal*.

HANK: It just doesn't always work out that way, Alan. No matter how you might want it to. And God knows, nobody ever wanted it more than I did. I really and truly felt that I was in love with my wife when I married her. It wasn't altogether my trying to prove something to myself. I did love her and she loved me. But . . . there was always that something there . . .

DONALD: You mean your attraction to your own sex.

HANK: Yes.

ALAN: Always?

HANK: I don't know. I suppose so.

EMORY: I've known what I was since I was four years old.

MICHAEL: Everybody's always known it about *you,* Emory.

DONALD: I've always known it about myself too.

HANK: I don't know when it was that I started admitting it to myself. For so long I either labeled it something else or denied it completely.

MICHAEL: Christ-was-I-drunk-last-night.

HANK: And then there came a time when I just couldn't lie to myself anymore . . . I thought about it but I never did anything about it. I think the first time was during my wife's last pregnancy. We lived near New Haven—in the country. She and the kids still live there. Well, anyway, there was a teachers' meeting here in New York. She didn't feel up to the trip and I came alone. And that day on the train I began to think about it and think about it and think about it. I thought of nothing else the whole trip. And within fifteen minutes after I had arrived I had picked up a guy in the men's room of Grand Central Station.

ALAN: [*Quietly*] Jesus.

HANK: I'd never done anything like that in my life before and I was scared to death. But he turned out to be a nice fellow. I've never seen him again and it's funny I can't even remember his name anymore. [*A beat*] Anyway, after that, it got easier.

HAROLD: Practice makes perfect.

HANK: And then . . . sometime later . . . not very long after, Larry was in New Haven and we met at a party my wife and I had gone in town for.

EMORY: And your real troubles began.

HANK: That was two years ago.

LARRY: Why am I always the goddamn villain in the piece! If I'm not thought of as a happy-home wrecker, I'm an impossible son of a bitch to live with!

HAROLD: Guilt turns to hostility. Isn't that right, Michael?

MICHAEL: Go stick your tweezers in your cheek.

LARRY: I'm fed up to the teeth with everybody feeling so goddamn sorry for poor shat-upon Hank.

EMORY: Aw, Larry, everybody knows you're Frieda Fickle.

LARRY: I've never made any promises and I never intend to. It's my right to lead my sex life without answering to *anybody*—Hank included! And if those terms are not acceptable, then we must not live together. Numerous relations is a part of the way I am!

EMORY: You don't have to be gay to be a wanton.

LARRY: By the way I am, I don't mean being gay—I mean my sexual appetite. And I don't think of myself as a wanton. Emory, you are the most promiscuous person I know.

EMORY: I am not promiscuous at all!

MICHAEL: Not by choice. By design. Why would anybody want to go to bed with a flaming little sissy like you?

BERNARD: Michael!

MICHAEL: [*To Emory*] Who'd make a pass at you—I'll tell you who—nobody. Except maybe some fugitive from the Braille Institute.

BERNARD: [*To Emory*] Why do you let him talk to you that way?

HAROLD: Physical beauty is not everything.

MICHAEL: Thank you, Quasimodo.

LARRY: What do you think it's like living with the goddamn gestapo! I can't breathe without getting the third degree!

MICHAEL: Larry, it's your turn to call.

LARRY: I can't take all that let's-be-faithful-and-never-look-at-another-person routine. It just doesn't work. If you want to promise that, fine. Then do it and stick to it. But if you *have* to promise it—as far as I'm concerned—nothing finishes a relationship faster.

HAROLD: Give me Librium or give me Meth.

BERNARD: [*Intoxicated now*] Yeah, freedom, baby! Freedom!

LARRY: You gotta have it! It can't work any other way. And the ones who swear their undying fidelity are lying. Most of them, anyway—ninety percent of them. They cheat on each other constantly and lie through their teeth. I'm sorry, I can't be like that and it drives Hank up the wall.

HANK: There is that ten percent.

LARRY: The only way it stands a chance is with some sort of an understanding.

HANK: I've tried to go along with that.

LARRY: Aw, *come on!*

HANK: I agreed to an agreement.

LARRY: Your agreement.

MICHAEL: What agreement?

LARRY: A ménage.

HAROLD: The lover's agreement.

LARRY: Look, I know a lot of people think it's the answer. They don't consider it cheating. But it's not my style.

HANK: Well, *I* certainly didn't want it.

LARRY: Then who suggested it?

HANK: It was a compromise.

LARRY: Exactly.

HANK: And you agreed.

LARRY: I didn't agree to anything. You agreed to your own proposal and *informed me* that I agreed.

COWBOY: I don't understand. What's a me . . . mena-a . . .

MICHAEL: A ménage à trois, baby. Two's company—three's a ménage.

COWBOY: Oh.

HANK: It works for some.

LARRY: Well, I'm not one for group therapy. I'm sorry, I can't relate to anyone or anything that way. I'm old-fashioned—I like 'em all, but I like 'em one at a time!

MICHAEL: [*To Larry*] Did you like Donald as a single side attraction?

[*Pause*]

LARRY: Yes. I did.

DONALD: So did I, Larry.

LARRY: [*To Donald, referring to Michael*] Did you tell him?

DONALD: No.

MICHAEL: It was perfectly obvious from the moment you walked in. What was the song and dance about having seen each other but never having met?

DONALD: It was true. We saw each other in the baths and went to bed together, but we never spoke a word and never knew each other's name.

EMORY: You have better luck than I do. If I don't get arrested, my trick announces upon departure that he's been exposed to hepatitis! One more shot of gamma globulin and my ass'll look like a pair of colanders!

MICHAEL: In spring a young man's fancy turns to a fancy young man.

LARRY: [*To Hank*] Don't look at me like that. You've been playing footsie with the Blue Book all night.

DONALD: I think he only wanted to show you what's good for the gander is good for the gander.

HANK: That's right.

LARRY: [*To Hank*] I suppose you'd like the three of us to have a go at it.

HANK: At least it'd be together.

LARRY: That point eludes me.

HANK: What kind of an understanding do you *want*!

LARRY: Respect—for each other's freedom. With no need to lie or pretend. In my own way, Hank, I love you, but you have to understand that even though I do want to go on living with you, sometimes there may be others. I don't want to flaunt it in your face. If it happens, I know I'll never mention it. But if you ask me, I'll tell you. I don't want to hurt you, but I won't lie to you if you want to know anything about me.

BERNARD: He gets points.

MICHAEL: What?

BERNARD: He said it. He said "I love you" to Hank. He gets the bonus.

MICHAEL: He didn't call him.

DONALD: He called him. He just didn't use the telephone.

MICHAEL: Then he doesn't get any points.

BERNARD: He gets five points!

MICHAEL: He didn't use the telephone. He doesn't get a goddamn thing!

[*Larry goes to the phone, picks up the receiver, looks at the number of the second line, dials. A beat. The phone rings*]

LARRY: It's for you, Hank. Why don't you take it upstairs?

[*The phone continues to ring. Hank gets up, goes up the stairs to the bedroom. Pause. He presses the second-line button, picks up the receiver. Everyone downstairs is silent*]

HANK: Hello?

BERNARD: One point.

LARRY: Hello, Hank.

BERNARD: Two points.

LARRY: . . . This is Larry.

BERNARD: Two more points!

LARRY: . . . For what it's worth, I love you.

BERNARD: Five points bonus!

HANK: I'll . . . I'll try.

LARRY: I will too.

[*Hangs up. Hank hangs up*]

BERNARD: That's ten points total!

EMORY: Larry's the winner!

HAROLD: Well, that wasn't as much fun as I thought it would be.

MICHAEL: THE GAME ISN'T OVER YET!

[*Hank moves toward the bed into darkness*]

Your turn, Alan.

[*Michael gets the phone, slams it down in front of Alan*]

PICK UP THE PHONE, BUSTER!

EMORY: Michael, don't!

MICHAEL: STAY OUT OF THIS!

EMORY: You don't have to, Alan. You don't have to.

ALAN: Emory . . . I'm sorry for what I did before.

[*A beat*]

EMORY: . . . Oh, forget it.

MICHAEL: Forgive us our trespasses. Christ, now you're both joined at the goddamn hip! You can decorate his home, Emory—and he can get you out of jail the next time you're arrested on a morals charge. [*A beat*] Who are you going to call, Alan? [*No response*] Can't remember anyone? Well, maybe you need a minute to think. Is that it?

[*No response*]

HAROLD: I believe this will be the final round.

COWBOY: Michael, aren't you going to call anyone?

HAROLD: How could he? He's never loved anyone.

MICHAEL: [*Sings the classic vaudeville walk-off to Harold*]
   "No matter how you figger,
    It's tough to be a nigger,
    But it's tougher
    To be a Jeeeew-ooouu-oo!"

DONALD: My God, Michael, you're a charming host.

HAROLD: Michael doesn't have charm, Donald. Michael has counter-charm.

[*Larry crosses to the stairs*]

MICHAEL: Going somewhere?

[*Larry stops, turns to Michael*]

LARRY: Yes. Excuse me. [*Turns, goes up the stairs*]

MICHAEL: You're going to miss the end of the game.

LARRY: [*Pauses on stairs*] You can tell me how it comes out.

MICHAEL: I never reveal an ending. And no one will be reseated during the climactic revelation.

LARRY: With any luck, I won't be back until it's all over. [*Turns, continues up the stairs into the dark*]

MICHAEL: [*Into Alan's ear*] What do you suppose is going on up there? Hmmm, Alan? What do you imagine Larry and Hank are doing? Hmmmmm? Shooting marbles?

EMORY: Whatever they're doing, they're not hurting anyone.

HAROLD: And they're minding their own business.

MICHAEL: And you mind yours, Harold. I'm warning you!

[*A beat*]

HAROLD: [*Coolly*] Are you now? Are you warning *me? Me?* I'm Harold. I'm the one person you don't warn, Michael. Because you and I are a match. And we tread very softly with each other because we both play each other's game too well. Oh, I know this game you're playing. I know it very well. And I play it very well. You play it very well too. But you know what, I'm the only one that's better at it than you are. I can beat you at it. So don't push me. I'm warning *you.*

[*A beat. Michael starts to laugh*]

MICHAEL: You're funny, Hallie. A laff riot. Isn't he funny, Alan? Or, as you might say, isn't he amusing? He's an amusing faggot, isn't he? Or, as you might say, freak. That's what you called Emory, wasn't it? A freak? A pansy? My, what an antiquated vocabulary you have. I'm surprised you didn't say sodomite or pederast. [*A beat*] You'd better let me bring you up to date. Now it's not so new, but it might be new to you— [*A beat*] Have you heard the term "closet queen"? Do you know what that means? Do you know what it means to be "in the closet"?

EMORY: Don't, Michael. It won't help anything to explain what it means.

MICHAEL: He already knows. He knows very, very well what a closet queen is. Don't you, Alan?

[*Pause*]

ALAN: Michael, if you are insinuating that I am homosexual, I can only say that you are mistaken.

MICHAEL: Am I? [*A beat*] What about Justin Stuart?

ALAN: . . . What about . . . Justin Stuart?

MICHAEL: You were in love with him, that's what about him. [*A beat*] And *that* is who you are going to call.

ALAN: Justin and I were very good friends. That is all. Unfortunately, we had a parting of the ways and that was the end of the friendship. We have not spoken for years. I most certainly will not call him now.

MICHAEL: According to Justin, the friendship was quite passionate.

ALAN: What do you mean?

MICHAEL: I mean that you slept with him in college. Several times.

ALAN: That is not true!

MICHAEL: Several times. One time, it's youth. Twice, a phase maybe. Several times, *you like it!*

ALAN: IT'S NOT TRUE!

MICHAEL: Yes, it is. Because Justin Stuart *is* homosexual. He comes to New York on occasion. He calls me. I've taken him to parties. Larry "had" him once. *I* have slept with Justin Stuart. And he has told me all about *you.*

ALAN: Then he told you a lie.

[*A beat*]

MICHAEL: You were obsessed with Justin. That's all you talked about, morning, noon, and night. You started doing it about Hank upstairs tonight. What an attractive fellow he is and all that transparent crap.

ALAN: He *is* an attractive fellow. What's wrong with saying so?

MICHAEL: Would you like to join him and Larry right now?

ALAN: I said he was attractive. That's all.

MICHAEL: How many times do you have to say it? How many times did you have to say it about Justin: what a good tennis player he was; what a good dancer he was; what a good body he had; what good taste he had; how bright he was—how *amusing* he was—how the girls were all mad for him—what close friends you were.

ALAN: We . . . we . . . were . . . very close . . . very good . . . friends. *That's all.*

MICHAEL: It was *obvious*—and when you did it around Fran it was downright embarrassing. Even she must have had her doubts about you.

ALAN: *Justin . . . lied.* If he told you that, he lied. It is a lie. A vicious lie. He'd say anything about me now to get even. He could never get over the fact that *I* dropped *him.* But I had to. I had to because . . . he told me . . . he told me about himself . . . he told me that he wanted to be my lover. And I . . . I . . . told him . . . he made me sick . . . I told him I pitied him.

[*A beat*]

MICHAEL: You ended the friendship, Alan, because you couldn't face the truth about yourself. You could go along, sleeping with Justin, as long as he lied to himself and you lied to yourself and you both dated girls and labeled yourselves men and called yourselves just fond friends. But Justin finally had to be honest about the truth, and you couldn't take it. You couldn't take it and so you destroyed the friendship and your friend along with it. [*Michael goes to the desk and gets address book*]

ALAN: No!

MICHAEL: Justin could never understand what he'd done wrong to make you cut him off. He blamed himself.

ALAN: No!

MICHAEL: He did until he eventually found out who he was and what he was.

ALAN: No!

MICHAEL: But to this day he still remembers the treatment—the scars he got from you. [*Puts address book in front of Alan on coffee table*]

ALAN: NO!

MICHAEL: Pick up this phone and call Justin. Call him and apologize and tell him what you should have told him twelve years ago. [*Picks up the phone, shoves it at Alan*]

ALAN: NO! HE LIED! NOT A WORD IS TRUE!

MICHAEL: CALL HIM! [*Alan won't take the phone*] All right then, *I'll dial!*

HAROLD: You're so helpful.

[*Michael starts to dial*]

ALAN: Give it to me. [*Michael hands Alan the receiver. Alan takes it, hangs up for a moment, lifts it again, starts to dial. Everyone watches silently. Alan finishes dialing, lifts the receiver to his ear*] . . . Hello?

MICHAEL: One point.

ALAN: . . . It's . . . it's Alan.

MICHAEL: Two points.

ALAN: . . . Yes, yes, it's *me*.

MICHAEL: Is it Justin?

ALAN: . . . You sound surprised.

MICHAEL: I should hope to think so—after twelve years! Two more points.

ALAN: I . . . I'm in New York. Yes. I . . . I won't explain now . . . I . . . I just called to tell you . . .

MICHAEL: THAT I LOVE YOU, GODDAMNIT! I LOVE YOU!

ALAN: I love you.

MICHAEL: You get the goddamn bonus. TEN POINTS TOTAL! JACKPOT!

ALAN: I love you and I beg you to forgive me.

MICHAEL: Give me that! [*Snatches the phone from Alan*] Justin! Did you hear what that son of a bitch said! [*A beat. Michael is speechless for a moment*] . . . Fran? [*A beat*] Well, of course I expected it to be you! . . . [*A beat*] How are you? Me too. Yes, yes . . . he told me everything. Oh, don't thank *me*. Please . . . Please . . . [*A beat*] I'll . . . I'll put him back on. [*A beat*] My love to the kids . . .

ALAN: . . . Darling? I'll take the first plane I can get. Yes. I'm sorry too. I love you very much. [*Hangs up, stands, crosses to the door, stops. Turns around, surveys the group*] Thank you, Michael.

[*Opens the door and exits. Silence. Michael slowly sinks down on the couch, covering his face. Pause*]

COWBOY: Who won?

DONALD: It was a tie.

[*Harold crosses to Michael*]

HAROLD: [*Calmly, coldly, clinically*] Now it is my turn. And ready or not, Michael, here goes. [*A beat*] You are a sad and pathetic man. You're a homosexual and you don't want to be. But there is nothing you can do to change it. Not all your prayers to your God, not all the analysis you can buy in all the years you've got left to live. You may very well one day be able to know a heterosexual life if you want it desperately enough—if you pursue it with the fervor with which you annihilate—but you will always be homosexual as well. Always, Michael. Always. Until the day you die.

[*Turns, gathers his gifts, goes to Emory. Emory stands up unsteadily*]

Oh, friends, thanks for the nifty party and the super gift. [*Looks toward Cowboy*] It's just what I needed.

[*Emory smiles. Harold gives him a hug, spots Bernard sitting on the floor, head bowed*]

. . . Bernard, thank you.

[*No response. To Emory*]

Will you get him home?

EMORY: Don't worry about her. I'll take care of everything.

[*Harold turns to Donald, who is at the bar making himself another drink*]

HAROLD: Donald, good to see you.

DONALD: Good night, Harold. See you again sometime.

HAROLD: Yeah. How about a year from Shavuoth? [*Harold goes to Cowboy*] Come on, Tex. Let's go to my place. [*Cowboy gets up, comes to him*] Are you good in bed?

COWBOY: Well . . . I'm not like the average hustler you'd meet. I try to show a little affection—it keeps me from feeling like such a whore.

[*A beat. Harold turns. Cowboy opens the door for them. They start out. Harold pauses*]

HAROLD: Oh, Michael . . . thanks for the laughs. Call you tomorrow.

[*No response. A beat. Harold and Cowboy exit*]

EMORY: Come on, Bernard. Time to go home. [*Emory, frail as he is, manages to pull Bernard's arm around his neck, gets him on his feet*] Oh, Mary, you're a heavy mother.

BERNARD: [*Practically inaudible mumble*] Why did I call? Why?

EMORY: Thank you, Michael. Good night, Donald.

DONALD: Goodbye, Emory.

BERNARD: Why . . .

EMORY: It's all right, Bernard. Everything's all right. I'm going to make you some coffee and everything's going to be all right.

[*Emory virtually carries Bernard out. Donald closes the door. Silence. Michael slowly slips from the couch onto the floor. A beat. Then slowly he begins a low moan that increases in volume—almost like a siren. Suddenly he slams his open hands to his ears*]

MICHAEL: [*In desperate panic*] Donald! Donald! DONALD! DONALD!

[*Donald puts down his drink, rushes to Michael. Michael is now white with fear, and tears are bursting from his eyes. He begins to gasp his words*]

Oh, no! No! What have I done! Oh, my God, what have I done!

[*Michael writhing. Donald holds him, cradles him in his arms*]

DONALD: Michael! Michael!

MICHAEL: [*Weeping*] Oh, no! NO! It's beginning! The liquor is starting to wear off and the anxiety is beginning! Oh, NO! No! I feel it! I know it's going to happen. Donald!! Donald! Don't leave me! Please! Please! Oh, my God, what have I done! Oh, Jesus, the guilt! I can't handle it anymore. I won't make it!

DONALD: [*Physically subduing him*]Michael! Michael! Stop it! Stop it! I'll give you a Valium—I've got some in my pocket!

MICHAEL: [*Hysterical*] No! No! Pills and alcohol—I'll die!

DONALD: I'm not going to give you the whole bottle! Come on, let go of me!

MICHAEL: [*Clutching him*] NO!

DONALD: Let go of me long enough for me to get my hand in my pocket!

MICHAEL: Don't leave!

[*Michael quiets down a bit, lets go of Donald enough for him to take a small plastic bottle from his pocket and open it to give Michael a tranquilizer*]

DONALD: Here.

MICHAEL: [*Sobbing*] I don't have any water to swallow it with!

DONALD: Well, if you'll wait one goddamn minute, I'll get you some! [*Michael lets go of him. He goes to the bar, gets a glass of water and returns*]Your water, your Majesty. [*A beat*] Michael, stop that goddamn crying and take this pill!

[*Michael straightens up, puts the pill into his mouth amid choking sobs, takes the water, drinks, returns the glass to Donald*]

MICHAEL: I'm like Ole Man River—tired of livin' and scared o' dyin'.

[*Donald puts the glass on the bar, comes back to the couch, sits down. Michael collapses into his arms, sobbing. Pause*]

DONALD: Shhhhh. Shhhhhh. Michael. Shhhhhh. Michael. Michael.

[*Donald rocks him back and forth. He quiets. Pause*]

MICHAEL: . . . If we . . . if we could just . . . not hate ourselves so much. That's it, you know. If we could just *learn* not to hate ourselves quite so very much.

DONALD: Yes, I know. I know. [*A beat*] Inconceivable as it may be, you used to be worse than you are now. [*A beat*] Maybe with a lot more work you can help yourself some more—if you try.

[*Michael straightens up, dries his eyes on his sleeve*]

MICHAEL: Who was it that used to always say, "You show me a happy homosexual, and I'll show you a gay corpse"?

DONALD: I don't know. Who was it who always used to say that?

MICHAEL: And how dare you come on with that holier-than-thou attitude with me! "A lot more work," "if I try," indeed! You've got a long row to hoe before you're perfect, you know.

DONALD: I never said I didn't.

MICHAEL: And while we're on the subject—I think your analyst is a quack.

[*Michael is sniffling. Donald hands him a handkerchief. He takes it and blows his nose*]

DONALD: Earlier you said he was a prick.

MICHAEL: That's right. He's a prick quack. Or a quack prick, whichever you prefer.

[*Donald gets up from the couch, goes for his drink*]

DONALD: [*Heaving a sigh*] Harold was right. You'll never change.

MICHAEL: Come back, Donald. Come back, Shane.

DONALD: I'll come back when you have another anxiety attack.

MICHAEL: I need you. Just like Mickey Mouse needs Minnie Mouse—just like Donald Duck needs Minnie Duck. Mickey needs Donnie.

DONALD: My name is Donald. I am called Donald. You must never call anyone called Donald Donnie . . .

MICHAEL: [*Grabs his head, moans*] Ohhhhh . . . icks! Icks! Terrible icks! Tomorrow is going to be an ick-packed day. It's going to be a bad day at Black Rock. A day of nerves, nerves, and more nerves! [*Michael gets up from the couch, surveys the wreckage of the dishes and gift wrappings*] Do you suppose there's any possibility of just burning this room?

[*A beat*]

DONALD: Why do you think he stayed, Michael? Why do you think he took all of that from you?

MICHAEL: There are no accidents. He was begging to get killed. He was dying for somebody to let him have it and he got what he wanted.

DONALD: He could have been telling the truth—Justin could have lied.

MICHAEL: Who knows? What time is it?

DONALD: It seems like it's day after tomorrow.

[*Michael goes to the kitchen door, pokes his head in. Comes back into the room carrying a raincoat*]

MICHAEL: It's early. [*Goes to a closet door, takes out a blazer, puts it on*]

DONALD: What does life *hold*? Where're you going?

MICHAEL: The bedroom is ocupado, and I don't want to go to sleep anyway until I try to walk off the booze. If I went to sleep like this, when I wake up they'd have to put me in a padded cell—not that that's where I don't belong. [*A beat*] And . . . and . . . there's a midnight mass at St. Malachy's that all the show people go to. I think I'll walk over there and catch it.

DONALD: [*Raises his glass*] Well, pray for me.

MICHAEL: [*Indicates bedroom*] Maybe they'll be gone by the time I get back.

DONALD: Well, *I* will be—just as soon as I knock off that bottle of brandy.

MICHAEL: Will I see you next Saturday?

DONALD: Unless you have other plans.

MICHAEL: No. [*Turns to go*]

DONALD: Michael?

MICHAEL: [*Stops, turns back*] What?

DONALD: Did he ever tell you why he was crying on the phone—what it was he *had* to tell you?

MICHAEL: No. It must have been that he'd left Fran. Or maybe it was something else and he changed his mind.

DONALD: Maybe so. [*A beat*] I wonder why he left her.

[*A pause*]

MICHAEL: . . . As my father said to me when he died in my arms, "I don't understand any of it. I never did." [*A beat. Donald goes to his stack of books, selects one, and sits in a chair*] Turn out the lights when you leave, will you? [*Donald nods. Michael looks at him for a long silent moment. Donald turns his attention to his book, starts to read. Michael opens the door and exits*]

END OF ACT II

END OF PLAY

# REMOTE ASYLUM

To
Marion Marshall Wagner
and
Robert John Wagner

*Remote Asylum* was originally presented by the Center Theatre Group [produced by arrangement with Zev Buffman] at the Ahmanson Theatre, Los Angeles, in December, 1970.

The scenery was designed by Ming Cho Lee, the costumes by Donald Brooks, and the lighting by Thomas Skelton. The play was directed by Edward Parone.

The cast was:

| | |
|---|---|
| Tom | *William Shatner* |
| Dinah | *Anne Francis* |
| Irene | *Nancy Kelly* |
| Ray | *Arthur O'Connell* |
| Michael | *Ralph Williams* |
| Carlos | *Carlos Rivas* |
| Juanito | *Roberto Roberi* |
| Girl | *Annette Cardona* |

About the set:

The terrace of a "contemporary" mansion, perched high on the coastline cliff at the most distant point of an unnamed Hispanic island in the Mediterranean [such as Majorca or Ibiza].

Across the width of the stage is the facade of the 1960's style house, something that suggests a fortress: two multi-floored "towers" at each end, connected by a single story center section. In the one-level middle portion, there is a big arch, leading inside to a foyer in which the front entrance is located [also the unseen side doors to the living and service rooms].

Stage left is the two-story "private tower"—a structure which contains Ray's bedroom suite on the ground floor with an exterior door onto the terrace. Beside Ray's door is a wall niche with a stature of the Virgin Mary. Irene's suite is directly above with an exterior door leading onto a balcony and stairway to the terrace.

Stage right is the "guest tower"—a three level stucco cylinder with suites on each floor, each with doors, balconies and stairways. The ground floor bedroom suite  #1], where Tom and Dinah will stay, should be open so action within is visible.

On the left side of the terrace there are wrought iron chairs and a table for dining, and to the right there are chaise longues for sunning. There is a rolling drinks trolley.

Finally, downstage left of the apron there are the "beach stairs" which lead into the orchestra pit.

# ACT I

*Light comes up to reveal the five principals standing at the very extreme of the stage apron, as if on the edge of a precipice. They are looking out over the audience, into space, at what would be the sea.*

*DINAH has on a pants suit and dark glasses and carries a small piece of hand-luggage. TOM wears a tennis hat, has a sheathed racquet under his arm and is looking through binoculars. MICHAEL carries a briefcase and a portable Olivetti typewriter. IRENE is in an expensive caftain. RAY is in linen trousers and a sport shirt with the tail hanging out.*

*[After a long moment . . .]*

TOM: Faaannn-tastic.

DINAH: Heavenly.

IRENE: [*Proudly*] It's something, isn't it?

DINAH: It's heavenly.

IRENE: It's *something!*

TOM: It's fantastic!

IRENE: Well, am I right—or am I right?!

DINAH: [*Final, flat*] It's *heavenly*, Irene. *Simply heavenly.*

IRENE: [*Not leaving it alone*] Whattaya think, Tom?

TOM: I think it's . . . fantastic.

IRENE: [*Imperiously*] It's like Dinah says—it's *heavenly*. Like heaven. [*to Ray*]—Isn't it, my darling?

[*Goes to Ray, cuddles, kisses him*]

IRENE: What does my baby think? Hmmm?

[*Ray mouths some indistinguishable words . . .*]

DINAH: [*Turns to Michael*] And what do you think, Signor Silencio?

MICHAEL: I think we've *done* the *view.*

IRENE: [*Breaks from Ray*] What did you say?

MICHAEL: [*Deferentially dry*] I think it's something like *you*: a little bit of heaven—like Dinah says.

IRENE: You bet it is! Right, Tom?

TOM: It's fannnnnn-fuckin'-tastic, sweetheart! Like Michael says—like *you!*

[*Tom throws his arms about Irene, lifts her, kisses her on the cheek . . .*]

DINAH: [*Lightly disapproving*] Honnneeeee!

IRENE: [*Squeels of mock protest*] Taaahhhmmmmm! Such *language!* You're a scandal!

TOM: [*Smooth charm*] Lady, you are something else!

[*Tom puts Irene down, slaps her lightly on the rear. Irene shrieks gleefully.*]

DINAH: [*To no one*] Honestly.

IRENE: [*Coy young girl*] Ray, did you see what Tom did to your mama?!

[*Tom picks up Irene again and swings her around*]

IRENE: [*Louder squeel, more protestation*] Ohhh! Oh, Tom, now, stop! Put me down! Ray, make him put me down! Raa-aayeee! [*Giggles*] Ohhh . . . I'm so dizzy. I'm so dizzzeeeeee!

[*Ray starts to chuckle. Dinah turns to observe Ray's private, mocking laugh*]

DINAH: [*Without effort*] That's enough, Tom.

[*Ray laughs more and more. Tom releases Irene as she becomes aware of Ray . . .*]

IRENE: [*Catching breath, to Ray*] Ohh, my darling! You're laughing! It's so wonderful to hear you laugh again! [*A beat*] You're not laughing at me, are you? Well, I don't care!

[*Rushes to Ray, puts her arms about him*]

IRENE: Tom! Tom, you've made Ray laugh again! Oh, thank God you're here!— [*Goes to Dinah*] Dinah, my dear . . . how can I ever thank you for coming?

DINAH: [*Evenly*] We're thankful to be here, too. You have no idea.

TOM: We all need a rest, Irene. We need to get away. We're tired.

DINAH: Bone tired. And I don't mean from the flight.

TOM: [*A weak swing with his racquet*] I'm afraid we're rather played-out. Pun intended. It's the end of the tour.

MICHAEL: [*To himself, looking over the "cliff"*] The end of the world—

IRENE: What?

MICHAEL: [*Correcting himself*] The *edge* of the world. [*Lightly*] It's only the end of the *map!* [*Moves to lip of apron*] As far as one can go. One more step and you're over the hill. One false step and it's man overboard!

IRENE: Young man, what are you trying to say?!

MICHAEL: I'm saying what I'm saying.

IRENE: Then what you are saying sounds morbid and this place is utterly *sans souci!* This place is *something!* And this is out-of season!

MICHAEL: [*Wipes his brow*] You're telling *me!*

IRENE: That's why we retired here—to get away from it all!

MICHAEL: "Retired." Now that sounds morbid.

IRENE: [*Sardonically, to Dinah and Tom*] Who is this charming friend of yours?

TOM: Michael's an old friend of *mine*.

DINAH: And now mine. We ran into him in Rome and he's been traveling with us since. We've become really quite attached. [*Puts her arm about Michael*] Haven't we, kiddo?

MICHAEL: [*Sweetly*] I love you, Dinah. You've saved my life. I hope that's what I wanted.

[*Dinah strokes Michael's hair, but he moves away, wanders off to himself*]

IRENE: [*Re: Michael*] What an odd duck.

DINAH: [*To Irene*] When he drinks too much he's like a child.

IRENE: [*Bluntly*] You don't need any more children.

[*Ray turns away, watches Michael*]

DINAH: [*Flatly, to Irene*] I need the ones I have.

[*Ray turns back to Dinah, gasps a few words*]

DINAH: Yes, Ray?— [*Ray mouths something*] The kids? How are my kids? [*Ray nods*] Just great. They're with their father in the south of France. He gets them for six weeks in the summer.

IRENE: [*Sarcastically*] And did you see dear Jerry?

DINAH: No, he sent a car and driver to Nice to collect the kids. Tom was in a tournament in Monte Carlo.

IRENE: [*Disdainfully*] My, my, living the high life in Beverly Hills and the Cote D'Azur! Jerry's come a long way for a cheap theatrical promoter.

DINAH: I admit he was always a bit grand, Irene. But cheap, *never!* And believe me, it sickens me to defend him. [*To Ray*] What, luv?

[*Ray leads her to some measures scratched on the wall of the house*]

DINAH: [*Laughs*] Oh, no, they've grown since then! [*Indicates on wall*] They're up to here now. Two little bean poles! [*To Tom*] Look, darling, the marks Ray made when the boys were here with me the last time.

TOM: Jesus, they *have* taken off!

[*Ray taps another marking*]

DINAH: Yes, Ray, I see the date. God, how time flies—even when you're *not* having a good time. [*To Tom*] Jerry and I had just separated.

TOM: But, Ray, you saw the kids at Christmas!

IRENE: He remembers very little from that ghastly trip.

TOM: [*To Ray*] You remember meeting me, don't you?

[*Ray nods*]

DINAH: [*To Ray*] How's your daughter?

[*Ray looks down*]

IRENE: [*Snaps*] We never see her.

DINAH: I'd die if I didn't see my children.

IRENE: No, you wouldn't.

DINAH: Oh, but I would. If I didn't have my kids, I wouldn't have anything to live for.

IRENE: You have Tom. He's all you need. And you know what, you don't even really need him. I'm sorry, Tom, but I have to say it: Dinah's too independent to need *anybody*. Dinah, you're like me.

DINAH: No, I'm not, Irene.

IRENE: [*Going right ahead*] I never wanted children, but if I had, I'd have liked to have a *daughter* like you, Dinah.

MICHAEL: [*To Irene*] But I thought you said you *have* a daughter.

IRENE: She's Ray's. By his first marriage. [*Changing subject*] How long is it from Nice these days?

DINAH: Oh, I don't know. We went from Nice to Madrid to . . .

MICHAEL: [*Turns*] I'd say it's about a two-martini flight. To Madrid. One and a half from there.

IRENE: [*To Dinah and Tom*] Would you like something cool to drink?

TOM: Beautiful.

IRENE: Some lemonade?

MICHAEL: *Lemonade*?!

IRENE: I'm sure you want to bathe and lie down a while . . . ?

DINAH: [*Exausted*] That would be heavenly—just to rest.

[*Irene indicates a bar cart . . .*]

IRENE: [*To Tom*] Make yourself at home.

TOM: [*Goes to bar. To Michael*] Swifty?

MICHAEL: I'm not sure our hostess approves. Or, maybe I should say, approves of *me*.

IRENE: Any friend of Dinah's . . .

MICHAEL: . . . had better watch their step with you.

[*Dinah laughs*]

IRENE: [*To Dinah, laughs*] Such *insolence!* I'm not at all sure I like your friend.

DINAH: [*Good-naturedly*] You will. When you met Tom at Christmas you didn't exactly think he was off the top of the tree.

IRENE: Nonsense! I *adored* Tom from the moment you introduced us!

DINAH: No, you didn't.

MICHAEL: [*To Irene, re Dinah*] Dinah tells the truth. And she's not going to let you do otherwise.

TOM: That's right. She'll nail you.

IRENE: [*Laughs*] That's right, Dinah. I didn't.

[*Tom moves away from bar. Michael's expression slides . . .*]

TOM: [*Insecurely*] You didn't like me?

IRENE: Couldn't you tell?

TOM: No.

DINAH: He could tell. [*To Tom*] Tell the truth. You had to work a little harder than usual to win Irene over.

TOM: [*With an edge*] Game, set and match to you, kiddo.

IRENE: Shhhh! Listen!

TOM: What, Irene?

IRENE: *SHHHH!*

[*A beat. Silence*]

IRENE: I heard it! Didn't you? Didn't you hear it?!

DINAH: Hear what, Irene?

IRENE: A baby. A baby, crying. Sometimes it sounds far away. Sometimes . . . not so far. Surely you heard it!

DINAH: No.

IRENE: Tom?

TOM: [*Shrugs*] Sorry.

MICHAEL: [*A mocking sound*] Waaaa–a–a–a!

[*Ray chuckles. Irene turns to glare at Michael*]

MICHAEL: [*To Irene, re: drink*] Sometimes when I don't get my bottle, I cry like a baby.

IRENE: Help yourself!—Put a nipple on it, if you like.

[*Michael goes to bar, fixes a drink. Ray contines to laugh. Irene goes to him*]

IRENE: [*To Ray*] Ray, you heard it this time, didn't you? Didn't you, my darling?

[*Ray laughs, a bit out of control*]

IRENE: Ray! Answer me! Stop that laughing! You'll have a heart attack right here in the middle of this million-dollar terrazzo!

[*Ray stops laughing*]

Did you hear the crying? The baby?—

[*He shakes his head*]

Are you telling me the truth? I don't think you're telling me the truth!

[*Dinah turns away*]

IRENE: [*Hears something*] SHHHHHHHH! LISTEN!

MICHAEL: [*Sipping his drink*] No one is talking but you, Irene.

IRENE: Quiet! I hear something! [*Silence. A beat*] No, it's only your luggage.

[*Juanito, a thin manservant with plucked eyebrows, dressed in tight jeans, a white housejacket and too much gold jewelry, chains, ear-ring and bracelets, stumbles onto the terrace, struggling with various "good" suitcases. He's angrily mumbling to himself in Spanish, idiosyncratic of Majorca or Ibiza. He drops the bags, kicks them, spewing vulgar slang.*]

IRENE: [*Crossing*] Juanito! Stop that! [*Heavy American accent*] Paren, me oyen?!

[*Juanito kicks the bags and screams epithets*]

IRENE: Paren! *He dicho paren!*

[*CARLOS enters, dressed in a black suit and chauffeurs's cap, carrying some more luggage under his arms*]

CARLOS: [*Cooly authorative*] Basta!

[*Juanito calms. Irene eyes Carlos disdainfully*]

IRENE: Just who's giving the orders around here?!

MICHAEL: Good question.

IRENE: [*Ignores remark*] Cargen estas maletas! [*to Dinah*]—You and Tom will have your old room. [*To Juanito*] Apartemento uno para la senora y el senor. [*To Carlos, re Michael*] El dos para el amigó del señor.

JUANITO: [*Taunting Carlos*] Y el tres?

CARLOS: [*Strikes Juanito*] Silenció!

IRENE: [*To Carlos*] How *dare* you! Ray, there's another example of this man's insubordination. I tell you, Carlos must be fired!

[*Ray panicks, rushes to her, gasping protest*]

IRENE: [*Restraining Ray*] Now, now, calm down! You mustn't excite yourself so! Ray! Please!

[*Ray continues hysterically until Carlos goes to him*]

CARLOS: Señor! Por favor calmense. Por favor a mi.

IRENE: [*To Carlos*] *TAKE YOUR HANDS OFF HIM!*

[*Ray calms*]

IRENE: Déjalo, vete!

[*Carlos backs away*]

IRENE: Ray, don't excite yourself with this. I'll deal with them later. Luego! Me ocupare de ustedes mas tardes. Vayanse!

[*Juanito fingers his gold chains, sucks a tooth, picks up the scattered luggage and goes into the ground floor guest suite #1. Carlos looks toward Ray, nods sightly. Ray responds, sees Irene catch him, turns away*]

IRENE: [*To Carlos*] He dicho, vayanse!

[*Carlos climbs the exterior stairs and goes into guest apartment #2. Irene crosses to Ray*]

IRENE: Sweetheart, what did Carlos nod to you about? Something is going on behind my back, isn't it?

[*Ray shakes his head as Carlos comes out of guest suite #2, checks Irene, then quietly goes up to enter #3*]

DINAH: [*To Michael*] I didn't know you spoke Spanish.

MICHAEL: I don't, but I get the drift.

DINAH: [*Smiles*] All that Latin as an altar boy finally coming in handy.

MICHAEL: That's not exactly what I meant.

IRENE: [*Warming a bit to Michael*] Ray was raised a Catholic. He left the church when he divorced his first wife for me, but he's still devout. I had the architect who did this house design that niche over there for him. He never misses Mass on Sunday. You can go with him.

[*Ray looks expectantly toward Michael . . .*]

MICHAEL: Well, I don't think . . . [*Sees how much it means to Ray*] Yes, sir. I'll go with you.

[*Ray takes Michael's hand, smiles*]

IRENE: I have no religion myself but I'm glad Ray has his faith. It's a source of great solace to him and for that, I'm grateful. Human beings need something to grasp onto in trying times—and I'm for anything that works. [*Crosses, puts her arms about Ray*] It's way past Ray's nap time. It's time we all had a siesta. A nice, long, long rest.

DINAH: Heavenly.

IRENE: Dinah, you know the way. [*Wryly*] Why don't you lead your . . . charges. After you've bathed and had a lie-down—cocktails here on the terrace. And then, I'll take you off to a party.

TOM: Fantastic.

IRENE: Our neighbor across the bay is having a little fiesta this evening and we're all invited. [*To Ray*] Come along, my darling, it's beddie-bye for you! [*Reacts to something*] *Ohhh!* Lucky is gone! [*To Tom*] Didn't you see the dog lying here?

TOM: As a matter of fact, I didn't.

IRENE: I chained him here myself. [*To Michael*] Didn't you see him?

MICHAEL: I'm a bad one to ask. Sometime I see all sorts of creatures.

DINAH: You take too many pills.

IRENE: [*Exhasperated*] Ray, you didn't let Lucky go again, did you? [*Ray shakes his head*] Now, don't tell me you didn't when I know you did! [*Ray chuckles, crosses to the bar, lifts a bottle of Scotch. Irene darts after him*] No, no, no! Bad boy! [*Takes the bottle away*] You know the doctor said only one before dinner. Now, come on—everybody off to bed! [*Catches herself*] To nap. Everybody off *to nap!*

[*Dinah and Tom cross to their suite #1] and enter. Michael climbs the stairs to his quarters #2], hesitates to observe Irene and Ray below . . .*]

IRENE: Ray, wait! [*Vulnerable, girlish*]— Why . . . why did you laugh when Tom slapped Irene on her tush? Huh? You weren't laughing *at* her, were you? [*No answer from Ray*] Say, "no." Please . . . say, "no." [*Finally, Ray shakes his head, walks off*] I didn't think you would. I knew you weren't laughing at . . . *me.*

[*Ray goes to his room off the terrace, shuts the door. Irene slowly climbs to her own quarters, goes inside. Michael then turns and enters the guest suite #2. [The stage is empty. A beat. There is the sound of a baby's cry. Momentarily, Carlos exits the "unoccupied" guest suite #3. He quickly descends all the way to the beach stairs. He whistles and momentarily, Lucky, the German Shepherd comes up. Carlos pats him on the head and quietly whispers to the dog in Spanish. Carlos quickly crosses to the bar, retrieves the bottle of Scotch and goes to Ray's door, knocks gently. Ray opens the door, pats the dog and accepts the whiskey. Carlos quickly recloses the door and exits through the foyer arch. Lights come up in guest suite #1. Tom is twirling his tennis racket. Diana is sitting on the bed, talking on the phone*]

DINAH: [*Into phone*] When will they be back? Quand seront-ils la? Is there anyone there who speaks English? Where's the children's governess? [*To Tom*] Gone, too. And Jerry didn't say where he was taking them. I don't understand this. [*Into phone*] Allo? Ou sont-ils alles? Priez de m'appeler a ce numero. Merci. [*Hangs up. To Tom*] Something's wrong. I know it. I just know it.

Tom: [*Unconcerned*] You sound like Irene.

Dinah: Paranoid?

Tom: [*Wearily*] The kids are okay, Dinah.

[*Dinah gets up, takes off her shoes, slacks and blouse, hangs them neatly*]

Dinah: I'm not worried about them, exactly. I mean, about their *safety* or anything like that. [*Directly*] I know they're "okay," thank you very much. It's not that.

Tom: It's Jerry. He's what's eating you.

Dinah: I wouldn't trust that son-of-a-bitch with the key to a can of sardines. Let alone with my . . . with my babies.

Tom: Relax. Seven and nine . . . they're not exactly babies anymore. They can take care of themselves.

Dinah: [*Somewhat proudly*] Yeah. They're tough, those kids. [*Locks eyes with Tom*] I know what you're thinking. Go ahead and say it: "Tough like their mother."

Tom: [*Turns away*] I wasn't thinking that. *You* were thinking that.

[*Dinah, barefoot, in her bra and pants, slips into a man's pajama top*]

Dinah: Okay. What *were* you thinking? You seem even farther away than usual.

Tom: [*Unbuttoning shirt*] I was wondering what you're gonna do when they grow-up and leave you.

Dinah: [*After a moment*] Try to be realistic. Let go.

[*Tom drops his shirt on a chair, slips off his pants, throws them on the chair*]

Tom: I hope you can manage it when the time comes to let go.

Dinah: [*Meaningfully*] And it's only a matter of time, isn't it?

Tom: [*Evasively*] It's good they're with Jerry. They need a father.

Dinah: [*Pointedly*] Don't you think *I* know that?

TOM: I'll give *you* a break if you'll give *me* a break.

DINAH: Jerry doesn't give a damn about those kids. It's *my* scalp he wants. He's just using them to get to me, and I know he's up to something. I know too well the way that bastard's mind works!

TOM: Alright, for Crissake! I don't wanna hear anymore about Jerry *or* the kids! It was a deal, remember? That's why we're here—to get away from it all—all of them, once and for all—or, at least, for a little while, right?

DINAH: [*Calmly*] And Karen, included.

TOM: [*Finally*] And Karen included.

[*Tom shakes his head, bounces the tennis ball with the raquet, catches the ball fiercely*]

TOM: Couldn't resist, could you?!

DINAH: I'm sorry. I'm jealous, I admit it. I'm not proud of it, but there it is.

[*There is a loud offstage crash of dishware, followed by a heated, indistinguishable exchange in Spanish*]

TOM: This place is like some kind of loonie bin.

DINAH: I said I'd come alone. I warned you.

TOM: [*Twirls his racquet*] What makes me think anything'll be different anywhere else? What makes me think with a passport and a plane ticket the pasture's any greener?

[*Another crash offstage. Irene's door opens. She comes down the stairs to enter the house*]

TOM: Jesus, I don't know if I can take it here!

DINAH: Give it a chance.

TOM: [*After a moment*] I *want* to stop running. Honest I do.

DINAH: If it doesn't work out, we can cut it short. She's afraid he's going to die and leave her all alone. I can understand that. That's why I had to come.

TOM: What made me think anything would be better here? Nothing is any different. The kids are still with us. Your husband is still with us.

DINAH: And your wife is still with us. And your *life* is still with you. No matter how far or how fast you travel.

TOM: [*Lightly*] Get off my back.

[*Another crash followed by more garbled yelling from Irene in terrible Spanish*]

DINAH: You think I don't know why you keep Michael around? As a pipeline to Karen.

TOM: [*Exhausted*] Get . . . off . . . my . . . back!

[*A final crash. Silence. A beat . . .*]

DINAH: Go on, go! To Rio or Rangoon or wherever you can smash a ball over a net and pull the wool over your baby blue eyes!

TOM: I can't go another step. Something inside me is broken in two.

DINAH: Then stay with me! [*Crossing to Tom*] I can put you back together, Humpty-Dumpty. I'm good at that, aren't I?

TOM: [*Puts his hand on her breast*] Are you . . . are you too tired?

DINAH: [*Directly*] Not if you mean it.

TOM: [*Turns away*] What the hell is that? I always mean it. Don't I?

DINAH: [*Coolly*] You tell me.

TOM: [*Viciously*] FUCK OFF!

DINAH: That's more like it. Direct contact. That wasn't so hard, now was it?

[*Tom turns and slaps Dinah*]

TOM: [*Instantly*] I'm sorry.

DINAH: [*Smooths her hair*] Your backhand's as strong as ever.

[*Tom turns away, looks out the door at the sea. Dinah takes a deck of cards from her handbag, starts to play solitaire on the bed. The door to Ray's room opens. He exits to return the partially depleted Scotch bottle to the bar. Irene can once again be heard babbling away in Spanish, her chatter punctuated with exclamations of "Carlos! Carlos!" Michael comes out onto his balcony, observes Ray straightening the liquor bottles. Irene is heard approaching. Ray quickly returns to his room, closing his door. Michael quickly comes down to the bar, pours another vodka. Irene's voice loudens. Michael straightens the bottles, heads for his room but doesn't*] *have time to make it and hides behind a potted palm. Irene bursts upon the terrace, followed by Juanito*]

IRENE: Carlos! Carlos!

JUANITO: [*Indicating Carlos has gone*] Desapareció.

IRENE: Yes, well, he *will* be gone! I can assure you that! By sundown! [*Spots liquor bottles*] ¿Que pasa aqui? ¿Quien has estado tomando esta bebida? [*Picks up Scotch*] I measured and marked this bottle this morning! Now, look! [*Sees vodka bottle*] And the vodka! Ray doesn't even drink vodka! [*Picks it up*] Mira! If I didn't know better I'd think you're turning into a lush! ¿Quién se has tomando esto?

JUANITO: [*Shakes his head*] No se, Señora.

IRENE: ¡Dime!

JUANITO: [*Indicates Ray's room*] Carlos le da whiskey a Señor.

IRENE: Lock up the bottles and give me the key! Encierren estas botellas . . .

JUANITO: Yeah, yeah, Señora.

[*Irene crosses to Ray's door, knocks gently*]

IRENE: Ray, are you asleep? Ray, I have to talk to you. [*Opens door, peeks inside*] Are you taking a nap, my darling? [*A beat*] Ray . . . do you drink behind my back? Does Carlos give you whiskey behind my back?

[*No response. She closes the door*]

—I'm sorry. Get your rest. I'm sorry. [*Sees Juanito watching her . . .* ] Well, go on! Vayanse!

[*Juanito goes to the bar cart, starts to push it away. Irene goes up the steps to her balcony, goes inside her room. Juanito stops, puts his hand on his hips, stars to mimick Irene, prancing and cackling low in Spanish with an American accent. Michael steps out from behind the plan. Juanito turns to see Michael and freezes, somewhat panic-stricken at first. Then, his attitude changes to one of hauteur and defiance as he pointedly snatches the vodka bottle from the bar, puts it under his arm and rolls the trolley away. Michael, drink in hand, goes to Dinah and Tom's room, knocks*]

MICHAEL: It's Michael. Can I come in?

DINAH: It's open.

[*Michael enters. Dinah continues to play cards on her side of the bed. Tom is propped on pillows on his side, under the covers. He is smoking, his tennis hat pushed down over his eyes*]

DINAH: [*Not looking up*] Well, how do you like it so far?

MICHAEL: *About your friends. And* their retinue.

DINAH: Perfect, aren't they?

MICHAEL: The original Dynamic Duo. Rather, she's the original Dynamic Duo. He's The Invisible Man.

TOM: She's chopped off his balls and stuffed 'em in his mouth so that poor son-of-a-bitch can't even say "Uncle!"

MICHAEL: [*Sardonically, re: Tom*] He's cute, Dinah! Why don't you marry him?

TOM: [*To Michael*] Shut up and sit down.

DINAH: I already married one asshole, what do I need with another? [*To Tom, re: his remark about Irene*] That's not really fair. She didn't personally give him cancer. Someone had to take charge.

MICHAEL: Coming to this quaint little haven has not, thus far, been the orgy of tranquillity we anticipated, am I correct?

TOM: What the hell do you care? You found the booze to wash down whatever shit you're taking, didn't you?

DINAH: [*Casually*] Tom may leave. You go with him. I'll catch up.

MICHAEL: [*Sloshes his drink*] Leave?! Before we know the answer to the riddle of "The Baby?"

TOM: [*Sliding down in bed, pulling up covers*] We're a little late folks, so g'night!

DINAH: [*To Michael, re: drink*] You're gonna be in great shape by dinner.

MICHAEL: Listen, I know you think I hear voices, but I did hear a baby cry. Who's locked in the attic? Ray's mad illegitimate child by the first wife?

TOM: You better lay off that shit.

MICHAEL: I've only had one drink and a valium. Don't you think that's fair? One *stolen* drink. A multi-million dollar layout like this and you have to cop a drink! Irene had her bangling, jangling, clanging amigo lock up the liquor. [*Michael sits on the foot of the bed*]

TOM: Pills and likker—stops your ticker.

DINAH: [*To Michael*] Listen, kiddo, will you please not knock my cards to hell and gone?

TOM: [*To Michael, over his shoulder*] Go to your room. You've had too much Christmas.

MICHAEL: [*To Dinah and Tom*] Can I get in bed with you?

TOM: It looks like you're already *in* bed with us.

MICHAEL: I mean under the covers. Even though it's sunny, I'm cold.

DINAH: Oh, honestly, Michael, you're worse than a two year old! Okay! Get in!

MICHAEL: Oh, goody, goody!

DINAH: Watch out, don't spill that martini!

[*Michael quickly crawls to the middle of the king-size bed, gets under the covers between them*]

MICHAEL: Ohh, this is fun! Here we are, all snuggled up, cozy and warm.

TOM: [*Turns away*] Jesus Christ! I don't believe this!

MICHAEL: Here we are in our house—we've made a little house for ourselves all cozy and warm and nothing can hurt us.

[*Dinah starts to laugh out loud. Tom pushes up on his arm, turns to look at Dinah*]

TOM: [*To Diana*] Are you ready for this crazy bastard? Is he beautiful?!

DINAH: [*Stops laughing*] Honestly. Do you have any idea how many times a day you say "fantastic" and "beautiful"?

TOM: Honestly, do you have any idea how many times you say "honestly"?

MICHAEL: Don't fight. Please don't fight.

DINAH: [*To Michael, re: Tom*] Hit him for me, will you?

TOM: Get off my back!

DINAH: That's another one!

MICHAEL: Please, please don't fight!

TOM: Nobody's fighting! Don't get hysterical!

MICHAEL: Sometimes I think you all fight just so you can have a fabulous reconcilation fuck.

[*A beat. Dinah bursts out with a loud laugh*]

TOM: [*Loud hoot*] Whoo-hooo! Oh, Jesus, Cuckoo City!

[*Tom starts to laugh, slap the bed. Michael spills some of his drink on Dinah. She screams, then laughs heartily . . .*]

DINAH: Ohh! I told you not to spill that fucking drink! Shit, I'm all wet!

TOM: [*Laughs*]Yeah, I'll say you're all wet!

DINAH: What're *you* laughing at?

TOM: You!

DINAH: You should see yourself in that stupid hat!

[*Tom gives her the Bronx cheer. She dips her fingers in Michael's drink, flicks it in Tom's face*]

MICHAEL: Hey! What makes you think I want somebody's fingers up my drink!

[*Tom takes the glass from Michael, pours it over his head. Michael lets of a shriek, they all collapse with laughter as the phone rings*]

DINAH: [*Seriously*] It's the phone! Maybe it's the kids! Michael, gimme the phone! Quick, baby!

[*Michael reaches over Tom to answer the phone on the night table*]

MICHAEL: [*Into phone*] Bellevue. Isolation ward. Just a minute. [*Hands Dinah receiver*] It's the head matron.

DINAH: [*Disappointed*] Oh. [*Brightly, into phone*] Yes, Irene? Ohh, the boys were just . . . cutting up.

MICHAEL: [*Cups hands megaphone style*] Cutting up before we cut out!

DINAH: [*Covering receiver*] Honeee!

[*Tom pops Michael on the head*]

MICHAEL: OW!

TOM: What's the matter, boy, have you lost your marbles?

MICHAEL: [*Singing with Castilian "lisp" to "I Left My Heart in San Francisco"*] "I los-th my mind . . . th-outh of Ibi-tha"

TOM: [*Mimicking Irene*] Don't be insolent. I'm not certain I like you.

[*Tom and Michael continue to giggle*]

DINAH: [*Into phone*] Yes, Irene. I'll come over.

DINAH: [*Hangs up phone*] Honestly, you two!

MICHAEL: What was that all about?

TOM: Orders from headquarters.

[*Dinah gets up, straightens her hair, slips on a robe*]

DINAH: Listen, if there're any long distance calls, I'll be with the head honcho.

[*She exits. They stop laughing. Michael moves over to Dinah's side of the bed*]

TOM: Shit, man, what am I doing here? What am I doing in this cracker factory at the end of . . .

MICHAEL: . . . the line.

TOM: What?

MICHAEL: Rope. The end of our rope.

TOM: [*Reflectively*] Man, I am so fucked-up. Like you wouldn't believe!

MICHAEL: I would believe.

[*Dinah pauses when she sees Ray's door open. She watches as Ray comes out unsteadily, leading the German Shepherd to the beach stairs, where he releases the animal. Ray crosses back to the niche, attempts to kneel, but stumbles, falls. Diana rushes to help him*]

DINAH: [*To Ray*] It's all right, dear. It's only me.

[*Ray looks at her, dazed. He finally smiles, as if he recognizes her. She helps him to his feet, leads him back inside his room*]

TOM: [*To Michael*] I can't tell you what it's been like to have you to talk to. Better than paying a psychiatrist.

MICHAEL: Costs about the same, having me around to listen. Maybe I'm a little cheaper. No comments, please.

TOM: I still win some pretty good purses—make a pretty good living, but . . . how much longer can I hold out?

MICHAEL: Actually, you don't pay me to listen. You pay me to talk. To tell you Karen stories.

TOM: Listen, Swifty, level with me. You think it's serious between her and that "king of the schlubs" or whatever it is he calls himself?

MICHAEL: The Shoe King of the Surburbs—*please*. He has an ad on TV.

TOM: Tell me the truth. How serious is it?

MICHAEL: What do I know?! How serious is it between you and Dinah? Well, make that, "How serious are *you?*"

TOM: [*Anxiously evasive*] Oh, Christ, I don't want to think about that! I'm getting in deeper and deeper and I don't know how to get out before it's too late. Man, I've gotten myself in the biggest fuckin' trap. And I've got to get out. Now. Fast. Before it's too late.

MICHAEL: Tom, I think she really loves you.

TOM: Karen?

MICHAEL: *Dinah!*

TOM: [*Deflates*] Oh. Listen, let's call Karen and tell her we're coming back. Both of us. That we're on our way home—whatta ya say?

[*He reaches for the phone. Michael stops him*]

MICHAEL: Tom—make sense. Things have changed. Karen's the one to come back if any coming-back's to be done. She's the one who walked out on you. You can't go back to something that's not there to go back to.

TOM: Swifty, I know we're going to get back together. I just *know* we are! Let's call her now! She'd get a kick out of hearing from both of us. Did she know you were going to meet me?

MICHAEL: No.

TOM: Where would she be, huh? What time is it there now?

MICHAEL: [*Warningly*] Tom. *Don't!*

TOM: Tell me where she is!

MICHAEL: [*After a moment*] At *his* place.

TOM: Oh. Well. You know what the number is, don't you?

[*Michael nods. Tom picks up the phone*]

How do you get Long Distance?

[*Dinah exits Ray's room and crosses to the "private" tower stairs as Irene comes out of her room*]

IRENE: Dinah, darling?

DINAH: Yes, Irene?

IRENE: Come up, come up! What took you so long?

DINAH: I was just . . . I was hoping maybe I'd hear from the kids. I have a call into them. I was waiting for them to call back.

IRENE: [*Settles on a chaise longue*] Come sit with me. Here beside me.

[*Dinah sits beside Irene*]

IRENE: Take this pillow and put it behind your back. There. Isn't that better? Aren't you comfortable?

DINAH: [*Puts pillow behind her*] Thank you.

IRENE: I can't tell you what a comfort it is for me to have you here. These last weeks have been . . . Would you like a drink?

DINAH: Nothing. Thank you.

IRENE: I have anything you want in my room. White wine, whiskey, anything.

DINAH: I don't want anything.

IRENE: [*Gets up*] Maybe some sherry. I generally have some sherry this time of the afternoon. Or a glass of champagne. Only that which comes from the grape. [*Irene goes into her room*]

DINAH: Nothing, really. Thank you.

IRENE: [*Returns with sherry*] I never take anything that does not come from the grape. You don't really drink, do you?

DINAH: Not really.

IRENE: Neither do I, really. But this is quite good this time of day. [*Pours

*Dinah a glass*] Here. Take it. I know you don't really want it, but I want you to try it.

DINAH: [*Takes glass, tries a sip*] Thank you.

IRENE: Like it?

DINAH: It's very nice.

IRENE: [*Sits beside Dinah*] I knew you'd like it. It's local. Are you comfortable?

DINAH: Yes.

IRENE: [*Takes Dinah's hand*] I can't tell you what a strain I've been under. How can I ever repay you for coming?

DINAH: Please, Irene. I don't want anything from you.

IRENE: I cannot believe that in life people can ever not want anything from anyone. But, Dinah, I believe *you*. I usually don't like women at all. But with you, I don't feel threatened by your friendship.

DINAH: What an odd thing to say. Threatened?

IRENE: We're all feeding off each other, my dear. Taking little bites out of each other. It's a universal condition. But you're different. I actually believe you are unselfish. Are you sure you're comfortable?

DINAH: Well . . .

IRENE: *I'm* not really comfortable. [*Gets up*] Come on, take your sherry and come with me. [*Moves across her balcony*] Ah, look at that sky! Just look at the colors in that sky!

[*Dinah follows Irene onto the center portion of the house over the foyer. They are now bathed in rays of pink and orange and magenta*]

DINAH: It's heavenly, Irene.

IRENE: It's overwhelming. It makes one aware of so many things that are— unanswerable.

[*Ray moans in his sleep*]

IRENE: Life. Limitation. Limitlessness. It makes one stop and take stock. Do you ever think about God, Dinah?

DINAH: Not much.

IRENE: Do you think there is one?

DINAH: I don't know.

IRENE: What do you think happens to us after we die?

DINAH: Personally, I don't think anything happens to us. I think it's over. I just think that's it. Peace. At last.

[*A beat*]

IRENE: Ray is dying, Dinah.

DINAH: I know.

IRENE: That's why I asked you to come here. *Ray is dying.*

DINAH: Well, Irene, forgive me if I sound glib—that's one thing we all have to do.

IRENE: [*Laughs*] You have such a remarkably simple way of looking at things.

DINAH: I just don't think there's any point wasting any time with things which cannot be changed or helped. I have as many short-comings and insecurities as anybody else. I feel as though it's a never ending battle to stay just this side of insanity—to not slip over the edge. I think . . . I hope that no matter the problem, I can deal with it without losing my footing. I think . . . I don't want to believe . . . I could go crazy over any*thing* . . . or any*one*.

IRENE: I envy you.

DINAH: Don't envy me. Of anything. I'm as scared as the next one.

IRENE: Could you stand it if Tom left?

DINAH: I don't know. I guess I'd find out. He may very well—any day. I think eventually, he will.

IRENE: And when your children grow up and leave you? And they will.

DINAH: That's a fact of life. It simply *is* the way it is. And if I cannot live with it—I will, quite simply, die.

[*Ray moans*]

IRENE: What am I going to do when Ray dies?

DINAH: You'll go on. You'll be the same . . . until you die. The only thing that will change when Ray dies is that he won't be here anymore.

IRENE: [*Vulnerably*] Oh, Dinah I'm . . . I'm terrified of being left alone. When Ray dies will you come and live here with me?

DINAH: I don't see how that would be realistic.

IRENE: I'm *panicked,* Dinah, that at my age I won't ever again find anyone! I'm not so old. I'm not so ugly—am I? Oh, it's cruel. The desire is still there, but look at me. That's cruel.

DINAH: Your looks are fine for a woman your age. And what does it matter? It all goes, finally. For all of us—male and female. No one, these days, knows better than I, that when something is over, *it is over.*

IRENE: Please, please don't leave, Dinah. I beg you.

DINAH: You helped me, Irene—once, when I was alone after Jerry and I broke up. That's why I came to you now—and, selfishly, I suppose, to take advantage of your lovely refuge and rest a while. I'm so exhausted from trying to stay on top of things. Stay one step ahead. But I'm losing ground, now. I'm losing my . . . [*Dinah sags a bit*]

IRENE: I know. I know what you mean, my dear. And you couldn't have come to a better place. Come with me. Give me your hand. [*Leads Dinah to her bedroom*] Rest inside. Lie down on my bed and rest. Stay here in my room. Stay as long as you like.

[*Irene leads Dinah into her rooms. Tom snores inside suite #1. Michael covers him with a sheet, quietly gets out of bed and wanders out onto the terrace, starts up to his own room, suite #2, in the guest tower.*]

[*Suddenly, there is the sound of a baby crying. Michael races up the stairs to suite #3, and goes inside.*]

[*Irene comes out of her room, listens. Ray moans again, which might be mistaken for the sound of the baby*]

[*Presently, Michael comes out of the "mystery" suite door, #3*]

IRENE: [*Looks up*] What are *you* doing up there?!

MICHAEL: Howling at the moon, what else? There's going to be a lovely moon tonight, haven't you noticed—or is that old hat to you, because *every* night there's a lovely . . .

IRENE: Lunatics howl at the moon.

MICHAEL: Exactly.

[*Dinah moans fitfully in Irene's room*]

MICHAEL: [*Descends stairs*] That *wasn't* me.

IRENE: I know very well who it was.

MICHAEL: Can you tell the sound of a baby's voice from a lunatic? Can you tell the sound of a woman's voice from the sound of a man's—when they cry out in their sleep?

IRENE: I think it is impossible to distinguish the age or the sex of a cry for help or a voice in pain. What were you doing in that room?

MICHAEL: Snooping. Sticking my nose where it doesn't belong. [*Yawns*] Excuse me, I think I'll have a little snooze myself. [*Michael goes into his suite and closes the door*]

[*Tom sits up in bed, shakes his head, gets up, picks up his tennis raquet, pantomimes a serve, comes out on the terrace, still wrapped in his towel [The terrace is now in deep shadow, illuminated only by the moon. Irene watches Tom intently. Tom yawns, stretches, looks up to see Irene*]

TOM: Are you looking at me?

IRENE: [*Flustered*] Of course not! But how could I miss you!

TOM: It's possible. It's gotten dark out here.

IRENE: I mean . . . dressed that way.

TOM: I'm decent, am I not? [*Re: towel*] This is longer than my tennis shorts.

IRENE: [*Melting, all charm*]I think you look as good in a towel as you do in a dinner jacket.

TOM: Where's Dinah?

IRENE: Lying down inside—resting.

TOM: What were you doing just now—besides looking at me?

IRENE: I thought I heard some noises down on the pier. Fishermen, I think, bring girls there. I think they pull up their boats after dark and use the cabanas for—"parties." I've got to put a stop to it.

TOM: If they're not hurting anything, why not let them have a few laughs on the rich?

IRENE: [*Descends stairs to terrace*] Would you like to come down there with me now—join me in a dip? You've already got your towel.

TOM: I don't have a bathing suit on.

IRENE I never bother, myself.

TOM: You mean, go skinny dipping?

IRENE: [*Crosses to Tom*] It's even darker down there. Your modesty won't be compromised.

TOM: [*Tactfully*] I don't think there's time. I'd better get dressed for the party.

IRENE: There's no rush. In hot countries, Tom, we take it slow.

TOM: [*Politely*] Listen, sweetheart, you and me in the dark in our birthday suits—I think I'd better sit this one out.

IRENE: [*Flirtatious*] Really, Tom, the way your mind works!

[*Irene musses Tom's hair, runs her hand down the nape of his neck as Dinah abruptly comes out of Irene's bedroom onto the balcony*]

TOM: [*Tactfully takes Irene's hand away, "gallently" kisses it*] Excuse me, beautiful.

[*Tom goes to Dinah; Irene "sulks"*]

TOM: [*To Dinah*] What's the matter? You have a nightmare?

DINAH: [*Catching her breath*] Why, could you hear me? Was I making sounds in my sleep?

IRENE: Like you were having an erotic dream.

[*Dinah comes down the stairs*]

DINAH: [*To Tom*] Oh, honey, I was so frightened.

[*Tom enfolds Dinah in his arms. There is some noise from the dock below. Irene turns*]

IRENE: [*Calling*] Who's down there? What's going on?!

DINAH: [*To Tom*] It was horrible. You were in the dream. And so was Jerry.

IRENE: [*Crossing to beach stairs*] That's private property! No tresspassing! Propiedad privada! No pase! [*Irene descends to the beach, into the pit*]

DINAH: Jerry was pushing me under some dark water—holding me down.

TOM: [*Slips his arm inside her robe*] Maybe you need a little artificial respiration.

DINAH: Honnneee!

TOM: And what did you do? When Jerry held you under?

DINAH: I woke up. Where's Irene?

TOM: Gone.

[*Tom kisses Dinah as Michael's door opens and he comes outside in a kind of daze*]

MICHAEL: [*Sees them below*] Don't . . . don't fight.

DINAH: Michael, what's wrong?

[*Michael descends the stairs. Tom and Dinah remain in an embrace*]

MICHAEL: I want the mommy and the daddy to be good to each other.

TOM: You're stoned outta your head!

DINAH: We're not fighting, darling. Don't you see? We have our arms around each other.

MICHAEL: [*To Tom, slurred*] Tell her you're sorry.

TOM: For what?

MICHAEL: For everything. And that you won't do it again. Tell her.

TOM: [*To Dinah*] I'm sorry—and I won't do it again.

MICHAEL: [*To Dinah*] Now, you tell him.

DINAH: I'm sorry, too. For everything.

MICHAEL: Now, kiss. [*They look at him*] Go on. Please. Kiss each other.

[*Tom and Dinah face each other and kiss. Michael sinks to his knees before them, encircles them with his arms and buries his face against their legs*]

MICHAEL: That's right. Love each other. Love each other.

[*Tom and Dinah hold their embrace. Michael gets up and goes back up to his room. Carlos comes out of the house*]

CARLOS: Buenos tardes.

DINAH: Good evening.

TOM: Carlos.

[*Tom and Dinah turn and go inside their suite as Carlos goes about the terrace lighting some hurricane lamps*]

[*Dinah and Tom sink onto their bed as the light in their suite dies out and the candle-lit glow on the terrace intensifies*]

[*Some latin music begins, as if wafting from across the water from a distance*]

[*Carlos moves to straighten the cusions on the lounges, then crosses to Ray's door. He knocks gently and enters as the music loudens*]

[*Irene comes up the stairs from the beach, passes Tom and Dinah's door. She stops, listens for a moment, then continues up to her own room, enters and closes the door*]

[*Michael's door opens and he steps outside, dressed in black tie. He is not drunk or drugged beyond reason, but is clearly feeling no pain. He begins to descend to the terrace as Juanito exits the house with the empty bar cart. Michael reacts. Juanitio leaves the cart, tosses his head haughtily, and goes back inside*]

[*Carlos opens the door to Ray's room and the old man exits, wearing dinner clothes. Carlos follows, carrying a freshly ironed handkerchief which he carefully arranges in Ray's breast pocket. Ray silently thanks him, pats him on the shoulder. Carlos goes back into the house as Ray toddles over to the niche, takes a match and lights a votive candle before the statue*]

MICHAEL: Good evening, sir.

[*Ray turns with surprise to see Michael, gives him a little wave of the hand. Michael bows slightly*]

[*Ray weaves over to the bar, sees there is no liquor*]

MICHAEL: Prohibition is back.

[*Ray waves a hand dismissively toward Irene's room, moves toward a chair, sits down unhappily*]

MICHAEL: You know, Ray, you remind me of my father. He was a devout Catholic.

[*Ray shakes his head, wags his hand negatively*]

MICHAEL: Yes, you are. I can tell. My father liked a good joke and you like a good joke. And, God knows, my father liked his liquor—and the rest goes without saying. And I liked my father—and the rest goes without saying.

[*Ray smiles, nods appreciatively*]

MICHAEL: [*Continuing*] Although I was closer to my mother as a child. I thought my father a villain of sorts. But, as I got older, I grew farther away from her and closer to him—the more I grew up—became more of a man. But, unfortunately, just as we were about to finally have some respect for each other, he died.

[*Ray's head drops slightly*]

MICHAEL: He died in my arms. And when he did, he said to me—after years of answers—or, at least, opinions—he looked up at me and said, "I don't understand any of it. I never did." [*Looks up at Irene's room*] In a odd way, Irene even reminds me of my mother. Oh, she's not really like her at all—nor you like him—but you both remind me of them. Does that make any sense to you? Do you understand?

[*Ray gently beckons Michael to come nearer. Michael crosses to him, kneels down beside him. Ray wiggles his hand: "Come si, come sa."*]

MICHAEL: Oh. Yes and no. Not completely.

[*Ray smiles, puts an elbow on the arm of his chair, turns his head away, but listens as Michael speaks—like a priest and penetant in a confessional*]

MICHAEL: My father was born very poor, but he made a lot of money . . .

[*Ray nods, taps himself on the chest, knowingly*]

MICHAEL: You, too?

[*Ray does the "Come si, come sa" bit again*]

MICHAEL: Oh. I see. You weren't poor, but you weren't rich. Just average.

[*Ray nods*]

MICHAEL: Yes, well, my father was poor. You probably went to college, didn't you?

[*Ray nods*]

MICHAEL: Umm, well, my father didn't. But he was very smart. He was really self-educated. He read. He was bright. Especially in ways in which I am not. A whiz at arithmetic and spelling. I can't spell my name and, to me, two and two is twenty-two!

[*Ray laughs*]

MICHAEL: Anyway, he made a success of himself. Nothing like what you've done. But to me, growing up in a one-horse town, it seemed like this much. Everybody thought we were rich—and I thought so, too. That's why I identify with you—sitting here in your elegant clothes, you are how I always wanted my father to be. [*A beat*] He died. I escaped.

[*Ray pats Michael on the head*]

MICHAEL: [*Ironically*] Can I go in peace now, father?

[*Michael takes Ray's hand, kisses it as the doors to Irene's suite are opened by Juanito. Irene comes outside, regally gowned all in black, coiffed, and bejewelled. She carries a handbag and a stole, trimmed in black ostrich*]

IRENE: What's going on down there? What are you two talking about? Me?

MICHAEL: [*Standing*] Oh, God! It's like that cliche—deja vu all over again? You look wonderful, Irene.

IRENE: [*Coquettishly*] Compliments will get you everywhere. How about a drink? And I don't mean lemonade.

MICHAEL: [*Charmingly*] Yes. And Ray and I would prefer a belt to a punch— if you know what I mean.

[*Ray laughs. Irene relents, smiles, descends to the terrace*]

IRENE: I see what Dinah means. You might get to grow on one—in spite of yourself. *Carlos!*

MICHAEL: [*To Ray*] Stick with me, chum.

[*Ray smiles gleefully as Carlos appears*]

CARLOS: Si, Senora?

IRENE: [*Takes key from busom, hands it over*] Trae la bebida y heillo.

CARLOS: En sequida, Senora.

[*Soft strains of a latin beat begin . . .*]

IRENE: Oh, listen, they've started the music. And look—lanterns strung across their terrace! And candles lit in cut-out paper bags on the stone stairs. Lovely. I must remember to steal that idea sometime. [*To Michael*] You and my husband seen to have become old friends.

MICHAEL: Ray and I understand each other.

[*Ray nods, pats Michael on the shoulder*]

IRENE: What are your plans from here—after Dinah and Tom leave?

MICHAEL: Why, to leave with them.

[*Carlos returns with a tray: several bottles of liquor and a bucket with champagne, glasses and ice. He takes them to the bar cart. Ray starts toward him*]

IRENE: [*Heading him off*] Now, now, Ray! I had this brought out for our guests.

MICHAEL: Oh, Irene! Ray's allowed one drink before dinner, you said so yourself.

IRENE: Huh! He had that and more this afternoon. Isn't that right, my darling? Tell me truth, Ray. Didn't Carlos bring you a bottle this afternoon?

[*Ray looks away. Irene goes to the bar cart, holds up the Scotch bottle*]

IRENE: [*To Carlos*] ¿Dime si le llevaste esta botella al Señor esta tarde, si o no?

CARLOS: No, Señora. No es verdad.

IRENE: ¡Mentiroso! [*To Michael*] He lies. He also steals wine and food and entertains women down in the cabanas. [*To Ray*] How many more insults must I bear before you will dismiss this man! [*Ray helplessly shakes his head*]

IRENE: [*To Carlos*] Go, get out! ¡Vete fuera! ¡FUERA!

[*Carlos exits*]

IRENE: [*To Michael*] I'd watch him if I were you. He'll probably offer himself to you for money.

MICHAEL: If I had the money I'd pay him.

IRENE: You know by now, I don't find insolence amusing. From Carlos or from you.

MICHAEL: I think it's unfair to make accusations of Carlos. He strikes me as a man of rather admirable principles. You're fortunate that he stays.

[*Ray nods in agreement*]

IRENE: Go ahead and gang up on me! See if I care.

[*Ray starts for the bar cart. Irene quickly intercepts him once more*]

IRENE: Ray, you can't have any of that! *The doctor says . . .*

[*Ray suddenly and violently pushes her away. Michael catches Irene before she falls. Ray tears off the Scotch bottle cap and pours himself a substantial drink*]

IRENE: [*To Michael*] Don't let him do it! Please! Please! It's bad for his heart! [*Starts to cry*] I'm not trying to be mean. I have to be strong with him. It's for his own good. Won't you help me, Michael? Please?

MICHAEL: [*Puts his arm about her, comforts her*] It doesn't matter, Irene. If it makes him happy, let him have it. Because it really doesn't matter.

[*Irene continues to cry as Michael rocks her gently and Ray downs the drink*]

MICHAEL: [*Softly*] Shhhh . . . quiet . . . don't cry. Don't cry, mama, don't cry.

[*Irene composes herself. The music across the bay changes to a Bossa Nova beat*]

MICHAEL: Come on, Irene, let's dance.

[*Michael makes an attempt at moving her about the terrace*]

IRENE: Oh, stop! I can't dance!

MICHAEL: I know you can. Can't she, Ray?

[*Ray laughs, nods*]

IRENE: [*To Ray*] What are you laughing at, you silly thing?! Don't try to make-up with me. I'm mad at you, Ray. Mad as can be!

[*Ray only laughs some more*]

MICHAEL: Come on, now, Irene, dance with me!

IRENE: Well, we can't dance *here*—not on this pavement. I'll ruin my evening slippers. If we want to dance—we've got a dance floor. Why don't we use it? Nobody ever *does!*

MICHAEL: Where?

IRENE: [*Indicating area over foyer*] Up there. It's inlaid with glazed tiles. This house was designed for parties! It was planned for living-it-up!

MICHAEL: Well, let's live-it-up! But first, how about a little drink?

IRENE: All right. I'll have one with you! Now, what do you think about that, Ray?!

MICHAEL: What'll it be—a martini?

IRENE: I never touch anything that does not come from the grape!

[*Michael goes to the bar cart, pours himself a vodka and a glass of champagne for Irene. Irene has headed up to the dance floor*]

MICHAEL: One on-the-rocks and a bit of the bubbly, literally coming up!

[*Michael climbs the stairs. Irene does a few turns about the floor. Michael gives her the glass of champagne. They toast each other*]

MICHAEL: Cheers!

IRENE: Oh, I hate saying, "Cheers." I think it's so common. But, all right, "Cheers!" [*They drink. Irene catches sight of Ray*]

IRENE: Ray? Raaa-aaayyy?! What's the matter? Huh? Are you mad at me, my darling? Yes, you are! I can tell. Well, I'm sorry. Okay? I said, I'm sorry, Ray. Am I forgiven?

[*After a moment, Ray gives in and nods*]

IRENE: Oh, good! I don't want us to be upset with each other. I just want . . . I just want you to . . . *enjoy your drink!*

[*Ray looks at her, inscrutably. Irene laughs a bit hysterically*]

[*The door to Tom and Dinah's room opens and they step outside. Tom is in black-tie. Dinah is resplendent in a long, simple dinner gown in a flattering warm color*]

DINAH: Well, well, well, this sounds like a happy group!

[*Irene stops laughing as Michael leaves her side and goes down the steps to Dinah*]

MICHAEL: Wow, do you look sensational! Gimme a kiss!

IRENE: [*Ignoring Dinah*] Michael! What about our dance?

MICHAEL: [*To Dinah*] Some dress! Where'd you get that?

DINAH: [*Kisses Michael's cheek*] You'd be surprised what I can do with a needle and thread.

MICHAEL: I'll bet!

TOM: [*To Michael*] How do *I* look? Don't I get a kiss?

MICHAEL: You're too ugly.

IRENE: [*Impatiently*] *Mii-chael!*

TOM: Well, Irene'll give me a kiss.

IRENE: [*To Tom, petulantly*] You had your chance.

TOM: Uh-oh. I'm in the doghouse.

IRENE: No, you're not! Not tonight. Not even the *dog* is in the doghouse, Even though he's left me, too.

DINAH: [*Kisses Ray on cheek*] Hello, handsome.

[*Rays basks in the attention*]

TOM: [*To Ray*] How're you doing, pal? [*They shake hands warmly. Ray indicates for Tom to make drinks*]

TOM: Champagne? Beautiful.

MICHAEL: [*To Dinah*] Ray looks great this evening, don't you think? Good color.

IRENE: [*Grimly, descending stairs to terrace*] It's the alcohol. It has him flushed.

DINAH: And I'd say the lady of the house looks pretty smashing.

IRENE: [*To Tom re: her dress*] Dior. Decades ago.

DINAH: And your hair—it's lovely. Did someone come in to do it?

IRENE: Juanito's been dressing my wigs ever since he's been here. You know that!

DINAH: Sometimes the really important things slip my mind.

MICHAEL: Come on, Dinah, let's dance. [*Michael takes Dinah's hand and leads her up to the floor. Ray follows slowly*]

IRENE: I thought you asked *me* to dance, Michael.

TOM: [*To Irene*] *We* can dance. It's you and me, baby! [*Irene gently shakes her head, moves away. Tom doesn't insist*]

[*Michael and Dinah glide across the tile dance floor, dancing to the music from across the bay: Cole Porter's* You're Sensational]

MICHAEL: [*Singing along*]
  "*I've no proof*
  *When people say*
  *You're more or less aloof*
  *'Cause you're sensational!*"

TOM: [*Applauding*] Yeah, yeah, yeah! Couple number one! Couple number one!

MICHAEL: [*Singing*]
   "*I don't care*
   *If you are called*
   *The fair Miss Frigidaire*
   *'Cause you're sensational!*"

[*There is the sound of a dog barking, down by the beach. Irene quickly crosses to the edge of the terrace*]

MICHAEL: Was there ever—will there ever be again—anyone quite as marvelous as Cole Porter?

IRENE: Somebody's down there on the dock! I think that's Lucky barking at them! [*Calling*] That's private property!—Propriedad privada! [*She hurries down the beach steps* [*into the pit*]. *Tom looks into the darkness. Dinah and Michael have stopped dancing*]

MICHAEL: [*To Dinah*] What are you looking at?

DINAH: At you. What have you taken?

MICHAEL: [*Simply*] A pain-killer. I had a headache. I just took something to kill the pain, Dinah.

DINAH: That's so tiresome.

MICHAEL: I know. Pretty soon it's going to be passe. Like stealing hub caps, which went out in the fifties.

[*The telephone in the foyer rings*]

[*Ray goes toward it, looks at it helplessly*]

DINAH: It's the kids!

[*Tom turns. Dinah breaks away from Michael, rushes down stairs to pick up the phone*]

DINAH: [*Into phone*] Hello?! Si, si? Who? Qui l'appelle? Oh. Just a minute [*She puts down the receiver, comes outside*]

DINAH: [*To Tom*] It's for you. It's your wife.

[*Tom goes into the foyer to the phone. Dinah sits on a chaise. Ray goes to sit by her, takes her hand. Dinah smiles at Ray appreciatively. Michael slowly descends the stairs to the terrace as the Cole Porter song ends*]

TOM: [*Into phone*] Karen? Darling?

[*Irene comes up from the beach*]

IRENE: [*Dejectedly*] There was no one. Not even Lucky—If there was anyone . . . they ran away. Lucky must have run away, too.

TOM: [*Into phone*] Well, when do you plan to file? Well, Jesus, darling, what's the rush? [*After a moment, he hangs up, returns outside, like a sleepwalker*]

MICHAEL: What's up, fella?

TOM: She—wants a divorce.

[*Dinah gets up, goes to Tom. He doesn't respond. Carlos enters with a tray of canapes*]

CARLOS: Hors d'oeurvres?

IRENE: [*Coolly*] Gracias. [*To group*] Come on, everybody, let's be festive!

[*Carlos serves the guests*]

MICHAEL: [*Apprehensively*] Dinah? Tom?

[*Dinah turns away from Tom, who has kept his back to her, and crosses to Michael. Tom still hasn't moved*]

IRENE: Tom? What's wrong?

TOM: [*Crosses to Irene, turns on the charm*] Nothing, sweetheart. Nothing a little party won't cure!

IRENE: You're going to like our friends. They have a marvelous chef. The fare is strictly local. *Authentic.* I never eat French food anywhere but France. Never Italian anywhere but Italy.

TOM: You've been everywhere—done everything.

IRENE: I've never been to Hawaii.

DINAH: Neither have I. I'd like to go there—if they just wouldn't play that music.

TOM: Hawaii's great. I played a tournament there.

IRENE: You like to follow the sun, don't you?

TOM: I like to keep on the move—keep active. It keeps one from too much thinking.

IRENE: When Ray and I were first married we went around the world on our honeymoon. We went places with names that don't even exist anymore—like Ceylon. Nothing in life is very permanent, I'm afraid.

DINAH: Not even countries are forever.

IRENE: Ray bought and sold land everywhere. We lived everywhere. Now, I want to stay in one place and let the world go around me.

MICHAEL: Do you think you've achieved that—having the world revolve around you?

IRENE: In a way, yes. Ray has attained everything important for survival—interest, work, ambition, accomplishment, fulfillment.

TOM: What about love?

[*There's an awkward silence*]

IRENE: [*To Carlos*] Carlos, traigan el auto!

CARLOS: Si, Senora.

[*Carlos puts down the tray and goes through the foyer and off*]

MICHAEL: I have no money and I'm nowhere. But I want to sing and dance and love and exhaust all possibilities by the time the end rolls around. So far, I'm making quiet a hash of it. I think Tom and Dinah are on the verge of a success, though.

DINAH: What makes you say that?

MICHAEL: [*Clearly*] Because you both know what's essential for each other's survival. And I think you're committed to it, whether you know it or not. You may think it's not enough—but it's all you need. It's all there is. I'm sure of it.

IRENE: I wonder if, at this point in his life, Ray feels the same way.

MICHAEL: Do *you*, Irene?

[*Ray reaches into his breast pocket, removes a small, elegant leather pad and a gold pencil. He writes something, pushes the pad to Tom*]

TOM: [*Reads*] "There's not much between us and the grave except some personally meaningful work and an honest give-and-take relationship with, at least, one other human being."

IRENE: Oh, Ray, that's so true. So true. [*Ray turns away. Irene covers . . .* ] Oh, look at the time. We must be going! Just put your glasses anywhere, Juanito will straighten up. Juanito, arreglen este desastre! Let's go, children.

[*Dinah's takes Ray's arm. Tom takes Irene's. Michael follows. The music from across the bay starts up again*]

IRENE: Tom, *I will* dance with you, if you like! Please, dance with me at the party! I want to dance and sing and have a good time, like Michael says, . . . before . . . before the night's over.

[*The group goes cut through the arch to the foyer and exits the front entrance*]

[*For a moment, there is silence, except for the music wafting over the water*]

[*The door to Irene's suite opens and Juanito steps outside, wearing Irene's high heel shoes, a feather boa, and one her wigs. He takes a lipstick and paints on a big, mocking mouth, then looks at himself in the mirror of a compact*]

JUANITO: ¡Ay, madre de Jesús! [*Juanito descends to the terrace floor, picks up one of the full glasses of champagne and gulps it down*]

[*Carlos comes through the foyer arch and out onto the terrace to see Juanito*]

CARLOS: [*Sardonically*] Brava. Brava.

[*Juanito is momentarilly chagrinned at being caught, then recovers with defiance*]

JUANITO: [*Lewdly*] ¿Me quieres?

CARLOS: No te metas con las cosas de la Señora. Te vas arrenpentir.

[*The door of suite #3 slowly opens and a lovely young peasant girl, steps out onto the balcony, holding a tiny baby, wrapped in a blanket*]

JUANITO: [*Looking up*] Ahhhhhh! ¡Que linda!

[*Carlos turns. The baby cries for a moment. The young mother rocks the infant in her arms as she descends the stairs. Carlos goes up to meet her halfway. He takes the baby from her, kisses her*]

JUANITO: [*Applauds*] Ah, bien. ¡Muy bien! [*Juanito descends to Ray's room and let's Lucky, the German Shepherd, out on a leash*]

JUANITO: Ay, Lucky!

[*The young woman and Carlos, holding the baby, come down to the terrace. For a moment, they all seem like one big, happy family*]

[*The music and their laughter loudens. Suddenly, the front door in the foyer is flung open and Irene, like a volcanic manifestation, erupts onto the terrace, screaming . . .*]

IRENE: Help! HELP! *HEEELLLLL-PP!!*

[*Juanito and the dog, the girl and Carlos, holding the baby, freeze as Tom enters, carrying Ray in his arms, with Irene, Dinah, and Michael quickly following*]

[*There is a breathless, flash-second when all action, all sound ceases and the two groups stare at each other for an instant, like a mirrored reflection. Lucky barks, Juanito releases him, and the dog runs down the beach stairs]*

IRENE: [*Simultaneously*] What—Who? Get a doctor! ¡UN MEDICO! ¡BUSCA UN MEDICO!

[*Tom carries Ray to a chaise. Diana follows and unfastens Ray's black tie and shirt*]

[*Carlos passes the baby to the girl and dashes to the telephone in the foyer*]

[*The girl clutches the baby and flees down the steps to the beach. Irene runs to the edge of the stage after her*]

IRENE: Come back, you! Who are you?! ¡Para! ¡*PARA!*

[*The girl disappears. Irene turns on Juanito, beating him, kicking at him . . .*]

IRENE: ¡Cabrona! ¡Loca cabrona!

JUANITO: ¡No, Señora, no!

[*Carlos slams the phone down, dashes out the front door, leaving it open. Momentarilly, there is the sound of a car motor pulling away*]

[*Michael goes slowly toward the niche by the door to Ray's room as the phone in the foyer begins to ring*]

IRENE: [*To Juanito*] ¡Contesta el telefono!

[*Juanito races to answer the phone. Ray revives a bit, tries to sit up*]

MICHAEL: [*Sinks to his knees*] Hail, Mary, full of grace . . . the Lord is with thee . . .

JUANITO: [*Into phone*] ¿Oigo? ¿Si? Siii. Un momento.

TOM: It's all right, Ray—you just fainted.

JUANITO: [*Coming outside*] Señora Dinah . . . teléfono.

[*Dinah rushes toward the foyer. Ray is making interrogative gasps . . .*]

TOM: We're home, Ray. We're back home.

MICHAEL: . . . Pray for us sinners now and at the hour . . .

DINAH: [*Into phone*] Hello? Yes? Yes! [*Devastated*] No . . . no . . . oh, NO!

MICHAEL: [*Murmuring*] . . . Blessed art thou among women, and blessed is the Fruit of thy womb . . .

[*Dinah hangs up the phone, walks dazedly outside and into guest suite #1. Juanito has dashed upstairs to Irene's room, removing the heels and wig en route*]

MICHAEL: . . . Holy Mary, mother of god. . .

[*Tom tries to restrain Ray from getting up*]

IRENE: [*To Ray*] No, no, my darling, you mustn't move! Not before the doctor gets here!

[*Ray pushes Irene away, tries to indicate something to Tom . . .*]

MICHAEL: . . . Amen.

IRENE: [*Crossing into foyer*] Oh, Tom, don't let him get up! Make him stay still! [*Exiting front door*] Where can the doctor be?! Oh, why doesn't he hurry?! [*Off stage*] Open the gates! Abre las rejas! Al medico!

MICHAEL: [*Gets up, goes to Ray*] Oh, Daddy, you shouldn't be up. Please . . . please. You shouldn't be in the bathroom. Go back and get in your bed!

TOM: [*Shaking Michael*] Michael! What's the matter with you?

MICHAEL: [*To Tom*] Take care of my mother. Take her to a room down the hall—don't let her see. I'll stay with him. I'll stay with him.

TOM: Michael! Michael! [*Slaps Michael*] Dinah! Dinah! Help me! [*Tom rushes to guest suite #1*]

TOM: Dinah, help me, please!

DINAH: [*Without affect*] Jerry's gotten a court order to take the kids. [*Begins to break*] . . . If he takes my kids from me I'll . . .

TOM: . . . You'll die.

DINAH: . . . I'll kill him! [*Picks up Tom's racquet, beats the bed*] . . . I'll kill that son–of–a–bitch. I'll kill him. I'll kill that bastard, I mean it, I'll kill him! [*Violently*] . . . Kill him! KILL HIM!

[*Tom rushes to Dinah. She collapses in his arms, sobbing*]

[*Ray makes the sign of the cross, falls backward into Michael's arms*]

MICHAEL: Oh, Daddy . . . oh, my father . . . don't leave me. You can't be leaving me, you haven't . . . you haven't said it . . .

IRENE: [*O.S.*] We need you! Help! HELP US, PLEASE!

[*Ray begins to move his lips*]

MICHAEL: Yes? . . . Yes? . . .

[*Ray moves his lips and Michael speaks the sentence in synchronization . . .*]

MICHAEL: I . . . I . . . don't . . . understand . . . any of it. I never did.

[*Michael closes his arms tightly around Ray. Ray's head drops backward and he dies. Michael rocks him gently back and forth*]

[*The light fades out*]

CURTAIN

END OF ACT I

# Act II

*The lights come up as daybreak would, with golden rays from the horizon [the balcony rail], continuing slowly to rise and intensify during the scene.*

*DINAH, clad in a terrycloth robe, is seated on the edge of the apron, looking out into space. MICHAEL, wearing a matching robe, comes up the steps from the beach.*

MICHAEL: What're you doing?

DINAH: Watching the luminous dawn—like in *Turandot*. What've *you* been doing? Having a swim?

MICHAEL: Just watching the pool drain. You know, we're like those plastic rafts and rings, having a last aimless float before it all runs out. Nice robe.

DINAH: Thanks. So's yours.

MICHAEL: Nice that they're in such great supply. Like a hotel in Hell.

DINAH: I wouldn't walk off with one.

MICHAEL: I wouldn't run the risk with La Reina. Are they back yet?

DINAH: Not yet.

MICHAEL: Any phone calls?

DINAH: [*Stops laughing*] No. Any sign of Lucky?

MICHAEL: None. We should be so lucky as Lucky. And no sign of Carlos and the girl. They all must have all gotten out while the getting was good. *About this night!*

DINAH: I'm going to be like Tom—close my eyes and hope it all goes away.

MICHAEL: It won't. There's no way out. I've tried all the exits. Except suicide. But, of course, that takes guts.

DINAH: [*Distressed at the thought*] Please, Michael, I've got such a headache.

MICHAEL: Take a pill. Take *two* pills: one for the headache and one to get high.

DINAH: I take it you've already taken your own advice?

MICHAEL: I don't pop anything serious.

DINAH: It's *all* serious. You were a mess last night.

MICHAEL: It's the weird grass I bought here. I've never been so spaced in my life. Grass is mostly my scene at the moment. *Good* grass. Viet Green, Panama Red, Acapulco Gold. I light up just like a traffic signal. Why didn't you drive in town with them?

DINAH: Coroners are *not* my favorite. No, that's not why I couldn't make it. For the first time in my life I just couldn't *do* something. I told them I wanted to stay in case the lawyer in New York called. But the truth is, Michael, I've run down. Down and out. And I'm . . . frightened. Why didn't *you* go?

MICHAEL: Irene didn't ask me. Frightened? *You?*

DINAH: Yeah, me. I can't think of anything but that rich kids' prison in the Alps that Jerry's taken the boys to.

MICHAEL: He going to put them in boarding school?! Didn't your lawyer have any suggestions?

DINAH: Just one.

MICHAEL: That Tom marry you.

DINAH: I wouldn't ask him to do such a thing. Never. Ever.

MICHAEL: What other cheery news did the lawyer have?

DINAH: I've been served with papers labeling me an unfit mother—living in sin in front of the children.

MICHAEL: "Living in sin." That *would* be grounds for damnation.

DINAH: *And* exposing them to a degenerate.

MICHAEL: *That* would be me.

DINAH: Just when you baby sit.

MICHAEL: Jerry knows I baby sit?

DINAH: He hired a private detective. He knew every time I went out with Tom and left them in a hotel with you.

MICHAEL: Did it ever occur to you that Jerry's an ex-chorus boy? I know there are *straight* chorus boys, just like there're straight hair dressers and decorators and florists. Be that as it may . . .

DINAH: Jerry's not gay. Although he *was* always plagued with itching asshole. But I'm sure that was something else.

MICHAEL: I'm sure. Gays are far less butt-centric, if you will, than most people think. What'd he do for it, or don't you know? The itching asshole, I mean.

DINAH: Well, I know he tried every salve or lotion or talcum known to man. He even put athlete's foot powder on it. I don't recommend that.

MICHAEL: Jerry *is* The Itching Asshole! Thank God, the kids take after you. Jerry's such a wimp—what the English call "wet"—he's soooo wet. But you . . . *you've* got guts.

DINAH: [*Drily*] You mean you think I have the courage to kill myself?

MICHAEL: That's not what I mean at all, and you know it.

DINAH: I'm not so strong. Honestly. I told you I was frightened. I haven't done so much for a little girl from Van Nuys, California.

MICHAEL: I'd say Boston, Beacon Hill or Philly. Went to . . .

DINAH: Farmington. I know that's what you'd say.

MICHAEL: Or Smith or Stephens.

DINAH: I'd say Santa Monica Junior College—and it's a wonder I made *that* for one semester.

MICHAEL: Flunk out?

DINAH: No. I won a beauty contest. And Jerry saw the photographs.

MICHAEL: And overnight it was searchlights in the sky and Twentieth Century-Fox presents . . . [*He lies back, waves his arms in a crisscross fashion, intones [badly] the famous fanfare*]

DINAH: Hardly. But Monroe and I *were* signed on the same day and given our names. She was M.M. and I was D.D. and I don't have to tell you how things alliteratively worked-out.

MICHAEL: I thought you were fabulous. Freckles and all.

DINAH: She got the bugle beads, I got the slacks and trench coats.

MICHAEL: I thought you were so chic and classy!

DINAH: Well, I never sat on cakes of ice on the fourth of July or jumped through paper hearts on Valentines's Day.

MICHAEL: You were sort of a man-woman symbol. Blurred the edges.

DINAH: Vaguely dykey, is what you're trying to say.

MICHAEL: Well, all the great ones were. And some of them not so vaguely.

DINAH: Sweetie, it takes a long time to find out what your style is, and when you find it, stick to it.

MICHAEL: You know, Dinah, if there were ever any chance of my . . . well, it could only be someone like you.

DINAH: Like me, or like that Hollywood image you have of me?

MICHAEL: Like I think you really are. You're real to the sprocket, Maude.

DINAH: You mean I'm a pal.

MICHAEL: Yeah. Why can't a gal be more like a pal? I wish I could have met you when you could have shown me the ropes. I love you, Dinah. I really do.

DINAH: Shut up and tell me why you think I didn't make it big in pictures.

[*There is a door slam. Tom, Irene and Juanito have come in the front entrance. Irene stops to speak to Juanito in the foyer as Tom comes out onto the terrace. The sun is higher and brighter with less color*]

IRENE: Haz cafe.

JUANITO: Si, Senora. [*Juanito exits from the foyer to the kitchen*]

TOM: [*To Dinah*] Have you heard anymore?

DINAH: [*Shakes her head*] I want to meet with the lawyers in person. I made a reservation on the noon plane to New York.

TOM: For how many?

DINAH: Only myself. I didn't know if you'd want to come—or if you and Michael would be going on someplace else.

IRENE: [*Comes outside*]—You're leaving?

DINAH: I have to, Irene.

IRENE: Just when I need you most.

DINAH: I'm sorry, but my children need me too. What arrangements have you made?

TOM: Jesus, you wouldn't believe the red tape!

IRENE: Cremation. But there are so many papers and legalities to be dealt with before I can . . . Tom has been a great help. I couldn't have managed without him. Won't you please stay just a little while longer? We can all go back to New York together.

DINAH: I can't wait.

IRENE: Tom?

TOM: I . . . have to go with Dinah.

DINAH: You don't *have* to. [*Tom goes to the bar, pours himself a straight Scotch*]

IRENE: [*To Tom*] Awfully early, isn't it? Juanito's making some coffee.

TOM: I'm a big boy, Irene. I can take care of myself.

IRENE: Really? And what about you, Michael? Will you stay and help me?

MICHAEL: Well . . . if Tom doesn't go with Dinah—I suppose I'll move on with him.

IRENE: But if they *do* go together, stay here. Stay here with *me*.

MICHAEL: Well, I . . .

IRENE: [*Crosses to Michael*] You won't have to worry about anything. Your company will be all that is required, and it will be such a consolation. You can simply live here and be taken care of. You can rest—and write.

[*Juanito enters with a tray of coffee and rolls, puts it down on the dining table*]

MICHAEL: It's a very gracious offer.

IRENE: Think about it. Coffee, Dinah?

DINAH: Thanks, no.

IRENE: [*To Juanito*] Where is the silver service? Why have you brought these horrid plastic things? These are the kitchen dishes. These are what the help use!

MICHAEL: I believe it's up top.

IRENE: What? What's up where?

[*Juanito sheepishly starts toward the foyer*]

MICHAEL: Your silver service.[*Points to guest suite #3*] It's up there.

TOM: What are you talking about, Swifty?

IRENE: Juanito! Ven aqui!

JUANITO: [*Stops*] Si, Senora.

IRENE: [*To Michael*] Explain yourself.

MICHAEL: [*After a beat*] After I heard the crying, I traced it up to the guest suite on top. And there was the baby. And Carlos and the girl—packing silver into some rather elegant suitcases. And canned goods and booze. They looked up at me, but said nothing, and neither did I, and I left. I went back up a while ago. The luggage is still there and so is all the stuff in it. I guess the family got out on shorter notice than expected. If you want your silver coffee pot, Irene, it's in Ray's Louis Vuitton in the upper guest quarters. I know it was Ray's because his initials were stencilled on it.

IRENE: [*Calmly*] Juanito, donde esta la cafetera de plata?

JUANITO: [*Shakes his head*] No se, Senora.

[*Irene turns and crosses to the stairs. Juanito follows*]

JUANITO: [*Panicking*] No, no, Senora! La culpa es de Carlos!

[*A heated altercation ensues, ad-libbed Spanish between Juanito and Irene as she leads the way up the stairs, and enters guest suite #3. Meanwhile . . .*]

DINAH: [*Crossing to Michael*] Michael, don't stay! Whatever you do—even if you just keep running, *keep running*—but don't stay here.

MICHAEL: Can I come with you?

DINAH: It's time for you to be on your own. But you must *get out.*

TOM: Dinah's right. If you stay here—it'll be the end of you.

MICHAEL: [*To Tom*] What are *you* going to do? Go with Dinah—or move on to somewhere new?

TOM: [*Turns away*] I don't know. I just don't know.

[*Irene appears on the balcony outside suite #3 with the silver coffee pot in her hand*]

IRENE: [*Calmly*] Well, well, well. Michael, you'd be invaluable to have around. [*Descending stairs*] Juanito blames Carlos. It was just as I suspected all along. That animal was taking this poor boy's hard-earned money in exchange for—an occasional favor. And to keep Juanito quiet, he was blackmailing him into harboring his pregnant slut who had his whining bastard in that very room. How do you like that?!

TOM: Fantastic.

IRENE: I'll say it's fantastic. It's *something!*

IRENE: Juanito tells me, Michael, that Carlos offered himself to you down on the beach. Did you find Carlos attractive?

MICHAEL: Yes. In a venereal sort of way.

IRENE: Juanito was quite jealous.

MICHAEL: Carlos had several things for sale. But the only thing I bought and paid for was a lid of local grass. I couldn't afford both it *and* Carlos, and I figure you have to be realistic and make up your mind what's most important to you. Priorities. It's something I've picked up from Dinah.

DINAH: That's my boy.

MICHAEL: Juanito has nothing to be jealous about. All that was blown was my fifty bucks. The really odd thing happened when I was smoking the dope on the beach. I found some fresh footprints, but there was no one around. I followed the tracks but they began to fade and were washed away. So I ran back to the spot where I'd first seen them and discovered a set of *new* tracks. I couldn't tell whether the same person had returned, as I had done, or whether a third party had passed by. But there was no one around and suddenly I thought, timing *is* everything.

IRENE: Is that all? So what?

MICHAEL: And so I masturbated into the footprints.

IRENE: [*After a moment*] I'll tell you as I have always told those who work for me—when you want things which you cannot afford, I will take care of such arrangements. If you stayed, Michael . . .

MICHAEL: I said I'll think about it.

IRENE: Very well. Did Lucky ever come back?

MICHAEL: Eh . . . no.

IRENE: Oh, well. I think I'll try to rest now. [*With an edge*] Dinah, I don't suppose you'd leave without saying goodbye.

DINAH: [*Slightly stung*] I wouldn't dream of it, Irene. Surely you know that.

[*Irene goes up the steps to her suite in the private tower. Juanito follows, carrying the silver coffee pot*]

IRENE: I don't know anything anymore. I merely want to avoid any further disappointment. Knock on my door even if I'm asleep. You know, that son-of-a-bitch Carlos probably stole Lucky too.

[*Irene enters her room. Juanito follows her and closes the door*]

DINAH: That woman has a P.H.D. in Guilt. [*Dinah begins to move*]

TOM: Where're you going?

DINAH: To get my clothes and get a taxi.

TOM: I'll—change the reservation. Make it for two.

DINAH: That's up to you.

TOM: Don't you *want* me to come with you?

DINAH: Oh, Tom, what I want is beside the point. The choice is yours.

[*She goes into suite #1. Tom goes to the bar*]

MICHAEL: Awfully early for that, Tom. Juanito's made some coffee.

TOM: [*Takes drink*] Screw you and the boat that brought you over!

MICHAEL: It was a plane this time, remember? [*Michael goes to pour some coffee*] Well, I'm gonna have some coffee in a plastic cup. What *will* the neighbors think?

TOM: What is it with me and women? Huh, Swifty? Can you tell me?

MICHAEL: Sorry, I'm gonna slither out of that one. How was it in town?

TOM: The laughs were *not* at the creamatorium.

MICHAEL: Well, it was fast.

TOM: It was a slow day. They were glad to see us.

MICHAEL: [*Puts on dark glasses*] Wow, that sun is getting hot!

TOM: Yeah, the heat's really on!

MICHAEL: By noon, it's going to be a blazing, blistering, unbreathable inferno. To Hell with tonight, there's going to be a hot time in the 'ol town by *noon!*

TOM: You wanna drink? Or are you half-in-the-bag already?

MICHAEL: I'm not anything. I'm not high, I'm not low, I'm nothing. Nada. Niente. Nicht. In spades.

TOM: [*Finishes his drink, pours another*] Come on, Swifty, have a silver bullet.

MICHAEL: No.

TOM: Well, that's a switch.

MICHAEL: Are you trying to *force* alcohol upon me?!

TOM: Don't get raggy with *me!*

MICHAEL: You're the one who's on the rag! What's with you? Belting 'em down like there's no tomorrow and it's not even high, hot noon!

TOM: [*Grimly*] I'm in a bind, man. I'm in one helluva spot.

MICHAEL: Umm. Actually, you're *on* the spot.

TOM: [*Takes a drink*] You better believe it. If I marry her—which is what I've got to do to get her off the hook, to save her kids for her—then I'm screwed. I'm stuck. My life's—well, not my own anymore.

MICHAEL: You wouldn't mind being "stuck" with Karen, would you?

TOM: On the other hand, if I walk—say, "bye-bye, thanks for shaping me up and the waltz around the park"—then I'm nailed for what I've done: let her down. Carry around that monkey on my back for whatever happens to her.

MICHAEL: And what do you think's going to happen to her?

TOM: She'll lose the kids and crack—split right down the middle—spin out in space for good. She's already seeing a psychiatrist. Did you know that?

MICHAEL: So? It wouldn't do *you* any harm.

TOM: A lot of good it's done *you*.

MICHAEL: It might have. I pissed all over it—stop, start, show, no show, show-up late, show-up late and drunk. That's no way to run a war.

TOM: Why don't you go back? Start over.

MICHAEL: Dinah says the same thing. Karen even offered to pay for it if I would go. I wonder what Irene would do? I know what Irene would do: pay the two dollars.

TOM: Your mothers. Did you ever get far enough for the doctor to point that out to you?

MICHAEL: They're *your* mothers too. You and I have a lot of the same hangups—except mine are gay and yours are straight. It's no coincidence that we are friends. It's not a big accident that with the females in our lives I do their hair and you marry them.

TOM: Why don't you have a drink?

MICHAEL: Because, goddamit, I don't want one!

TOM: Now, now, take it easy.

MICHAEL: I'm already shaking my guts out, and I want to try to make one lucid decision. If you can believe it—I'm trying to sober up.

TOM: Well, I'm trying to get drunk.

MICHAEL: That much seems obvious.

TOM: Swifty?

MICHAEL: What?

TOM: What am I going to do?

MICHAEL: Whatever it is you *have* to do. To keep your . . . for lack of a better word . . . integrity. To keep your sanity. You've been brought up to do the right thing. You could never do anything less.

TOM: And what's that?

MICHAEL: I can't live your life for you, Tom—make your decisions for you. Dinah can't. Karen couldn't. For once you're going to have to do it yourself. *For* yourself. All *by* yourself. And when you do, you have no idea the relief you'll feel.

TOM: You dirty, cocksucking bastard.

MICHAEL: Now, now, take it easy.

TOM: Swifty?

MICHAEL: What?

TOM: You know what?

MICHAEL: You're gonna tell me how much you love me.

TOM: You son-of-a-bitch.

MICHAEL: You've called me worse names. And in the recent past, I might add.

TOM: You know I don't mean it. You know I *do* love you.

MICHAEL: Yeah, I know. I'll have a pitcher of stingers and a box of Kleenex, please.

TOM: [*Enthusiastic about Michael's drinking*] Good!

MICHAEL: No, Tom, I'm kidding. I know it's hard to believe, but I really don't want a drink. I want to try and stop. What you said just now is a high in itself.

[*The front bell is rung by hand*]

TOM: What's that?

MICHAEL: The gate bell out front, I think.

[*It rings again. Tom goes to the bar to replenish his drink. Michael goes into the foyer to open the front entrance. Tom downs his drink and follows*]

[*Juanito comes out of Irene's door and goes up to guest suite #3. Momentarilly, he returns with a large Louis Vuitton suitcase. He serruptitiously comes down the stairs, but quickly has to take refuge in Michael's suite #2, as Michael returns with Ray's ashes, wrapped in a box from a crematorium*]

TOM: [*Re: box of ashes*] Where're you going to put them?

MICHAEL: I'll leave that up to Irene. Meanwhile, how about over here beneath the statue. [*Michael crosses to place the box in the niche below the statue of the Virgin Mary*]

TOM: That's good. Christ, can you believe this is how we're all gonna end up?

MICHAEL: Air mailed to New York? We make the mistake of thinking that "If we could just get away from it all, everything would be okay." But it never is.

TOM: You mean trying to escape with booze and pills.

MICHAEL: And sex and religion and time and space. [*re: box of ashes*] This is the only escape.

TOM: I just shut off my brain, no matter where I am.

MICHAEL: It's the same thing. We all seek some refuge right down the line, from the day we come into the world. As if we want to go back into the womb. Maybe we just don't want to be born in the first place.

TOM: Stop it, Swifty.

MICHAEL: Too "down" for you?

TOM: *I* want to live. I don't want to go backwards, keep doing the same things over and over.

MICHAEL: Is that why you drink your breakfast?

TOM: I'm just *afraid* of going forward. What if I can't cut it? It's safer being a kid all one's life. Look at you.

MICHAEL: Yeah, I'm the poster boy for arrested development.

TOM: What if I can't make it as a adult? As a man?

[*They look at each other for a moment. Tom picks up his glass and the bottle of Scotch, crosses to guest suite #1 and enters. Michael goes to the niche, kneels down to pray*]

[*The door to guest suite #2 opens and Juanito struggles down the stair with Ray's Vuitton case and Michael's Olivetti typewriter*]

[*Juanito sees the box of Ray's ashes in the niche, lets out a little cry, drops the cases and makes the sign of the cross*]

MICHAEL: Going somewhere? Marbella? Madrid? Maybe just to Hell in a Vuitton handbag with the rest of us. [*Michael crosses to Juanito. A moment later and they engage in a fierce struggle. There are muffled screams, ad libs in Spanish, some garments are torn, and above all, the jangling sound of Juanito's gold jewelry*]

[*Juanito eventually triumphs over Michael, hurls him aside. Juanito hastens to pick up Ray's Vuitton case. It is all he can manage. Michael gets to his feet and chases him off stage right*]

[*Michael stops, gets his breath, picks up his Olivetti and painfully climbs the stairs to his door, guest suite #2*]

[*After a moment, Irene comes out of her bedroom, rubbing her eyes, having had a fitful nap. The light comes up in Tom and Dinah's room on the ground floor, guest suite #1. He's sitting on the bed, drinking. Dinah is now dressed in a pants suit and is finishing her packing, about to close her luggage*]

[*Irene descends to the terrace, sees the box with Ray's ashes in the niche*]

IRENE: [*Panicked*] Dinah! DINAH! [*Dinah rushes outside. Irene is weaving, as if she's about to faint. Dinah's helps her to a chaise longue. Irene clings to Dinah's hand*]

IRENE: [*Indicating the niche*] Look. Look. I *can't* look.

DINAH: [*Glances at niche*] Yes. Tom told me. Did you get any sleep?

IRENE: [*Gasps*] Such as it was. Such horrible nightmares. [*Fans the air*] Such heat and humidity.

DINAH: Yes, I can hardly get my breath too.

IRENE: You're not really serious about going.

DINAH: Yes, Irene. I'm dead earnest.

IRENE: But you can't be!

DINAH: I've called the Hilton. The concierge is sending a car.

IRENE: [*Standing*] No! You can't go!

DINAH: I *have* to go. I'm sorry, but it's what I have to do.

IRENE: I said you can't go off and leave me like this!

DINAH: Irene, don't . . . don't misunderstand. It's not my intention to abandon you, it's what I must do. Don't make it difficult for both of us.

IRENE: I understand. And I *want* to make it difficult!

DINAH: Honestly, Irene, there's nothing more to say. [*Dinah turns, starts away. Irene dashes after her, blocks her*]

IRENE: [*Desperately*] Dinah, Tom doesn't love you. He'll leave you. Stay with me and I'll take care of Jerry. My lawyers will handle everything. Tell Tom to leave without you. Tell him you don't need him.

DINAH: [*Coolly*] Excuse me.

IRENE: [*Lashes out*] All right! Go on and chase after him. Rope him, tie him to you, drag him with you across the world.

[*Dinah stops, stunned by the barrage. Inside suite #1, Tom listens silently*]

IRENE: [*Relentlessly*] You can't make him love you if he doesn't. You may make him marry you but you can't make him love you because he loves his ex-wife. And he always will, even if you never let him out of your sight. You'll always know, he doesn't love you.

DINAH: Aren't you talking about yourself, Irene?

IRENE: What do you mean?!

DINAH: I mean you're talking about you and what you've done with your life, and the man in your life. You're not talking about *me*—not about *Tom.*

IRENE: Oh, yes, I am!

DINAH: Oh, no, no, no, dear lady. You're talking about yourself and I'm not like you. If I were ever headed in that direction, I hope I've found out in time. I hope I'll never let myself be like you.

IRENE: Like me? Like what?

DINAH: Bitter and barren.

IRENE: That's not the truth!

DINAH: You've built this house in the hot sun and it is as cold as an icecap. You've reduced your friends to neuter toys, hired one servant who's was no threat and got rid of the one who was. You made a eunuch of your husband.

IRENE: You don't know anything about me! Everything I ever got in life was because I was shrewd and strong. Ray was a smart man but he never would have achieved what he did if it hadn't been for me. And if I got bitter along the way it was because I got tired. I was never a part of anything in my life. I was never just naturally included. I was never attractive and wanted for myself. I had to force my way, *all* the way. You don't know anything about that. And you don't know anything about *me.*

DINAH: [*Turns*] I must . . . get out of here.

IRENE: [*Warningly*] You're going to lose. You're going to lose your Tom, you're going to lose your children, you're going to lose your mind!

[*Dinah goes inside guest suite #1. Tom stands. They silently stare at each other. She goes to close her luggage*]

IRENE: [*Stumbling about*] Michael?—Michael—*MIIICHAELLLLLL!!!*

TOM: [*To Dinah*] Wait!

DINAH: I'm through waiting for nothing. Through hanging around.

TOM: [*Indecisively*] I mean . . . I don't know what I mean, but . . . wait!

DINAH: You don't want me to go. You don't want to go *with* me. Tom. what *do* you want?

TOM: [*Ruthlessly*] I don't want you to *change* things!

DINAH: [*Realizes*] You're drunk! And you only get down to business when you're blotto. It's bye-bye to the charmer. The polite little rich boy with all the manners tucks his tail and the real you shows his face.

TOM: [*Irrationally*] *You're forcing me to make a decision!*

[*Dinah picks up her bags, Tom rushes to snatch them from her, hurl them across the room*]

TOM: *WAIT!* Things'll be the same! For a minute they will be!

DINAH: If I just stand here in one spot, not move, not breathe, nothing will change! Is that it?

TOM: For a minute, no.

DINAH: Have you taken leave of your senses? Or just reverted to childhood? You're like the kids when I wake them in the morning to go to school. All I hear is give me five more minutes—one more minute—anything, anything to put off, postpone, avoid the unavoidable—having to face the world, face life!

TOM: You think you know me pretty well. You pick up a guy in a strange town . . .

DINAH: It wasn't strange to me, I lived there. You were the foreigner. The stranger. And I didn't pick you up—I picked-up with you.

TOM: You picked me up off the ground, Dinah. I was flat.

DINAH: Yeah, I did. And don't you forget it.

TOM: You gave me a place to live . . .

DINAH: You weren't exactly out on the street. A suite at the Connaught is hardly what one would call "roughing it."

TOM: Believe me, it was rough. Until you gave me a place . . . at your table . . . in your house . . . in your bed.

DINAH: I gave you nothing but a hard time.

TOM: You figured out what my next move was.

DINAH: I boiled you an egg. I made you shave. I pressed your pants.

TOM: You pressed my brain. You changed my life.

DINAH: What was I thinking of? Myself, I guess. I was lonely. I fell in love.

TOM: And now, you think you know me. Know my traits—hide from reality—keep my head under a rock.

[*Dinah is silent*]

TOM: Dinah, talk to me.

DINAH: Why can't you talk unless you're drunk?

TOM: The booze helps me.

DINAH: No wonder you drove Karen nuts.

TOM: Who's drunk—me or you?

DINAH: I'm *not*.

TOM: Then I'm the one who's suppose to be hostile.

DINAH: That never made it all right.

TOM: I know.

DINAH: How did Karen stand it?

TOM: She couldn't.

DINAH: Silence. Denial. A fight. And the next day . . .

TOM: Flowers.

DINAH: And never any mention of the night before. All very proper. All very well brought up. All very un-real.

Tom: I wonder if Karen will marry that guy she's going with? I wonder if they talk to each other? I wonder if they'll live in our house?

Dinah: You were two kids *playing* house. *Playing* married. *Playing* grownup!

Tom: She was growing up. She was trying. I wouldn't let her. She wanted us to get help, but in my family, if you saw a psychiatrist, it meant you were . . . it was something shameful. [*Tom dissolves into tears. Dinah goes to him, tries to hold him in her arms*]

Dinah: Tom . . . Tommy . . . darling . . . don't . . . don't . . .

Tom: [*Pushes her, harshly*] Get away from me! Don't come around smothering me with your goddamn understanding! Mothering me like Irene did Ray, like you do Michael! Mother your kids, but lay off me! You may think I'm a child, but I'm not!

Dinah: [*Letting him have it*] Then act like it, goddamit! Grow-up and act like it!

Tom: Stop making me feel guilty for something I'm not guilty of! Why the fuck should I be responsible for you?!

Dinah: You're drunk! Drunk and crazy!

Tom: You've made me that way! You've put me in the middle and locked me in!

Dinah: Nobody's holding you! Tom, for Chrissake—for your own sake—take a look at yourself.

Tom: I'm afraid.

Dinah: Of what?

Tom: I don't want to talk about it now.

Dinah: Talk about it! For once, *talk!* Afraid of what—giving up this golden boy image you have of yourself?

Tom: Isn't that really why you were attracted to me? Isn't that about all the . . . all the . . . power I have? Isn't that all there is to me?

Dinah: You can't believe that. You *are* attractive. That's a very real part of you—but only a part. You can't believe that's all I see in you.

Tom: I think maybe now you only want to . . . use me.

Dinah: To get the children back?

TOM: Well?

DINAH: I think we'd better clear the air on that score right this minute. Let me tell you here and now I want to let you off the hook—if you think you're *on* the hook. I couldn't live with that. I don't want anything from you that you don't want to give.

TOM: And right here and now, I want to tell you that if it hadn't been for meeting you in London when I did, I *would* be locked-up somewhere for real. Or dead. I know I thought about killing myself. Who knows whether I would or not if it weren't for you.

[*Dinah goes to collect her two bags which have been scattered across the room*]

TOM: If we were to get married . . . would you think I was doing it because I love you, or would you think I was doing it out of my guilt over a sense of responsibility toward you?

DINAH: If I were to get married . . . would you think I was doing it because I love you, or would you think I was doing it simply to hang on to my kids?

TOM: I know which one I feel you'd be doing.

DINAH: I know which one I feel you'd be doing.

TOM: I don't think it's the one you think I think it is.

DINAH: Well, I certainly hope it's not the one you think I think it is.

[*Silence between them. Dinah exits the room with her bags. Tom goes into the bath and closes the door*]

[*The terrace is empty. Dinah puts down her cases, shields her eyes from the sun. Tears pour forth and she sits on a piece of luggage and cries*]

[*Michael exits his suite, showered and changed, but still noticeably weak. He catches sight of Dinah . . .*]

MICHAEL: Dinah, if you've got to have a nervous breakdown, the Costa-Schmosta, out-of-season, is not the place to do it.

DINAH: [*Straightens, wipes eyes, digs in bag*] It's just so fucking bright I can't even see to find my sun glasses.

[*Irene comes up the beach steps.*]

IRENE: [*To Michael*] There you are. I've been calling. Where were you?

MICHAEL: [*Descending to terrace*] I've been—in a daze. But now, I think I've finally come to.

[*Tom exits the bath in guest suite #1, carrying his valise. He continues onto the terrace, stops, looks at the group . . .*]

MICHAEL: Tom, are you going to marry Dinah?

TOM: [*Firmly*] Yes.

IRENE: Do you love her?

TOM: Irene, if you tried to make it on that alone, the whole thing would be over before you'd get the wedding presents unwrapped.

IRENE: What'll hold you together—guilt?

TOM: Decisions. Who can make them and who can stick to them. And money. Who's got it and who needs it—who can pay the bills. And, of course, kids. Those goddamn little beasts. The only thing worse than having them is not having them. All of that holds you together. That's the real stuff, that's what makes you know what the word *"responsible"* means. Being responsible—for yourself, for others—that spells survival. And you have to hang on to survive. To hang on to each other. If that's not love, I don't know what it is. Does that answer your question?

DINAH: You forgot your tennis racquet.

[*There is an offstage car horn, followed by the gate bell*]

TOM: [*To Dinah*] Would you get it for me? I'll take care of the bags and meet you at the gate.

[*Dinah nods sweetly, hurries back inside guest suite #1*]

TOM: So long, Swifty.

MICHAEL: G'bye, gorgeous.

[*Tom and Michael hug each other. Tom picks up his and Dinah's luggage.*]

TOM: Thank you, Irene. You have my most sincere sympathy. [*He exits through the foyer out the front entrance*]

[*Dinah comes out of suite #1 with Tom's racquet.*]

DINAH: I'll write to you, Irene. And please believe me, when I say I feel truly and deeply saddened. [*She moves to Michael*] Keep cool, kid. And keep *moving!*

[*Michael smiles. Dinah exits out the front entrance. Michael turns to go upstairs*]

IRENE: [*Apprehensively*] Where are you going?

MICHAEL: To get my things and get on my way.

IRENE: Not you too.

MICHAEL: I know it's what I must do.

IRENE: You all can't desert me here with just servants and a dead man!

MICHAEL: The servants have left too.

[*Michael starts up toward guest suite #2. Irene charges after him, grabs his arm.*]

IRENE: What are you saying? Where's Juanito?

MICHAEL: Stole you out of house and home and hit the high road.

IRENE: You're lying!

MICHAEL: Call him and see if he comes. All that remains are the remains of your husband.

[*Michael continues up to suite #2. Irene rushes about*]

IRENE: [*Calling*] Juanito! Vuelvan! Juan, come back! VUELVAN! VUELVAN! There *is* no one here! There's no one left! [*She rushes to the niche, picks up the box with Ray's ashes, clutches them to her*]

[*Michael exits suite #2, carrying his bag. He descends to the terrace as Irene goes to him*]

IRENE: Michael: ! Don't go! Please!

MICHAEL: Irene, you would suffocate me and, eventually, I'd finish you.

IRENE: We'd be friends!

MICHAEL: We'd be perfect victims for each other. You'd make me into another Ray and I'd make you into another mother—just as I've done with so many women before you.

IRENE: We'd be different!

MICHAEL: We'd destroy each other so neatly, so sweetly—it almost seems unthinkable not to proceed.

IRENE: What am I going to do?

MICHAEL: Let go, Irene. Let Ray rest in the Mediterranean. Where he retired to, where he was happy for a while.

IRENE: I only did what I thought was best for him. I only did what I thought was right.

MICHAEL: Perhaps. But now it's time to think what's best for yourself.

[*Irene looks over Michael's shoulder, screams.*]

IRENE: No!—Go away! Michael, help me! *Vayanse!* He dicho *vayanse! VAYANSE!*

[*Carlos comes up the beach steps, followed by the young peasant girl, carrying the baby, wrapped in a blanket. Carlos has Lucky, the German shepherd, on a leash*]

[*The light is now brighter, whiter and higher and more colorless than ever*]

CARLOS: I came back to pay my respects to the Senor. I heard that he has died.

IRENE: You stole our motor boat!

CARLOS: When we left last night—with our child—we took the boat, yes, but we have returned it.

IRENE: You were harboring this woman and child behind my back, hoarding food and liquor. Planning to steal my silver—you've come back for those things! I'm going to call the police!

CARLOS: [*Calmly*] No, Senora, that is not the truth.

MICHAEL: It doesn't matter anyway. They've already been stolen. If you're going to report a theft, Irene, Juanito is the culprit, not this man.

IRENE: [*To Carlos*] You hate me! You always have! You've come back to harm me!

CARLOS: We have come back to see if we can help you.

IRENE: You want something! You want money!

CARLOS: If you wish my services—then I will work for you. For money, yes. I consider the exchange a fair one. I looked after the Senor's needs and he gave me money. Extra money. He wanted me to bring my family here. He wanted me to have his fine things—his luggage and tea set. He said it belonged to his mother. He wanted me to take his suitcases because he knew he was never going to use them again. He told me to take the food and liquor. I stole nothing.

IRENE: You lie!

CARLOS: I tell the truth.

MICHAEL: In the end, it's simply easier to tell the truth. I must go now. Thank you for your hospitality. Will you . . . kiss me good-bye?

[*Irene doesn't move. Michael picks up his bags and crosses to her, kisses her on each cheek*]

MICHAEL: Adios, Senora.

IRENE: [*Quietly*] Adios, Senor.

[*Michael exits through the front entrance. Irene turns to Carlos as the light intensifies*]

IRENE: Your wife . . . can take . . . your child . . . up to your room.

CARLOS: [*To girl*] Sube la criatura—nosotros nos quedamos. [*Carlos gives the girl the leash. She moves quickly up the stairs to guest suite #3 and goes inside with the baby and the animal*]

[*Irene looks at Carlos, raises the box of Ray's ashes slightly . . .*]

IRENE: At sunset. When it's cool. We'll use the motorboat.

[*Carlos nods. After a moment, he crosses to Irene and puts his arms around her. Irene gently rests her head against his chest*]

[*The baby cries offstage*]

[*The predomanant source of light is now directly overhead, as if the sun is at the highest and hottest time of the day . . .*]


BLACKOUT

END OF ACT II


THE END

# A Breeze from the Gulf

for
My Mother and My Father

*A Breeze From the Gulf* was first produced on the New York stage by Charles Hollerith Jr. and Barnard S. Straus at the Eastside Playhouse on October 15, 1973. The scenery was designed by Douglas W. Schmidt, the lighting by Ken Billington, and the costumes by Stanley Simmons. The play was directed by John Going.

The original cast was:

| | |
|---|---|
| LORAINE | *Ruth Ford* |
| TEDDY | *Scott McKay* |
| MICHAEL: | *Robert Drivas* |

The play is in two acts representing the passage of ten years—1950 to 1960.

The scenery should consist simply of levels and stairs of varied and interesting heights, with only the most basic and essential set and hand props employed to identify a playing area as a particular room or place or as an exterior locale.

Much of the action takes place in the Connelly home, the basic level representing the living room, another the kitchen, three others three bedrooms in which there are only three simple beds. Whenever the action occurs away from the Connelly home—on the beach, in an institution, in a hospital, in a coastline bar—a "screen drop" consisting of three separate panels flies in to mask the three permanent beds. MICHAEL is to be portrayed by an actor of mature comprehension, yet one who physically belongs to that vague period between puberty and manhood. Within the convention of the play he must communicate an age range from fifteen to twenty-five years old. Because of the convention of the play, because he "remembers" the other two characters, he is outside of time, even though he appears in the scenes. Therefore, with the exception of an ordinary bathrobe, I would like him costumed in a dark blue suit, a dark blue necktie, and a beige raincoat throughout. Of course, he doesn't wear all the garments at the same time *all* of the time. Sometimes he wears only his under-shorts, and other times he may wear the suit trousers and his shirt with the sleeves rolled up and the collar open. It depends on the age he is playing and the context of the scene.

LORAINE and TEDDY, the other two characters, change both costumes and makeup in accordance with the requirements and chronology of the material.

Although this play takes place in the state of Mississippi, I do not want it to drip with magnolias. Hence, only LORAINE speaks with a Southern accent. MICHAEL is basically a stranger in a foreign country from the very beginning, and TEDDY's speeches and the jargon employed will, hopefully, take care of his origins and current environment.

Characters:
| | |
|---|---|
| LORAINE | The mother |
| TEDDY | The father |
| MICHAEL: | The son |

# Act I

## SCENE 1

*As the houselights dim, MICHAEL's silhouette appears, slowly tracing a path from bed to bed, from level to level, finally emerging through the panels of the screen drop, to be picked up by a spotlight as he comes down to the stage apron.*

LORAINE: [*Offstage*] MIICHAEL! OHHHH, MIIIIICHAELLLLLLL!

[*A light comes up on LORAINE, standing on the opposite side of the stage, calling . . . out front*]

MIIICHAEL! Come on inside, honey, and look at the house. Oh, Michael!

MICHAEL: [*After a pause, out front*] Yeeeeessuuuuummmmmmmm. [*Michael removes his suit jacket and his necktie, unbuttons his shirt collar, pulls the shirttail out, starts to roll up his sleeves and kick off his loafers*]

LORAINE: [*Turns to face him*] Come on inside and see the front room. [*Michael turns slowly to face her but doesn't leave his position*] Stop that runnin'! Just slow up!

MICHAEL: [*Still standing in place*] Yessum.

LORAINE: [*Exasperated*] Ohh, Michael, how many times do I have to tell you, *don't run!* [*Michael now begins to move, walking slowly toward Loraine as she speaks*] I sound like a broken record. Don't run, don't run, don't run, don't run . . .

MICHAEL: I know better than to run.

LORAINE: You're just wringin' wet with perspiration! You're gonna have the croup tonight just as sure as shootin'!

MICHAEL: P-U! It stinks in here.

LORAINE: No wonder—there hasn't been a breath of fresh air in here in twenty years. Did you notice the roof? Don't you just love it—terra-cotta tile.

MICHAEL: And there's a triple-car garage!

LORAINE: They must have had automobiles to let! Oh, boy, oh, boy, I sure hope your daddy's gettin' warm after all the buildin' up I've been doin'. After all the times I've been drivin' by this place watchin' and watchin' that old "for sale" sign. I've just gotta think of a way to convince him.

MICHAEL: Maybe if we say an "Our Father" real hard, it'll help.

LORAINE: Well, you pray and I'll think.

MICHAEL: No. You have to pray too or else it won't work.

LORAINE: [Sighs] Well, anything's worth a try. [Looks heavenward] Please, dear God. For God's sake, don't trouble the water when I'm just gettin' a bite.

[TEDDY raps "shave-and-a-haircut-two-bits" and enters, dressed in a suit and tie and wearing a hat]

MICHAEL: Daddy!

TEDDY: [To Michael] Hello, Joe, whadda-ya know!

MICHAEL: Just got back from the picture show!

LORAINE: [Ignoring Teddy] Where's the real-estate man?

TEDDY: [Removing his hat] Good afternoon. How are you today, you yummy tootsie-wootsie.

LORAINE: [To Michael] I'm married to a clown. [To Teddy] Teddy, be serious. Where's the real-estate man?

TEDDY: He's not coming.

LORAINE: Not comin'! I don't believe it!

TEDDY: Would I shit a blind girl?

LORAINE: Honey, don't talk that way in front of your son. Lord only knows what language he'll grow up to use.

TEDDY: [*To Michael*] Oh, I beg your pardon.

LORAINE: What went wrong?

TEDDY: It's already been sold. [*Silence. A pause. Then he pulls a set of keys from his pocket and jingles them*] Santy Claus!

LORAINE: Oh, honey! I don't believe it! Oh, my stars!

[*She rushes to him and throws her arms around his neck*]

MICHAEL: Oh-boy-oh-boy-oh-boy!

LORAINE: [*Hugging Teddy ecstatically*] You devil you!

TEDDY: I just hope it makes you happy.

LORAINE: Happy! I've never been so happy in all my life!

MICHAEL: Me too! Me too! Me too! Me too!

[*He rushes to embrace the two of them as they embrace each other*]

LORAINE: [*To Teddy*] You're happy too, aren't you?

TEDDY: [*Breaks away gently*] You know me, Mama. I don't really care. To me, it's an awful lot of show. But if it's what you and Michael want, that's all that matters.

LORAINE: [*Sincerely*] Oh, honey, thank you. [*She kisses him, turns to Michael*] You know, I just knew we were goin' to get this place. I knew it from the moment I asked the man why the livin'-room floor sagged in the middle and he said it was from so much dancin' at so many parties! He said one night at a party everybody was high as Georgia pines doin' the Charleston when suddenly the whole thing dropped four inches and they had to go into the basement and prop it up. But once they did, everybody picked up where they left off and never skipped a beat! Well. I knew I liked this house and this house liked me.

TEDDY: Are you planning on doing some entertaining?

LORAINE: Of course I'm not. You know I've never been one for socializin'. Thank God, we don't have any friends so we won't *have* to entertain.

LORAINE (CONT'D): But that's what this house was built for. This livin' room is more like a ballroom. Imagine! Eleven doors in four walls!

MICHAEL: And some of them seem to go nowhere.

LORAINE: But you'll notice most of them go to the porches all around. People must have just danced out through one and had a cigarette and danced right back in through another! I suppose we can seal up some of the dead ends—like that botched-up affair that covers the old built-in bar.

MICHAEL: [*Disappointed*] Awww, the bar is my favorite!

LORAINE: I wonder who you get that from.

TEDDY: Tear it out! I don't care. I'll have my toddies in the kitchen anyway.

MICHAEL: [*At the bar*] It's even got a built-in radio!

LORAINE: I'm just gonna stucco over that whole space.

MICHAEL: And it still works! Listen!

[*"The Very Thought of You" starts to play. Teddy starts to sing along . . . Teddy grabs Loraine and starts to dance*]

TEDDY: ". . . the little ordinary things that everyone ought to do. I see your face in every flower, your eyes in skies . . . "

MICHAEL: [*Interrupts their dance*] What do you suppose this is?

[*Teddy gives up—walks away*]

LORAINE: Oh! It's an ice shaver!

TEDDY: In case your ice has got five o'clock shadow at three a.m.

MICHAEL: [*Singing*] Shave-and-a-haircut-two-bits!

LORAINE: [*To Michael*] It's to shave ice for frozen daiquiris and silver fizzes.

MICHAEL: First time I've ever seen one.

LORAINE: The first time I ever saw one was in the bar of the Edgewater Gulf Hotel in Biloxi. Remember, Daddy? Or was it the bar in the Palmettos? Well, it was on the coast somewhere. Sure never saw one till I saw you.

MICHAEL: Ouuuu! There's a dead mouse in the sink.

TEDDY: He's probably just passed out. Run a little water on him—maybe he'll come to.

LORAINE: Don't touch him! He's probably riddled with disease. That's where that ghastly odor is comin' from.

MICHAEL: [*To Teddy*] I'm afraid he's a goner.

TEDDY: Cirrhosis strikes again!

LORAINE: Open a door! Let's open all the doors! Let's let the sunset in!

[*She and Michael open what would be all the doors to the porches, and the light changes*]

MICHAEL: Open sesame.

TEDDY: Now we got two nigger maids: Willy Mae and sesame.

LORAINE: Isn't it glorious! I know just how I'm gonna fix it up. I'm gonna paint everything green.

TEDDY: Well, I love green.

LORAINE: I don't mean Kelly green—a rich green, a luscious forest green with brilliant white enamel woodwork. [*To Michael*] And I'm gonna do our bedroom in wallpaper of giant cabbage roses. I can see it now.

TEDDY: I can see you're gonna put me back in the poorhouse.

MICHAEL: Don't I get to have a bedroom of my own now?

LORAINE: Whatever for?

MICHAEL: Mama, I'm fifteen years old—it's beginning to make me nervous.

LORAINE: [*Reflectively*] You know, although I'm a Southerner, I'm glad we didn't try and buy any of those antebellum or mainline magnolia homes. I think you really have to be aristocracy to live in them. Of course, I can put up a good front right along with the best of 'em if I have to—but I don't think I have to here. I feel like this house has just been sittin' here waitin' for me.

MICHAEL: Daddy, are you considered a rebel, being born in St. Louis?

LORAINE: No, honey. Missouri's not in the South! Missouri's not even in the North. Missouri's nowhere.

TEDDY: [*To Michael*] In answer to your question, I am from what is known by most intelligent people as the Midwest. Your mother never heard of it.

LORAINE: You know, your daddy and I were always livin' in the spirit of this place even if we *were broke* and livin' out of suitcases and taxicabs.

TEDDY: [*To Michael*] You were too little to remember it, but once we drove past the hotel where you were born and I said, "Look, baby, that's where Jesus brought you." And you looked up at me and said, "Did he bring me in a taxi?"

LORAINE: [*In her own world*] I'm so beside myself with joy, I feel like doin' a dance!

[*Loraine takes Michael and starts to dance*]

TEDDY: Well, let's do one. [*Pushes Michael away*] Turn up the music, son.

[*Michael turns up the volume on the radio. "Deep Purple" is playing. Teddy joins Loraine in the middle of the floor, puts his left hand up to her right one, and wraps his right arm around her spine to rest his palm on her behind. She reaches back, slaps his hand, pushes it up to the small of her back*]

LORAINE: Come on, Daddy. Don't act dirty.

TEDDY: Oh, excuse me. I thought I was dancing with the aristocracy.

LORAINE: You've had a drink, haven't you?

TEDDY: Just a little toddy to be somebody.

LORAINE: I know it's the truth. You can't fool me.

TEDDY: I'm not trying to.

LORAINE: Well, let's not argue about it now. I'm too happy. I don't know why, but I feel like, at long last, we've come home!

TEDDY: Heaven is *my* home.

LORAINE: Well, I don't know about you, but *I* am *in* heaven!

[*She exits*]

TEDDY: [*Surveys the house, slaps and rubs his hands together in a gesture of luck as if he has a pair of dice; rolls them as he speaks out front*]

Oh, Lawdy, Lawdy! I wonder what the po' folks are doin' tonight!

[*Michael continues to dance as the light fades, but a spot stays on him. Music fades; he stops, a pause, puts hands in his pockets, reflects for a moment. . .*]

## SCENE 2

*An automobile horn toots "shave-and-a-haircut-two-bits."*

MICHAEL: [*Out front, singsongs*] Daddy's home!

[*A light comes up on Teddy in the kitchen area holding a brown paper bag behind his back*]

TEDDY: [*To Michael*] Santy Claus!

MICHAEL: I've been waiting up for you— Did you bring a sack?

TEDDY: [*Flatly*] Aren't you even gonna say hello?

MICHAEL: Hello-did-you-bring-a-sack?

TEDDY: Where's that blond woman I live with?

MICHAEL: Upstairs lying down. What'd you bring?

LORAINE: [*Offstage*] Yoo-hoo!

TEDDY: Who you yoo-hooin'?

LORAINE: [*Entering*] I'm yoo-hooing you! Aren't you gonna say hello to *me*?

TEDDY: Hello, you.

[*He attempts to kiss her, she turns away. Michael sees the paper bag*]

MICHAEL: [*Elated*] You brought one!

TEDDY: [*To Loraine*] What's the matter—my breath bad?

LORAINE: No, indeed. You smell sweet—like always. You always smell just like orange juice.

TEDDY: That's just my natural fragrance. You sure look pretty tonight.

LORAINE: Why, thank you.

MICHAEL: What'd you bring?

LORAINE: [*To Michael*] Oh, honey, let the man get in the door!

MICHAEL: I want to know what's in the sack tonight!

TEDDY: Some real good ham—sliced thin as a whistle. Some Wisconsin cheese and some Swiss. You want some?

MICHAEL: Uh-uh.

TEDDY: Say, no sir, don't gimme any of that uh-uh business.

MICHAEL: *No sir.*

LORAINE: He couldn't eat another thing—we just got in a while ago. We went to Ambrosiani's and he had spaghetti.

MICHAEL: Smell *my* breath.

LORAINE: I had saltimbocca alla Romana.

TEDDY: Oh.

LORAINE: I told you I was gonna take him there this Saturday.

TEDDY: I forgot. [*To Michael*] And I brought you some new movie magazines.

MICHAEL: Oh, boy!

[*Teddy takes the magazines out of the bag, hands them to Michael, puts the bag on the kitchen table*]

LORAINE: [*To Michael*] Let me see! Let me see who's on the covers!—Oh, I can't stand *her*. [*Flips to another magazine*] Oh, I love *him*. [*Flips to another* Oh, I can't stand *her*.

TEDDY: The score is two to one. The girls lose.

[*Meanwhile, Teddy has proceeded to empty his pockets of their contents—money, glasses, pill bottles, leaflets, keys, and, lastly, his rosary, with which he reverently makes the sign of the cross and then places it with the other things on the table*]

LORAINE: [*Picking up a leaflet*] What's this?

TEDDY: A pamphlet on the Immaculate Conception.

LORAINE: Oh.

TEDDY: I know—you can't stand *her*.

LORAINE: Honey!

TEDDY: [*Goes to Loraine*] How do you feel?

LORAINE: [*Pulling away*] Pretty good. I've had a little old naggin' headache all day—but other than that I'm OK. [*Moving toward the kitchen counter*] Think I'll just take another one of my pills. [*She gets a glass of water and a bottle of pills and takes one*] You look tired.

TEDDY: It's not that I'm so tired, it's just that my damn ankles have begun to swell up so much.

[*He loosens his tie; places his jacket on the back of a chair*]

LORAINE: It's from standin' on your feet long hours. How are things at the place?

TEDDY: Hand over fist. I only hope the good Lord will let it hold out till I get the building paid for and the last note on this house. Then we'll really be in clover.

[*He has taken a bottle of gin out of the paper bag. Loraine reacts unfavorably as he picks up a glass and pours himself a drink*]

LORAINE: [*Picking up the empty sack with disdain, throwing it away. Moving off*] They say it may snow.

MICHAEL: Just think! Wouldn't it be wonderful if we had snow for Christmas this year!

TEDDY: Well, if my in-laws show up, I can guarantee a little frost.

LORAINE: [*Bristling*] Well, they'll be here!

TEDDY: In-laws and outlaws!

LORAINE: If you had any family left, I'm sure they'd be right here on top of us too!

MICHAEL: Daddy, does it snow a lot in St. Louis?

TEDDY: All the time. Why, I can remember when I was your age, my Aunt Maureen having to break the ice in the water pitcher before she could wash her face. She always made me stay in the bed till she got up and lit the stove and *heated* the water for me.

MICHAEL: [*Lamely*] Where was your . . . Uncle Brian?

LORAINE: Out drunk somewhere, no doubt.

TEDDY: Probably.

MICHAEL: [*Rather distantly*] I remember it was cold the night you threw Uncle Brian out of our old house.

LORAINE: That was too good for him—that dirty old s.o.b.—I went by the funeral parlor today to see Dr. Valkenberg and his Mexican matador. What a scandal *that's* been. It has just rocked this town. They found strychnine in the bottle of wine they were drinkin'—so it was murder as well as suicide.

TEDDY: That's too fancy for me.

LORAINE: You should have seen them. They looked just like wax. I declare, they were the most gorgeous corpses I've ever seen!

TEDDY: Sounds creepy to me.

LORAINE: I always liked Dr. Valkenberg. I was always sorry he wasn't a gynecologist so I could have tried him out. He was so nice to me when I was out to the hospital to have my partial hysterectomy. But you know and I know I could never leave Dr. LaSalle. He's just like a father to me.

TEDDY: I was thinking this year we might go to the Sugar Bowl game for Christmas.

MICHAEL: You mean go to New Orleans?

TEDDY: How would you like that, Mama?

LORAINE: You know me! I just love to travel! Boy, howdy! If I had my way, I'd keep one foot in the middle of the big road.

TEDDY: Well, I think we ought to try and plan on it. We could go to the track, have some good food, maybe take in a stage show, and see the game on New Year's Day.

LORAINE: [*To Michael*] I know you'll adore the clubhouse at the race track. It's not just like bein' *at* a movie, it's like bein' *in* a movie!

TEDDY: [*To Michael*] I can't see it myself. Stuck off to one side with those stuckups, when you can have box seats right down on the finish line!

LORAINE: [*Remembering. Deflated*] Oh. What'll I do about Hattiebeth?

TEDDY: All you have to do is write to her and politely inform her and her husband that we have other plans this Christmas.

LORAINE: I hope she won't get her nose out of joint.

TEDDY: Why are you bothered about what those heathens think!

LORAINE: [*Bluntly*] Listen, Teddy, regardless of what you think of my sister and her husband, they have been damned nice to us.

TEDDY: I never did like that goddamn baby carriage!

MICHAEL: What baby carriage?

LORAINE: *Your* baby carriage! If it hadn't been for Aunt Hattiebeth and the Captain, we'd have been pushin' you in a wheelbarrow!

TEDDY: [*Unlacing his shoes*] And, Jesus, I'll never hear the end of it.

MICHAEL: Don't fight. Please.

TEDDY: We're not fighting.

LORAINE: Do you have to undress in the kitchen and empty your pockets out all over creation! [*Gathering up the articles on the table*] Michael, take your daddy's things up to his room.

TEDDY: Can't I even relax in my own kitchen?

LORAINE: No.

TEDDY: Why not?

LORAINE: Because if your ankles are swollen, what you need is to elevate them. What you need is to lie down. So, come on, I'll turn down your bed.

[*She takes his coat and his hat and exits*]

TEDDY: What I need is my head examined for putting up with this. I wonder what a psychiatrist would say.

LORAINE: [*Going up the stairs*] That you're crazy in the head.

[*Michael has put Teddy's things in Teddy's bedroom. Loraine enters, puts his coat and hat down, and starts to turn down the bed with Michael's help*]

TEDDY: [*Picking up his shoes and his drink and heading for the stairs*] Did I tell you the joke about the cripple who went to the psychiatrist?—Well, this one cripple was telling this other one that he'd been to a psychiatrist to see if the reason he couldn't walk was because it was all in his head. [*He stops on a step; has a sip of his drink*] So the other one said, "So, what happened?" And the first cripple said, "Well, the psychiatrist said there's only one way to find out—throw away your crutches and take a step!" [*He resumes ascending the stairs*] So the other one said, "So then what happened?" And the first cripple said, "Well, then I threw away my right crutch." And the other one said, "So then what happened?" And the cripple said, "And then I threw away my left crutch." And the other one said, "And then what happened?" [*He appears in the bedroom*] And the first cripple said, "And then I fell on my fucking face!"

[*Michael starts to giggle. Loraine starts to snicker, then laughs out loud as Teddy starts to laugh, sets his glass down, and pushes Loraine over onto the bed with him. Michael collapses from the other side and the three of them lie in a heap, roaring with laughter. Finally, Loraine sits up, wiping tears from her face*]

LORAINE: [*Still through a few guffaws*] . . . Oh! . . . that is the funniest thing I ever heard—my headache is just killin' me!

[*Her laughter dies away; she kisses Teddy*]

Good night, honey.

[*She gets up and goes to her room and lies in a seductive pose on her bed, allowing the slit of her negligee to part and reveal her legs*]

MICHAEL: [*Crawls up and kisses Teddy*] Good night, Daddy.

[*Michael goes to his bedroom, removes his shirt and pants, and gets into bed as Teddy calls to him*]

TEDDY: Good night, son. Are you going to Holy Communion in the morning?

MICHAEL: Yes, sir.

TEDDY: Well, remember, don't have anything to eat or drink afterward until you swallow a few sips of water—in case any of the sacred host remains in your mouth. You hear?

MICHAEL: Yes, sir.

LORAINE: [*From her bed*] Good night, darlin'.

MICHAEL: [*From his bed*] Good night, Mama.

LORAINE: I love you.

MICHAEL: I love you too.

TEDDY: [*From his bed*] I love you three.

[*And he takes the pamphlet and glasses out of his coat pocket, puts the glasses on, starts to read and sip his drink as the lights dim out on him and Loraine while a spot holds on Michael. Pause. The sound of the Gulf surf comes up. Michael gets out of bed, picks up a beach towel, and comes center as the screen drop flies in . . .*]

## SCENE 3

*A light picks up Teddy in beach clothes and dark glasses. He has a pair of binoculars on a strap around his neck.*

TEDDY: [*Looking off through the binoculars*] Get set. Here she comes.

MICHAEL: I'm ready. Are you ready?

TEDDY: Yeah, yeah, now remember, don't say a word and for Jesus' sake, don't laugh.

MICHAEL: I won't laugh. Don't *you* laugh.

TEDDY: Don't worry about me.

LORAINE: Teddy?

TEDDY: Now, hurry up! Here she comes.

[*Michael puts an arm around Teddy's neck and hops into his arms. Once Teddy is holding him, Michael releases his grip and bends backward, letting his head and arms dangle as his feet do*]

LORAINE: [*Offstage*] What's goin' on? What're y'all doin'? Teddy?

[*Teddy has a glazed expression and moves forward a step at a time. Michael allows his head to wobble as Loraine darts onstage wearing beach clothes and carrying a Kodak*]

Teddy, what happened? What's wrong? ANSWER ME!

[*Simultaneously on cue, Michael flips up and . . .*]

TEDDY AND MICHAEL: *BOO!!!*

LORAINE: [*Recoils with fright, then recovers*] . . . You bastards!

[*Teddy and Michael fall to the ground, laughing*]

. . . I've told you not to do that to me!

MICHAEL: Oh, Mama, not again!

TEDDY: [*To Michael, with his arm around him*] You see! What'd I tell you—she fell for it again! What a sucker you are, Loraine!

LORAINE: [*Furious*] Because I'm always terrified somethin' has really happened to my child!

MICHAEL: I'm not a child anymore.

LORAINE: I don't care if you're seventy! You'll always be my baby!

TEDDY: [*Shaking his head, patting Michael*] She fell for it again! I don't believe it!

[*Loraine picks up the towel, which has fallen on the ground, and goes to put it around Michael's shoulders. He does not see her at first, is startled by her proximity, and flinches*]

LORAINE: Watcha flinchin' for? You thought I was gonna pop you one, didn't you? 'Cause you know you need it. Here.

[*Pulling Michael away from Teddy*]

Put this towel around your shoulders. You're gonna get blistered and make yourself sick.

MICHAEL: [*Dully*] Let's go for a walk.

TEDDY: Good deal. Let's walk a ways so Mama can cool off. She's mighty hot under the collar.

LORAINE: I rue the day you ever floated down the Mississippi! I should have taken one look at you and run for dear life in the other direction!

[*Pause. They stroll*]

TEDDY: Look, Loraine!

LORAINE: What?

TEDDY: That big open space over yonder.

LORAINE: That empty lot across the highway?

TEDDY: Yeah.

LORAINE: Well, I see it. What about it? [*Gasps*] Oh, my goodness! Oh, my goodness gracious!

TEDDY: Ain't that somethin'!

MICHAEL: What?

LORAINE: That's where the Palmettos was! Have you ever! What happened, Teddy? Did a hurricane get it?

TEDDY: I don't know. Maybe they tore it down.

LORAINE: Gone! Oh, that just gets away with me so!

TEDDY: I'm just as glad it's gone.

LORAINE: Oh, Daddy, how can you say that?

TEDDY: I'm glad those days are over and done with.

MICHAEL: What was it like?

LORAINE: Well, from the outside it appeared to be one of the most swell-elegant private residences along this entire coastline. But inside it was the swankiest casino on the Gulf of Mexico. Your daddy and I worked there years ago. My God, Teddy, what do you suppose ever became of Clayton?

TEDDY: Who knows?

MICHAEL: Who?

LORAINE: Clayton Reed. The Reed brothers. There were three of them—Clayton and Ramsey and Bubber Reed. And they were all the best-lookin' things you ever laid eyes on. And rich as Croesus!

TEDDY: I always thought maybe you took a shine to Clayton.

LORAINE: I did no such thing! Clayton was my favorite and that's all there was to it! [*To Michael*] They were born gamblers—had it in their blood just like your daddy. That's why they got along so well.

TEDDY: We got along because they trusted me. Clayton knew if they were gonna be successful crooks, they needed an honest crook to help 'em.

LORAINE: The story was that they had won the Palmettos in a poker game, but no one knew for sure. Daddy and I had just been married and I wasn't dry behind the ears. I used to hang around the bar late at night, playin' the slot machines, waitin' for Daddy to get off—when one night Clayton came up to me and said, "Lollie, you sure are a pretty thing. How'd you like to make a little somethin' on the side?" And I said, "Doin' what, I'd like to know." And he told me. And the next day he took me in this limousine to the best shop in Biloxi and bought me a lime-green evenin' dress. I'll never forget it as long as I live. He did all the talkin'—said, "We'd like to be shown the finest dinner dresses you have." And with that they brought out the most gorgeous clothes I've ever seen in my life. One after another—satin and beaded and spangles, and I was just ga-ga! But Clayton didn't react to a single thing until they showed us this one made of lime-green crepe de chine with no trim on it at all. And then he said, "Lollie, why don't you try on that one?" And I did. It had kind of a flared skirt and long, full, full puff sleeves that hung down and were gathered up by a band at the wrists. And it was high in the front and had no back at all. And I floated out of the dressin' room like green smoke. And Clayton said, "We'll take it!" I asked him why he had chosen that particular one. He said, "Because it was the simplest and the most dignified—and because of those big, beautiful sleeves. I hope you like it." And I said, "I think it was my favorite all along and I just never knew it till you told me."

MICHAEL: What was your job?

LORAINE: I was the shill. Clayton said people would watch my good looks rather than the dice and so they gave me money to play with and I stood on the left side of Daddy, who was ridin' the stick. On a big bet I would place a chip on the field, and my big, beautiful sleeve would spread on the board and cover Daddy's hand as he switched dice. God! We had nerve in those days! I did that time and time again and never batted a beaded eyelash, and now it scares me just to think of it.

TEDDY: Oh, yeah, I think you were stuck on Clayton all right.

LORAINE: Oh, honey, he didn't mean a thing to me. I liked him like a father. He was so reserved and genteel.

MICHAEL: What ever became of him?

LORAINE: Well, Clayton just played out and picked up and moved on. No one has seen nor heard of him since. That's one thing in this life—we never know what will happen to us.

TEDDY: [*Looking through the binoculars*] Look at what's become of that big old place over there.

LORAINE: I can see a cross above the porch, but what does the sign say?

TEDDY: Retreat House.

LORAINE: Is that like a monastery?

TEDDY: Yeah. But more. Michael, tell your mama what a retreat house is.

MICHAEL: It's a place where you can sort of be a monk for a day. Or two days or a week, depending on how long the retreat lasts. For ladies I guess it's like temporarily taking the veil. You read and meditate and listen to talks and keep a vow of silence. I don't think you'd like it.

LORAINE: Do you have to abstain from alcohol?

TEDDY: *I* would never drink while making a retreat.

LORAINE: Then I'm all for your makin' one.

TEDDY: It would defeat the point. I'd take a pledge—I'd promise God that I wouldn't drink.

MICHAEL: For how long?

TEDDY: Well, certainly during the time of the retreat—but maybe longer.

LORAINE: That's too good to be true.

TEDDY: You don't think I could do it, do you?

LORAINE: Oh, honey, I know you could do it. When you make up your mind to do somethin', you do it. You've got a will of iron. I only wish a little of that could rub off on me.

MICHAEL: Will you, Daddy?

TEDDY: We'll see. We'll see. [*Looking back at the house through the binoculars*] Sure is a snazzy layout—don't you think?

LORAINE: Uh-huh.

TEDDY: I think it's a dilly!

LORAINE: [*Looking in the opposite direction*] I just can't get over it bein' gone. Poor Clayton . . .

[*Lights fade on Loraine and Teddy. The spot stays on Michael, looking back and forth from Teddy to Loraine, from Loraine to Teddy, almost as if he were watching a tennis match, as sound of surf comes up . . .*]

## SCENE 4

*Michael slowly crosses to the proscenium, where he exchanges the beach towel for two white turkish ones. He throws one over his shoulder and wraps the other around his waist and then removes his boxer shorts. Over the above action Loraine can be heard.*

LORAINE: [*Offstage*] Michael: ! Ohh, Michael!

MICHAEL: [*Out front*] Yessum!

LORAINE: [*Offstage*] What's takin' you so long up there?

MICHAEL: [*Out front*] I'm taking a bath.

LORAINE: [*Offstage*] Your supper's ready.

MICHAEL: What'd Willy leave on the stove?

LORAINE: [*Offstage*] Nothin' but goodwill. *I* am the chef tonight!

MICHAEL: [*Incredulous but delighted*] *You* cooked? What'd you fix?

LORAINE: [*Offstage*] It's *suppose* to be a surprise! Now stop that dawdlin' and come on! You could have taken ten baths as long as you've been up there. And with as much water as you always put in that tub!

MICHAEL: You need a lot of water to take a bubble bath.

LORAINE: [*Offstage*] Bubble bath! Honestly, Michael, you should have been a girl.

[*Loraine enters to catch Michael in a pose—perhaps wrapping his head in a towel as if it were a nun's wimple, dipping his fingers into the washbasin as if it were a holy-water font, making a pious sign of the cross before his mirror*]

MICHAEL: [*With a start*] Ohhh!

LORAINE: [*Surprised as well*] What's the matter?!

MICHAEL: You scared me!

LORAINE: Whatcha scared of—your shadow?

MICHAEL: You might as well *be* my shadow. Why don't you knock?

LORAINE: Why do I have to knock? I'm your mother. Now, let me see behind your ears.

MICHAEL: Don't pull 'em!

LORAINE: I'm not gonna pull 'em.

MICHAEL: You do sometimes.

LORAINE: Only when you need it.

[*She pushes him by the shoulders to sit down and investigates his ears. He grimaces*]

Just look!—there's a blackhead! Now, let me get it!

MICHAEL: NO!

LORAINE: [*Firmly*] *M*ichael: , stop squirmin' and sit still. I'm not gonna have you with filthy ears!

MICHAEL: Well, do it fast!

LORAINE: I'm not gonna hurt you.

MICHAEL: You always say that.

LORAINE: [*Commanding*] Hush!

[*She bends his head to one side and commences her excavation. He begins a low moan . . .*]

MICHAEL: Ooowwwwwww!

LORAINE: Whatcha yellin' about—it's all over!

MICHAEL: [*Rubbing his ear*] You lied, you hurt!

LORAINE: Look at it! Big as a tick! Believe you me, you didn't have dirt in your ears as long as I bathed you in the tub with me.

MICHAEL: Well, don't get any ideas—we won't fit anymore!

LORAINE: Oh, my nails are just horrible! Now let me see your little thing.

MICHAEL: No!

LORAINE: Come on, Michael, let me look at your talliwacker.

MICHAEL: *No!* I don't have any blackheads there.

LORAINE: Stop stallin' and let me look!

MICHAEL: Mama!

LORAINE: Michael. *You hear me.*

MICHAEL: [*Defeated*] Ohhh, *all right!*

[*And he snaps his towel open upstage. She has a look and a poke*]

LORAINE: . . . Well . . . OK.

[*He glumly closes his towel*]

Now, that wasn't so bad, was it?

[*Observing Michael, who is still drying himself*]

Now, put on your robe this instant—I don't want you catchin' cold. And hurry up about it!

[*She exits and quickly goes downstairs. He pulls on his robe, steps into his slippers, and follows her down to the kitchen*]

MICHAEL: [*En route*] Can I listen to *Lux Presents Hollywood* tonight?

LORAINE: Not until you do your lessons.

[*He enters the kitchen*]

Go sit down and put your napkin in your lap.

MICHAEL: What's the menu on this special occasion?

LORAINE: [*Serving him*] Peas and okra—stop playin' with the silver—fried corn, smothered steak, sliced tomatoes! How's that suit your apparatus?

[*He smiles broadly for the first time*]

What're you grinnin' at? Huh? Sweet thing. Who do you love?

[*She bends and kisses him. He giggles*]

Silly willy! [*She goes for a bowl, returns holding it with pads*] Watch out for this one—hot, hot, hot. Stop singin' at the table! Honestly, Michael, everyone always tells me what lovely table manners you have, but God knows, one would never know it when you're at home!

MICHAEL: [*Through a mouthful of food*] Mama, please . . .

LORAINE: And don't talk with your mouth full. How is it?

MICHAEL: [*Through clenched teeth*] Mmmmmmmmmmmmmmmm.

LORAINE: I think I'll tidy up here. I just can't stand things out of place.

MICHAEL: Aren't you gonna eat any supper?

LORAINE: Oh, honey, I couldn't eat a mouthful right now. I just can't cook food and smell it and have any appetite left. By the time you've finished foolin' with it, it makes you sick at your stomach to look at it— Why aren't you eatin' your good supper?

MICHAEL: I'm full.

LORAINE: [*Incredulous*] Whaaat? Michael, all I ever hear is "Why don't we ever have meals like other people?" And when I *do* cook, you won't eat.

MICHAEL: Why don't we ever eat together?

LORAINE: Well, you know why . . . your daddy's at work. He has to work to keep this terra-cotta tile roof over our heads. And I . . . Well, I just told you, I'd be sick if I tried to eat right now. [*Pause. She sees the look on his face*] Ohhh, I know what you mean. But I gave up a long time ago, tryin' to get this family together for a meal. And if we ever do, you know how it ends up.

MICHAEL: *Excuse me.*

[*Pointedly polite, he gets up from the table and goes upstairs*]

LORAINE: Where're you goin'? [*Blankly staring at the food*] Looks like I cooked it just so I could throw it out. What're you doin' up there?

MICHAEL: Turning on the radio. The program goes on in a minute.

LORAINE: [*Clearing away the table*] You haven't done your lessons yet. You heard what I told you!

MICHAEL: I don't have any homework. The sisters never give any the first week.

LORAINE: Well, the summer is over. We are not on the coast now. You know what that means. You know your daddy's rules—no picture shows except only on Friday and Saturday, and no radio until after you do your lessons.

MICHAEL: What time is he coming home?

LORAINE: How would I know?

MICHAEL: [*Finding the radio station*] Hurry up! It's just about to start!

LORAINE: [*Excited*] I'm comin'! I'm comin'! Get out my negligee and the nail-polish remover and my emery boards.

[*There are muffled sounds from the radio as he adjusts it. Then he retrieves the manicure articles. She continues talking as if he were still in the room, during which she opens a bottle of beer*]

I think I'll just work on myself tonight. Give myself a manicure, shampoo my hair. Roll it, set it, pluck my eyebrows, and try to get myself lookin' like a halfway-decent human bein' for Mass Sunday. What story's on tonight?

MICHAEL: *Rebecca*—hurry up!

[*She starts up the stairs with the beer and two glasses*]

LORAINE: Oh, that was a grand picture—Laurence Olivier and Jo Ann Fontaine.

MICHAEL: *Joan* Fontaine.

LORAINE: She's Olivia de Havilland's sister. They were born in China, you know.

RADIO VOICE: [*Following fanfare*] *Lux Presents Hollywood!*

LORAINE: [*Enters bedroom*] Boy! Put your feet under that cover!

[*He does. She hands him a glass and pours hers full; he unzips her dress for her*]

You're just bound and determined to get the croup, aren't you?

[*She slips out of her housedress and into her negligee as Michael stares at her, filing his nails*]

MICHAEL: I don't have croup anymore. I have asthma.

LORAINE: Well, asthma then.

MICHAEL: [*Extending his glass*] Just a tap, thank you.

LORAINE: [*Pouring Michael beer. Studying her glass of beer*] I don't really like beer. Beer just goes through me like Sherman went through Georgia.

[*And she has a big swallow*]

MICHAEL: Shhhhh!!!

RADIO VOICE: And now, Daphne du Maurier's *Rebecca*.

LORAINE: [*Sits on bed, hugs Michael*] Are you warm enough?

MICHAEL: [*Smiles*] Um-hum. Warm as toast.

LORAINE: It's still the best bed in the world.

[*She snuggles closer as the lights dim, leaving only Michael in a spot. The radio voice begins. A pause, and he gets out of bed and moves to his own room as the narration finishes*]

RADIO VOICE: "Last night I dreamt I went to Manderley again. It seemed to me I stood by the iron gate leading to the drive, but the way was barred to me by a padlock and chain. I called to the lodge keeper but, peering closer through the rusted spokes of the gate, I saw that the lodge was un-inhabited."

## SCENE 5

*Lights come up full on Teddy in the kitchen and Loraine in her bed. Michael is visible in his room, eavesdropping as he dresses.*

TEDDY: Get your ass down here now and answer me.

[*Pouring a drink*]

LORAINE: Please, Teddy, I've got cramps pretty severe and I'm on edge and I want to stay on the bed.

TEDDY: You've always got cramps or a headache or you're down in your back or some damn thing when I want you to account for something.

LORAINE: [*Taking pills from a bottle by her bed*] Look, I'm nervous as hell and I don't feel like arguin'.

TEDDY: Are you nervous because you've got something to hide?

LORAINE: I most certainly am not! I'm late and I'm afraid when I do start I'll start floodin' again! And if that keeps up, I'll have to have another operation.

TEDDY: Yeah, so LaSalle can have another Cadillac.

LORAINE: I wouldn't be alive today without that man.

TEDDY: Alive so you can live it up on the sly.

LORAINE: Leave me alone, please.

TEDDY: I said, get your ass down here.

[*Loraine gets out of her bed and slowly comes downstairs*]

LORAINE: Anyone else drinks on the job, you fire them.

TEDDY: It's my place of business—I can do as I damn well please—and while I'm workin' at night, you go out! And you take Michael with you and pick up your friends.

LORAINE: I do not. I don't have any friends to speak of. I don't want any friends.

TEDDY: Well, then, where are you while I'm at work?

LORAINE: Right here in this house! Alone with my child. Night after night, except on the weekends when Michael and I go for rides—or window shoppin'! I'd take an oath.

TEDDY: You act like I never take you anywhere.

LORAINE: [*Getting a glass of water and taking a pill*] I didn't say that, Teddy.

TEDDY: We go to the coast.

LORAINE: Yes, and I love it when we do . . .

TEDDY: I took you to the World Series last year, didn't I?

LORAINE: The less said about that, the better.

TEDDY: You're just guilty about the way you acted.

LORAINE: The way *I* acted!

TEDDY: The same damn way you've always acted in front of other men.

LORAINE: That's not fair to say that of me! Because it's not true!

[*Michael has come into view a few speeches back, edging his way down the stairs, listening to this exchange. He is now wearing his shirt and trousers*]

MICHAEL: [*Entering*] What are you two arguing about?

LORAINE: Go back upstairs, honey.

MICHAEL: I can hear you upstairs.

TEDDY: Do what your mother said!

LORAINE: I can't help it if men look at me!

TEDDY: You don't have to look back! You don't have to *smile* back!

LORAINE: If they smile at me, I do. I'm flattered.

TEDDY: You're just like your sister!

LORAINE: *No, I'm not!*

MICHAEL: Please. Please, don't fight.

LORAINE: I have never been man-crazy in my life!

TEDDY: It's no news to anybody that I'm not keen on my brother-in-law—in fact, I despise his guts. But sometimes I feel sorry for the poor son of a bitch because you pair of heathens make such a sucker out of him.

LORAINE: He's not all that easy to live with—fogy as hell.

TEDDY: She put her ass in a butter tub is what she did. If we don't go to the Sugar Bowl, I am not having those barbarians in this house at Christmastime!

LORAINE: Well, they're comin'! It's already been settled.

TEDDY: If I so much as see that goddamn black Buick in the driveway, I'm gonna get the pistol out of the safe and blow their fucking heathen heads off!

LORAINE: You'll have to kill me first!

TEDDY: With pleasure! You'll be target practice!

MICHAEL: Daddy!

LORAINE: It won't be the first time. There's already one bullet hole in my bedroom to prove what a mean and crazy bastard you are!

MICHAEL: Mama!

TEDDY: I will not subject myself to that bitch taking over around here. I will not sit still and watch you slobber all over the old man.

MICHAEL: I like Aunt Hattiebeth.

TEDDY: Oh, sure. Oh, sure.

MICHAEL: And I like going to visit them during vacation.

TEDDY: Because they let you run hog-wild! Feed you chocolate candy till you start gasping for breath or puke all over the place. Not to mention letting you hang around roadhouse honky-tonks all night playing the jukebox while they tank up!

LORAINE: Look who's talkin'!

TEDDY: I don't want him with people who have no concern for his spiritual welfare.

LORAINE: Hattiebeth always makes him go to Mass on Sunday when he's up there visitin'— He is the one who doesn't want to go and who talks her into lettin' him skip it!

TEDDY: You'd let him stay in bed too if I didn't stand over you like some wild-animal trainer in the circus! You only agreed to be married by a priest to shut me up. You don't believe in anything!

LORAINE: What do you know about what I think or feel? Just because I'm not a fanatic like you!—in the front pew every time the bell rings! One thing I'll say for my sister and brother-in-law, at least *my* relatives never molested your son!

TEDDY: [*Lunges at her*] Don't you dare throw that in my face!

MICHAEL: [*Running between them*] NO! No! Keep away from her!

TEDDY: [*Trying to push him aside*] Get out of the way!

LORAINE: Go ahead, beat me to a pulp! Set some good example!

MICHAEL: Mama, please . . .

TEDDY: [*To Loraine*] You shut up!

MICHAEL: Both of you, please! Stop it!

LORAINE: [*To Michael as Teddy goes to retrieve a bottle and a glass and pours himself a drink*] You asked me about those photographs taken at the Stork Club and at Leon and Eddie's—why I had taken a razor blade and cut out my face. Well, I'll tell you. Because my eyes were so blacked and my cheeks so swollen you wouldn't have known it was your mother!

TEDDY: [*Taking a gulp of his drink*] You slut.

LORAINE: You got me mixed up with some of your friends.

TEDDY: You shut up!

LORAINE: Don't you accuse me of anything after the mornings you've stumbled in dead drunk after having holed up with God knows who—so soused you didn't even know you were wearin' a pair of satin bedroom mules!

[*Teddy throws the drink in her face*]

MICHAEL: DADDY!

[*And Michael rushes to Loraine*]

LORAINE: It's all right. It's all right.

MICHAEL: Oh, Mama, Mama . . . here . . . sit down. Sit down and let me dry your face.

[*He grabs a dishcloth and starts to gently blot her tears and the drink from her face*]

. . . Don't cry. Mama, shhh, don't . . . don't cry.

[*Teddy silently watches for a second, then turns, weaves unsteadily away and out of sight*]

LORAINE: Oh, *I'm* all right. He didn't hurt *you*, did he?

MICHAEL: No.

LORAINE: [*Drying her eyes, getting up*] Well, come on, we're gonna pack our things and get out of here.

MICHAEL: We are?

LORAINE: I'm just afraid of him when he's like this.

MICHAEL: I was hoping you'd say we'd leave! This time, let's never come back.

LORAINE: What do you mean?

MICHAEL: If you got a divorce, then we'd never have to come back! Then we could move away together somewhere. To a city— Say yes. Oh, please, say yes.

LORAINE: Oh, Michael. I don't know about any of that right now. I just want to get away from here before he has any more and starts in on me again.

MICHAEL: Then where will we go? To Aunt Hattie's?

LORAINE: No. I don't want to go there. A little of her goes a long ways. I don't feel well and I've got to take a little somethin' for it and be quiet for a while.

MICHAEL: I wish I could drive. I wish I could drive us far, far away.

LORAINE: We'll go out on the edge of town and find some little motor court for the night. And tomorrow or the next day he'll be himself again and then we can come back.

MICHAEL: But I don't want for us to come back.

[*Pause*]

LORAINE: [*Quite calmly and directly*] Michael—he's your father. And you know I've always tried to teach you to love him, no matter what he's done. He means well. And he tries. I will just have to try a little harder too. But I want you to respect him—I mean that. Because, after all, he is your father.

[*Michael is silent*]

Now, come and help me pack.

[*Lights fade, leaving only Michael illuminated by the follow spot. He slowly crosses to the proscenium to retrieve his raincoat, a Kotex box wrapped in plain brown paper, and a pharmacy bag. Throughout this action Loraine can be heard emitting a faint moan . . .*]

## SCENE 6

*Lights come up on Loraine in bed.*

LORAINE: Darlin', is that you?

MICHAEL: [*Entering*] Yes, ma'am.

LORAINE: Did you bring the Demerol?

MICHAEL: Yes, ma'am.

LORAINE: . . . and the Kotex?

MICHAEL: Yes.

LORAINE: Did you have enough money?

MICHAEL: I charged it. How do you feel?

LORAINE: [*Anxiously taking the bag from him, removing a pharmacy bottle*] I'll be OK just as soon as this medicine takes effect.

[*Michael gets a spoon from the bed table, kneels on the mattress beside her*]

Oh, honey, don't shake the bed! Just the slightest touch is like a knife goin' through my brain.

MICHAEL: [*Taking the bottle from her, rising*] I'm sorry.

LORAINE: Don't spill it! Don't spill it!

[*Michael carefully pours out a spoonful; she opens her mouth and he gives it to her*]

I thank you.

[*He replaces the cap on the bottle and moves toward the bathroom*]

And, baby, pick up your feet. Please, tiptoe. Tiptoe.

MICHAEL: I'm sorry. I'll put this in the medicine cabinet.

LORAINE: No. Just leave it here by my bed.

[*He returns the bottle and spoon to her bedside table*]

Have you got many lessons?

MICHAEL: I did them at recess.

LORAINE: Whatcha starin' at?

MICHAEL: I think I'll go out in the yard for a while.

[*He tiptoes into Teddy's room to get the binoculars*]

LORAINE: Well, be sure and button up. And don't run.

MICHAEL: I never run. The boys down the street are playing basketball and I just want to watch them through the binoculars.

LORAINE: Willy left your supper on the stove whenever you're hungry.

MICHAEL: I'm not hungry.

LORAINE: You didn't buy any chocolate at the drugstore and spoil your appetite, did you?

MICHAEL: You know I'd get asthma if I did that.

LORAINE: Thank you for stoppin' by Dr. LaSalle's to pick up the prescription.

MICHAEL: You're welcome.

[*Over this action, there is a distant, prolonged train whistle*]

LORAINE: Listen at that train. It makes me want to travel. I wonder where it's headed.

MICHAEL: No telling.

[*He tiptoes out— She continues the weak, rhythmic moan. He comes down the stairs and walks slowly out to the apron of the stage. Kneeling, clasping his hands together and looking up*]

MICHAEL: Dear God, I want to make a deal with you. Please don't punish my mama for my sins. I'm sorry for offending you—and I promise you that if you let her get well, I won't commit any more acts of self-abuse. No matter how strong the temptation. So please, let me have wet dreams and I'll keep my end of the bargain if you'll keep yours.

[*And then he takes a Tootsie Roll out of his raincoat pocket, tears off the wrapper, and starts to eat it as he raises the binoculars to his eyes. The light on Loraine fades out, but the spot holds on Michael . . .*]

## SCENE 7

*Thunder. Teddy lights a candle to reveal basement stairs. Sound of rain is heard. Michael runs to Teddy's protective arms and they huddle tightly every time there is a roll of thunder.*

TEDDY: . . . And stay away from water and never turn on a light switch with a wet hand.

MICHAEL: Yes, sir. [*Pause. A thunderclap. It subsides. Michael is now seated a step or two below so that Teddy's knees form a kind of armchair*] I wish we could fix it up down here.

TEDDY: You and your mama can think of more ways to spend money.

MICHAEL: To have a place where I could bring some people and we could dance. It's comfortable and cozy down here.

TEDDY: That's because it is what it is—a cozy cellar. If you fix it all up, it would be like the rest of the house. A little more concentration in the area of your studies and a little less time spent on becoming the local Fred Astaire might not be a bad idea.

MICHAEL: You're not gonna yell at me anymore, are you?

TEDDY: I'm through yelling. I'm now going to give you a quiet ultimatum. If you don't bring your marks up by next term, every privilege gets taken away. If you only knew how many people in this world don't have the opportunity . . .

MICHAEL: I know. I know all about it.

TEDDY: Well, if you know so much, why the hell don't you do something about it!

MICHAEL: Don't yell at me. That doesn't do any good. It just makes it worse—like the time I misspelled the word on the card of your Christmas present. All it did was make me sick.

TEDDY: I'll never get over that. How could anybody spell a simple word like "from" with an e! "To Daddy, *frome* your son!"

[*He pronounces the word "frommy." There is a clap of thunder. Michael makes a dive back into Teddy's arms. Teddy holds on to him and ducks his head. Then, after it has passed, slowly looks up*]. . .

TEDDY (CONT'D): Mainly you shouldn't be around trees. When it rains a lot of people run and stand under a tree. Well, there's nowhere more dangerous to be when lightning strikes. So remember—stay away from trees.

MICHAEL: Yes, sir.

[*Michael gets up again, takes a few steps in a different direction. He stops, picks up an old, partially deflated basketball, tries to bounce it. Dust billows out as it plops to the floor and softly rolls away*]

TEDDY: I was sure happy when you asked me to buy that. Of course I never disapproved of your having dolls. But I can't deny, when you asked for a basketball I was really thrilled. Not to mention that I nearly fell over in the toy store.

MICHAEL: I wanted to learn how to catch. I hate it when people throw things at me and expect me to catch them—like books and key rings . . . and basketballs.

TEDDY: I can't understand it. You've got good coordination and timing—you can dance. You should be able to find some rewarding athletic outlet. I don't mean football, of course. But . . . *possibly* . . . basketball. Tennis surely. Or golf—which has always looked boring as hell to me, but you might like it.

MICHAEL: I'd get asthma if I tried any of those things. You know that!

TEDDY: Maybe you'd overcome it by doing them.

MICHAEL: Maybe if we lived up north I could learn to ski. Skiing requires coordination and timing but there's no exertion required. All you have to do is stand there and slide down the hill.

TEDDY: I'm sure there must be more to it than that. If there isn't, that sounds boring as hell too.

[*Another roll of thunder. Michael runs back to Teddy and they huddle together until it dies away. A door opens at the top of the stairs, spilling a shaft of light on Teddy and Michael as Loraine is revealed, wearing a negligee. She never comes down the steps toward them but remains above them throughout her appearance*]

MICHAEL: [*Holding up his arms defensively toward her*] Shut the door!

LORAINE: [*Amused*] Well, if you two aren't a couple of screwballs!

TEDDY: Ohhhh, Jesus.

LORAINE: I felt like I needed a good laugh so I thought I'd come down and take a look at you two chicken-hearted cuckoos.

MICHAEL: Shut the door because of the draft!

LORAINE: I always know where to find y'all when it's rainin'.

MICHAEL: *Drafts attract lightning!*

LORAINE: Now who told you that, as if I don't know.

TEDDY: I didn't tell him that. He told *me!*

LORAINE: What are y'all talkin' about?

MICHAEL: Nothing.

LORAINE: Are you talkin' about me?

TEDDY: No, we're not talking about you!

LORAINE: Well, what *are* you talkin' about?

TEDDY: We were talking about your son's rotten, stinking grades.

LORAINE: Y'all are not fightin', are you?

TEDDY: Not yet.

LORAINE: [*To Michael*] What's the matter, honey? Did you get a bad report card?

MICHAEL: Well . . . not as good as they have been.

TEDDY: It was a thoroughly disgusting stinkeroo.

LORAINE: What could be causin' this?

MICHAEL: I don't know.

LORAINE: I used to be able to help you with your lessons when you were smaller. I used to drill you and drill you on your catechism. You didn't fail your catechism, did you?

MICHAEL: It's called religion now. I failed math.

LORAINE: Arithmetic?

TEDDY: He better not have failed religion or you really would hear some yelling around here.

LORAINE: [*All clear to her now*] Oh, well. I never could help you on arithmetic. Although I did drill you on the multiplication table.

MICHAEL: I still don't know the twelves.

LORAINE: Well, honey, who does?

TEDDY: You taught him to count on his fingers, which is positively the wrong way to even begin to go about it!

LORAINE: Well, you're *teachin'* him to be afraid of lightnin'! Which is positively crackpot!

MICHAEL: Will you please shut the door.

TEDDY: On your way *out!*

LORAINE: Lightnin' can't hurt you, honey. Why, I used to love to play in the rain when I was a child—couldn't wait for it to pour down so I could get wringin' wet!—or make paper boats and watch 'em go sailin' down the gutter and get swallowed up by the sewer! Of course, once Eldred Barlow was swingin' on a limb when lightnin' struck the tree, and he was split in half and burned to a crisp.

TEDDY: What did I tell you about trees?

LORAINE: But that was a freak accident! Freak accidents happen all the time—not just when it's rainin'. You ought to just gimme your hand right this very minute and let's march outside together and just stand there and say, *I am not afraid!*

MICHAEL: No!

TEDDY: Defy the elements! That's the rule of thumb you apply to everything!

[*Thunder and lightning. Michael and Teddy huddle*]

LORAINE: Rain is so relaxin'. I love to sleep in rainy weather. I think I'll get back on the bed right now and try and relax a bit. Excuse me.

[*And she moves out of sight, leaving the door ajar. Pause*]

TEDDY: I don't suppose she's told you, but I'm going to have to take her to Memphis to a hospital.

MICHAEL: Why Memphis?

TEDDY: It's a private place. It's been highly recommended by Dr. LaSalle.

MICHAEL: Why doesn't Dr. LaSalle treat her like he always has?

TEDDY: That old French-fried fart says it's beyond him now. Too many pills and shots for migraines and female trouble and nerves. She's hooked. And I'm going to have to take her to this hospital to get her off and back to where she can manage without being dependent on anything. Willy Mae can take care of you.

[*Loraine is up in her bedroom by now and has begun to sing "Red River Valley"*]

MICHAEL: [*Hearing her*] She didn't shut the door.

TEDDY: The rain has stopped anyway. We can go out now.

[*Loraine continues to sing as Michael blows out the candle. Light fades from the scene but he alone remains encircled in the spotlight. He picks up his raincoat and removes a letter in an envelope from his pocket . . .*]

## SCENE 8

MICHAEL: [*Out front*] Peabody Hotel, Memphis, Tennessee, Dear Son . . .

[*A spot comes up on Teddy on opposite side of stage*]

TEDDY: [*Out front*] Got a kick out of your note and I don't mean to be critical but you spelled "towel" with two *l*'s and "pursue" p-*e*-r-s-u-e. Now, two misspelled words on one penny postcard is a bit strong to my way of thinking, so I would appreciate it if you would get the dictionary and check these out.

Mama is doing fine. All our fears seem to have been utterly unfounded. I always suspected she might be a bit of a schizo, but the doctors say she is as sane as sane can be. They also say that she is uncooperative as hell, but this is my side of it.

I think you would like the Peabody. It has a very swanky dining room—maître d' and all—and right in the middle of the lobby there's a fountain with a lily pond around it and real live ducks quacking and paddling about. It's all a little rich for my blood, but Mama wanted to stay here and I wanted to do everything in my power to smooth things over and keep peace before I had to admit her to the hospital. Memphis, however, is one of the deadliest holes I've ever been caught with my pants down in. I just can't understand it for a river town. Absolutely no action. You practically have to go to the Arkansas side to piss, and once you go, there's nothing but a couple of buckets of blood laughingly called nightclubs, and one or two package stores. Man, I've really got the Beale Street Blues. So, as soon as I have another consultation with the head of the joint to find out how long she's going to have to stay to get straight, and pay the bill, I'm going to catch the Panama and leave this burg in the shade.

MICHAEL: [*Out front*] I.L.U.B.I.T.W.

TEDDY: [*Out front*] I love you best in the world.

[*Light fades on Teddy. Spot holds on Michael as he puts on his raincoat and . . .*]

## SCENE 9

*Marian Anderson begins to belt out "Ave Maria" at an earsplitting volume. Lights come up to reveal Teddy, prone on the kitchen floor, passed out amid scattered phonograph records, snoring. Michael crosses to look at Teddy a moment, walks around him to turn off the portable phonograph, pick up and look at an empty gin bottle. He raps "shave-and-a-haircut" on the top of the cabinet, waits for a moment . . .*

MICHAEL: Hello? Anybody home?

[*Another snore from Teddy*]

Oh. Out for the evening, as it were. [*Pause*] Here, catch. [*And he tosses a set of keys on the floor*] Thank you kindly for the use of your new car. It's a dilly!

[*He heads for the stairs, starts to ascend them, stops, looks back, turns, walks back to stand over Teddy. Michael takes off his raincoat and spreads it over him and goes up the stairs to his room to undress as Teddy continues to snore, then gets up, gets his bearings, and heads for Michael's room. Teddy enters the room to find Michael asleep. He sits on the edge of the bed and picks up Michael's hand. Pause*]

MICHAEL: Daddy!

TEDDY: [*Hushed*] Yeah, it's only me. Shhhh . . .

MICHAEL: You scared me!

TEDDY: Oh. Sorry. Shhh . . .

MICHAEL: Why are you shushing? There's no one to wake up but me.

TEDDY: Oh. Forgot. Sorry. Can't seem to keep track of when the madame is "at home" or the madame is "at sea."

MICHAEL: What are you doing up?

TEDDY: Just holding your hand. Just listening to you breathe.

MICHAEL: I have to get up at five fifteen—I have to serve six o'clock mass.

TEDDY: Oh, I'm so sorry I woke you up. Go back to sleep.

MICHAEL: OK. Good night.

[*He takes his hand from Teddy's, turns away*]

TEDDY: I'm sure proud of you. Serving Mass has always been a secret yen of mine. Maybe we could go by the church some time when it's empty and you could give me a few tips.

MICHAEL: It's a deal. Some time, but not now.

[*He turns over again*]

TEDDY: What's that nice odor? Kinda like lemons.

MICHAEL: It's some aftershave I bought.

TEDDY: [*Reaching to touch him*] I can't believe you have to shave already—your face is still so smooth.

MICHAEL: That's because I shave. Twice a week.

TEDDY: [*Laughs*] I smell like oranges and you smell like lemons. All we need is a couple of bells and we'd hit the jackpot!

MICHAEL: [*Laughs, then stops*] By the way, I didn't pay for it, I charged it.

TEDDY: [*Stops laughing*] Michael, you know I don't like that.

MICHAEL: I know, but I needed it and I had spent my allowance.

TEDDY: Son, you have to watch running up debts that you cannot pay. Your word *must* be your bond. *No compromising.*

MICHAEL: Yes, sir.

TEDDY: [*Going right on*] It's not that I don't want you to have luxuries. And the money's not important to me—it's the *principle*.

MICHAEL: Yes, sir. I know.

TEDDY: Jesus once said, when someone criticized Mary Magdalene for using the perfume on his feet instead of giving the price of same to the poor—"The poor you will always have with you." So, he meant some things to be used for adornment. But he didn't say anything about charging them.

MICHAEL: Yes, sir. I won't do it again.

TEDDY: Mary Magdalene, by the way, is one of my favorite saints. And one of Jesus' too. This is one of the most consoling lessons in the life of Christ—to love deeply the acknowledged sinner.

MICHAEL: Five fifteen is going to come awfully early.

[*Pause*]

TEDDY: Would it make you happy if I went on the wagon?

MICHAEL: [*Sitting up*] What did you say?

TEDDY: I don't mean, take a pledge. I don't mean, swear before God in writing. But I will give you my word that, for a while, I'll dry out. At least till Mama gets home once again.

MICHAEL: [*Elated*] Ohhhh, Daddy!

[*He throws his arms around Teddy and hugs him*]

TEDDY: Now, you better get to sleep. [*Teddy lowers Michael back onto his pillow and then kisses him on the forehead and tucks him in*] Good night. I love you best in the world.

MICHAEL: I love you three.

[*Teddy exits as lights dim to spot on Michael. Pause. Michael begins to get out of bed and put on his pants and shirt as . . .*]


## SCENE 10

*A light comes up on Loraine in her room on the telephone.*

LORAINE: [*Desperately and irately*] . . . What do you mean, Dr. Dillon is not in his office—not in his office to *me*? Is that what you mean! This is the thirty-seven-thousandth time I've called in the past two days, so you tell that bastard he'd better get on the line or I'm gonna have the law on his tail for everything from sellin' morphine to performin' abortions quicker'n he can say Booker T. Washington! [*Pause*] Hello? . . . Hello!

[*And she rapidly starts flashing the telephone bar as all the lights come up*]

MICHAEL: [*Entering her bedroom*] Dr. Dillon won't help you anymore, Mama. He told you to stop calling him.

LORAINE: [*Putting down the phone*] I wasn't callin' Dillon! I was tryin' to call your daddy.

MICHAEL: [*Hopelessly shaking his head*] Oh, come on. You've been hiding from him all day yesterday and today—pretending you're asleep when he leaves; pretending you're asleep when he comes in.

LORAINE: He's not comin' in early tonight, is he?

MICHAEL: Let's hope the hell not.

LORAINE: You think he knows?

MICHAEL: He knows it's just a matter of time.

LORAINE: I'm not goin' back to Memphis again! I've been in and out of that place too many times, and it just does no good! He's gonna have to try it *my way* for a change.

MICHAEL: You know he'll never go for that.

LORAINE: Maybe if you tried to convince him. [*Michael doesn't answer*] Well, what am I gonna do?

MICHAEL: I've tried to offer a solution.

LORAINE: Oh, Michael, that's so far-fetched.

MICHAEL: You won't listen to me, just like he'll never listen to you. It's a vicious circle.

LORAINE: Everything's a circle and it's all vicious. First, I'm overdue and get one of those unbearable migraines, or else start floodin', or both. And how long do you think any human bein' could stand such pain without takin' something to kill it? The last headache went on for eleven days before I finally gave in—and then there's no turnin' back. And then, sooner or later, it runs out. And here we are—right back where we were—not a c.c. of anything left, not even a bottle of paregoric, and me goin' into withdrawal like greased lightnin'! I tell you, when the Lord put me together, I think it must have been from the leftovers.

MICHAEL: [*Quickly retrieves a slop jar from behind the bed*] Are you going to be sick again?

LORAINE: No. But I better get back on the bed. [*Michael helps her to lie down, covers her*] Is it cold in here to you?

MICHAEL: No.

LORAINE: Oh. How are things at St. Iggy's?

MICHAEL: Winding up slowly but surely. Boy, will I ever be glad to get away from that bunch of meatheads.

LORAINE: I just can't feature your graduatin' and goin' off to college in the fall. Where has the time gone?

MICHAEL: It's seemed like forever to me.

LORAINE: That's because you're young. I was the same way when I was your age. Only I never finished high school. Hattiebeth did. But I never had the chance. I went to work when I was in the tenth grade as a switchboard operator.

MICHAEL: Aunt Hattie was the favorite, wasn't she?

LORAINE: That's puttin' it mild. After my pa died, my ma took everything we had and gave it to her. All I ever got was my ears boxed if I didn't chop enough wood or pump enough water from the cistern, while Hattiebeth stayed dressed up like a department-store dummy lookin' out the window at me work.

MICHAEL: Is that why you didn't go to Grandma's funeral?

LORAINE: I had a sick headache that day. You know, I've often thought that might be one of the reasons I have these headaches—'cause my ma made me see stars so many times. I used to think it was from bleachin' my hair—that the peroxide seeped right straight through to my brain. And, of course, I never had anything to take for them. I'd just crawl up to the edge of the back porch and let my head hang over the side and vomit and vomit. Nobody ever bothered me. Nobody even knew I was there.

[*Pause*]

MICHAEL: Are you all right?

LORAINE: Oh, darlin', I wish I could answer yes, but I'm beginnin' to shake to pieces.

MICHAEL: [*Insistent but encouraging*] Mama, please, instead of thinking of ways of trying to get more stuff—and since you don't want to have to go anyplace again—let's do it here; go through it together. Right now, before Daddy gets home.

LORAINE: Oh, darlin'!

MICHAEL: How long does it take?

LORAINE: You don't understand what it's like.

MICHAEL: Yes, I do. It won't scare me.

LORAINE: No. It takes time. I'd lose control. You couldn't manage me.

MICHAEL: Please, Mama, trust me.

LORAINE: Oh, I do trust you. But it's dangerous. I won't be able to stand it. I can tell that now. I'm chilled.

MICHAEL: I'll fill the tub up with hot, hot water—it'll relax you.

[*He dashes offstage into the bathroom*]

LORAINE: What if I went into convulsions and your daddy caught us! [*The sound of running water begins. Michael reappears . . .*] . . . I can't. It's no use.

MICHAEL: Please. Please try. It'll be the answer to everything. You won't have to go anywhere and Daddy will never have to know. I'm sure we can do it together. Now, come on!

LORAINE: No! No, darlin', don't try to pick me up. I'm too heavy for you.

MICHAEL: No, you're not.

LORAINE: You'll hurt yourself.

MICHAEL: No, I won't.

[*He pulls her to a sitting position on the bed*]

LORAINE: Oh, I'm cold. I'm so cold!

MICHAEL: The water will warm you up and relax you too. Come on!

LORAINE: [*With a touch of panic*] Oh, Michael . . . honey . . . what am I gonna do?

MICHAEL: Please, Mama. Let me help you!

LORAINE: [*Unsteadily approaching him*] OK—OK—whatever you say.

MICHAEL: Come on, now. Please, come on!

LORAINE: [*Near the bathroom entrance*] . . . My nightgown. [*She tries to pull the straps down over her arms*] . . . I can't get it off.

MICHAEL: Never mind. Just get in the tub with it on. I'll find the scissors and cut it off you after you relax. Now . . . please, please . . .

LORAINE: I'm comin'! I am.

[*Michael helps her out. Teddy enters the kitchen. He has a paper bag with him. He climbs the stairs to his room, retrieves a glass, removes a half-empty fifth of gin, and pours himself a drink. He is drunk but with a lucidity that alcohol produces when it removes inhibitions— He is in an articulate but violent rage. The following dialogue is offstage*]

MICHAEL'S VOICE: Now, be careful. Don't slip. Don't slip.

[*There is the sound of mild splashing and stirring of water*]

LORAINE'S VOICE: . . . Ohhhh . . . Ohhhh . . .

MICHAEL'S VOICE: Does that feel good?

LORAINE'S VOICE: . . . Yes . . . Ohhh, yes . . .

MICHAEL'S VOICE: Is it too hot?

LORAINE'S VOICE: . . . Ohhhh! Michael! . . . I'm cold . . . I'm cold!

MICHAEL'S VOICE: I'll turn on the tap—let some more hot run . . .

LORAINE'S VOICE: No! It's too deep! I've got to get out! I've got to get out!

MICHAEL'S VOICE: Then grab me around the neck. That's right. Careful now . . . careful.

[*Teddy polishes off the drink, sets the bottle and glass down in his bedroom*]

LORAINE'S VOICE: I've got to get back on the bed!

MICHAEL'S VOICE: Hang on! Hang on!

[*Teddy enters Loraine's bedroom just as Michael appears, carrying Loraine in his arms. The ends of her hair and her nightgown are thoroughly soaked, causing the fabric to become partially transparent and to stick to her skin and reveal her body. Michael's shirt front and sleeves are wet*]

TEDDY: What the fuck do you think you're doing?

LORAINE: [*After a moment*] Put me down, honey. I'm all right. I'm all right! Put me down and get my bathrobe!

[*Michael stands her up and rushes back into the bathroom*]

LORAINE: You've fallen off the wagon.

TEDDY: What did you fall off—a diving board?

LORAINE: No, dear. Just the deep end. I only fell off the deep end. [*Michael returns with a thick, full-length terry-cloth robe. He assists her to put it on*] Thank you, my angel.

TEDDY: A certain doctor came to see me today. It seems you owe him a bit of a bill.

LORAINE: Teddy, don't fuss at me now. Please.

[*She ties the robe, moves to sit on the bed*]

TEDDY: Michael, I want to talk to your mother in private.

MICHAEL: [*Flatly*] I already know about Dr. Dillon. I picked up one of the prescriptions and had it filled myself.

TEDDY: You *what?!*

MICHAEL: She needed it! She said it would be the last!

TEDDY: You fool! You punk!

LORAINE: Leave him alone, Teddy! I made him do it. So Dillon came by to collect in person. Well, I guess everybody and his sister Sue knows now.

TEDDY: I guess they do—'cause there we sat in my place of business for all to see—me and the biggest nigger doctor in town!

LORAINE: *All right!* So now you know. I get it when and where I can— behind your back, under your nose! Now maybe you'll listen to reason and try it my way!

TEDDY: Reason! What you're talking about don't make good sense!

LORAINE: It makes as much sense to me as whiskey does to you. I got along just fine until I couldn't get any more. If I stay in Memphis six weeks or six months, I shall always be as I am now. I want and need a shot. Why not let's try it this way for once. Let me have a shot every four hours and I'll never try any way of gettin' any more. Let me live the rest of my life in as much peace as possible. I think this will be agreeable with Michael.

[*Teddy is silent. Michael is silent. Loraine turns to Michael . . .*]

Tell him, Michael. Tell him it's all right with you.

MICHAEL: [*Softly*] It's . . . all right with me.

TEDDY: [*Cynically*] It's OK by you, is it?

MICHAEL: Maybe it would work.

LORAINE: [*Trying to be firm but really being desperate*] I would like to know one way or the other as I'll try and make other plans.

TEDDY: [*Mockingly*] Oh, I see.

MICHAEL: We've tried everything else, it seems.

TEDDY: [*Same attitude as before*] I see. I see. I have to check with my adolescent son if it's OK to supply you with dope—oh, but it's all right because he gives me his approval. And my wife, the dopehead, lays it on the line that if I do not *approve,* she will make other plans.

LORAINE: Now, don't take it the wrong way. *Please.*

TEDDY: [*Heated*] What's the right way to take it? And why should I take it at all! [*To Michael*] I don't have to ask your permission for anything! [*To Loraine*] And go ahead with your other plans. I'd like to know what they are. If you're gonna leave me—all right then, get out! [*To Michael*] And you get out with her! You seem to prefer her company—to be in cahoots with her—so be it!

[*He goes back into his bedroom, takes the bottle of gin, starts to pour another one. Michael quickly follows him but keeps his distance*]

MICHAEL: [*Mock disbelief*] You're not gonna take another drink!

TEDDY: I am. I most certainly am. And I don't need nor want your permission.

LORAINE: Michael, come away. Leave him alone.

[*Teddy pushes past Michael, going back to Loraine's bedroom to confront Loraine directly*]

TEDDY: [*Deliberate innuendo*] And not *everything* has been tried!

LORAINE: You wouldn't let them give me those treatments! You promised you'd never let them do that to me!

TEDDY: You promised every trip to Memphis would be the last one!

LORAINE: The last one *was* the last one, as far as I'm concerned! I'm never goin' back there again.

TEDDY: You better believe it, you're not! Because I'm not throwing good money after bad. I'll be damned if I let you break me when you have no intention of changing!

LORAINE: That's right! As long as it is there to take, *I am goin' to take it!*

TEDDY: [*Grabs hold of her*] I am going to have you committed! I'm going to have the shit shocked out of that crazy brain of yours!

LORAINE: [*Rushing to Michael*] NO! Michael! Michael, take me away from here!

TEDDY: And it won't be in some fancy joint either! I am going to have you put away in the state institution!

MICHAEL: [*Lashing out*] You shut up! Don't you say those things to her!

TEDDY: [*Boiling*] You just shut up your mouth, you impudent little shitass!

MICHAEL: You're the one who's crazy!

LORAINE: Michael!

TEDDY: *What did you say to me?*

MICHAEL: I said, you're the one who's crazy, you goddamn drunk!

[*Teddy lunges at Michael*]

LORAINE: Teddy!

MICHAEL: [*Pulling away from him; fiercely*] Get your goddamn paws off me, you drunken son of a bitch!

[*Teddy swings at Michael, misses. But Michael violently pushes him in the same direction he has swung, which causes Teddy to fall to his knees. The moment he is down, Michael rushes upon him, beating him with his fists*]

TEDDY: [*Bellowing drunkenly*] Go on! Go on! Hit me! Hit me! HIT ME! HIT ME!

[*And he starts to laugh. Meanwhile, Loraine runs between them, tries desperately to pull Michael off Teddy*]

LORAINE: Michael, stop it! *Stop it! He's your father!* HE'S YOUR FATHER!

[*Teddy stops laughing, grabs Loraine by both her arms and hurls her aside with such force that she is thrown to the floor. She screams. Teddy now subdues Michael's arms, pulling himself to his feet at the same time. The moment he is up, he knocks Michael back onto the landing. Loraine screams again*]

LORAINE: NO! NO! NOOOOOOOO!

[*Teddy starts to come at Michael again. Michael backs into Teddy's room, grabs the gin bottle, and cracks it over his skull, smashing the bottle. Teddy is genuinely physically stunned by the impact—stops, staggers forward a step or two, loses balance—one knee bends and he falls. Michael is frozen with fear. Loraine is still crouched on the floor, whimpering. A moment . . .a tick of the clock or a heartbeat when all are breathlessly still. Then Teddy grabs his head as blood begins to stream down over his face. Loraine sees it and covers her mouth to suppress a still-audible, monotonous moan. Michael remains immobile—transfixed. Teddy removes his hand from his head, holds it before him to see his bloody palm*]

TEDDY: [*Incredulously; glazed look at Michael*] . . . You! . . . You've hurt me.

[*He loses his equilibrium and falls forward to catch himself with his free arm*]

MICHAEL: [*With increasing volume*] . . .Willy! *Willy Mae!* WILLY MAE! [*And he bolts down the stairs, yelling*] CALL AN AMBULANCE! CALL AN AMBULANCE!

[*He stops at the foot of the stairs, trembling visibly. Loraine has gotten to her feet, staggered to her bed where she collapses, sobbing . . . Teddy has now crawled to the top of the stairs, Michael turns to see him*]

MICHAEL: . . . Oh, God, oh, God, oh, God, oh, God, oh, God . . . [*And he starts to run—this direction, then that direction—then another, and another, until he bolts to the apron of the stage and doubles up on his knees, sobbing . . . Lifts his head heavenward and screams through clenched teeth*] . . . Oh, God! Oh, God— Goddamn you, God. You broke your end of the bargain! *GODDAMN YOU!*


BLACKOUT

END OF ACT 1

# Act II

## SCENE 1

*A spot comes up on MICHAEL, lying in his bed. Then lights come up to reveal LORAINE in her room. A brief pause, and she crosses toward MICHAEL's room. She is wearing a jersey negligee. The fabric clings to her curves and falls to the floor in soft, flowing folds; however, she is dissipated, slightly disheveled, and ill.*

LORAINE: Darlin'? Can I come in?

MICHAEL: [*Tonelessly*] Sure.

LORAINE: [*Entering*] It's so dark in here—don't you want me to open the Venetian blinds?

MICHAEL: No, ma'am.

LORAINE: . . . Or turn on a lamp?

MICHAEL: No, ma'am.

LORAINE: Or turn down the air conditioner—it's like the North Pole in here.

MICHAEL: No. I like to listen to the hum.

LORAINE: Well, it's gonna rain this afternoon and cool off. Have you got a headache?

MICHAEL: No. How's yours?

LORAINE: Better. There's still a little throbbin' in one temple and I'm weak as a kitten but I just need some rest. [*Picking up a box of candy by his bed*] Chocolate bonbons! Where'd they come from?

MICHAEL: I bought them. Would you like one?

LORAINE: No thank you. Kinda heavy. Maybe that's what got you feelin' bad.

MICHAEL: I eat chocolate all the time now.

LORAINE: No more asthma attacks?

MICHAEL: No.

LORAINE: Why, that's the best news I've had since Hector was a pup! You must have outgrown it.

MICHAEL: I must have.

LORAINE: Well, don't eat too much of it or it'll make you sick anyway.

MICHAEL: I won't.

[*There is a roll of thunder*]

LORAINE: Ohhh! Just listen at that thunder! [*Peeping out through the Venetian blinds*] We are goin' to have an electrical storm. It is just as hot and still as it can be. Clouds have covered the sun and the trees, and the grass looks like green neon. [*Turns back to Michael, crosses slowly toward his bed*] . . . Is that why you're lyin' here in the dark, honey? Are you still scared of the lightnin'?

MICHAEL: No.

LORAINE: [*Sits on bed, takes his hand*] Why, your little hand is like ice! Michael, you've got me worried. All you've done this entire week is mope. Seems like the only reason you came home from college was to deliver your dirty laundry.

MICHAEL: [*Distantly*] Has it only been a week?

LORAINE: You remind me of some of those vegetables I've been locked up with who do nothin' but stare into space.

MICHAEL: I just don't feel like getting up, that's all.

LORAINE: [*Continuing to warm his hand*] Do you miss Washington and your friends at school?

MICHAEL: Some of them.

[*Another roll of thunder. She embraces him*]

LORAINE: I know what's wrong with you—you need a girl. Come on, now. Why don't you get up and call up some of your old friends here? Maybe they'll take you out to the country club for a swim. You like goin' out there, don't you?

MICHAEL: Not always as their guest.

LORAINE: Well, you know your daddy and I don't care a thing about that crowd of social climbers. He would *never* join, but he has always said he'll pay for your membership as soon as you're old enough to be accepted on your own.

MICHAEL: I wouldn't go near any swimming pool with it so threatening out.

LORAINE: Well . . . why don't you give a party?

MICHAEL: When?

LORAINE: Tonight!

MICHAEL: A party—with you sick in bed?

LORAINE: Oh, honey, don't mind me—you're young! You've got to have your friends!

[*Pause*]

MICHAEL: Wouldn't all the noise . . .

LORAINE: I won't hear a thing way upstairs in my room.

MICHAEL: But what about Daddy?

LORAINE: Oh, you know he won't care—he wants you to enjoy your summer vacation. Why don't you get on the phone right now and call everybody and say you've just decided to have a bash!

MICHAEL: I'd have to have something to serve them when they showed up.

LORAINE: Tell Willy to boil a pot of shrimp and fry some chickens and make a great big bowl of potato salad.

MICHAEL: Willy won't like the idea.

LORAINE: She ain't got nothin' to say about it. There's plenty of liquor in the house, and if you run out, there's plenty more where that came from!

[*There is a flash of lightning, followed by a clap of thunder. Michael flinches visibly, buries his face in his pillow. She puts her arms around him*]

Don't be such a scaredy-cat. No matter what Daddy says, lightnin' won't hurt you. It's really pretty. Look at it sometimes.

[*No response*]

Move over and let me lie down. My headache is just killin' me.

[*He slides over a bit and she gets under the covers with him, holding him in her arms. As the light dims on them, light comes up on Teddy, glass in hand, slowly climbing the back stairs to his room. He picks up a pamphlet, settles on bed to read it while sipping his drink. A spot comes up on Michael, tying his tie. A piano is playing some Cole Porter in the background. Michael goes to the door, raps "shave-and-a-haircut" on it, then quietly enters*]

MICHAEL: [*Sotto voce*] Daddy?

TEDDY: Hi. Whatcha doing up here?

MICHAEL: I'm just checking to see if you're home. I didn't hear you come in.

TEDDY: Been here about an hour. Took some of your ice from the kitchen and came up the back way. Didn't want to interrupt anything.

MICHAEL: You always say that. You wouldn't have interrupted anything. You should have come in for once and said hello to everyone.

TEDDY: Now, Michael, you know that's not my speed.

MICHAEL: Just to say hello?

TEDDY: Let's not argue about it, shall we?

MICHAEL: Why are we whispering?

TEDDY: Why did you tiptoe in? We're conditioned not to wake the sleeping beauty in the next room.

MICHAEL: If she can sleep through the music from downstairs, she's not going to hear us through a closed door.

TEDDY: I wouldn't take odds on it. Our whispers produce an effect on her eardrums not yet discovered by RCA Victor!

MICHAEL: What are you reading?

TEDDY: Some new religious literature I sent away for and the *What's On in Las Vegas* magazine.

MICHAEL: Well. What's on?

[*Sits on bed beside Teddy and lights cigarette*]

TEDDY: I haven't gotten there yet. I'm still stumbling through the desert with Thomas Aquinas.

MICHAEL: Sure you won't stumble downstairs with me for just a second?

TEDDY: Honey, don't put me on the spot. I'm all for you and I want you to be right along with the next one—but all that to-do is just too strong for me. Let me enjoy my nip by myself.

MICHAEL: . . . Well . . . OK. Please don't drink too much.

TEDDY: Don't worry about me getting swacked; just watch out for yourself.

MICHAEL: Do I seem high to you?

TEDDY: No. But you seem mellow as hell.

MICHAEL: Well, let's not argue about that, shall we?

TEDDY: I have nothing against your choice of friends—I mean the fact that they are quite a bit older than you—that doesn't matter. I always ran with an older crowd—it's a great way to learn the score. But they are adults and they can really put the sauce away—so don't you feel like you have to match 'em or you'll wind up on your ass.

[*Loraine sweeps in, dressed to the nines—hair, jewelry, the works*]

LORAINE: I thought I heard you two in here.

TEDDY: Well now, looka here. I'd say you're dressed up enough to go to a party.

LORAINE: How do I look?

MICHAEL: Like you've recovered.

TEDDY: I thought you weren't feeling well today.

LORAINE: You know me, I can put up a good front. I felt like it wasn't fair to our son not to have one of his parents put in an appearance.

TEDDY: [*To Michael*] She doesn't want them to think that we're myths! [*To Loraine*] Where'd you get the snazzy outfit?

LORAINE: I bought it ages ago. But it's still in style—simple things always are! [*To Michael*] Why aren't you downstairs? What were you two talkin' about?

MICHAEL: Nothing.

LORAINE: Were y'all talkin' about me?

TEDDY: No, God, no, we weren't talking about you.

LORAINE: [*To Michael*] Well, you ought not to be away from your guests so long.

TEDDY: Then I guess it's left up to you to rectify the situation.

LORAINE: I'm only goin' to stay for a second. Just long enough to let everybody know you do have a mother.

TEDDY: There'll be little doubt of that by the time you leave.

LORAINE: Fortunately I *have* been blessed with the gift of gab. But you can just about win anybody over if you are warm and charmin'. [*To Michael*] Don't you be long. I don't want them to think *you're* rude.

MICHAEL: I'll be right down.

LORAINE: [*Takes Michael's cigarette*] Tell me who's here so I'll know what to expect.

MICHAEL: Oh, Mary Jo and Charleen and Jerome and the same old crew.

LORAINE: Charleen Cunningham! Why, she's got children as old as you!

MICHAEL: I don't like her children. I like her.

LORAINE: Well, wish me luck! [*She exits the bedroom and sweeps down the stairs . . . Descending grandly*] Why, Charleen, what a surprise to see you here! And Jerome! I haven't seen you since the Valkenberg-Ortega rites. Weren't they the most gorgeous corpses you've ever seen?

[*She exits as the lights dim, except for the spot which follows Michael as he comes center. Pause. He goes to the proscenium. . . .*]

## SCENE 2

*. . . To get his raincoat and a valise. Lights come up full on Teddy in the living room. He is wearing pajamas and a dressing gown. Michael enters the scene.*

MICHAEL: I still don't understand why you haven't written a word since you were in Washington. What's going on? Have you been on a tear ever since you got back—you were well on your way when you left.

TEDDY: I hope you have the Christmas spirit.

[*Michael sets down the valise, notices an oxygen tank on a dolly*]

MICHAEL: [*Removing his raincoat*] What's the lowdown on this attractive accessory for the home?

TEDDY: In case of emergency. The living room is now my bedroom. Stairways are not advised.

MICHAEL: What happened?

TEDDY: I'd been back from seeing about you for almost three weeks when I just ran down. The doctor said that digitalis wouldn't get my ticker back on the track and that I'd better check into the hospital. The following morning I had a spell, which was later diagnosed as angina pectoris. After the storm and treatment I was released and have been here ever since.

MICHAEL: I knew something was up.

TEDDY: That has absolutely nothing whatsoever to do with why I have not answered your letters.

MICHAEL: [*Referring to the tank*] I guess one is not supposed to smoke around this thing.

TEDDY: Not unless you'd like us to personally attend Jesus' birthday party. We can go in the next room.

MICHAEL: Never mind. Don't keep me in suspense any longer.

TEDDY: It was impossible for me to write because I was terribly upset by the disrespect shown me, particularly the night I took you and your friend to supper. It's taken time for me to think it out and try to understand why I am always to blame.

MICHAEL: Has it ever occurred to you that you might start by considering your behavior?

TEDDY: Believe it or not, I was trying my damnedest to be on my *good* behavior. When I found out that your impacted tooth was nothing and that you'd already recovered, I thought we might celebrate and shoot the works.

MICHAEL: Well, you shot a little wide of the mark. Your behavior, if there can be any doubt in your mind, was insulting and embarrassing to me and to my friend.

TEDDY: A great deal of it could have been avoided by a little tact on your part.

MICHAEL: Why should I have to account for *your* conduct! You *are* an adult, aren't you?

TEDDY: You're damn right, I am. And I am your father too!

MICHAEL: So that's it. What you want is for *me* to apologize to *you*.

TEDDY: No matter what you believe, I did not come to Washington to get drunk. I can do that here. I did pretty well until that night.

MICHAEL: Yeah, and then you got smashed and made up for lost time. Made an ass of yourself in the restaurant and fell asleep in the theater. Snored so loudly that you had to be dragged back to the Willard and undressed and dumped into bed like a heap of garbage.

TEDDY: And you told me that you *hated* me!

MICHAEL: I *did!* And I've got a witness!

TEDDY: And that your mother and I had no love for you.

MICHAEL: You've got a keen memory even when you're fried!

TEDDY: Not such a very long while back, here in this very house, I heard you say to your mother that you wished she were dead. And now, in a hotel room in Washington D.C., you tell me that you . . . hate me!

MICHAEL: Jeeezuz, we haven't been together five minutes and . . .

TEDDY: Who held you when you were a baby and had the croup and couldn't breathe? Your mama used to sit up all night in a rocker with you on a pillow. You might not believe it, but I did get up occasionally to check on you. And when you were still frail, Mama would drive to St. Ignatius' Academy and feed you hot soup on the backseat. Several of these times your father was present.

MICHAEL: What do you want, a medal for not letting me suffocate or starve?

TEDDY: I insisted on your being an altar boy throughout school . . .

MICHAEL: *That* you certainly did.

TEDDY: Besides which, you had all the material things of life: toys, clothes, money, warm home, the use of a car at an early age, and either one or two idiots worrying about the time of night, watching every passing vehicle to see if it would turn safely into the driveway.

MICHAEL: [*Boiling*] I still say that if you really loved me so much, you wouldn't have tried to pay me off so but would have tried to do something about your sorry state of affairs.

TEDDY: What your mother and I do to ourselves has got nothing to do with *you!*

MICHAEL: But it does! I am included whether you want me to be or not! All the three of us do is torture each other. You call this a home? A home to come home to? It's a nightmare!

TEDDY: I never wanted this place.

MICHAEL: I know! It was for *me*. Always for me.

TEDDY: Your mama wanted it too. And don't say you didn't.

MICHAEL: Of course I did. I was dumb enough to believe that if it looked legit from the outside, it must be legit inside! How many times do you think I've watched that same street for hours wondering where the hell either of you were, and when you *did* show up, wondering if you could make it by the side of the house without taking off half the porch—which you have accomplished on occasion.

TEDDY: Since you were eleven years of age you seemed to have a contempt for me. I figured it would wear off with the years. But I see you now resent me more than ever. Certainly you know the only way to overcome this is to bring it out in the open. According to what you say, the trouble with me seems to be overdrinking. Is that really all?

MICHAEL: That's too cryptic for me. I'm afraid you'll have to bring that out in the open!

TEDDY: I remember once I was ashamed of your Aunt Maureen and our home in St. Louis because I ran with a better financial class of boys. We had neither electricity nor bath facilities, and your Aunt Maureen was dressed about fifteen years behind the times, and it made me feel backward.

MICHAEL: I am not exactly reluctant to invite my so-called "social-climbing" friends into this house. Everyone in this town knows exactly who we are— your place of business is on display on the busiest corner of the main drag.

TEDDY: Everyone in this town is a cornball and you know it.

MICHAEL: It is you who signs hotel registers with your occupation as "merchant."

TEDDY: It's a good word to cover a lot of things! Besides, that is what I am. A tobacco merchant. But I am not unaware for one minute that Connelly's Smoke House has nothin' to do with sausages. It's a pool hall. And there are punch boards and tips on the games and dominoes and a bar that serves liquor in a dry state and a lunch counter with one of the best short-order cooks this side of the penitentiary. But beyond that, it is a sports center, a fine one, like it says on the stationery, "Where All Good Fellows Meet." And you never need be ashamed of the Connelly background—my grandmother was a nun!

MICHAEL: What do you mean she was a nun?

TEDDY: A novice, that is, and she hightailed it over the wall to marry a brick contractor who was working in the convent. He was one of the best, mind you, laid every brick street in St. Louis.

MICHAEL: Among other things.

TEDDY: That friend of yours who was the witness to the debacle in the capital city— he was a nice boy, but I daresay he'd seen a drunk before in his life. And if he hadn't, it was an enlightening experience for him. What was his name?

MICHAEL: David Zimmerman.

TEDDY: Oh, yes. Well, maybe he never *had* seen one before. I understand there's not a high rate of alcoholism at B'nai B'rith. [*He picks up a liquor bottle, looks at the bottle, shakes his head, looks back to Michael, puts it down*] I received a letter today from Mama telling me that she had convulsions and chewed up her tongue pretty bad.

MICHAEL: I don't care if she chewed it up, swallowed it, and digested it. At least I'd never have to listen to her again.

TEDDY: She had to have three blood transfusions—they had to cut into her arms to find the veins.

MICHAEL: I don't care if they had to amputate her arms—then *I'd* never have to get another letter from her.

TEDDY: [*Incensed*] She said to tell you she received her birthday gift and was most pleased. And to tell you that she is not able to write you.

MICHAEL: Able to write you but not me.

TEDDY: I didn't think you wanted to hear from her!

MICHAEL: I don't want to hear that shit! That's all I've ever heard. Do you know how I dread getting a letter from her? I start shaking the moment I see the goddamn envelope. I break out in a cold sweat and get dizzy when I finally tear it open, and after I read it, I cry and throw up. If once, if only once, I could get a letter that wasn't a horror story! I am so goddamn sick of highballs and hypodermics, attempted suicides and oxygen tanks, remorse, self-delusions, broken promises, and, on top of it all, God, God, God. God, God!

TEDDY: Stop it! I can't take it!

MICHAEL: You can take it. If you can dish it out, you can take it. And if you can't, have a heart attack right here on the spot and let me watch. Yes, yes, yes, I said it before and I'll say it again, *I wish she were dead and I hate you and I hate her and I wish you were dead!*

TEDDY: GODDAMN YOU, YOU ARROGANT SNOB! I'm going to tell you the same as I told your mother the day you left home to go away to college. I said I had your entire education paid for and it was a tremendous pressure off of me and I was not going to be abused anymore by anybody!

MICHAEL: ALL RIGHT THEN, GODDAMNIT. ALL RIGHT, YOU WIN. I'M SORRY! If that's what you want to hear, then Christ Jesus all right, I'M SORRY! PLEASE FORGIVE ME! FORGIVE ME, FATHER. FORGIVE MY SINS. OK? OK? [*Sighs*] No. I mean it. I do. I am sorry. I am. I am. And I guess I *am* sorry that you aren't a doctor or a lawyer but a cigar-store Indian chief. And that she always behaved like Betty Grable and Lana Turner and never did what Claudette Colbert did or what Irene Dunne done.

[*Quiet. Pause*]

TEDDY: I hope you will not continue to profane God's name. That's reducing yourself to my class.

MICHAEL: Do we *have* to drag God into this?

TEDDY: And I don't mean, by any measure, I expect you to be a goody-goody. I have no time for them.

MICHAEL: You don't have to worry about that with me.

TEDDY: We do not know who is right or wrong. God will judge us all— So I ask you . . . that as long as you live . . . don't ever try to get even with anyone.

[*Lights dim on Teddy, spot stays on Michael . . .*]

## SCENE 3

*. . . As he moves and sits down.*

MICHAEL: [*Out front*] Dear David . . . I think the main reason you and I never write to each other is because we feel that if we write we have to write well. I say to hell with that—so for better or worse, here goes. I miss you, you dumb Jew! How I wish I'd accepted your parents' invitation for the holidays.

MICHAEL (cont'd.): Here it's strictly the same song, second verse. The past few New Years seem only to have introduced a new illness or another operation. Consequently, we've been skipping the Sugar Bowl jaunt and deluding ourselves that it's so much nicer to plan a *real* Christmas at home with just the three of us. This usually consists of my extravagant overdecoration of the house, only to have Loraine spend the day in the local clinic singing, "Red River Valley," for me to eat dinner at someone else's home, and for Teddy to wind up blotto on the kitchen linoleum with "Ave Maria." Oh, how I wish I were with you, blotto on your living room rug, singing, "Rio Rita"!

But again this year she broke down like clockwork around the end of November, so Teddy has revived the New Orleans gambit in an attempt, I suppose, to take the curse off things. He and I are about to leave now. But first we have to go visit her on our way.

The scenario goes like this: After you turn off Highway 80, just outside of Jackson, there is a short drive on a country road before you reach Whitfield, Mississippi. And to anyone who's ever heard of it, that word in itself is synonymous with, and euphemistic for, insane asylum. Because, after all, that's what it is—primarily. But there are others who are not there on mental papers but who have been legally committed for alcoholism and narcotic addiction.

After you've ridden along the side road for a way, the first indication that you are nearing the place is the appearance of a long double row of tall shade trees on either side of the blacktop. It's one thing to me to drive beneath those welcoming trees in the summertime; whether it is taking her out there once again or passing back through them after a visit, either way, coming or going, in summer that phalanx of green means *freedom*.

But always at this time of the year—or rather, at this time of day on this very same day of the year, the bare branches against the December light are never a thrilling indication that, at last, at least for a while, it is almost over. On this day, there is always a sense of disappointment that already, we have arrived . . .

[*A spot comes up on Teddy, holding a tray on which there are several brown paper bags covering various pots and pans*]

TEDDY: [*Out front*] Give her the signal on the horn.

MICHAEL: There's no need to—there she is waving through that upstairs window.

[*A spot comes up on Loraine, waving*]

TEDDY: [*Out front*] Give it to her anyway.

MICHAEL: [*Out front*] Daddy, it's a hospital.

TEDDY: [*Out front*] Shit, it's Christmas too.

[*Car horn sounds "shave-and-a-haircut-two-bits" as Michael rises and goes to the proscenium to collect a gift-wrapped package*]

LORAINE: [*Out front*] Hurry up there! Hurry up with the key to this ward! Woman, you are as slow as molasses in January!

MICHAEL: [*Out front*] My God, you can hear her even through a steel door. I sure would hate to be cooped up with her with nothing stronger than vitamin B12.

TEDDY: [*Out front*] She was a wonderful mother to you when you were young. She helped you when you couldn't help yourself. She can't help herself now. Be kind to her.

[*All the lights come up*]

LORAINE: Hey there!

MICHAEL: Hi.

TEDDY: Santy Claus!

LORAINE: [*Rushing forward*] Oh, my goodness gracious! You both look just beautiful!

[*They all embrace and kiss simultaneously*]

. . . Oh, look at that package! It's just wrapped grand! [*To Michael*] Did you do that, darlin'?

MICHAEL: Not this year. I had it done at the Special Wrapping Desk at Julius Garfinckel's.

TEDDY: [*Indicating the tray*] And we got a sack!

LORAINE: Oh, and I bet I know what's in it.

TEDDY: Good old cornbread dressing that Willy Mae made. And giblet gravy.

MICHAEL: And turkey . . .

TEDDY: And sweet potatoes with marshmallows on the top that Hattiebeth sent.

LORAINE: Well, you know I've never been one for sweets. But it all sounds delicious. Here, put these down a minute so I can get a good look at my husband and my child. [*To Michael*] I guess I should say my son— you're a grown man, aren't you? But you'll always be my baby. I love your haircut—shaped so becomin'. And that's a gorgeous suit. Is it new?

MICHAEL: Uh-huh. I got it at the Georgetown Shop. It's Ivy League.

TEDDY: [*To Loraine*] The Ivy League sounds like the Big League, don't it?

LORAINE: [*To Teddy, flirty*] You look pretty Big League to me yourself.

TEDDY: [*Tongue-in-cheek*] I still smell like orange juice.

LORAINE: [*Kissing him, nuzzling his cheek*] Mmmmmmmmmm. You sure do. And a little something else too.

TEDDY: [*Breaking away*] Oh, Lordy, here we go.

LORAINE: [*Defensively*] Now, did I say something? I'll change the subject.

TEDDY: [*Directly*] I told you, Mama, I took a pledge till Christmas Day and I have honored that pledge.

LORAINE: I know you've been good. Your word is as good as gold. I didn't mean anything. You look wonderful. You do.

TEDDY: And so do you.

LORAINE: [*Flattered, fishing for a compliment*] Do I?

TEDDY: [*Sincerely*] You sure do. You look just as pretty as the first day I ever saw you.

LORAINE: Well, I tried. I was so excited about seein' the two of you—I've been up half the night tryin' to decide what to wear—laid out my clothes a hundred times. It seems like no matter what I do to *myself*, I take such good care of my things—*they* just never wear out. I hope I don't look tired, do I? I'm not. Just nervous as a cat with a crocheted tail. Guess you can tell that, though.

TEDDY: You seem fine.

MICHAEL: Yes. Just fine. You look marvelous.

LORAINE: It's just gonna take a little time, that's all.

MICHAEL: Sure.

[*Teddy is silent. Loraine senses this*]

LORAINE: What Mass did you go to?

MICHAEL: Eleven.

LORAINE: Did you both go to Communion?

MICHAEL: [*Flatly*] Side by side.

LORAINE: Well, have you had anything to eat?

MICHAEL: I had a glass of water and then a piece of turkey.

TEDDY: I had a drink. Just one. Just a little toddy to be somebody.

LORAINE: [*Exasperated*] Oh, I declare, you two! A piece of turkey and a toddy!

TEDDY: We're savin' space for all that good rich food in Noo Awlens.

LORAINE: And all the bourbon on Bourbon Street.

TEDDY: Now, Mama, don't razz me.

LORAINE: What y'all got planned?

TEDDY: Same thing as always.

MICHAEL: Drive down by way of the coast so Daddy can stop at the monastery and see some of those priests who conduct those retreats.

TEDDY: Just to say hello and slip 'em a fin.

LORAINE: You can't buy your way into heaven, you know.

TEDDY: Don't have to. Heaven is my home.

LORAINE: And I know *you* in our old stompin' ground. You'll have to stop at the Edgewater or Paradise Point . . .

TEDDY: [*Pleasurably and acknowledgingly*] . . . and have one good jolt and some great seafood.

LORAINE: Well, all I ask is, please be careful.

TEDDY: I'm not going to be driving, *he* is.

LORAINE: I know he'll be drivin'—but not all the drunks on the highway are behind the wheel. I mean, be careful about your health. If you don't know it by now, you never will—that when you lose your health nothin' else is worth very much.

TEDDY: That's right. If I don't know it by now . . .

MICHAEL: Please, let's not have a fight right here.

TEDDY: Who's fighting?

MICHAEL: *We are about to.*

LORAINE: That's another thing—I don't want you two fightin' on this trip!

MICHAEL: We never fight when there's just two of us. Well, not as much. [*To Loraine*] Just like you and I don't fight when there's just the two of us. And the two of you get along better without me.

TEDDY: I guess we don't work in threes as well as we do in twos.

LORAINE: Well, then, since *I* won't be there, try to have a good time.

TEDDY: We *always* have a good time.

MICHAEL: Better every year. Really.

TEDDY: Careful what you say—she might not be in here when you get home next Christmas.

LORAINE: Oh, I'm not jealous of you two! It's just that when you talk about nice places and lovely things, it sure makes me want to be out of here. I wonder just how long I really will be here.

TEDDY: Well, if you would cooperate with the doctors for a change, instead of *defying* them to help you . . .

LORAINE: I want to do everything in my power to do the right thing this time. Nobody believes me!

MICHAEL: Mama . . .

LORAINE: I'm really gonna be well and my old self again after this trip here. I *want to* be like I used to be—and I intend to be. I just don't know what happened to me along the way. [*She looks to each of them for corroboration—both are silent*] I get so put out with myself for thinkin' I'm not able to do somethin' better with my life. I simply *have* to find a remedy for my situation.

MICHAEL: Mama, don't cry . . . please.

LORAINE: Oh, hell, I'm not cryin'. You think I want to be here! You don't know what goes on—it gets pretty rough.

TEDDY: Aw, Christ Almighty, woman, if you start now, I'm gonna sing "Jingle Bells."

MICHAEL: Daddy!

TEDDY: I'm sorry.

LORAINE: No, I'm the one who's sorry.

TEDDY: Oh, come on, let *me* be sorry.

MICHAEL: Daddy, please . . .

LORAINE: It's just gonna take time—and plenty of it. But that's what I do have plenty of. [*Brightly*] One thing for sure—it can't be for always.

[*Neither answers for a moment*]

TEDDY: Here comes the nurse.

LORAINE: [*Looks to Michael*] Already?

MICHAEL: Good-bye, Mama.

LORAINE: Good-bye, my angel. Drive careful and have fun and go back to school and study real hard. Are you learnin' some French?

MICHAEL: I'm in third year.

LORAINE: That's good. Most everything I read has a lot of French words in it, which, of course, leaves me blank.

TEDDY: Merry Christmas, Mama.

LORAINE: [*Turns to Teddy*] Merry Christmas, Daddy.

[*They kiss each other*]

It's a shame you have to be married to someone like me. I'll try some way to make up for everything I've left out all these years.

MICHAEL: I love you.

LORAINE: I love you too.

TEDDY: I love you three.

[*Loraine moves off as the lights dim to leave only the spot on Michael, and the sound of the Gulf surf comes up . . .*]

## SCENE 4

*Michael joins Teddy on a barstool. They both have drinks. In the background a saxophone, wailing some progressive jazz, replaces the sound of the surf.*

TEDDY: The thing I like about this bar—apart from the view and the salt-sea air—is that it never changes year after year. Been the same since the Depression. Makes me feel young.

MICHAEL: Well, they've stopped asking me for my draft card, so *I* feel older.

TEDDY: If *I* lived up in New York City, my hair'd turn white overnight!

MICHAEL: Heaven may be *your* home, but Manhattan is *mine.*

TEDDY: Well, as long as you're doing what makes you happy. And even though the magazines haven't yet bought any of your material, the reports seem to be universally positive.

MICHAEL: It's all Russian roulette, but I love it.

TEDDY: Now, tell me the truth, wasn't Father O'Reilly a honey?

MICHAEL: I liked him.

TEDDY: Only one who ever convinced me I could learn to serve mass at my age.

MICHAEL: I liked him—for a priest.

TEDDY: Oh, I know what must have been going through your mind when I up and write you and say I want you to take an Irish missionary out to a Broadway show and buy him a steak in Sardi's.

MICHAEL: As long as you sent the money, I was delighted.

TEDDY: Mama said when I got his thank-you note, I was grinning ear to ear. You played your hand and your heart perfectly.

MICHAEL: I had a wonderful time.

TEDDY: I'm sure you both had a wonderful time—real people! Keep like that and you'll find lots of happy moments regardless of your down-in-the-dumps periods. Don't lose faith in humanity because you run into a few dogs now and then.

MICHAEL: Yes, sir.

TEDDY: [*Takes a sip of his drink. Pause*] You know that time with Uncle Brian . . .

MICHAEL: What about it?

TEDDY: I never have forgiven myself for leaving you alone in the house with him.

MICHAEL: You didn't know he'd do what he did.

TEDDY: I should have. He did the same thing to me. Worse, I think, 'cause I was older. He made me bend over. He didn't do that to you, did he?

MICHAEL: No.

[*Pause*]

TEDDY: How's David Zimmerman?

MICHAEL: Boring as hell, probably. He has a sense of humor like a cement matzoh.

TEDDY: You haven't fallen out, have you?

MICHAEL: No, I just smile and mentally do my laundry list while he bores on. I haven't seen him in a while. He's going to graduate school in Washington.

TEDDY: He knows his stuff, though. He's strictly on the ball.

MICHAEL: You liked his parents, didn't you?

TEDDY: I thought they were jam-up!

MICHAEL: I thought you'd like them.

TEDDY: Just don't quite understand why they would choose to send their boy to a Catholic university.

MICHAEL: They're very broad-minded.

TEDDY: Well, I have nothing but praise for them.

MICHAEL: In a crazy way, they remind me at times of you and Loraine.

TEDDY: Please don't compare me with them. They are extraordinary people in my book.

MICHAEL: I just meant . . .

TEDDY: First of all, the Zimmerman family is a family of love—mother, father, offspring, and in-laws. Mama makes the home and runs the family—

as it should be. Mr. Zimmerman has money and a fine legitimate racket. I don't know how long he has been making the dough, but it don't take long with wholesale maternity dresses.

MICHAEL: And the Connelly family?

TEDDY: Is a family of . . .

MICHAEL: Of?

TEDDY: Of mother, father, son, in-laws, and outlaws.

MICHAEL: And who runs the family?

TEDDY: Daddy grabs the reins and holds on and tries to run the family. But Daddy is a thirty-year-old loser who has spent his life being smart-aleck, Casanova, ne'er-do-well black sheep!

MICHAEL: How old are you?

TEDDY: I was thirty when you were born. The previous ten years of manhood practically a parasite. Quit school, ran away, lived in crap games and whorehouses. Finally, *with* one *in* one. Daddy was a dude.

MICHAEL: [*Finally understanding, at last*] The satin bedroom slippers.

TEDDY: Got syphilis, got arrested, got wise. Daddy at this turn is not near as smart as Papa Zimmerman. Daddy doesn't make much money—Daddy doesn't *make* any money, and he meets sweet Loraine. And shows her the ropes and falls in love. And marries her. And for a while life is duck soup. Win or lose. Then the little man comes along and Daddy is really determined to grow up, go to work, and be the breadwinner. But things don't happen overnight.

Daddy is weak as hell through this early period, but as usual, he has his bottle to fall back on. Daddy and Mama don't seem to hit it off anymore since he isn't successful at this time—he just don't seem to come up with the bright ideas that the Cap'n does who, by now, is everybody's boy!

The little man is fondled and wooed and pampered by Mama and Aunt Hattiebeth and Uncle Bright Boy, the Cap'n—try to buck that combo with nothin' and then check your blood pressure. Daddy is all wrong—no good, nuts, fanatic, religious crank. Makes no difference, Daddy is determined to bring the little man up to amount to something. Daddy didn't do it right, but he didn't have Mama Zimmerman. Result: interference—no harmony. Outcome: I am still the big louse. Reward: THE KID MADE IT!

[*A moment*]

TEDDY (CONT'D): I feel the difference between the Zimmermans and the Connellys is this: Zimmermans—give proper love, you receive same. Connellys—if you can't figure out your child's resentment, then check up on Daddy and you'll find out that Daddy caused it somewhere along the line. I don't blame *you*—but I will blame you if you don't come through now. Not anytime soon—no rush—just try. I'm glad that you are patient and understanding with your friends. It's a mark of compassion—how I love that word. A great and happy virtue. One that if cultivated can be your source of future great joy; to give and to give in. Just remember, be good, be meek, be humble, but don't let no son of a bitch walk over you!

[*A moment*]

MICHAEL: Funny how warm the breeze is for this time of year.

[*Lights dim. Spot remains on Michael . . .*]

## SCENE 5

*A light comes up on Loraine.*

LORAINE: [*Out front*] My goodness, this is such a grand connection, you sound like you're across the street!

MICHAEL: [*Out front; puzzled*] Where are *you*?

LORAINE: I'm home again! [*Sincerely*] And for the first time in many, many times, Michael, I feel like I can make it on my own and never have to take anything again.

MICHAEL: When were you released?

LORAINE: Last week. Hattiebeth came and picked me up.

MICHAEL: Why didn't Teddy come for you?

[*Pause*]

LORAINE: Well, that's really why I'm callin' you. He's in Good Samaritan Clinic.

MICHAEL: How bad off is he?

[*Pause*]

LORAINE: Could you manage to get away from your work for a day or two?

MICHAEL: I'm not working.

LORAINE: Do you have the money for plane fare, honey?

MICHAEL: I'll use a credit card. Now listen, Loraine, you hang on till I get there, you hear me?

LORAINE: Don't worry about me. I'm the rock of Gibraltar when the chips are down.

[*Pause. He and Loraine join each other in the playing area*]

LORAINE: He's asleep now so let's not disturb him.

MICHAEL: How are you holding up?

LORAINE: You couldn't kill me with a meat cleaver. All I want is for *you* to get quieted down.

MICHAEL: I'm great. You know, just great. Really.

LORAINE: God, you sound like a Yankee! How do you like my hair?

MICHAEL: When can I talk to his doctor?

LORAINE: He's makin' rounds right now, so it won't be too long.

MICHAEL: Well, what's the story?

LORAINE: Well, his heart is enlarged twenty-nine percent and his ankles are swollen up mighty bad—caused from his heart not bein' able to pump all of the water through his kidneys. So it settles in his ankles. It's called . . . edema. That's the way the nuns explain it to me, I think. They are so educated, and they seem to think everyone else is.

MICHAEL: What do *you* think?

LORAINE: I think it's a serious business. He goes off at times and has a wild look, and then again he'll talk perfect sense. But don't get me wrong, with time we'll get everything back in place and try again to make a happier life.

MICHAEL: Are you . . . are you taking anything?—for your nerves, I mean?

LORAINE: [*Looking him squarely in the eye*] I haven't had as much as an aspirin tablet!

MICHAEL: [*Gently but wryly*] You wouldn't tell me a tale, would you?

LORAINE: [*Defensively serious*] I'd take an oath!

[*Teddy moans, Michael reacts, gets up, moves over to where the sickroom would be . . . Loraine gets up; sotto voce*]

Tiptoe! Tiptoe!

[*Light comes up on another area to reveal Teddy lying in a hospital bed*]

TEDDY: [*Weakly*] . . . Mama . . . Mama?

LORAINE: I'm right here, darlin'. And guess who else is here.

MICHAEL: Daddy?

TEDDY: . . . Who is that? . . . Son? Son? Is that *you*?

MICHAEL: Yes, Daddy, it's me.

[*He goes to Teddy, kisses him*]

TEDDY: Oh, Jesus-Mary-and-Joseph, I must really be in bad shape! Now, who called you? Who told you about all this mess?

LORAINE: [*Winks at Michael*] He just decided he wanted to come home.

TEDDY: That'll be the day.

MICHAEL: How do you feel?

TEDDY: Like cutting a rug.

LORAINE: I know it's the truth.

TEDDY: I'm OK—if I could just get my damn kidneys to act. I keep telling myself that if I think about having to have the good sisters catheterize me, I'll pee from now till doomsday. But it seems to have a reverse effect.

LORAINE: That's 'cause you'd like any woman foolin' with your talliwacker, even if she's married to God.

[*Michael laughs*]

TEDDY: Don't make me laugh. Believe me, it's no picnic. [*To Michael*] Always remember, don't kid around with your kidneys!

LORAINE: Oh, I think you're gettin' well. You're actin' mighty feisty!

TEDDY: You been getting my letters and clippings?

MICHAEL: Every one of them.

TEDDY: I particularly like that little poem I cut out of the *Clarion-Ledger*. "Year after year I plainly see my son is growing more like me— And for his sake I'm just a bit regretful I'm like me so much."

LORAINE: Awwwww, Daddy!

MICHAEL: I love the letters the most.

LORAINE: What did he say? Things about me?

MICHAEL: Sometimes. But only good things.

TEDDY: I'm happy that you said you had a good time in Noo Awlens at the Sugar Bowl—even though it did wind up in a free-for-all in Antoine's.

MICHAEL: Give and give in, isn't that it?—even via airmail.

TEDDY: I was a little concerned about how the tone of my last few sermons might affect you.

MICHAEL: I know my spelling is a washout.

LORAINE: You get that from me. You get all the bad things from me. Of course, you get your artistic nature from me—although Daddy does love pretty things.

TEDDY: I'm not beefing about your spelling at the moment; however, there is no excuse for a college graduate to misspell "forty" f-o-u-r-t-y. And on a bank check too—that's unpardonable! I am referring to the fact I felt you were being complacent and getting in a rut.

MICHAEL: I'm sorry if I sounded down in the mouth. I'm really very optimistic about my career—even though I can soon paper my apartment with editors' rejection slips.

TEDDY: I'm sure everything will work out on schedule. After all, you've only been out of school a little over a year and a half. With your temperament— if you'd gotten anywhere too quickly—your head might have swelled up bigger than my bladder.

[*Michael and Loraine laugh*]

Mama wants to come to New York as soon as the weather is nice.

LORAINE: That can wait till Daddy gets on his feet again and I get a little more time behind *me*. But we do want to see your livin' quarters—we don't understand what a cold-water flat is. What, no hot water—no heat?

MICHAEL: No, no, it has heat.

LORAINE: Can you cook in one?

MICHAEL: The kitchen's the biggest room. It even has a bathtub in it.

LORAINE: It just sounds godawful to me. Do you have a warm bed?

MICHAEL: Of course I have a warm bed.

LORAINE: Well, I just want to know what you have in the way of comfort. To think of you in real need would kill *both* of us.

TEDDY: You get your tact from her too.

LORAINE: We'll just never get used to your bein' gone. If you're not sellin' your stories, are you doin' anything else? I don't seem to know anything much about you anymore.

TEDDY: Leave him alone, Mama. That's his business. He's a young man out in the world on his own. [*To Michael*] And on that score I have this to say: If you commit a mortal sin, say an act of contrition immediately and then go to confession as soon as possible. Gamble if you must, but don't gamble with your soul. I know you already know this—just a reminder. And now, I think I'd like to try to use the toilet.

LORAINE: Oh, good! Let me ring for the orderly.

TEDDY: No. I want Michael to help me.

[*Pause. Michael comes to the opposite side of the bed from Loraine; Teddy weakly extends an arm. Michael takes it, begins to gently pull him from the pillow, slipping his other arm behind Teddy's back. As Teddy is raised and his feet swing out to dangle in space, Loraine hurries closer to be of assistance. During this, Teddy gives out with a faint gasp and all freeze silently once he is in a sitting position. He is pale as a dead man. Pause*]

Oh, Lord, I don't want any cheese—I just want to get my head out of the trap!

[*There is a moment before both Michael and Loraine begin to assist him to stand. Then, as they simultaneously start to lift him, he hesitates and gently pushes Loraine away*]

No, Mama. Michael can handle me.

[*Loraine helplessly backs away, then looks to Michael and gives him a little sign, as if to say he has her permission to continue. Michael kneels to put Teddy's slippers on him*]

Now ain't this some fine come-off! I never thought I'd hear myself say this—but if somebody offered me cold beer right now, I'd have to turn 'em down.

LORAINE: Don't waste your breath, darlin'. Concentrate on what you're doin'.

TEDDY: Since Mama is looking so sharp, if the Yankees win again, I think we'll surely have to bring her to the World Series, but I see no real reason to wait till then. So as soon as you get back, I want you to get tickets to whatever shows you think we should see.

MICHAEL: Yes, sir.

TEDDY: There'll be no trouble selling mine in case at the last minute I can't go. But get those tickets *immediately* and I will reimburse you.

MICHAEL: Yes, sir.

LORAINE: It's too cold yet!

TEDDY: Well, Easter is next Sunday. Maybe the temperature will rise with the Lord.

[*Michael helps Teddy to stand and assists him to move slowly toward the area that would be the bathroom*]

LORAINE: I pray we don't have a dark and rainy day on Easter. All the little children will be disappointed they can't show off in their new spring clothes.

TEDDY: Old Bess Donahue is out here too—supposed to have died last Tuesday, but she's rallied some and they say, if she recovers, she'll be mental the rest of her life. Cirrhosis of the liver, et cetera . . .

LORAINE: *Alcohol.*

TEDDY: [*Barman's yell*] Last call for alcohol!

[*He pauses*]

MICHAEL: You wanna stop for a minute?

TEDDY: Hell no! I can't wait to get there—when we do, I just want you to turn on the faucet and step away a bit so I won't feel self-conscious.

LORAINE: [*Alarmed*] Who's gonna hold you up, honey?

TEDDY: I'm gonna hold myself up. I'm gonna hold on to the wall! [*On his way again*] Joe Ambrosiani has been serving six-o'clock mass with me every morning till I had to come out here . . .

LORAINE: On the Q.T., the food in that restaurant has gone down, down, down.

TEDDY: One morning he said to me, "Does Michael still go to church?" And I said, "Sho', Joe! Did you ever meet a Connelly without the purpose to become involved? Well, this is involvement in the world and concern for the individual *is* the church!"

LORAINE: Slow up, Teddy. You're just bound and determined to overdo it.

TEDDY: All I'm worried about is whether I can *do it* or not.

MICHAEL: We'll soon see.

[*They have arrived at the entrance to the bathroom*]

TEDDY: Now stay out of here, Mama.

LORAINE: Hold on to him tight, Michael. He's so weak he couldn't swat a fly.

TEDDY: Now stand back—stand back for your life!

[*Michael has led Teddy to a point where he faces upstage. Michael secures him and steps away. Loraine is a distance apart from them as if she is still in the other room. Pause. Teddy, looking down, then with a horrible, frightened moan . . .*]

OHHHHHHHH!!!!

[*Michael dashes to him, looks down . . .*]

MICHAEL: OH, MY GOD, THERE'S BLOOD IN HIS URINE! MAMA! GET THE DOCTOR!

TEDDY: OHHHHHH, NO! OHHHHHHH, *SHIT!*

[*Loraine gasps but does not scream; lunges out into what would be the corridor, running . . .*]

LORAINE: [*In a desperate, earsplitting whisper*] Doctor! Doctor! Nurse!

MICHAEL: GET MY MOTHER OUT OF HERE, DON'T LET HER SEE!

LORAINE: [*Then, farther away, she increases the volume, exiting hysterically*] SOMEBODY! HELP! GET A PRIEST! GET A PRIEST!

[*Simultaneous to this action, Teddy collapses backward into Michael's arms and Michael swiftly drags him back toward the bed, but Teddy collapses to floor, center*]

TEDDY: [*Wildly in shock*] Aunt Maureen? Don't leave me! I gotta get out of here! Who are *you*?

MICHAEL: Daddy, Daddy! This is Michael! I am Michael!

TEDDY: Michael? Son?

MICHAEL: *Yes! Yes!* Your son! Now, listen! I want you to say the act of contrition with me. Do you understand?

TEDDY: Michael? Michael?

MICHAEL: Yes, yes, I'm here. Now, help me say the prayer. I need you to help me. Come on, now! . . . "Oh, my God, I am heartily sorry . . ."

[*Mumbling in unison, audibly, inaudibly . . .*]

TEDDY: I . . . I . . .

MICHAEL: . . . for having offended Thee . . .

TEDDY: . . . offended . . .

MICHAEL: . . . and I detest all my sins . . .

TEDDY: . . . all my . . . sins . . .

MICHAEL: . . . because I dread the loss of heaven and the pains of hell.

TEDDY: . . . pains of hell . . .

MICHAEL: . . . but, most of all because they have offended Thee my God, who art all good and deserving of all my love.

TEDDY: . . . love.

MICHAEL: I firmly resolve . . .

[*He stops. Pause*]

TEDDY: [*Looking up directly at Michael*] I don't understand any of it. I never did.

[*He goes limp, and Michael sobs and cradles him in his arms and rocks him back and forth . . . Slow dim to black*]

## SCENE 6

*Spots come up simultaneously on Michael leaning against the proscenium with his back to the audience and Loraine seated center.*

LORAINE: [*Out front*] Dear Michael: Ohh! It's so good to be home again and out of Whitfield. I am gonna put a curl in my hair and work on my clothes and try to look like somebody again. Please take care of yourself, for you are all I have now and I love you more than anything else left in this world.

[*Light change*]

I am back in the A and N building after ten days in hydro, which I wouldn't describe even if the mail from here wasn't censored. But I am feelin' fine. I am also *cooperatin'*. I am gonna stay here this time until I know I can walk out of here and never come back.

[*Light change*]

As soon as I got back home, I decided to let Willy Mae go. I can do what little there is to do around here. I tried to call you but your answerin' service picked up. I know you don't like me to call if it's just for nothin', but it's been so long since I've seen you, I just wanted to hear your voice. I worry about you up there by yourself. You know that as long as I have a place to sleep, so do you.

[*Light change*]

I had a long talk with the doctor today and told him how I regret all the years of not lettin' him help me in some way to help myself. I am disgusted with myself for not tryin' to see things as they really are. I would certainly hate to ever let myself believe that your and my dreams were all in vain.

[*Light change*]

It's imperative that I sell the house. The upkeep here is just too much. I remember a little dollhouse on the coast that I always admired. Who knows, maybe it's just sittin' there waitin' for me. Please let me hear from you and please try not to disagree. This place is just too full of memories.

[*Light fades on Loraine but holds on Michael*]

## SCENE 7

*. . . Michael reaches for his coat as lights come up. He walks into Loraine's bedroom. She is in a negligee seen earlier, but now it is terribly faded and worn— not soiled or torn; it looks as if it had been washed and ironed too many times.*

MICHAEL: I suppose you're gonna tell me you haven't had anything more than an aspirin tablet.

LORAINE: [*Heavily drugged*] I suppose you're gonna start in on me again.

MICHAEL: I stopped by the garage where they towed the car to have a look at it. It's a miracle you got out of it alive. It's a total loss—you had let the insurance expire.

LORAINE: It's probably for the best.

MICHAEL: Oh, sure. Now we can't collect a cent, and we can't even sell it—except for scrap.

LORAINE: I mean, it's best I don't have a car. Good riddance, I say.

MICHAEL: It's a good thing you feel that way—especially since you have been booked and arrested and your driver's license revoked permanently.

LORAINE: And if I *wanted to* drive this minute, I'd damn well do it!

MICHAEL: It's a pity you've never felt that hell-bent about your rehabilitation.

LORAINE: What did you do with the paregoric? It's missin' from the medicine cabinet.

MICHAEL: Never you mind what I did with it.

LORAINE: All right then, don't tell me. I couldn't care less.

MICHAEL: You look like you need a dose of paregoric!

LORAINE: You didn't pour it out, did you?

MICHAEL: You're so full of goofballs right now, it's all you can do to speak.

LORAINE: And if I wanted a dose of somethin', I'd get it!

MICHAEL: What would you bargain with at the drugstore? Warmth and charmth?

LORAINE: I don't need any of your cocky college-degree remarks.

MICHAEL: When you are down to taking paregoric, it means one thing—

you're broke. And you can't afford anything better. And times have changed. The days of bribing a black doctor are over.

LORAINE: Black, white, or polka-dotted, the day that money ceases to talk will be the day Atlas drops the ball!

MICHAEL: I also found out a few other details which you forgot to fill me in on.

LORAINE: Go on, chew my head off.

MICHAEL: The lawyers informed me that you told the judge in court that you *deliberately* ran into those people in that pickup truck.

LORAINE: I *did!* They were takin' up all the highway. I kept honkin' the horn for them to move over and let me pass—but they were deliberately drivin' slow and right down the middle of the road just so I couldn't get by. So I fixed them—I stepped on the gas and tore off the back end of that rattletrap!

MICHAEL: You could have killed them!

LORAINE: I was so mad I didn't care! Still don't.

MICHAEL: It's beyond me why those farmers haven't sued.

LORAINE: What the hell do those rednecks know!

MICHAEL: We could have lost this house—which is about all we've got left. And now there's nothing to do but sell it before we lose it, or you let it fall down around you.

LORAINE: And the quicker it's sold, the better.

MICHAEL: Well, it's not going to be grabbed up overnight. I only hope we can get a reasonable price for it. [*Directly and cutting*] One that will allow me to reclaim some of our possessions!

LORAINE: I don't have the slightest idea what you're referrin' to.

MICHAEL: To this. [*He holds up a yellow receipt*] It's a pawn ticket, in case your memory needs refreshing.

LORAINE: Where did you get that?

MICHAEL: I found it in your *empty* change purse. I went by the pawnshop to find out what you've hocked—and the only thing that surprised me is how little was there.

LORAINE: [*Pathetically concerned*] Did that old man sell my silver? Time hasn't run out! He didn't go against his word, did he?

MICHAEL: No. All the flatware is still there, and your tea set—and the candelabra . . .

LORAINE: [*Greatly relieved*] Oh, thank the Lord!

MICHAEL: What I want to know is, *where is your jewelry!* Your solitaire and your sapphire bracelet and the diamond wristwatch!

LORAINE: You know I never wear any of those unless I'm puttin' on the dog.

MICHAEL: And what is all this about a gun, and where the hell have you hidden it?

LORAINE: The only thing that's been hidden is the paregoric.

MICHAEL: The man said that along with the other stuff you also pawned a gun, but a week or so later you came back and claimed it. *What* gun? And for *what*?

LORAINE: It's just that little pearl-handled pistol Daddy used to keep downtown in the safe. I need it now—for protection!

MICHAEL: Protection from what?

LORAINE: Anybody and everybody—thieves—riffraff! I am a woman alone in a large house!

MICHAEL: I'm asking you again, where is your jewelry? It's not at the pawnshop, it's not on your hands, and it's not on a safety pin in your brassiere! I looked! All that's between your tits is a St. Christopher medal.

LORAINE: All of it's in my jewelry box.

MICHAEL: Show it to me.

LORAINE: And that's in the safety-deposit vault at the bank.

MICHAEL: There's nothing in that tin can at the bank!

[*She is trapped and knows it*]

LORAINE: [*Defiant admission*] They were stolen, goddamnit! And that's all there is to it! I was brutally taken advantage of by someone I trusted. And I don't mean what you think! He and I were friends and that's all. He was a very nice man. Cultivated. Only he was a dope fiend from way back. And he told me he could get me anything I wanted and that I wouldn't have to pay black-market prices. He said he had some connections in Shreveport. And like a fool I believed him. Don't look at me that way. I can't be to blame every time the wind changes!

MICHAEL: [*Quietly disgusted*] Ohhhh, shit. I feel like beating your brains out just to see if they are really there.

LORAINE: Don't say that, honey. It's already beat me so. But I am not gonna let this throw me. For some reason, I can't help but think it's for the best.

MICHAEL: Is there anything to drink in the house?

LORAINE: I'm sorry, honey, you know I don't drink.

[*Michael starts to laugh—a little hysterically—not much, just a little, and a little sadly, and trails off, shaking his head, as Loraine asks . . .*]

. . . What did you do with the paregoric?

MICHAEL: I poured it out.

LORAINE: Oh, no! You didn't!

MICHAEL: Of course I didn't. But if you think I'm gonna give it to you, you *are* nuts!

LORAINE: You give me that paregoric or else, I'm warnin' you!

MICHAEL: I'm not afraid of you anymore. The days of your digging your sharp red fingernails into my flesh and twisting my earlobes off are long gone!

LORAINE: I just wanted you to have some manners and trainin' and be a gentleman. You don't know what the meanin' of bein' whipped is! I was beaten all my life. And so I can tell you one thing, mister, I am not gonna take it from you now. I'll kill you first!

MICHAEL: Give me the gun, Loraine!

LORAINE: You give me the paregoric and I'll give you the gun.

[*He starts toward her; she flinches*]

*Don't you hit me!*

MICHAEL: You know you need it. Where's that goddamn gun!?

[*He pushes Loraine aside, goes to the bureau, tears open a drawer, starts flinging the contents into the air—little glass cylinders clink together and fly out along with lingerie and scarves . . .*]

LORAINE: You stay out of there! Those are my personal belongin's!

MICHAEL: Christ! Every goddamn receptacle in this house has got needles and syringes tucked into it! I bet you've got hypos hidden in the inner springs!

LORAINE: NO!

[*They both instantly look at the bed, then back to each other. Suddenly she makes a dash for the bed and scampers into it, up against the pillows and headboard*]

MICHAEL: [*Quickly coming toward her*] Get out of that bed!

LORAINE: You keep away from this bed!

MICHAEL: Get off that bed or I'm gonna pull you off bodily!

LORAINE: You do and you'll regret it!

MICHAEL: [*Quickly moving closer*] You heard me.

LORAINE: Don't you come another step!

MICHAEL: You think I'm talking to myself? Get away from those goddamn pillows!

[*He lunges at her*]

LORAINE: DON'T YOU TOUCH ME!

[*He starts to rip the pillows away; she recovers, fighting to prevent his getting the gun. The gun now flashes into view and they are both desperately struggling for it*]

MICHAEL: Give me that fucking gun!

LORAINE: Let go of me, YOU PRICK!

MICHAEL: LET GO!

LORAINE: NOOOOOOOO!!! [*Screams*] IT'S MINE! GIVE IT TO ME AND LET ME STICK IT IN MY MOUTH AND PULL THE TRIGGER!!!

MICHAEL: [*Struggling with her*] If only you had the guts, you cunt! If only you had the nerve to kill your worthless self on your own time! But you won't! AND I'M NOT GOING TO LET YOU DO IT ON MINE!

[*The gun goes off! She screams again and he finally manages to wrench it from her hands. She collapses back onto the remaining pillows, sobbing hysterically*]

LORAINE: I wish I was in hell with my back broke!

MICHAEL: [*Removing the bullets*] You *are* in hell! And I am now going to escort you to Whitfield.

LORAINE: [*Springing upright*] NO!! You wouldn't do that to me!

MICHAEL: [*Puts the bullets in his pocket, tosses the gun into the open bureau drawer*] Oh, yes I would and *am*—just as soon as I pack a few of your precious garments, of which you take such remarkable care.

LORAINE: [*Forcefully; getting off the bed*] Oh, no! Oh, no, Mister Big Shot! You're not gonna put me behind bars and walk off to New York City on *my* allowance.

MICHAEL: [*Gathering articles of clothing*] You have no allowance! You have run through everything he left you and you're in debt over your head. And so am I. I haven't got a nickel to my name. I'm going back to New York the way I came—on my credit card—my *bad* credit card!

LORAINE: Your daddy would die.

MICHAEL: My daddy *is* dead.

LORAINE: Poor Daddy.

[*Michael has now retrieved a small suitcase and is stuffing things into it*]

MICHAEL: Poor Daddy, my ass.

LORAINE: He was good!

MICHAEL: He was a maniac!

LORAINE: Don't you say a word against him!!!

MICHAEL: Don't you defend him to *me!* And damnit, put your clothes on!

LORAINE: You can't take me anywhere! You've gotta have the papers!

MICHAEL: I've *got* the papers! And I've got the fifty dollars—I borrowed it from Willy Mae. And I've got a tankful of gasoline. And when I see those big green trees on either side of the road, I'm gonna let out a yell that'll shake the ghost of Teddy Connelly!

[*Loraine is wide-eyed with fright. She runs in panic. Michael races after her, clutches her*]

You come back here! I'm through having you run out in the street half naked. So help me God, if there is one—this is the last time I'm dragging you to the goddamn loony bin!

LORAINE: [*Breaks*] Please, Michael! For God's sake, show a little mercy.

MICHAEL: [*Releasing his grip hostilely*] My mercy has run out. We are fresh out of mercy, and understanding and patience, and forgiveness forever!

LORAINE: [*Terrified*] They'll put me in hydro! You don't know what that means!

MICHAEL: I did not put you in this position.

LORAINE: [*Lashing out savagely*] Well, your life is far from perfection!

MICHAEL: GET DRESSED! OR I AM GOING TO DRESS YOU!

LORAINE: [*Instantaneous switch to a soft, pleading tone*] Please, Michael! I beg you.

MICHAEL: There's no use begging me!

[*Loraine finally realizes that he is serious . . .*]

LORAINE: Then please . . . please have the charity to give me the paregoric. If you don't, I'll go into convulsions before we get there.

MICHAEL: No! You're not getting it!

LORAINE: [*Desperately sincere*] Believe me, baby. I'll be in acute withdrawal before we're even halfway there. And God knows what I'll put you through. And . . . and . . . Michael . . . I'm scared. This time . . . If I go into a coma—I'm scared I'll die.

[*Quiet. Pause. He goes, picks up Loraine's Kodak, opens the back, and lets five small bottles of paregoric fall out onto the mattress*]

MICHAEL: That's all there was left.

[*Before the words are out, she has pounced upon the bottles, tearing one after another open, drinking them dry, and letting them fall to the floor until all five empties lie scattered at her feet. Pause*]

LORAINE: I thank you. [*She slowly gets up from the bed*] What shall I wear?

MICHAEL: Whatever you'll be comfortable in.

LORAINE: I wanna *look* decent.

[*She starts to wander off to her clothes closet*]

MICHAEL: Mama . . . [*She stops*] . . . I apologize.

LORAINE: [*She retrieves a dress from the debris on the bed*] I know you don't mean it, darlin'. I know you're sorry. And if you can believe it, I am too. Here. Help me get this off. [*He helps her out of her nightgown and into her dress*] . . . Please believe me when I say I never meant to hurt you—of all people. Or anyone, for that matter. And I *want* you to get as far away from all this as you can. There's no need of you grievin' your life away over my shortcomings. [*He turns away. She goes to the living-room area*] You didn't mean what you said about Daddy, did you?

MICHAEL: Of course not.

LORAINE: I didn't think so. We all say things when we're aggravated we don't really mean at all.

[*Michael returns to stand before her with a pair of her shoes*]

MICHAEL: [*Extending them*] Put on your traveling shoes, sweet Loraine.

[*She hesitates. He kneels and slips them on her feet*]

LORAINE: [*Looking around*] Well. That's the second bullet in the wall. Whoever buys this place is gonna think there was a firin' squad in that room.

MICHAEL: They'll just know we lived here.

LORAINE: I guess you're right. If I only had the ability to put into words what I would really love to say to you. It's times like this I realize how insecure and no good for nothin' I really am.

MICHAEL: Hush, Mama. I won't hear a word of that.

LORAINE: I know it may sound peculiar, but this living room has always been more like a ballroom, and if you squint your eyes, you would think it's the beach. Let's just sit here a moment with our eyes shut and pretend that a lovely breeze is blowin' in off the Gulf. If we think about it, that's where we spent our happiest moments. We had only moments of happiness—and they were always on the Gulf Coast—but they were enough to make up for a lifetime. [*Pause*] Do you mind if I sing? It might lighten things.

MICHAEL: Be my guest. Sing to your heart's content.

[*Loraine starts to sing gently "Red River Valley" as the lights dim, till only a spot remains on Michael . . .*]

LORAINE: Michael? Michael?

MICHAEL: Yessum.


SPOT FADES TO BLACK

END OF ACT II

END OF PLAY

# AVEC SCHMALTZ

For
Glynnis and Marty
[Mr. & Mrs. Mark Snow]

*Avec Schmaltz* was originally performed [in an earler version] under the title *The Spirit Of It All* on August 11, 1984, in The New Play Series at the Williamstown Theatre Festival, Williamstown, Ma., Nicos Psacharopoulous, Artistic Director. The play was directed by Steve Lawson.

The cast was:

| | |
|---|---|
| KIT | Marsha Mason |
| NELLIE | Erica Auerbach |
| JOSH | Kiefer Sutherland |
| NICK | Frank Hankey |
| MANNY | James Naughton |
| WENDY | Wendy Kahn |
| COLIN | Kevin Spacey |

# ACT I

*The living room of a Connecticut farm which might be characterized as "under glass". The architecture is dreamhouse American colonial—the ambiance, magazine cover charm. It's about seven p.m. and the room is cheerful with holiday decorations.*

*The front door is UPSTAGE in the RIGHT wall; when it is opened a wreath of holly can be seen, hanging around a brass knocker. UP CENTER are the stairs which have an evergreen garland, scalloped up the bannister. Beneath the stairs is a short closet door. UP CENTER LEFT of the stairs is an open French armoire which serves as a bar, generously stocked with liquor, tumblers, and stemware. On a middle shelf there is a big crystal pitcher of eggnog and an open bottle of white wine in an ice bucket. UP LEFT of the armoire is a swinging door to the kitchen.*

*The LEFT wall has floor to ceiling bookshelves on either side of a stone fireplace which, at present, is not lighted. Two empty needlepoint stockings hang from the mantel. UPSTAGE of the hearth there is a comfortable overstuffed chair with a loose faded chintz slipcover. A rustic table with a tolle Chinese tea cannister lamp is beside it. On the DOWNSTAGE side of the table is a Windsor chair.*

*OFF CENTER LEFT, angled toward the fireplace is a sofa with a matching slipcover. In front of it, a butler's tray "coffee table" with a silver cigarette box and striker, filled with kitchen matches. There is also a large spherical bowl with goldfish swimming in it. Behind the sofa is a rustic French desk and chair. On the desk is a telephone and a brass student's lamp.*

*Overhead CENTER is an old lantern under which a branch of misteletoe is tied with a brilliant red bow.*

*In the LEFT wall there is a large bay window with a semi-circular seat, heaped with colorfully wrapped presents. Standing in the curve of the window is a tall tree, presently being trimmed by KIT and JOSH and NELLIE.*

*KIT is mid-thirties with strikingly lovely features and glorious red hair. She's dressed in a loose, man's plaid work shirt over a turtleneck and jeans. She wears thick, wooly sox without shoes. JOSH is a handsome boy of fifteen with dark eyes and dark hair. Nellie is seven and has her mother's fair complexion and flaming curls. Both kids have on winter country apparel.*

*KIT is on a stepladder, stringing ropes of popcorn onto the tree. Nellie is by the coffee table, feeding the goldfish in the bowl. JOSH is seated at the desk, reading a book. It's a very pretty picture. It could be a Hallmark card or a window in Bloomingdale's.*

KIT: Well? Anybody here conscious? It can't be the triptophan, we haven't had the turkey yet. [*After a moment*] Well . . . can I have *some* kind of response?

NELLIE: [*Looks up from fishbowl, loudly*] Beautifulfabulousgreat!!

KIT: [*Laughs*] Now, that's more like it!

NELLIE: Don't ask me to spell it.

KIT: I'll just settle for a little approval, Nellie, dear. [*Looks at Josh*] I'm afraid your brother doesn't seem to share your opinion.

NELLIE: What's the matter, Joshie, don't you like it?

JOSH: [*Not looking up; glumly*] It's okay.

KIT: That good, huh? Not beautifulfabulousgreat?

JOSH: [*Gets up, crosses to Kit*] I think it was more *human* last Christmas. This year it seems—how shall I put it—so resolutely "happy hands at home."

[*Kit's expressions slides. She comes down the ladder.*]

KIT: [*Glares at Josh*] Come on. You get up there. These "happy hands" have—how shall I put it—so resolutely *had* it!

[*She dumps the popcorn ropes into Josh's arms.*]

JOSH: [*Groans*] Ohh, God, must we behave as if we're in the colorized version of *It's A Wonderful Life*?

[*Kit raises an eyebrow as Josh reluctantly mounts the ladder. Nellie crosses to kneel on the window seat and look outside at the falling snow. Kit finally crosses to the coffee table, takes a cigarette out of a box, starts to light it with a kitchen match from a striker, stops, thinks better of it, blows out the match and returns the ciagarette to the box.*]

NELLIE: If you go to all the trouble to put them out in boxes and to play with them, why you don't smoke them?

KIT: [*Dryly*] I get a sense of satisfaction out of not being able to enjoy one.

[*Nellie and Josh just stare at her*]

—Well, it's an answer. I know it makes no sense, but it's an answer.

JOSH: [*After a moment*] Mom . . . when he gets here—do I have to kiss him?

KIT: [*Tries to appear unruffled*] Well . . . I think that would be very . . . appropriate. . . .

JOSH: Really?

KIT: Yes, I do. I think that would be a very warm and welcoming thing for a son to . . .

NELLIE: [*Interrupting, crossing to the tree*] Don't put the angel on, Josh! That's what I get to do! Right, mom?

KIT: Right . . . [*To Josh*] After all, you haven't seen him since the summer and, in spite of what you may think, your father loves you very much.

JOSH: That's just it, though.

KIT: [*Tonelessly*] *What's* just it, though?

JOSH: I don't know if *I* love *him*.

[*Silence. Kit can't or doesn't choose to speak. Not so, Nellie . . .*]

NELLIE: Well, I'm going to kiss him! Not so much because I love him especially, but because I love kissing!

JOSH: [*To Kit*] Can you imagine what she's going to be like by the time she gets her period?

KIT: [*Annoyed*] Joshua, *really*! I've asked you repeatedly to please not . . .

JOSH: She doesn't understand.

KIT: That's not for you to decide and that's hardly the point!

JOSH: Okay, okay, I'm sorry!

NELLIE: [*To Josh*] And I understand. And I'm going to sing to him, too! [*Bellowing*] "SI-E-LENT NIGHT . . . HO-O-LEE NIGHT . . ."

JOSH: YOU'RE SUPPOSED TO SING "SILENT NIGHT" *SILENTLY*!!

NELLIE: THEN HOW COULD YOU *HEAR* IT?! THAT'S DUMB!

KIT: Shhhshhh! . . . quiet! . . . your brother means *softly*, sweetheart. [*Musically*] You should sing it *softly*.

NELLIE: [*Quickly, to Kit*] I love Daddy even if Josh doesn't!

JOSH: [*Loudly*] I never said I *didn't*, I said I didn't *know*!

[*He snatches at a rope of popcorn which shakes the limbs, causing some of the ornament to clatter. Nellie screams.*]

NELLIE: NO, NO! YOU'RE RUINING IT! STOP IT, STOP IT!!

JOSH: WILL YOU SHUT UP?!!

[*Kit sticks her fingers in her mouth and whistles loudly. The kids quiet.*]

KIT: [*Crossing to CENTER*] TIME OUT! Back to your corners! Or should I say, *cages*! [*Softly, to Nellie*] Ready to put the angel on top, sweetie?

NELLIE: [*Excitedly; then, for Josh's sake*] I'm ready to bust some bozo's nose!

JOSH: That would be me.

KIT: Now, now, Nell. [*To Josh, re: ladder*] Come on, down, Josh. It's time for *It's A Wonderful Life*, The Sequel.

[*Josh comes down the ladder and goes to slump into the Windsor chair. Nellie mounts the ladder, Kit minding her.*]

NELLIE: I just love Christmas! It's so red and green!

[*Kit smiles. Nellie takes the angel and places it on top of the tree.*[

NELLIE: There! How does she look?

KIT: [*Softly, looking at Nellie*] She looks . . . beautiful, fabulous, great . . .
NELLIE: [*Privately, to Kit*] I hope Daddy thinks so, too.

[*Nellie comes down the ladder into Kit's arms.*]

KIT: [*Kissing Nellie on the cheek*] He will, darling. I know he will.

JOSH: He doesn't like Christmas at all. He's Jewish.

[*Kit sets Nellie down, turns to Josh, fed up.*]

KIT: [*Flatly*] He likes Christmas *just fine!* He just never celebrated it as a child so it doesn't mean that much to him. But he likes it . . . *evah* so much! [*Turns to Nellie, sweetly*] Especially angels. [*To Josh, through her teeth*] And *we're* going to like it, too!

JOSH: [*Groans loudly*] Oh, it's some wonderful fucking life, all right!

KIT: *Joshua*! I will not have you using such thoroughly apalling . . .

JOSH: SOR-*REEEE*!!

NELLIE: Are you gonna kiss him when he gets here, Mommie?

KIT: [*Lightly*] Don't I always when he comes to see us?

[*Kit "nonchalantly" hangs the remainder of the ornaments on the tree.*]

JOSH: [*Grimly*] You kiss him on the cheek.

KIT: [*With an edge*] Well, *that's kissing,* is it not?

NELLIE: [*Hanging an ornament*] You kiss Nick on the mouth.

JOSH: Yeah. Great big wet toilet plungers.

KIT: [*To Josh, dryly*] Exquisitely put.

[*Josh makes a rude popping sound with his lips. Kit throws a Christmas ball at him. Josh is pleased to get a rise out of her.*]

NELLIE: Does that mean you love Nick and you don't love Daddy anymore?

KIT: [*With a certain "great lady" air*] *No,* that does *not* necessarily mean that I love Nick at all. Though I do love him in a *certain* way—which is not to say that I don't still love your father in a *certain* way, too, but . . . well, we *are* divorced and although I will always have a *certain* kind of . . . well, *loving feeling* for him, it's certainly not at all what I feel for Nick, whether you call it love or not. Does that make sense?

NELLIE: *Certainly not.*

JOSH: Yeah, mom, it needs work. And I don't mean the tree.

[*Kit gives them both a look, sighs with a modicum of defeat.*]

NELLIE: Is that why you're not still married? Is it because Daddy doesn't love you anymore?

KIT: You'll have to ask *him* that.

NELLIE: Is it because he loves Wendy now?

KIT: You'll have to ask him that, too.

JOSH: I bet he doesn't kiss *her* on the cheek. I bet he gives her a big wet . . . Well—something *e*xquisitely put.

NELLIE: He gives her jewelry, too. Well, I guess he does. She's got it, anyway. I saw it in the picture he sent. The blurry one where everything looks like stars, including the middles of her eyes.

KIT: *Everybody* named Wendy has jewelry.

NELLIE: Not in *Peter Pan.* Of course, that Wendy's wearing a nightgown, so it could be in the vault.

[*Nellie drapes a rope of popcorn around her neck as if they were pearls. Josh catches Kit's eye . . .*]

JOSH: My sister, the material midget. I'll bet she's gonna have jewels. Big, *angry* jewels like Grandma Corinne.

NELLIE: I'm *not* a midget! I'm petite. Grandma Corinne says so!

[*Kit freezes at the mention of the name.*]

KIT: Come on, Nell, you've got to be in bed so Santa Claus can come.

NELLIE: There ain't no Santa Claus.

KIT: Oh, there ain't, ain't there? Where'd you get that idea, as-if-I-didn't-know.

[*Kit looks at Josh.*]

JOSH: I never said a word!

KIT: [*Calmly, to Nellie*] Go on up and get started with your bath—I'll be there in a minute. Not too much water.

NELLIE: I hope you're gonna say something to Josh about his language.

[*Kit glares at Nellie. . . . Nellie goes to Josh, throws her arms abouut his neck . . .*]

NELLIE: [*Too adorably*] 'Night, 'night, Joshie darling.

JOSH: Bitch.

[*Kit gives him a barely tolerant look, scoots Nellie up the stairs, laughing "wickedly." After she is out of sight, Kit and Josh lock eyes.*]

JOSH: I *never* said a word! Besides, do you honestly think she doesn't . . .

KIT: [*Matter-of-fact*] Well, I hope not. It's probably the last Christmas she'll even *wonder* about *anything!* Where babies come from. Whether there's a God or not. And, oh, God, Josh, I *do* wish you wouldn't use such unnecessary, ghastly . . .

JOSH: I know, I know. What I said just slipped out.

KIT: Well, try to get a little more traction on the four-letter words.

JOSH: Yeah, yeah.

KIT: And I wish you'd get a little yuletide spirit! It wouldn't kill you to go along with things for a little while.

[*Kit takes a cardboard box which the decorations were in and begins to deposit the clutter in it . . . Josh goes to the stepladder, folds it, stops . . .*]

JOSH: Mom, is he gonna sleep with you?

KIT: Who, Santa Claus?

JOSH: You know who I mean.

KIT: He's going to sleep in the guest room like last time.

[*Josh takes the ladder to the closet beneath the stairs, puts it inside.*]

JOSH: I guess Nick won't be staying overnight as long as *he's* here.

KIT: [*Mildly irritated*] Nick has never stayed overnight in this house ever, and you know it!

JOSH: But you do sleep with him, don't deny it.

KIT: [*"Grandly" defensive*] *Not in this house!*

JOSH: At his place? Or in motels?

KIT: Just in motels. Just in wretched little fleabag motels. And when one isn't available, the odd sordid flophouse.

JOSH: How does Nick compare to Dad? In the sack, I mean.

[*Kit stops, puts down the box, faces Josh directly.*]

KIT: [*Evenly*] Look, I don't like this conversation. I don't like your smutty, smug impudence—the relentless way you've been trying your best to spoil this holiday. [*Josh turns away from her.*] I know we've been having a rocky time lately. Are you furious at me and your father because we broke up? Because we wrecked something for *you*? Well, I can understand that. It was a big disappointment for us, too. A *very* big one. And it wasn't anybody's fault but your father's and mine. Not your's. Not Nell's. Just the two people who happen to be your parents. The two people who happen to love you the most!

[*A moment, then Josh hurls a box of ornaments across the room and runs upstairs. Kit releases a deep sigh, slowly goes to pick up the scattered ornaments. The phone rings, she moves to the desk to answer it . . .*]

KIT: Hello? [*Dully*] Oh, hello, mother. Ohh . . . decorating. I was just watching Josh finish off the ornaments. Yes, the tree's lovely. Maybe a tad too "Hallmark card-ish" this year but . . . No, nothing's the matter, I'm fine—is it snowing in the city? The weather man on TV said it might. I don't know which one—just somebody with a good haircut in front of one of those big, swirling maps which are fascinating but tell you nothing. [*She picks up the instrument, brings it around to the sofa and sinks back in its cushions.*] No, nary a flake here, neither. Oh? Is that a double negative? Sorry. No, he hasn't arrived and I haven't heard from him. No, I haven't heard from Linda, yet, either—*neither*? I don't know what's correct but no calls from Paris. But you know how that goes with my dear sister . . . Yes, mother, I know she's a very, very busy person with very, very important things on her mind like the fate of the world and all, but . . . no, I'm *not* being catty and, yes, I *do* have the Christmas spirit. Listen, what time are you coming tomorrow? Oh, I don't know, I suppose we'll eat around four so come anytime you like . . . *after three.* Is Lucky driving you up or did you give him the day off? Oh. [*Suddenly sits bolt upright.*] No, mother, *don't*! I do not need any extra help so *do not* bring Rolando and Arlene! Didn't you let them off, either? *Neither* one of them—I mean, *none* of them? They must all have the Christmas spirit, too! [*Change of tone*] Oh, so sorry—no, for heaven's sake don't let me keep you! Whose party? Un, well, give everyone at Gracie Mansion my seasons greetings. Yeah, see you tomorrow . . . [*Quickly*] —and Mother, please . . . *one* request in advance: [*Takes a deep breath, then rattles of a littany*] Try to like my hair, my clothes, my children's hair and clothes, my house, my hospitality and my ex-husband. No, I'm not trying to be snide, I'm just trying to *lay it on the line for you.* Yeah, have a good time at the mayor's. Uh-huh, to you, too. [*She hangs up, says to herself through clenched teeth . . .*] I hate her. Oh, God, how I hate her.

[*Kit reaches for the cigarette box on the coffee table, opens it, removes one, stops, thinks, tosses it back into the box, thinks . . . suddenly picks up the whole box and crosses to the fireplace to throw the entire contents onto the hearth.*]

NELLIE: Building a fire?

[*Kit looks up to see Nellie leaning over the bannister, wearing a nightgown which could be out of* Peter Pan.]

KIT: Yes, darling, with Mommie's old cigarettes.

[*Kit strikes a match and lights the little pile, picks up a poker. Nellie descends the stairs.*]

NELLIE: You've been doing real good. Those patches seem to work—but they aren't very pretty.

KIT: You don't see them under my clothes.

NELLIE: I know. But I know they're there. [*She crosses to Kit*] Are we going to light the tree?

KIT: [*Not letting the last remark faze her*] We sure are, but we have to call Joshie first. My, my, don't you smell divine.

NELLIE: [*Sheepishly*] I cheated and opened my present from Grandma Corinne. Bath oil. Gardenia. I knew it would be.

KIT: [*Grimly*] Mmmm, you seem to know an awful lot of stuff. Well, thank her when she comes tomorrow and be sure to write her a little note, too. That means a lot to her. Like the difference between life and death.

[*Kit pokes hostily at the fire and it flames up.*]

NELLIE: Grandma Corinne says I take after her.

KIT: [*Bluntly*] Don't even *think* it!

[*The doorbell RINGS.*]

NELLIE: [*Runs toward the front door*] Oh, Daddy's home! Daddy's home!

[*Kit straightens, replaces the poker and crosses to the front door, nervously smoothing her hair. She pulls the front door open to reveal NICK. He's about her age, very handsome, dressed in a good business suit, a cashmere overcoat, and silk scarf. His arms are full of presents.*]

KIT: Oh, Nick, it's you! We thought you were an ex-husband but we'll settle.

NICK: Is that a compliment? I can't tell.

NELLIE: Hiya, Uncle Nick!

KIT: Looks more like *Saint* Nick, I'd say. Here, let me help you.

NELLIE: You're looking mighty handsome.

NICK: Well, thanks. [*To Kit*] Someone wouldn't be softening me up for their present, would they?

KIT: [*Sardonically*] Whatever would give you that idea? It's just an evening of *relentless* good cheer, that's all.

[*Nellie has intervened to take a couple of packages and go to put them under the tree. Kit searches the darkness outside the house before closing the front door. Nick moves into the room.*]

KIT: [*To Nick*] Want a drink? There's eggnog and white wine and . . .

NICK: Wine sounds good.

NELLIE: Want some fruit cake? We have some left from last year.

NICK: No, thanks.

NELLIE: I'd hate to drop it on my toe.

[*Kit has gone to the armoire to pour the wine into a stem glass.*]

KIT: Bourbon or brandy will soften it up.

NELLIE: Soften it, maybe, but not sell it.

KIT: *Sell* it? You can't *give* fruit cake away. Why is that?

NICK: [*Shrugs*] I don't know, but even drunks don't want it.

KIT: [*Brings Nick the drink*] I thought you had to play Santa at the club tonight.

NICK: So I'll be a little late. [*Takes the drink, gives Kit the remainder of the presents*] Thanks. I wanted to play Santa here first.

NELLIE: Hooray for our side!

[*The swinging door pops open and Josh enters.*]

JOSH: [*Bluntly*] There *is* no Santa Claus, didn't you hear?

NELLIE: YES THERE IS!!

KIT: Quiet, Nell! [*To Nick, irritated by Josh*] You've met my son, Ebaneezer somebody.

NICK: [*Holding out a hand*] Merry Christmas, Josh.

[*Josh does not shake hands. Nick self-consciously puts his hand in his pocket.*]

JOSH: [*To Nick*] Are you spending the night?

KIT: [*Levelly*] If you can't be civil, Josh, be good enough to leave us in peace.

JOSH: [*Continuing to Nick*] Tonight might not be a good night to stay. We're expecting someone. And I *don't* mean down the chimney.

NICK: Yes, I thought your dad might have arrived already.

NELLIE: You never can be too sure with the Christmas rush, you know.

KIT: [*Amused by Nellie's remark*] Come on, Nell, time for bed.

NELLIE: [*Petulantly*] But I have to stay up to see Daddy!

KIT: [*Dryly*] Well, with the Christmas rush he may have to come on skates. You can see him in the morning.

NELLIE: But I'm not at all sleepy.

KIT: When are you ever? You're the original party girl! I wonder who you get that from?

NICK: Your mother probably.

KIT: [*To Nick*] I had a sinking feeling you were going to say that.

JOSH: Well, Nell certainly doesn't get it from you.

KIT: [*Indulgently*] Heavens, no, I'm just old "Happy-Hands-At-Home," the Shut-in.

NELLIE: Nick, when are you going to take me sailing on your ship?

NICK: [*Pleasantly*] In the spring, if you like. But you don't call it a ship, Nell, you call it a sloop.

NELLIE: Oh. Does it have a living room?

NICK: Uh-huh, but you call that the cabin.

NELLIE: And a kitchen?

NICK: [*Nods, laughs*] Uh-huh, but you call that the galley.

NELLIE: [*Thinks, after a moment*] What do you call a tomato on a boat?

[*Nick is nonplussed, stops laughing. Kit laughs. Even Josh snickers.*]

KIT: [*To Nellie*] Say goodnight to Nick.

[*Nick bends to one knee. Nellie goes to him, puts her arms around his neck, kisses him on the mouth. Nick is chagrinned.*]

NELLIE: Goodnight, old Nick. Is my present expensive?

JOSH: Little *bitch*!

[*Kit takes Nellie by the hand . . .*]

KIT: [*Re: Josh's remark*] If the charm gets too thick in here, there's an ax in the woodbin.

[*Kit takes Nellie up the stairs. When they are out of sight, Nick turns to Josh.*]

NICK: Now, come on, Josh, don't tell me you don't have the Christmas spirit?

JOSH: Oh, we've got the Christmas spirit by the gallon. But *you* seem to be fresh out. Let me fill you up again. [*Josh takes Nick's empty wine glass from him, goes to the armoire, pours him another. Nick eyes him curiously.*] How come your first marriage failed?

NICK: [*Smoothly*] Married the wrong girl, I guess.

JOSH: Now you've found the right one.

[*Josh crosses to Nick with his refilled glass, hands it to Nick.*]

NICK: [*Takes drink*] Thanks. I think so. And I hope she feels the same.

JOSH: How would you like it being our father, Nick?

NICK: How would *you* like it?

JOSH: You go first.

NICK: [*Without hesitation*] I'd like it. Your turn.

[*Nick takes a big swallow of wine, watches Josh.*]

JOSH: Well . . . Grandmother would *really* like it. "Old money," WASP, all the right cliques and all the right clubs. "Good goods," is how she refers to you. Did you know that? Did you know you were "good goods."

NICK: You didn't answer my question.

JOSH: [*Bluntly*] I think you want to marry my mother but I think you'd prefer it if she didn't have us—my sister and me. I don't think you really give a shit about the two of us, no matter how many presents you bring. Now, in answer to your question . . .

[*Kit comes down the stairs. Nick and Josh turn toward her . . .*]

KIT: She's like something shot out of a cannon—going to be awake all night. We'll have to be extra quiet putting out the toys . . . [*Realizes . . .*] Oh, am I stepping on the punchline?

NICK: The one before you came in had the wallop.

[*Josh starts for the stairs. Kit has reached the bottom and catches him in her arms and hangs on to him for a moment, even though Josh resists and pulls away.*]

KIT: Hey, where're you going? We don't want privacy.

JOSH: *I* do. I've got presents to wrap.

KIT: Well, bring them down when you're finished and put them under the tree. I'm counting on you to help me out with the toys. You know I never know Tab A from Slot B.

JOSH: You're Slot A, he's Tab B. Any kid can figure that out.

[*Josh starts to run up the stairs.*]

NICK: Josh.

[*Josh stops.*]

NICK: [*Directly, but gently*] You have every right to be suspicious of me, but that just isn't true—what you said. I'm *very* fond of you. And Nellie, too. More than you know. I hope you believe that. I want to try and be a good father to you both.

[*Josh doesn't respond, turns and runs up the rest of the stairs and OFF. Kit looks at Nick quickly, goes over to the fireplace, stokes the fire which is now burning beautifully.*]

KIT: I don't even want to think what all of that was about.

NICK: I'm afraid he feels that if we get married, it will officially put an end to his ever having Manny as a father.

KIT: [*Flatly*] I thought that was what that was about.

NICK: Josh doesn't think I like him and Nellie—that I only want you and they'll be left out in the cold. That isn't true. You know it isn't.

KIT: [Distressed] I know, Nick. Oh, I know.

NICK: Of, course, I botched it the first time, but there were reasons. And thank God, there weren't any kids to suffer from my mistakes.

KIT: I botched it, too, the first time—and, I'm afraid, there *are* kids to suffer from my mistakes.

NICK: It couldn't have been all your fault.

[*Nick puts down his wine glass, crosses to her.*]

NICK: Darling . . . this may be the last few minutes of the holiday we have together. I want to give you my present— [*Takes a small plush box from his pocket*] Now, please don't say, "Oh, Nick, you shouldn't have."

[*He hands her the box. She goes to take it, but when she sees what kind of a box it is, she draws her hand back as if it were red hot.*]

KIT: [*Grimly*] Oh, Nick, you shouldn't have.

NICK: You don't even know what it is!

KIT: I know mittens don't come in a tiny plush box.

NICK: It's not a ring, if that's what you think.

KIT: [*Brightly*] Oh, it's not? What is it?

NICK: Just a little trimming of my own, you'll be relieved to know. Open it.

[*Kit opens the box.*]

KIT: [*Dazzled, gaily*] Oh, Nick, you really shouldn't have but I'm *sooo* glad you did! They're absolutely exquisite! The most beautiful earrings I've ever seen!

NICK: They were my mother's. My father gave them to her at Christmastime, too—when he asked her to marry him.

KIT: [*Her face slides*] Ohhh, you really shouldn't have.

NICK: [*Re: the earrings*] Put them on, Kit. I want you to have them. I can wait. I'm good at that. I've waited a long time. Put them on. Please.

KIT: [*Put her head in her hands*] Oh, I'm so confused, Nick. About so many things. About Manny. About me. You. Us.

NICK: I know you are. But I love you, Kit. I honestly am in love with you. And I think it's for always.

KIT: [*Sincerely*] Nick, you're such a fine man. You're thoughtful and attentive and generous and . . . well, decent. And you don't hardly meet none of them no more.

NICK: "Good goods." Isn't that what Corinne calls me?

KIT: You're better than that. Much better than anything my mother would ever take you for. So good, in fact, I know we could make it work. I know I'd work at making it work.

NICK: That doesn't sound like much fun—all that work.

KIT: Oh, Nick, don't say another syllable. Not tonight. I don't want to spoil it. I don't even know what it is I don't want to spoil, but I know I don't want to do it tonight. It's just that I'm . . .

NICK: Still in love with him.

KIT: . . . confused.

[*Nick nods understandingly. Kit takes the earrings out of the box and he helps her put them on. She puts her arms about his neck.*]

[*They kiss. A moment . . . and the swinging door to the kitchen is pushed open and Manny enters. He's in his late thirties with a lean, athletic body, dark eyes and dark hair. He has a decidedly impish quality, something devlishly attractive about him. He is dressed in cords and an expensive sweater and car coat. He has a duffel bag slung over his shoulder.*]

MANNY: Pardon me, but aren't you suppose to be standing under the mistletoe for that sort of thing?

[*Kit and Nick break apart, startled.*]

KIT: Manny!

MANNY: I guess you might say you *missed* the mistletoe. About ten feet and several toes. God, I hate that. I hate that like poison. [*Extends a hand to Nick*] Hello, I'm the alimony man.

NICK: [*Formally*] I'm Nick. . . .

MANNY: [*Brightly*] "*Good goods*"!! [*To Kit*] Isn't that what you mother calls him? [*To Nick*] You should hear what her mother calls *me*!

KIT: [*Seething*] Why did you come in the back?! Trying to sneak up on us?

MANNY: How'd I know you and loverboy were being kissy-wissy in front of the fire? I put my car in the garage next to yours— [*To Nick*] Such a pretty picture—just like slippers under the bed.

NICK: [*Looks at his watch. To Kit*] Sorry, darling, but I'm late. You're sure there's no way for you to get away?

KIT: [*Shakes her head*] Even if there were, you know me and parties.

MANNY: [*To Kit, going on*] I love that old VD of yours.

KIT: VW.

MANNY: [*To Kit*] What did I say?

KIT: [*Stonily*] Nevermind.

MANNY: [*To Nick*] Kit used to pick me up in it. Yes, sir, whenever I was suicidal, we'd get in the back seat and she'd make my spirit rise.

KIT: [*To Nick*] Manny's the most interesting teller of dull tales I know.

MANNY: [*To Kit*] The first time we met you picked me up. And I don't mean in your Volkswagen.

KIT: [*To Nick, nervously*] He was playing with some rotten rock group in some wretched disco and . . .

MANNY: And you asked me if I had hair on my back.

KIT: [*To Manny, irritated*] I seriously doubt that, but, yes, I was the first to speak. [*To Nick, lightly*] Terrified he was going to be turned down. Manny seriously can't handle rejection.

NICK: [*To Manny*] Then I hope you won't be distressed by my saying goodbye.

MANNY: [*To Nick*] I'll walk you out.

KIT: [TO NICK] *I'll* walk you out. [*To Manny*] If . . . you don't mind.

[*Kit takes Nick's arm, they turn for the front door. . .*]

MANNY: [*Dreamily*] I just ran my hand over your seat—of your VW—feeling-it-up sorta, remembering those lip-smackin', finger-licking good ol' times! [*To Nick*] Did she pick you up, too?

NICK: Well, she's helped me manage lift-off.

KIT: "Tira Mi Su" is my middle name.

[*Nick turns and crosses to the front door.*]

MANNY: Nice little baubles on your ears, Kit. Who's been stuffing your stocking?

[*Kit fumes, turns and hurries after Nick . . .*]

KIT: We're just lucky he didn't pull down his pants and moon for us! That's one of his specialties!

NICK: You mean, show us what an asshole he is!

[*Nick and Kit exit, leaving the door open. Manny rushes to the open door . . .*]

MANNY: [*Yells*] *Would you like me to do that?!* [*Starts to unbuckle his pants*] I'd be happy to . . . [*Suddenly stops*] Son-of-a-bitch! He's giving her a . . . a big wet toilet plunger!!

[*Manny stands back and slams the door loudly. He crosses the room, takes off his car coat, throws it on the arm of the sofa. Kit enters . . .*]

KIT: [*Slamming front door*] Well, I must say, *that* was attractive!

MANNY: [*Pleading whine*] Don't yell at me, *pleeese*.

KIT: Don't whine! And just let me tell you what I am not going to put up with this trip! Not one more minute of your goddamn stupid, fucking infantile behavior! It's Christmas for Christsake! So let's just call a truce and goddamn well try to relax and fucking A enjoy it!

*Silence.*

MANNY: [*Calmly, quietly; comic righteousness*] Kit! I've been meaning to talk to you about your language! Who've you been hanging around with?

KIT: Our son.

MANNY: [*"Saintly"*] Well, you know how I hate scenes. How I hate confrontations.

KIT: Now I suppose you'll sulk for the duration!

MANNY: [*Softly angelic*] If I've done something wrong, I'm sorry.

KIT: [*Furiously*] You're always sorry after you've provoked everyone into a frenzy!

[*Manny is silent, hangs his head.*]

KIT: Better not pout, Manny. *You-Know-Who's* coming to town.

[*Josh has come midway down the stairs. Kit quickly pulls off the diamond earrings before Josh can see them and unceremoniously plops them in the fishbowl.*]

JOSH: [*To Manny*] I figured you must have arrived from the sound of the artillery down here.

[*Both Manny and Kit turn toward Josh*]

MANNY: [*Tentatively, but with great warmth*] Hi, handsome.

JOSH: [*Tonelessly*] Hi.

MANNY: Do I get a kiss?

[*Manny crosses to the bottom of the stairs, holds out his arms. Josh looks at Kit. She doesn't move or react. Finally, Josh comes down the remainder of the stairs and kisses Manny on the cheek and Manny hugs him. Kit restrains a smile, looks away.*]

MANNY: How've you been?

JOSH: Okay.

MANNY: How's school?

JOSH: Okay.

MANNY: You're looking great.

JOSH: So do you. How do you keep a tan in December?

MANNY: It's easy in California. There's a tanning salon on every corner.

[Feebly laughs at his joke. Josh doesn't]

—Do you watch the show?

JOSH: It comes on too late for a school night.

MANNY: Well, I have all of them on tape. You can see them when you come to visit. Or I can send them to you. That is, if you want me to. [An awkward pause] Hey, I have some presents for you. They're out in the kitchen . . .

[Manny starts for the swinging door.]

JOSH: I'll open them tomorrow, with Nell.

MANNY: [Stops] Okay. Where is my Nellie?

JOSH: Asleep. If you can believe it. [Looks at Kit] And you have the nerve to talk about my language.

[Josh turns and starts up the stairs.]

MANNY: [To Josh] Goodnight.

[Josh doesn't answer, continues up. Kit watches him disappear, looks a bit worried. Manny turns to her.]

MANNY: How are they?

KIT: Ohh, Nell's a wonder.

MANNY: Yeah . . . and Josh? Not so wonderful?

[Kit has gone to the foot of the stairs to look up. She gestures silently to Manny.]

KIT: [Quietly] Later.

MANNY: [Nods, shrugs, changes the subject] Well . . . you look nice.

KIT: [Sweetly] Thanks. You look nice, too.

MANNY: Nice is such a nice word, isn't it?

KIT: Isn't it though. But that's how you always wanted things, right?

MANNY: Right. Just always wanted everything to be nice.

KIT: [*Re: the house*] How does the house look?

MANNY: Like something out of Currier and Ives. [*Thinking he may have said the wrong thing*] Only *cozier*. Warm and homey. Even . . . sexy.

KIT: Thanks.

MANNY: You could always make a place look cozy and warm and homey and sexy and . . . *nice*.

KIT: [*After a moment*] How's Wendy?

MANNY: Fine.

KIT: And you?

MANNY: Fine.

KIT: Fine is such a *nice* word.

MANNY: Isn't it, though. But that's how *you* always wanted everything. I wanted everything to be nice and you wanted everything to be fine. And how are *you*?

KIT: Fine—*what else*?! It's what nice people answer no matter what. People say it when they're falling apart inside—although that is not necessarily the case at the moment.

[*A pause. They look at each other.*]

MANNY: Wendy's pregnant. And that's not nice. And she wants to get married. And that's not fine. And I'm falling apart inside.

KIT: [*Seriously*] I'm sorry you're not happy, Manny.

MANNY: Oh, I'm happy! I didn't say I wasn't happy. I said I was . . .

KIT: I heard you. What are you and Wendy going to do?

MANNY: Well, I don't want to get married and she doesn't want an abortion so, I don't know—a double suicide, I suppose.

[*Kit is silent.*]

MANNY: [*After a moment*] But everything's gonna be just fine. Life's good. I like myself—most of the time. I like Wendy, most of the time—like my house, like my Mercedes.

KIT: A Mercedes . . . well. I hear there're as common as avocadoes out there.

[*Manny lets that pass. Kit goes to the sofa, sits down.*]

MANNY: Bernie's blossomed, really. Got color. Gets exercise. Gone Hollywood.

KIT: And the lady with the hat?

MANNY: The lady with the hat is a different story. As you know, Mable never wanted to move out there in the first place. She *loves* the city. Loves the streets, adores the filth, craves the noise, can't get enough of the violence.

KIT: I like your mother so much more than I like mine.

MANNY: All she ever wanted was to live in a building with a doorman on Park Avenue. That all I've heard ever since I was a kid in Brooklyn. Well, a building with a doorman she got.

KIT: She wrote me you bought them a condominium.

MANNY: Yeah, and it has a pimply-faced kid with a funny hat who *sometimes* opens the door. But it's not on Park Avenue in Manhattan—it's on Ocean Avenue in Santa Monica. And Mabel doesn't give a fuck-all for the climate or the cleanliness or the security of it all! She's starved for some pissing freezing cold muggins, some sky-high garbage, a few blistering insults. The lady in the hat wants *action!* They both make me nuts!

[*Kit laughs. Manny moves to the sofa.*]

MANNY: How's Corinne?

KIT: Still making *me* nuts. Still complaining. Always about the heaviest of issues like . . . they've stopped making satin lingerie cases in her color of champagne beige.

MANNY: Your mother is sort of champagne beige head to toe. Her hair, her skin, her clothes. In fact, Corinne is sort of a champagne beige name.

KIT: No wonder my father was an alcoholic.

MANNY: Do you suppose our kids are going to feel the same about us? Love us. Hate us.

KIT: They already do.

MANNY: [*Mild panic attack*] Oh, God, oh, God, I'm going to faint!

KIT: [*Not indulging him*] No you're not. Take a deep breath and you'll be fine.

MANNY: Oh, my God, I left my blood-pressure machine in the car!

KIT: Do you still have that stupid thing?

[*Slight pause as Manny inhales, exhales deeply, then sits down beside her, resting his head on the back of the sofa, feeling his pulse.*]

KIT: [*After a moment*] Why is it that you still go out of your way to insult anyone in whom I have the least bit of interest?

MANNY: [*Sits up*] Oh, well, you can't be serious about *him*! He looks like he's been delivering balloons all his life!

KIT: When you used to do it on the road, I'd flatter myself that you were being the jealous husband—though why I was ever fool enough to make you breakfast when you stumbled in after fucking some little groupie all night, I'll never know.

MANNY: [*Mock sweetly, almost batting his eyes*] I always came home though, didn't I? Didn't I, *darling*?

KIT: You did it when you were here this summer—with that fellow on the Yale faculty I was seeing.

MANNY: Oh, well, he was a joke! I mean, do you know he actually said to me that rock and roll was *declasse*?! God, am I glad you dumped *him*!

KIT: [*Laughs.*] You know what? I am, too.

MANNY: [*Laughing at himself*] Declasse, that's me. Can you believe this rock and roll schmuck is now an honest-to-God Hollywood composer?

KIT: I knew you'd make it. [*Sweetly*] I hope you get everything you want, Manny. I want you to be happy.

[*He smiles warmly at her, brushes her chin with his fingertip. She takes his hand—at first it is to discourage his being too intimate . . . then, she looks at his hand thoughtfully, holds on to it a second before letting it go.*]

KIT: You always had the most beautiful hands—graceful as a dancer's. I always loved the curve in your wrists, the way your long, slender fingers stay together, cupped ever so slightly—like the head of a swan. Music just has to come out of them.

[*Sight pause . . . Manny is entranced.*]

MANNY: [*Hushed*] What can I tell you, Kit, I'm jealous. When I see you with someone else I just hate it like poison.

[*Kit looks into Manny's eyes.*]

KIT: You've done well for yourself, Manny. Maybe the divorce brought you luck.

MANNY: [*Horrified*] Oh, Kit, don't say that!

[*A pause as they continue to look at each other. Finally, she gets up, moves away. He tries to break the mood, too, gets up and heads for the swinging door.*]

MANNY: [*En route*] There are presents from my folks, too—for the kids and for you. And some things from me, of course.

[*He exits to the kitchen. She goes over to the fireplace, and with the poker fishes out an unburned cigarette, puts it in her lips, lets it rest there a moment, then jerks it out and hurls it back in the fire.*]

KIT: [*Loud enough for Manny to hear*] I hope they didn't buy me clothes. They always buy me things I have to take back—and then I always feel so guilty and unappreciative.

[*Manny re-enters with an armful of wrapped presents and his garment bag. Kit goes to help him.*]

MANNY: Here, this one's for you from them.

[*He hands her a large hexagonal box.*]

KIT: [*Anxiously*] Oh, God, you don't suppose it's a hat, do you? This looks like it could be a hatbox.

MANNY: [*Dismissively*] Oh, they've learned their lesson. They said they've never seen you wear a thing they've given you so this year they were getting you something very "blah." Mabel's exact word.

KIT: What's blah that could come in a hexigon box? Oh, I just know it's a hat. An *eight-sided* hat!

[*Manny has hung his garment bag on the newell post, taken the other presents over to the tree . . .*]

MANNY: Listen, they know how hard you are to please.

KIT: [*Incredulously*] Hard to please?

MANNY: [*Quickly*] I mean, how *precise* you are. How you like things your way.

KIT: [*Glares*] *My* way?

MANNY: You know what I mean—"just so."

KIT: We just have very different taste, that's all!

MANNY: Yes, that's true—but you must admit, you can be very rigid.

KIT: [*Tightly*] Yes, I admit I *can* be. *Could* be. I'm different than I used to be!

MANNY: Good! How?

KIT: I'm actually *trying*. Can't you see how there're coffee stains on the slipcovers? And I never run around fluffing up the down cushions everytime they're sat on.

MANNY: Well, congratulations.

KIT: I'm not quite out of the woods yet, but I'm working on it. Actually, it's my New Year's resolution: to be more flexible—less rigid about everything.

MANNY: Great! God, how I hated it when you'd get a case of the "perfects."

KIT: The "perfects?"

MANNY: Just like your mother.

KIT: What a thoroughly shitty thing to say to me!

MANNY: And when the holidays rolled around it really would be nuclear family launchpad!

KIT: You hated the holidays long before you ever met *me*!

MANNY: Right. I'd like to mow down shoppers! I'd like to slaughter reindeer! I'd like to detonate the North Pole!

KIT: Well, I happen to love the holidays! *All* of them! I always have!

MANNY: Yeah, who needs a calendar with you around—homemade Valentines, satin hearts and paper lace. And pretty soon it's Easter baskets and Easter bunnies and bunnysuits and dyed eggs and dyed chicks and dead ducks and chocolate-covered everything but chocolate-covered crucifixes!

KIT: [*Defensively*] I just love getting in the spirit of things! I see nothing wrong with that!

MANNY: [*Hardly drawing breath*] And bammo! before you know it, it's homebaked birthday cakes with special sayings and party hats and pin-the-tail on the donkey, and lookout, folks! it's fireworks for the fourth of July, bakeoffs and cookouts and hoop-dee-do and *hello,* it's Halloween! Pumpkins stabbed into jack-o-lanterns and funny faces and trick or treat, and before-you-know-it, *tahdahmm!* it's a turkey for Thanksgiving, and a *goose* for Christmas and *whoops,* thank-you-very-much!

KIT: Cynical bastard!

MANNY: [*Really rolling*] . . . And Ho, ho, ho, it's Christmas cards and a Christmas tree, hand-picked and hand-hewn, and wreathes and garlands and boughs and bows on boxes stacked to the ceiling!—and enough food for a famine, and none of that sto' bought business for you, oh, no, your little oven's sayin' lovin' morning, noon, and night with pies and puds and nogs and grogs, and gimme a break!—and Godalmighty when and where does it ever for fuckin' sake end??!!

[*A pause.*]

KIT: So I overdid it.

MANNY: And you wonder why I tried to pretend the holidays didn't exist—tried to look the other way?!

KIT: [*Flaring*] Okay! Overdone! Overdecorated! Over-the-top! I wanted a home.

MANNY: Oh, was that it?!

KIT: It's all I ever wanted! All my life! A real home with a real family—a family that looks at each other and speaks to each other and *screams* at each other! One that doesn't just take each other for granted and shut each other out. One that's *alive!* Not like the dead thing I grew up with. Not like what I had with you: nobody at home, nobody ever in! [*Pause; calmly*] What's *your* New Year's resolution?

MANNY: [*Calmly*] Ohh, I don't know, I haven't thought about it. Let's see . . . try to thaw the Wall-Of-Silence, I guess.

KIT: [*Applauds*] Congratulations to you, too!

MANNY: Well, I'm still working on it. Not quite there yet, either. But I'm *trying* to communicate. Trying not to shy away from confontations, trying not to tune out, turn off . . .

KIT: The trouble is that you think saying what's on your mind is always a confontation. You think talking to each other has to turn into a war. All I ever wanted was a simple exchange of thoughts and words—so that some molehill wouldn't turn into some Mont Blanc which you could misunderstand and sulk about!

MANNY: [*After a moment*] Well, with a little luck, maybe we'll both come through. Change is possible. Growth is possible. I believe that.

[*Pause. He stares at her. She looks away.*]

MANNY: [*Simply*] It's good to see you.

KIT: [*Looks directly at him*] It's good to see you, too. [*Slight, awkward pause, then*] Let me help you put your things upstairs. In your room.

[*She goes to take the garment bag. He picks up the duffel bag and joins her at the stairs.*]

MANNY: You know Mabel and Bernie tell me everytime they speak to you.

KIT: That reminds me, I owe them a call. Oh, god, how I despise Alexander Graham Bell.

MANNY: Everytime you call *them,* they call *me.*

KIT: Well, I do try to make an effort on birthdays . . . and special occasions. I want the kids to know their grandparents.

[*Kit has turned and started up the stairs but Manny's next speech stops her midway*]

MANNY: My mother said you told her, "Just because Manny and I are divorced, it doesn't mean *we* can't be friends."— That meant a lot to them. They love you, you know.

KIT: And I love *them.*

MANNY: I hope we can be friends, too.

KIT: [*Sincerely*] We are friends, Manny. We always have been. Let's just try to be better ones. For everybody's sake.

MANNY: [*Sincerely*] It's a deal. Shake it like you mean it?

[*He hold out a hand. She holds out her hand. But Manny doesn't take it. Rather, after a beat, he sticks out his rear end and shakes it.*]

[*Kit doesn't react, just silently stares at him and lowers her hand. Manny stops, realizes his joke has fallen flat.*]

MANNY: [*Apologetic plea*] Sorry! I'm going to try to stop acting like a clown, too! Honest, I am—but, oh, Kit, I just hate being so goddamn solemn about it. I hate it like "pois*son*"—French for poison.

KIT: [*Coolly*] "Poisson" is French for fish.

MANNY: Well, pardonez-moi for living.

[*A moment, then Kit silently extends her hand again. He leaps upon it, shaking her hand vigorously and gratefully.*]

MANNY: [*Ecstatically*] Christ, this new year's not going to be *long* enough or *wide* enough or *tall* enough to contain our mental health!

[*Kit laughs, turns and goes upstairs and Manny follows.*]

[*The stage is empty for a moment. Then, the swinging door is slowly pushed open and Josh comes into the room. He looks toward the stairs, then turns to see Manny's coat lying on the arm of the sofa. He slowly crosses to it, picks it up and tries it on.*]

[*Josh walks about, getting the feel of the coast, obviously not disliking it. He spots the presents Manny has brought which were put under the tree. He crosses to pick them up and look at the cards until he find the one that's meant for him. He holds it a moment, shakes it, and then puts it back.*]

[*Now Josh reaches for the switch and turns the tree on and it illuminates with a spirited glow.*]

[*There is an OFFSTAGE sound—voices and footsteps at the top of the stairs. Josh snaps his head in that direction, quickly jumps up and takes off the coat and puts it back where it was, then runs out the swinging door.*]

[*Momentarily, Manny comes down the stairs, pausing in the center of the room, sensing that someone has just been there. He looks to see that the tree is lit as Kit comes downstairs.*]

MANNY: Is it my imagination or was the tree not lit when we went upstairs?

KIT: [*Not getting the question*] Ohh, it looks lovely! Did you turn it on?

MANNY: I didn't touch it.

KIT: Who, then? Some little elf?

MANNY: Yeah, some little fifteen-year-old elf.

KIT: [*Comprehending*] Ohh. Want a drink?

MANNY: Got any club soda?

KIT: No egg nog? Or fruit cake?

MANNY: Fruit cake?!

KIT: Forget I said that.

[*She goes to the bar, opens a bottle of soda and puts it over ice.*]

MANNY: [*Re: playing Santa*] So where do we begin?

KIT: The closet. Behind the coats and ladder and stuff . . .

[*Manny goes to the closet door under the stairs, opens it, removes the stepladder, pushes coats aside, removes several pieces of luggage to reveal an old steamer trunk, plastered with hotel stickers.*]

MANNY: [*Pulling out the trunk*] Oh, you've still got this great old trunk of your dad's.

KIT: [*Crosses to hand him the soda*] The toys are inside.

[*Manny takes the soda, drinks, sets it down. He opens the trunk to reveal some toys—some in boxes, some unwrapped. Kit starts to place some of them around the room. Manny does likewise.*]

KIT: How's your friend? And I don't mean Wendy.

MANNY: Who?

KIT: The violin player. Colin—?

MANNY: Oh! Well, now, Colin is probably the first close friend I've had in my life. I mean, other than you. He's fine now. What's this?

[*He holds a long, narrow, soft carrying case made of a synthetic material.*]

KIT: [*Looks up*] Josh's BB gun. And his friend died?

MANNY: [*Shakes his head*] Yeah. AIDS. Terrible. He was *my* age! I never really thought of anyone *my age* dying. His death really shook me up.

KIT: [*Sardonically*] Not to mention what it must have done to Colin.

MANNY: Oh, he was a mess. I must say—and I say this in all modesty—if it hadn't been for me, I think he would have cracked up.

KIT: I'm glad you were there for him.

MANNY: Yeah, I'm a much more generous person than I used to be.

KIT: I'm glad to hear that.

MANNY: How's your sister?

KIT: She got married again. To the same guy.

MANNY: The Frog?

KIT: [*Nods*] The rich, powerful, socially correct Frog.

MANNY: I wonder what it is that draws two people back together again and makes them get married all over.

KIT: [*Looks at him directly*] Masochism. Sadomasochism.

[*Manny gives her a look, wheels out a miniature baby carriage, then removes a kite-shaped object in a felt cloth bag, gathered with a drawstring at one end. He unties the sack to peer inside.*]

]MANNY: What's this wicked looking thing?

[*He starts to remove it from the sack . . .*]

KIT: [*Looks over*] Josh's crossbow.

[*Manny takes out a modern steel version of the medieval variety . . .*]

MANNY: Hmmmmm. [*Hangs the crossbow on the armoire door*] You know, I knew. I knew from the first time I saw you.

KIT: Knew what?

MANNY: From the first moment I laid eyes on you, I knew we were gonna get in some trouble together. And I think you knew it, too.

KIT: I did. And I think that about says it: "get in some trouble together." Why not, "support, extend, enrich each other?" Rather than cause each other some trouble.

MANNY: I don't know. I wonder what it is? There was this tremendous physical attraction, of course, but there was something behind your eyes, something that let me know . . . *here's the one.*

KIT: [*Stops, says softly*] Yes, Manny, I saw something behind your eyes, too.

[*They look at each other for a moment. She turns away, begins to gather up some wrapping and put it into a cardboard box.*]

[*Manny has removed a baby doll and two other items. He holds one up to Kit . . .*]

MANNY: This, I take it, is Josh's hunting knife.

[*Manny puts the doll under his arm and pulls the knife from its scabbard, flashing the blade . . .*]

KIT: That's right.

MANNY: And this?

[*Manny brandishes the second item.*]

KIT: . . . is his foil for his fencing lessons.

MANNY: You don't think it means anything, do you, that he only requested weapons for Christmas?

KIT: Listen, I drew the line at the Do-It-Yourself W.M.D. Kit.

[*She pulls out a baseball bat, hands it to him*]

—Here. Add this to the arsenal.

MANNY: I'm serious!

KIT: I'm so glad you are. Because it *is* serious.

MANNY: What is? What is going on?

[*Kit has moves to the stairs, looks up.*]

KIT: [*Looks back to Manny, softly*] Later.

MANNY: [*Picks-up her hushed tone*] You keep saying, "Later. Later." Why not *now, now?*

KIT: [*Hushed*] He's still up. I can hear him. And he can hear us.

[*Manny sighs, nods, goes to get a particular present he has brought—something that looks like a dress box from an expensive store.*]

MANNY: This is for you from me.

KIT: Shouldn't I wait for the kids?

MANNY: [*Shakes his head*]] Uh-uh.

KIT: [*Takes the package, looks at label*] Oh, my, Rodeo Drive, Beverly Hills, no less!

MANNY: No smart, East Coast cracks, please.

[*She opens the box to remove an expensive, hand-made black satin bra and pair of black satin panties, trimmed with sheer black lace.*]

KIT: Oh, my, they're . . . they're lovely.

MANNY: The lace—blind nuns or something.

KIT: At the very least. Thank you. They're . . . well, they're *stunning*. I'm truly . . . *stunned*.

MANNY: You really mean it? You don't hate them?

KIT: I really mean it, Manny—and I don't mean to sound ungrateful, but do you think they're appropriate?

MANNY: Appropriate? You mean, for the climate? I figured you had enough longjohns.

KIT: I mean isn't it the sort of thing you ought to give to Wendy rather than me?

MANNY: I only know it's probably something I wouldn't have given you when we were married. [*Thinks; after a moment*] Maybe I've learned something from Wendy.

KIT: Yes, maybe you have. [*Puts the lingerie back in the box*] I hope you don't mind, but I think I'm actually more interested in hearing about Colin than I am about Wendy.

MANNY: Oh. Okay. He's, well . . . he's a terrific musician. He and his fiddle are very much in demand. I always use him on the recording dates for the show. He does "avec schmaltz" great.

KIT: Avec what?

MANNY: Schmaltz. The lovey-dovey string stuff. That's how all those European composers who wound up in Hollywood used to mark the romantic passages in their scores. Especially the violin solos. Colin's fingers are more sentimental than Mother's Day.

KIT: Can we leave mothers out of this?

MANNY: [*Shrugs*] I love Colin. We have lunch at the studio and play tennis sometime and schmooze about our careers and, of course, the life and times of Manny Boy.

KIT: [*Dryly*] Mmmm. Well, who else?!

MANNY: You'd like him. You have a lot in common. You could talk about music and books and old movies . . . and you could talk about me.

KIT: You're so endlessly fascinating, I can't see how we'd have much time to cover anything else.

MANNY: You two have the same sort of sensitivity toward "*The Rules.*"

KIT: What rules would those be?

MANNY: You know, *The Unwritten Rules*. He would never come over without calling first. He would never cancel at the last minute, and if he were going to be late, he'd call to say he was going to be late. And he always calls the next day to say, thank you—or worse, writes a note. And he never forgets holidays, birthdays or anniversaries. He's just brimming over with all them there decent, humane, civilized qualities I never heard of.

KIT: Are you making fun of me?

MANNY: Would I do such a thing?

KIT: *Would* and *have* and *are*. I think.

MANNY: Don't be ridiculous. If anything, I'm lamenting my own short-comings.

KIT: Well, maybe there's hope for you yet. You used to not know you *had* any shortcomings. Just keep hanging around Colin. I approve.

MANNY: Yeah, what happened to "Goodtime Manny," our irresposible, emotionally adolescent friend—sex and drugs and rock and rollin' down the runway of life! I'm so sedentary now Wendy and I are almost like an old married couple. Different from the way *we* were a married couple. Different priorities. Different arrangement. Different sexually.

KIT: This is where I came in. I take it you're referring to what you've learned from Wendy. Well, okay, what is it? Can you *say*? *Will* you say?

[*She crosses with a basket of goodies: candy canes, nuts, trinkets, etc. She starts to fill the stockings.*]

MANNY: So you *are* interested. You're sure you really want to know?

KIT: You know goddamn well I want to know! I'm a big girl, Manny. I can take it.

MANNY: [*Sip of his soda*] Well . . . it's not that she's better than you—or that it's better with her than it was with you—or that it was lousy with *us* . . .

KIT: [*Stops, turns to him*] *Sometimes* it was lousy! And then, again, sometimes it was great.

MANNY: Yeah, when it was good it was great. For me, anyway.

KIT: When it was great it was good for me, too.

[*She turns back to the business of the stockings.*]

MANNY: With Wendy, it's just *different,* that's all. She's more . . . well, *I'm* more . . . well . . .

KIT: What?

MANNY: Free-er. There's something with her that allows me to be less inhibited. To be . . . well, for lack of a better word: *wilder.* I do things with her I never dreamt of doing with you.

KIT: [*Tolerantly, her back still to him*] I never knew you were inhibited with me. That I inhibited you.

MANNY: I know you never meant to.

KIT: [*Wheels around*] Never *meant* to! I had no idea that's how you perceived me!

MANNY: [*Staying cool—or trying to*] I'm saying that it was coming from me, not from you. Anyway, that's how it was.

[*Kit throws the basket into the overstuffed chair, steps forward to confront him.*]

KIT: Well, you certainly were a pretty good actor, that's all I can say! You certainly gave one helluva fine performance!

MANNY: I wasn't performing *all the time.*

KIT: [*Boiling*] Just *some* of the time.

MANNY: I really meant it *most* of the time. And *always* up to a certain point.

KIT: What *point,* may I inquire, was that?!

MANNY: I think it's because I don't love Wendy that I can have more fun in bed with her. There don't seem to be any terrible consequences involved.

KIT: [*Incredulous*] *What* terrible consequences?! What are you talking about?!

MANNY: I knew you weren't going to take this well.

KIT: [*Sardonically*] *Did* you?! I wonder why?!

MANNY: I think we ought to just drop it. I don't want to talk about it anymore.

KIT: [*Quickly*] Oh, no you don't! You're not going to pull that with me now!

MANNY: You know how I hate . . .

KIT: *Communication!*

MANNY: [*Softly*] I just want everything nice!

KIT: [*Bluntly*] Is this the old wife vs. mistress story? You can't enjoy fucking your wife because she's your mother and she's on a pedestal?! But you can really get–it–off with some bimbo?!

MANNY: Wendy's not a bimbo! She's an executive!

KIT: I don't care what she is, I know the type—her hair is longer than her skirt!

MANNY: Bimbo!

KIT: This girl sounds very talented.

MANNY: [*Grinning*] Ohh, she's *verr-y* talented.

KIT: You like it better with her than with me!

MANNY: I didn't say that. I said it was *different!*

KIT: What?! Toys?! Donkeys?! Chandeliers?! *What?!*

MANNY: That's not what I'm talking about and you know it!

KIT: I don't know *what* you're talking about! Why don't you just say what you're talking about and then I'll know. You always expect me to be some kind of a goddamn mind reader. I guess I was expected to be clairvoyant in bed.

MANNY: [*Slightly pouty*] That's not what I'm talking about at all.

KIT: [*An exhausted plea*] Speak, Manny! *Tell me* what you're talking about! [*Quieter*] You said I was your friend. Well, I was and I am. I still am. For God's sake for once, open up and say what's on your mind.

[*Pause. Manny sits in the overstuffed chair.*]

MANNY: [*Quietly, evenly*] I'm not afraid to let go with her. With you I always felt like I had to stay in control. The more you enjoyed it, the more you let yourself go, the more you got into it, the more anxious I'd get. The more I'd get scared. Terrified. Petrified. With her I can let myself go and get lost in it and enjoy it and not be afraid. I only wish I could do that with someone I love.

[*Pause. Kit sits on the arm of the chair beside him.*]

KIT: [*Sincerely*] Thanks for telling me. I mean that. Thank you for, at last, letting me in on exactly what's going on in your head. It helps. It really helps. [*Silence from Manny*] Do you have any idea what you were terrified of? What the consequences really are? [*Silence from Manny*] Manny . . . please . . .

MANNY: [*After a long moment*] I just know that the way you loved me scared the shit out of me. And I felt that if I went with it, that I'd fall apart—that I might even go crazy. That I might not get back. That I might die.

KIT: How very sad.

MANNY: I guess making contact with someone I love is something so unknown to me that it quite simply frightens me to death.

KIT: [*Going easy*] And why shouldn't it? You don't have much practice with people unless they're right on top of you or three feet away.

[*Pause. Manny puts his hands over his face. Kit puts her arm around him.*]

MANNY: Yeah . . . Either Bernie all over me like some infestation of locusts or Mabel never quite within reach. Sat by me and taught me to play the piano. But always from a distance . . . well, about . . .

KIT: Three feet.

MANNY: [*Nods*] And I'd chase her and grab her, but it didn't work. She didn't exactly pull away or push me away . . . she'd just *melt* away. Evaporate. Her laugh would die, her smile would fade and she'd . . . remove . . . herself just about three feet in distance.

KIT: [*Almost to herself*] No happy medium. Never. For either one of us. No . . . *reality.*

[*A moment and Manny straightens up and Kit removes her arm. He takes the last swallow of his soda, gets up, goes to the armoire, empties the remainder of the bottle into his glass.*]

MANNY: Colin's all for our getting back together again.

[*Kit doesn't respond, gets up, picks up the basket, resumes stuffing the stockings.*]

MANNY: He thinks you're wonderful. He knows everything about you. Everything. The works.

KIT: How odd—having someone you never laid eyes on know how you are in bed.

[*Manny crosses to her.*]

MANNY: Oh, Kit, I've made such a mess of things! I've really come here this time to tell you that!

[*She stops, puts down the basket, crosses to the tree, adjusts some ornaments.*]

MANNY: [*Urgently*] I realized it when I was here this summer. And when I got back to California and told Colin how I felt, it all came clear. I know what a fuck-up I am. What an impossible son-of-a-bitch I've been, but I've changed . . . I'm *trying* to change. Can't we . . . can't *we* give it another try?

KIT: [*Goes to bay window, looks out; simply*] You'd leave me again. I just know it. If you don't actually leave town, you mentally check out. What do you think it's like living with a goddamn zombie?

MANNY: No laughs, to say the least.

KIT: You got it. No laughs *at all*. When Josh was six years old, do you remember what he said? "Who is that man who lives with us?"

MANNY: You think that didn't get to me?

KIT: You'd hole-up in a room for days on end and when you'd finally emerge, you'd come into the kitchen and never speak to us, never say one word—just devour a box of jelly doughnuts, standing over the sink, then go back and close the door again. "Who is that man who lives with us?" It was a good question. And one to which I did not have the answer.

MANNY: I didn't know who I was myself.

KIT: You weren't there when Josh was born. I told people you were on the road, but you were . . . where *were* you?

MANNY: Just sitting in our apartment in shock. Twenty years old and a *father*!

KIT: It happens.

MANNY: Not to me. Not to Manny—loverboy, lunatic, life-of-the-party! I didn't even want to get married, so who wanted a kid?!

KIT: I wanted a kid.

MANNY: I wanted you to get rid of it.

KIT: I wanted to get married.

MANNY: I wanted to run. I remember Bernie came to find me—said everyone had been looking high and low and lo' and behold!—where was I? In bed with my clothes on under the covers, staring at the ceiling. [*Crosses to the fireplace, hyperventilating*] Jesus, is it hot in here?!

KIT: [*Sardonically*] Not for us grownups.

[*He turns, gives her a look, crosses back to pick up his glass and return to the armoire to fill it with ice cubes.*]

[*Kit crosses to the fireplace, takes the poker, adjusts the fire.*]

MANNY: You know what, Kit? I can see me in Josh and it makes me want to kill myself. God, I don't want him to be like me. I wouldn't wish that on . . . on *Nick,* let alone my own kid!

KIT: [*Turns to him, calmly*] I'm worried about Josh, Manny. He's so smart and so sensitive. Sensitive as a leaf and just about as sturdy in a windstorm. He's so hurt. And *sooo* angry. Some part of him feels deeply responsible for our breaking up. I'm afraid he's going to do something senseless to somebody—or to himself.

MANNY: [*Puts down his glass*] What exactly is going on? What happened?

KIT: Two weeks ago Friday he asked me if he could spend the night at his friend's, a really good kid I like—even though he's a bit older, he's about the only one I'm not totally terrified about Josh being around. Three-thirty Saturday morning, the police arrived at the door . . .

MANNY: Police?! Shit! What?!

KIT: He had totaled his friend's car. The other boy has a fractured pelvis and is still in the hospital. Josh wasn't hurt—just shook up and in shock. There're weren't any drugs or alcohol involved, but anyway, Manny—he's dancing near the flame.

MANNY: [*Anxiously*] Oh, Jesus, Josh and Nellie—when I think of where I've failed them and how their little minds are turning and twisting, my pulse plays the Minute Waltz in thirty-seven seconds!

KIT: Will you take him aside tomorrow—talk to him and try to get him to talk to you? I know it's not your style, but . . .

MANNY: My style! My style sucks! [*Sighs*] Sure. I'll give it my best shot. God knows, I love him and I'm glad he's ours. You do believe that, don't you?

KIT: Of course, I do.

MANNY: [*After a moment*] You know, it's lucky for some we married each other. Instead of four people being unhappy, only two were. [*Looks at her very directly*] I know it's not enough to say I'm sorry. But I am. Couldn't we . . . ?

KIT: [*Tearing, stops him*] No, Manny, no. I could never take your silences again. I could never allow you to freeze me out anymore. Ever again.

[*He pulls a silk scarf from his jacket pocket, hands it to her. She dries her tears.*]

MANNY: Oh, Kit, I love your eyes—they're so . . . so . . .

KIT: . . . so red and green?

MANNY: Kit, I know it sounds crazy but . . . come to California with me!

KIT: [*Moving away from him*] What??

MANNY: [*Following*] For New Year's! We'll do Christmas here together, but then let's leave! Together! All of us! Kids and all, Kit and kaboodle!

KIT: Manny, I just happen to be practically engaged to another guy.

MANNY: Oh, you don't care about *him*! Not *that* way! I know you don't. Say yes! Say you will! Say you'll come and celebrate with me—caviar and champagne, corks popping like cannon fire!

KIT: This doesn't sound like you, Manny. You were never a virtuoso with romantic underscoring.

MANNY: It's the new me! Ring out the old, ring in the bright, shiny new—filled with promise and hope, resolves and resolutions. Ring, ring, ring!

[*The doorbell RINGS . . .*]

KIT: Who could that be?

MANNY: [*Furious*] I don't know, but if it's Santa Claus his timing is shit!

[*Kit runs to the front door . . .*]

KIT: [*Crossing*] I hope it's not the police! I hope Josh didn't sneak out the back and bludgeon someone.

[*She tears the door open to reveal . . . Santa Claus!—or someone in a red suit and a white beard.*]

MANNY: [*Crossing*] I was just saying what lousy timing you have!!

KIT: [*Rattled*] NICK!!—What are you *doing* here?!

[*Nick steps inside, Kit closes the door.*]

NICK: [*Excitedly*] Forgive me, Kit, but I just know he's come here to pull something funny and I had to come back!

MANNY: GET OUT! GET OUT!

NICK: You're too important to me to risk . . .

MANNY: OUT-OUT!

NICK: I love you, Kit, and I want you to marry me! [*Takes a plush box from his pocket*] This *is* what it looks like! A plush box with a ring in it! [*Notices her bare ears*] Where are the earrings I gave you?

KIT: Uh . . . in the fishbowl.

NICK: The *fishbowl*?!

[*Manny has gone to grab Josh's BB gun, points it at Nick . . .*]

MANNY: Get out or I'm gonna shoot you!!

KIT: *Manny, put that down!*

NICK: OH-MY-GOD, KIT, IS THAT LOADED?!

MANNY: You better believe it's loaded!

KIT: [*To Nick*] Don't worry, darling, it's only a BB gun.

NICK: So what! It could still put a hole in me!

[*Manny takes aim, jumps to a crouched position.*]

MANNY: [*Warrior-like*] Ah-ha!

KIT: *Manny!!*

[*Suddenly, Nick grabs the crossbow . . .*]

NICK: *AH-HA!*

KIT: [*Alarmed*] NICK!!

MANNY: [*Jumps back*] HEY! ARE YOU CRAZY!

[*Pulling the trigger over and over, but nothing happens*]

—THIS FUCKING THING *ISN'T* LOADED!

NICK: [*Raises the crossbow*] BUT *THIS* FUCKING THING IS!

MANNY: OH-MY-GOD, KIT, *DO SOMETHING!*

KIT: NICK! MANNY!

[*Manny starts to run around the room, Nick in pursuit. Kit suddenly picks up the baseball bat, waits for them to pass, swings to hit Nick. He steps out of the way and she clips Manny!*]

MANNY: AAAAOOOOOOWWWWW!!!

KIT: [*Cringes*] Ooooouuuuuuuuuu!!!

[*Manny grabs his head, drops the BB gun, stumbles about like a stunned drunk. Kit gasps. Manny picks up the fencing foil, Nick raises the crossbow to aim at Manny and Kit conks Nick on the head. Nick stumbles about, his beard and hat falling off.*]

[*Simultaneously, Nellie runs down the stairs, followed by Josh who is now also dressed in pajamas*]

NELLIE: DADDY! DADDY! ARE YOU ALL RIGHT?!

[*Manny has wobbled and fallen to the floor in front of the tree as Nellie reaches him . . .*]

MANNY: [*Ga-ga*] Hello, my angel . . .

[*Nick has wobbled and fallen onto the sofa and Kit has gone to him . . .*]

KIT: Ohh, Nick, I'm *sooo* sorry!

MANNY: [*Gives her a look*] You're telling *him* you're sorry!

*[Josh covers his mouth with his hands, stiffling a laugh. Nellie has grabbed Manny about the neck, gives him a bear hug and a big kiss and starts to sing to him . . .]*

NELLIE: *[Bellowing]* "SI-E-LENT NIGHGHT!! HOL-LI-EEE NIGHT!!! ALL IS CALM!!! . . ."

CURTAIN

# Act II

## SCENE 1

*The living room of a nineteen-thirties Beverly Hills "hacienda." The architecture is Hollywood Hispanic—the ambience California casual. Everything is stucco, tile and wrought iron. And everything has been re-done by an expensive decorator in what might be called the "Santa Fe" school.*

*The entrance is in the CENTER RIGHT wall, an iron-hindged, heavy wood-paneled door with a semi-circular top. There is a smaller replica of the door at eye-level: the peephole.*

*DOWNSTAGE of the entrance in the LEFT wall is a built-in contemporary bar with lighted shelves, stocked with handsome crystal bar ware. [We can't see behind the bar, but it would have a stainlesss sink, a fridge and ice machine.]*

*Just RIGHT of the entrance is a semi-circle arch which leads to the dining room and kitchen. Just RIGHT of the arch is a curved staircase which fans up to the bedrooms OFF. Beneath the stairs is an arched niche, not for religious statury, but for a telephone.*

*UP CENTER LEFT there is a larger semicircle arch, framing window-doors which open onto a blossoming patio, drenched in late-afternoon sunlight. [This is the route to the pool and garage, OFF RIGHT.]*

*In the RIGHT wall is a third [smaller] arch which frames a fireplace.*

*All the furniture is up-to-the-minute. Everything is upholstered and painted in pale pastel desert shades: a sofa with end tables and a coffee table. Two comfortable chairs at either side with tables and lamps. A highest-tech possible TV and CD components are stacked on a space-age stand DOWN EXTREME LEFT. Here and there are gigantic ceramic planters containing enormous cacti.*

*Lastly, there is a small shocking pink artificial Christmas tree, sparsely decorated with a few shocking pink balls, standing alone, forlorn in the middle of the coffee table. Like the tree, the entire place is coordinated, detached, impersonal— another kind of shop window.*

*A Word To The Designer:* this may appear to be a complicated and expensive production with seven characters and two specific sets. Well, the play's always going to have seven characters so there's not much to be done about that but, I have divised a way for both the sets to be constructed on one turn table [even a manual one, which could be wound by-hand between the acts.] The colonial stairs in the "traditional" set lead up to an alcove behind which [on the other side of the scenery], flows the "mediterranean" cascade of steps. The side walls are on wheels and reversable:The RIGHT wall and door of the colonial house, flips and becomes the hindged-panel door entrance of the LEFT wall. The LEFT stone colonial fireplace, surrounded by books in shelves, flips and becomes the solid center medeterainian wall and a "plug" is struck [where the stone fireplace would be] for the indicated CENTER LEFT patio doors in the California house. The design for this show should be considered to be practical, economic, and clever, as opposed to a drawback.*

*At the top of Act II, the pastel, postmodern "mediteranian" room is empty. Presently, the front door is flung open and Nellie races in, carrying her small suitcase. She's followed by Josh, carrying his duffel bag as well as his sister's larger pieces of luggage. Both Josh and Nellie drop their things, awstruck by the place . . .*

NELLIE: *Ai, caramba!* Looks sorta like that restaurant on 46th Street where we get the enchilladas when we go to a matinee.

JOSH: El Cayote Loco?

NELLIE: [*Looks around*] Yeah, El Cayote Loco's—but with a better bar.

JOSH: Yeah, only this doesn't look quite as authentic.

[*Manny has dashed inside carrying Kit's suitcase and his duffel bag, both of which he drops, catching his breath. He has heard Josh's last line . . .*]

MANNY: Not authentic as *what*?!

JOSH: This Mexican joint in Hell's Kitchen.

MANNY: What do you mean, this is the *real thing*! The border's only about a block from here!

[*Josh hands Manny the house keys and Manny rushes back outside. Nellie has gone to look at the little shocking pink Christmas tree on the coffee table. Josh comes over to her . . .*]

JOSH: Rather pitiful looking isn't it?

NELLIE: It's so pink and . . . pink. And the wrong pink, at that.

JOSH: Well, let's not say anything.

[*Nellie nods and turns to start up the stairs. Josh turns and begins to follow when Manny dashes back in, carrying another one of Kit's bags as well as his own.*]

MANNY: [*Stopping them*] Oh, you two aren't up there! Mommie is going to be up there!

NELLIE: [*Innocently*] In Wendy's room?

MANNY: [*Tolerantly*] In the *guest* room.

JOSH: [*To Nellie*] What do you mean, in Wendy's room! They sleep together. You know that. Why play dumb?

NELLIE: [*Sotto*] I don't think he's ready for us to know what really goes on around here.

[*Manny pretends not to hear the remark, sets down the bags, quickly goes to throw the terrace doors open.*]

MANNY: [*Pitching*] You've got your own place all to yourselves out here! There's a two-bedroom suite right over the garage, all newly decorated.

NELLIE: [*Crossing*] The Pool House?

MANNY: [*Taking their bags, self-satisfied*] *Above* the pool house and *beside* the racquet ball court.

JOSH: My, my, ain't this grand!

NELLIE: Ain't it! What's a raquet ball court?

MANNY: [*Facetiously*] Where you make racket. You'll feel right at home.

NELLIE: [*Knows the put-on*] No, it's not. It's that game Nick plays.

MANNY: In his youth, perhaps.

[*Manny has swept out the terrace door and disappeared around the side of the house. Nellie and Josh exit after him.*]

[*A moment, and Kit enters the front door, carrying a small case and waving to the limosine chauffeur . . .*]

KIT: [*Graciously*] Thank you very, very much for our first "stretch experience" and I hope you drive us again when we leave! Happy New Year!

[*She smiles and closes the door. She's wearing gabardine slacks and a camel polo coat around her shoulders. She stops, puts down the case and looks around the room to spot the Christmas tree. She crosses to it . . .*]

KIT: [*Quietly, to herself*] How pitiful.

[*Kit turns her attention to a silver framed photopraph of Wendy that is sitting on the bar. She crosses to it, picks it up and studies it. Manny enter from the terrace, sees her. Kit looks up, sees him, replaces the frame on top of the bar.*]

MANNY: [*Re: picture*] I called her and asked her if she'd mind moving her things out while you were here. Actually, there wasn't much stuff—she has her own apartment. [*Indicates the photograph*] She must have missed that.

KIT: Maybe she doesn't consider it her possession—it's signed, "To Manny, from Wendy with oceans of love."

MANNY: It doesn't say "oceans," you're making that up!

[*The phone rings. Manny goes to the niche under the stairs answer it.*]

MANNY: [*Into phone*] Hello? [*Forced lightly*] Oh, hi, Ma! No, the plane didn't crash! Just this very minute, I *swear* . . . oh, hi, Pop! Oh, you're on the cellular extension by the pool? Uh-huh, Great. Don't fall in—you could be electrocuted. [*Forces a tight smile at Kit*] Yeah, we flew *very carefully.* Oh, they're out back unpacking. I'll get 'em to call you, but she's right here, hang on. . . [*Covers receiver; Sotto*] *Pleeease*!!! *Do not invite them over now.* Say you've got twenty-four-hour typhoid or something . . .

KIT: [*Into phone*] Hi, there! Well . . . my first impression is that it's so amazingly spring-has-sprung, it's a pleasure to sneeze to flatter the pollen. Yes, it was snowing when we left. [*Looks at Manny, quotes Mabel*] Yes, "real weather." Sure. New Year's brunch at your place sounds great! [*Modestly*] Oh, you're welcome, I'm just glad you liked everything. [*Clears throat*] Yes . . . I got the blouse . . . It was . . .

MANNY: Unthinkable.

KIT: *Unexpected*! I never in my life expected what was in that . . . well, *unique* box until I saw the muttonchop sleeves!— [*Incredulous*] You kept it since the fifties—the *box*. Oh, well! that's exactly why I didn't bring it!—the box is a collector's item and the blouse was so hard get back in it without getting it crushed. I'd have never forgiven myself if it'd been crushed.

MANNY: [*From the background*] Crushed is what it ought to be! Crushed to death! Crushed like *The Fly*'s head and claw.

KIT: [*"Shooing" him; Warmly*] Well, I long to see you and I love you both very, very much. Bye for now!— [*Hangs up*] Bernie says they can take the *real* weather back East and shovel it where the sun don't shine.

MANNY: What's the E.T.A. for the bagels and root canal?

KIT: Tomorrow morning at ten. They're dying to know what I think of their place.

MANNY: [*Proudly, expansively re: his house*] *Their* place?! Well . . . I'm dying to know what you think of *mine*!

KIT: [*Looking around*] Oh, Manny, it's . . . it's horribly marvelous.

MANNY: [*Wilts*] You don't like it.

KIT: [*Softer*] Listen, I know you think I'm very old-stuffed-sofa-pillow and I guess I am, but it's really . . . well, terribly impressive. Especially for someone like you who used to keep green bologna sandwiches in with your sox and underwear. It's *awfully attractive*. Honestly. [*Re: the tree*] Old tannenebaum is pathetic, of course, but the house couldn't be any nicer.

MANNY: [*Assuaged*] Thanks. I did the tree myself. Just in case you took me up on my offer to come out, I wanted things to look nice and Christmasy. I wanted it all to be as "perfect" as I can make it, so I had the house all done by a decorator. I know it's not your taste but . . .

KIT: Can't you take "yes" for an answer? I wouldn't want to stay in Southern California in anything else but a Spanish style house. I wouldn't want any of those things we passed on the way—English Tudor, French Normandy, Greek temple, Hanzel and Gretel's cottage. I like to know where I am.

MANNY: Stop right there! I'll take that as a compliment. Come on, let me show you your room. [*He starts to pick up the bags*] It's so strange how I find myself explaining to our children that we have separate bedrooms. It's *me*, not *them*.

KIT: [*Ascending stairs*] It's on their minds, too, though. Once, Nellie's homework was to write a word with each of the letters of the alphabet. So she wrote pretty much the usual—you know, apple, boy, cat, dog, and so on. When she got to "X" do you know what she put down? Ex-husband.

[*They have reached the top of the stairs. Manny bursts out laughing, suddenly stops, gasps for air, feels his heart.*]

KIT: What the matter?

MANNY: Oh, God, when I think of those kid having little minds of their own, growing and thinking and . . . *twisting*. I feel like I'm going to faint. Feel my heart and don't say, "*What* heart?"

KIT: [*Feels his heart*] Yes, yes, it pumping away as uncomplaining as a waterfall.

MANNY: [*Trembling lip*] I think I'd better lie down and be quiet. I'll just put your things in the Sand Room and I'll be in the Sage Room.

KIT: [*Incredulously*] The Sand Room, the Sage Room?

MANNY: I know it sounds like a Vegas casino, but I swear to God that's what the decorator called them. Desert colors, get it? Will you come in later and check on me?

KIT: [*Nods*] Soon as I check on the "kinder"—make sure they haven't drained the pool or burned down the garage.

MANNY: [*Lip-trembling whimper*] Promise to come see if *I'm* still alive.

KIT: [*Nods*] Yes, I promise.

MANNY: [*Indicates the terrace doors, starts up the stairs*] Go right out through there. Ohh, God, Kit, how am I ever going to talk to Josh? How am I ever going to face my own son? How am I ever going to be different from my own parents?

KIT: [*Heads toward terrace*] Meditate. They tell me it's an old California custom.

MANNY: That reminds me, I still have an outstanding bill at the Ashram, so maybe they've blocked my meditation privileges.

[*Kit laughs, goes out the terrace doors. Manny continues up the stairs as dramatically as if he were on his way to the guillotine. He exits OFF RIGHT.*]

[*The stage is empty and silent for a moment. Then, the front door is unlocked and presently, it is opened by a very beautiful YOUNG WOMAN in her late twenties, dressed in slacks and wearing dark glasses. This is WENDY.*]

[*She enters, quite unconcerned that anyone is at home. She is carrying a canvas shopping bag and goes directly to the bar, takes the framed photograph of herself and stuffs it into the bag.*]

[*Momentarily, Kit re-enters from the terrace, sees her, stops. After a moment, Kit speaks . . .*]

KIT: Don't let me frighten you.

WENDY: [*Spins around, startled, takes off glasses, recognizes Kit*] Oh, my God, you're here already!

KIT: Well, yes. Manny said that he had called you.

WENDY: He did. I just didn't think you'd get here so . . . hello, I'm Wendy.

KIT: Yes, I recognize you from your picture. [*Glances toward the bar*] Where *is* your picture?

WENDY: [*Sheepishly*] In the bag. That's what I came back for. I took everything else when Manny called—but I guess I forgot the picture. I suppose that sounds deeply Freudian or something. Maybe not even so deeply. Anyway, when I finally remembered having forgotten it, I dashed right over. I didn't see Manny's car or I certainly wouldn't have . . .

KIT: [*Rather pleased*] We came in a stretch limo. My first. I think they're brilliant—like mobile coffins—you can lie down the whole way. [*Re: Wendy's photograph*] There's no need to take your picture—that is, unless *you* want it removed. We've all seen it.

WENDY: [*Chagrined*] The kids, too?

KIT: Oh, they know all about you! I'm *glad* there was a picture of you here. It satisfies their curiosity and besides, that's the way things are. I want them to know the facts. *Please,* do put it back. For the family's sake.

WENDY: [*After a moment*] Okay.

[*She takes the picture out of the canvas shopping bag and replaces it on the bar.*]

KIT: Would you like something? Some tea or coffee or a drink?

WENDY: No, thanks. Would *you*? After all, you just got here and I know where everything is. It would be easier for me to fix it.

KIT: Oh, no thanks, but that's very considerate of you to offer. [*Sits on a chair, center*] Did you meet Manny on the show?

WENDY: Yes, I'm with the network.

KIT: Oh, I know. He told me. I just didn't know if you had known each other from before.

WENDY: [*Sits on the couch*] No, it was when we were doing the pilot. I came on the scoring stage when he was recording the main title and I looked at him and he looked at me and . . .

KIT: . . . And you both instantly knew you were going to get in some trouble together.

WENDY: That's right. How did you know?

KIT: I know the feeling. And I know *he* knows the feeling.

WENDY: I suppose you would. Of course, I made the first move. You probably also know that's essential with Manny.

KIT: Oh, my, yes. He's much too insecure to make the first move. His precious little ego's much too fragile to ever risk a turndown. The only way he's ever had a girl was if she came on to him first. I know *I* did.

WENDY: I know *I* did. And I have no idea at all what I saw in him—he's not all that good looking, really.

KIT: Oh, he's not all that good looking at all.

WENDY: Not in a conventional way. At best, he's offbeat.

KIT: At best. Offbeat—which is a funny thing to say about a musician. Now, the fellow I'm practically engaged to is a knockout in a conventional way. Definitely on-the-beat. He's so good looking, in fact, that it really intimidated Manny when they met. I could tell.

WENDY: You mean Nick?

KIT: You know about Nick?

WENDY: Oh, God, yes! Manny never shuts up about him, he's so jealous. But I probably know less about Nick than you know about me because, let's face it, Manny has a far bigger mouth than *you* could ever have.

KIT: [*Simply*] Yes. Manny's talked about you quite comprehensively.

WENDY: Honestly, he's impossible!

KIT: Totally impossible!

WENDY: He's got all the things I go for: he says he doesn't love me, he says he doesn't want a relationship, he says he certainly doesn't want to get married again, so he's perfect. It's guaranteed to fail. It's doomed from the start. I keep wondering—if I'm so aware of what I'm doing to myself, why am I doing what I'm doing to myself? I'm a reasonably attractive, reasonably intelligent person—so what do I need this shit for?

KIT: You're very beautiful and Manny says you're smart as hell.

WENDY: If I'm so smart, why'd I allow myself to get pregnant. Did he tell you that, too?

KIT: Well . . .

WENDY: Of course he told you that! It was probably the first thing out of his mouth!

KIT: No. I'd say, it was actually the third thing out of his mouth.

WENDY: Mind if I have a cigarette? I'll go outside to smoke it.

KIT: No, no, make yourself at home. After all, it *is* your home.

WENDY: I probably do spend more time here than I do at my own apartment.

[*Wendy takes a pack of cigarettes and a book of matches out of her handbag, offers one to Kit.*]

KIT: [*Shakes her head*] Thanks. I don't smoke. Anymore. Mostly.

WENDY: Good on you, as the Australians say. Have you ever been to Australia?

KIT: No.

WENDY: We filmed a show there. Had a ball. The food was wonderful. And the drinks. Oh, would you like an Australian cigarette? They're a more like "cigarillos."

[*She begins to dig in her bag . . .*]

KIT: Thanks, but I'm serious about giving them up. Well, I'm *trying*. It's one of several things I'm trying.

[*Slight pause. Wendy lights up, drops the book of matches on the coffee table.*]

WENDY: [*Seriously*] I don't think it would be so smart of me to have a baby. Not good for anybody at this particular moment—Manny or me or especially, *the baby*. So, I had an abortion. Not the cheeriest of weeks for it but then, not the cheeriest of tasks *any* week.

KIT: Are you all right?

WENDY: Oh, physically I'm okay, but emotionally, I'm pretty shaky. I have very complicated feelings about it. But somehow, for me, anyway, I felt I was doing the right thing for right now. I didn't tell Manny what I was planning to do while he was away. I don't know what he would have said.

[*Kit is silent. Another brief pause. Wendy flicks her ash into an ashtray on the coffee table.*]

WENDY: [*After a moment*] You know he's still in love with you and I can see why. You seem so . . . sensible. And sensitive. So *real*.

KIT: Real?

WENDY: Yeah. No bullshit.

KIT: Thanks.

WENDY: Why'd you come out here?

KIT: I'm not sure. But I hope it's not like getting pregnant in the Outback.

WENDY: Do you want to get together? I mean you and Manny.

KIT: [*Directly*] I guess that's what I thought I'd try to find out.

WENDY: When he asked me to take my things and stay in my apartment, I thought to myself, "Fuck *him*."

KIT: I can appreciate that. Totally.

WENDY: I thought, "This is it! I'm never coming back to this house again."— I wasn't angry at *him*, just at myself. At what I'd done to myself yet again with yet another guy. The funny thing is, now that it's over, I feel sad but it's a *good* sadness. I feel like there just might be a chance for a fresh start . . . [*She starts to cry, takes another drag on her cigarette*] I'm sorry.

[*Kit gets up, moves over, sits beside her on the couch and puts her arms around her.*]

KIT: It's okay.

WENDY: [*Weeping*] I'm so embarrassed.

KIT: Oh, don't be. I always wanted to be able to smoke and cry at the same time—like Simone Signoret in *Room At The Top*.

WENDY: I'm sorry, but that was before my time.

KIT: [*Indulgently*] Mine too. I've seen it on television.

[*Wendy looks at the pink tree, begins to laugh.*]

WENDY: Is that tree the most pathetic looking thing you've ever seen?

KIT: [*Laughs*] The *most!*

[*Manny has appeared at the top of the stairs, dressed only in his shirt  [now very rumpled], jockey shorts and sox. His hair is wildly disheveled from lying down.*]

[*He stops, looks down to see Kit and Wendy and reacts incredulously! He can't believe he's actually seeing the two of them together—and not just talking, but laughing and hugging each other.*]

[*He starts to creep down the stairs, his eyes widening, his jaw dropping further and further . . .*]

WENDY: [*Digs in her purse, finds a Kleenex*] Oh, I feel so much better now! And I don't mean just because of the good cry, though that certainly helped.

KIT: Me, too! I feel a hundred times better!

WENDY: You're *so* nice!

[*Now she throws her arms about Kit, hugs her. Manny is now down the stairs and coming up behind them.*]

MANNY: [*Heatedly*] Pardon me, but I had no idea that you two had met!

[*Wendy releases Kit.*]

KIT: [*Flatly*] Manny, you really must stop sneaking up on people from behind!

MANNY: Let alone had time to get all huggy-wuggy on the couch!

KIT: We're complete strangers who've know each other all our lives.

WENDY: [*Laughing at the sight of Manny*] Oh, Manny, you look so funny. You've got major Bed Hair!

KIT: [*Amused*] And I'd forgotten what witty knees you have!—they wrinkle just like those stupid "Smiley Faces"— Where're your pants?

MANNY: [*Haughtily*] *Who cares*?! You both have seen me without them before! And I've seen both of you with Bed Hair! But neither of your kneecaps are anywhere as witty as mine! [*Indignantly, to Wendy*] *What are you doing here?*

KIT: [*Off-handedly*] Just getting acquainted.

[*Josh runs in from the terrace where the light, by now, has gone orange and lavender with the sunset. He is in a bathing suit with a beach towel wrapped around him. His hair is wet.*]

JOSH: Mom! Mom, come here a minute . . . [*Sees Wendy, stops*] . . . Oh, hi!— [*Dryly*] You're The Other Woman, aren't you?

WENDY: [*Tentatively*] Yes, I guess I am.

JOSH: You're even sexier looking than your picture.

KIT: [*Appalled*] Oh, Josh!

[*Josh and Wendy shake hands. Manny is incredulous.*]

WENDY: [*To Josh*] That's a very sweet of you to say.

JOSH: Nice to finally meet you. I guess I'll be seeing more of you later. Mom, come watch me do this cool new dive I've just invented.

KIT: In a minute. Is Nell in the pool, too?

JOSH: Yeah, why don't you come in, too! It's great!

KIT: Better not leave her alone out there. [*Looking outside*] Oh, it's almost dark.

JOSH: There're colored lights everywhere—even in the palm trees. Imagine being able to snorkle in winter! You have all the luck, Dad!

[*He runs back out the terrace doors.*]

MANNY: Lucky, that's me! The luckiest little snorkler in the world.

WENDY: Well, I guess I'd better be going.

MANNY: [*Mock gracious*] Oh, why go? I think it's so civilized that you're here and getting acquainted with everyone so wonderfully, so why leave now?

WENDY: Actually, I have a date and I really better start pulling myself together.

MANNY: A *date*?! *Who with*?!

WENDY: [*Calmly*] Well, you didn't think I was going to sit at home on New Year's Eve, did you?

MANNY: That's what *I'm* doing!

[*Wendy and Kit exchange tight, knowing smiles.*]

WENDY: [*To Kit*] I can see this is going to take a turn for the worse. Goodbye and thank you for being so . . . so . . .

KIT: [*Sincerely, protesting*] Please. I'm just happy we got the chance to meet and talk.

[*Manny stares at them slack-jawed. Nellie races in from the terrace in a swimsuit, wet hair, her body wrapped in a beach towel.*]

MANNY: [*Bluntly, to Nellie*] Yes?! May we help you?!

NELLIE: Josh said The Other Woman was here and I just wanted to get a look.

KIT: Nell!

[*Wendy laughs . . .*]

NELLIE: [*Giving Wendy the once-over*] NOT BAD! BYE!

[*She barrels back out the terrace doors.*]

MANNY: [*Mock calm*] I feel like this is a hallucination. A really bad trip.

KIT: Relax, Manny. No one's taking this very seriously but you.

MANNY: [*Snapping at Kit*] Well, I *do* take it seriously! Call me old-fashioned! Call me fuddy-duddy! Call me Manny-wanny!

[*The doorbell RINGS. The evening light on the terrace should be gone by now. Manny whips around in the direction of the front door, starts for it, stops, realizes he doesn't have on any pants. He turns back to Kit and Wendy . . .*]

MANNY: You two seem to be wearing the pants around here—why don't one of you answer it?!

[*Kit and Wendy look at each other.*]

KIT: [*To Wendy*] Well, you actually live here. I'm just a guest.

MANNY: [*To Kit*] Yes, you're only staying here but you live somewhere else—while she's staying somewhere else but actually lives here. Explain *that* to your mother!

WENDY: [*Passing Manny, going to the door*] Oh, go hide under your desert-colored duvet!

[*Wendy opens the door and COLIN is standing there. He's forty-something, average looking, dressed in black-tie. He carries a jeroboam of Dom Perignon which has a silver bow tied around the neck of the bottle.*]

WENDY: [*Brightly*] Colin! Come in!

MANNY: Oh, my, yes, come one, come all! We're having Open House. And you've dressed—you shouldn't have! *I* didn't. [*Sarcastically*] I thought you always called before you dropped in. I thought it was one of your unwritten rules.

[*Colin is a bit thrown by what he has walked into, but manages it smoothly.*]

COLIN: I could go to my car phone if it'll keep my record unblemished. Am I getting you at an awkward time?

MANNY: An *awkward time*? No, nooo! Why would you think that?

COLIN: Well, I'm only staying a minute, I'm on my way to . . .

MANNY: No, no, no, come in and stay as long as you like!

[*He pulls Colin into the room.*]

WENDY: [*Shuts the door*] Hi, Collie!

COLIN: Wendola! You look positively sleek with happiness.

WENDY: Thanks. I think I am, rather.

MANNY: [*To Colin*] Allow me to introduce my wife—uh, my ex-wife!

[*Colin goes to Kit, shakes her hand warmly.*]

COLIN: [*Dryly*] Welcome to our city.

KIT: [*To Colin*] I understand we almost don't need an introduction.

COLIN: He must have mentioned me, too.

KIT: [*With meaning*] Not . . . in as intimate detail, I don't believe.

COLIN: Well, I hope you won't hold it against me. I loved everything I heard about you.

KIT: I like what I heard about you, too.

MANNY: [*To Wendy*] Isn't that *sweet*? They're instant old friends, too! I seem to be the only outsider!

COLIN: [*Hands Manny the jeroboam*] Here. I thought this might come in handy later this evening.

KIT: [*Brightly*] How lovely!

MANNY: Isn't it lovely?! Chilled, too! See, Kit, I told you he was thoughtful.

WENDY: I'm leaving before one drop of alcohol is consumed.

[*To Kit re: her photograph*]

—If you don't mind, I think I will take that after all.

KIT: I understand perfectly.

[*Wendy goes to the bar, takes the picture, stuffs in back in the canvas shopping bag.*]

MANNY: [*To Wendy*] What are you doing?!

WENDY: Never mind, Manny.

MANNY: [*To Kit*] Maybe *you'll* explain since you understand so much!

KIT: I think she's leaving you.

[*Josh comes in from the kitchen door, wearing a terry cloth robe, drying his hair with a small towel.*]

JOSH: Excuse me, Mom, but Nell's hungry. What are we gonna do about dinner?

KIT: I don't know yet. Is there something in the fridge to tide you over?

JOSH: Not much. Some diet soda and a pound of caviar. Gift wrapped.

MANNY: [*Generally*] A Christmas present from my agent.

WENDY: [*Apologetically*] Oh, I'm afraid I cleaned out the fridge—I didn't want things to spoil while Manny was away.

MANNY: [*To Josh*] Well, how about some diet soda and caviar?

COLIN: [*To Kit*] I could drive you to the market.

WENDY: No, *I* will. It's my fault.

MANNY: [*To Wendy and Colin*] Why don't the two of you fight over it!

KIT: [*Appreciative, but negative*] Thank you both, but we'll figure something out . . .

JOSH: Could we go out for pizza?

WENDY: Oh, there's a terrific pizza place right on Beverly Drive. And they deliver fast. Shall I call?

MANNY: [*To Wendy*] *Please don't*! You've been helpful enough! [*To Josh, bluntly*] We'll figure out what and where you'll *eat* as soon as the guests get out of here!

JOSH: What's eating you, dad? [*To all*] Excuse me.

[*Josh exits out the terrace doors. Wendy turns to Kit.*]

WENDY: Goodbye, Kit, and thanks.

KIT: No need to thank me. It was nothing. Really.

WENDY: [*Goes to Colin*] Bye, Collie.

COLIN: [*Kisses Wendy on the cheek*] Happy New Year.

WENDY: [*Goes to Manny*] So long, Manny. Here's your house key. Call me after your family leaves. We ought to have a serious chat about how to proceed with our lives next year—which is tomorrow.

[*Wendy goes out the front door and closes it. Manny turns back to Kit and Colin.*]

COLIN: [*Incredulously*] Is that a pink tree?

MANNY: Yes, and make something of it!

COLIN: How about a fire?

[*Kit laughs. Manny boils.*]

KIT: [*To Colin, forced lightly*] I know it sounds weird, but that tree reminds me of Maureen O'Hara. [*Touches her hair*] Maybe it's because she was the first redhead to have the courage to wear pink. Not that shade of pink, of course.

COLIN: [*Charmingly*] You have very lovely red hair.

KIT: [*Diffidently*] And the freckles to match, I'm afraid—but thank you.

MANNY: [*With an edge*] If I may interrupt, I think I'll slip into something a little more uncomfortable and order a pizza for my children.

[*Manny shoves the bottle of Dom Perignon into Kit's hands, turns and pounds up the stairs. When he is out of sight, Kit turns to Colin.*]

KIT: Why wait for midnight? Why not open this heavenly bottle and have a cup of kindness right now?

COLIN: Why not?

KIT: Will you do the honors?

COLIN: I'd be honored to do the honors.

[*Kit hands Colin the bottle. He starts to untwist the wire around the cork.*]

KIT: I'll get two lovely long-stem glasses . . .

[*She heads behind the bar when the doorbell RINGS.*]

COLIN: [*To Kit*] They can't deliver *that* fast!

[*Kit has taken two glasses from a shelf and placed them on the counter top. She goes to the front door. Colin crosses behind the bar, gets a towel, starts to pull the cork.*]

[*Kit opens the miniature door peephole, looks out, reacts.*]

KIT: [*Astounded*] Oh, *my!*

COLIN: [*Agog*] You mean it *is* the pizza man?!

KIT: I don't quite know who or *what* it is!

[*She opens the door, steps outside, out of sight.*]

KIT: [*Offstage*] Good evening! Thank you, very much! They're . . . they're *wonderful!*

[*A moment, and through the front door there begins to emerge an enormous bouquet of helieum-filled rubber balloons. There must be three dozen of them in silver and gold and white, tied with the same colored ribbons, gathered and weighted with a silver top-hat filled with noise-makers and an envelope.*]

[*Colin is arrested by the sight, stops what he's doing as Kit shuts the door and "floats" back into the room.*]

COLIN: Well! That's pretty splendid! Who'd send Manny . . . ?

KIT: [*Placing the top hat on the bar*] No, they're not for Manny—they're for *me!* There's a card here in the hat with my name on it! [*She tears open the envelope and reads the card*] Ohh, how sweet! They're from a friend in Connecticut.

COLIN: "Good goods"?

KIT: [*Reacts*] *Honestly!* Manny's tongue should be cut out. Manny said, rather rudely, that Nick looks like he's been delivering balloons all his life. And Josh heard him and told Nick.

COLIN: It's nice that Nick has a sense of humor about Manny's sense of humor. How'd Nick feel about your coming out here?

KIT: Well, he wasn't laughing.

COLIN: No one has that much of a sense of humor.

KIT: But he was very understanding. At least, he tried very hard to be understanding.

COLIN: He's in love with you. He'll try anything.

[*Colin pops the cork!*]

KIT: Oh, what a glorious sound!

COLIN: [*Pours, hands her a glass*] I can't think of anything clever to say except you're everything I'd imagined and much, much more.

KIT: That's clever enough for this redhead.

COLIN: Cheers!

KIT: Cheers!

[*They clink glasses and drink as Manny comes down the stairs. He has changed into a black silk shirt and a pair of black velour trousers. He sees the bouquet of balloons.*]

MANNY: [*To Colin*] What's *that*?!

COLIN: Balloons. From her lover, The Balloon Man. You remember him.

KIT: Sweet of Nick, don't you think?

MANNY: [*To Colin*] You ought to see this creep. So WASP he makes *you* look hamish. Really got a broom up his ass.

[*Manny picks up the card, but Kit snaps it out of his hand . . .*]

KIT: I believe that has my name on it.

MANNY: It's still my name, too. [*To Colin*] I see we're not waiting for midnight to dive into the shampoo.

COLIN: Why stand on ceremony?

MANNY: Why stand on ceremony when you can stand on your ear? Why don't we break out the gift-wrapped caviar!

COLIN: Why not?!

[*Colin gets another glass for Manny.*]

COLIN: [*To Manny*] Here. Have a bit of the bubbly to take the cramp out of your soul.

[*Manny tosses the card back into the hat with disgust, holds up a hand to Colin before he pours.*]

MANNY: None for me, thanks. I have my own method for getting a glow on.

[*Manny turns and exits to the kitchen. Colin picks up a steel trash basket and begins to prepare it with ice from the machine.*]

COLIN: I'm afraid the real ice bucket isn't going to do the trick. Anyway, when you have Italian trash baskets from Ogetti, who could ask for anything more?

KIT: [*Holding her glass*] God, isn't champagne wonderful?! One should really be dressed like you, Colin, to drink champagne on New Year's Eve!

COLIN: [*Re: his watch*] Oh, look at the time!

KIT: [*Disappointed*] Aw, you're not going already, are you?

COLIN: Don't you want me to?

KIT: Not if you don't want to.

COLIN: I don't want to go and I don't want to go to the party anyway. [*Smiles*] Maybe I'll just call and cancel.

[*Manny returns with the tin of caviar in one hand and a caviar bowl with a place for crushed ice, in the other.*]

MANNY: [*General announcement*] Toast triangles with the crusts trimmed, coming up!

[*Colin is placing the jeroboam of Dom Perignon in trash basket.*]

MANNY: [*Extending the caviar bowl to Colin*] Here, put some ice in this thing.

COLIN: [*Taking the bowl*] What do you know, a proper caviar server! I'm impressed.

MANNY: Yeah, well, we run a tight ship! Which reminds me, why are you using my imported Italian trash can as an ice bucket?

COLIN: It's jeroboam size.

MANNY: [*Re: trash basket*] Ah, well as you see, it certainly wasn't chock-full of discarded masterpieces of musical composition.

COLIN: Blocked again?

MANNY: From the moment I laid eyes on The Balloon Man, my bowels blocked and locked and threw away the key.

COLIN: [*Re: champagne*] A little of this will keep you as regular as your alimony checks.

[*Manny exits to the kitchen, giving Colin a look en route.*]

KIT: [*Toying with the card*] Nick really does possess the most outstanding qualities and character.

COLIN: I'm sure he deserves the Nobel Prize for being noble—but do you love him?

KIT: [*Picks up her champagne*] In my own . . . very warm and . . . respectful way.

COLIN: [*Refilling her glass*] Sounds rather fraternal.

KIT: Maybe so. I never had a brother, more's the pity. Thanks.

COLIN: Neither did I. Nor a sister, for that matter. But that's how I'd like to feel toward one if I had.

KIT: You're an only child?

COLIN: 'Fraid so.

KIT: So's Manny.

COLIN: Oh, yes, I know. [*Crossing to the coffee table*] I think there's so much to be profited from sibling rivalry. So many of the slings and arrows of childhood can be shared. And that can come in very handy later in life.

KIT: I'm not so sure. I have one sister and I think I'd rather *get* her with a sling and arrow, rather than *share* one with her.

COLIN: [*Laughs*] Is she older or younger?

KIT: A year younger. She lives and works in Paris. She's a correspondent for CNN.

COLIN: Oh, yes, I've seen her on TV. Manny told me she was your sister— rather, *his* sister-in-law.

KIT: Yes, she was "The Right One"—the one who, "Did something with her life." I'm the one who, as my mother puts it: "Never did anything but marry an exotic."

[*Manny swings in from the kitchen, a basket of toast triangles in hand.*]

MANNY: [*To Colin*] And you know what she means by "exotic," don't you?

[*He puts the toast on the bar.*]

MANNY: Toast isosceleses! [*To Kit*] *Perfect* enough for you?

KIT: [*Ignores the question, picks up last remark*] My mother means you were an unwashed, uncombed, filthy, long-haired, pot-head from the dregs of the seventies.

MANNY: She *means* I'm Jewish.

KIT: *She does not!*

MANNY: [*To Kit*] She doesn't say that, but that's what she means.

KIT: My mother is a lot of horrendous things, Manny, but what she is *not* is a bigot!

MANNY: I didn't say she was a bigot. She's just Episcopalian.

[*He turns and exits to the kitchen.*]

KIT: [*To Colin*] She *is* pretty white bread.

COLIN: Mine too. Born and bred white bread.

KIT: Boston is it?

COLIN: No, but I went to school there. Charleston.

KIT: God, you don't sound it.

COLIN: Didn't spend too much time there. Always in school somewhere. Boarding school. Prep school. You get the picture.

KIT: Oh, yes. Me, too. Actually, I'm considering sending Josh to boarding school, but I don't want him to misunderstand. I don't want him to think because he's gotten into trouble lately, I'm trying to punish him by shipping him out.

COLIN: My two boys are at a wonderful place in Colorado. I could tell you about it.

KIT: [*Crossing to him*] Oh, please do. How old are they?

COLIN: Sixteen and fifteen. God, I can't believe I said that. They're getting old and I'm getting older.

KIT: Josh is going to be seventeen on his next birthday. I feel like I'm a hundred.

COLIN: You look about seventeen yourself.

KIT: You *are* from the south. That's gotta be what they call gallantry.

COLIN: I mean it.

KIT: Thanks. I didn't know you'd been married.

COLIN: I suppose Manny only told you about Jim.

KIT: Yes and he didn't even tell me his name—he just referred to him as "Colin's friend."— I'm very sorry. I know that's not enough, but I am sorry.

COLIN: Thanks.

[*Manny breezes in.*]

MANNY: What's going on in here behind my back? And I'm not being paranoid.

COLIN: It's not behind your back, it's under your nose.

MANNY: [*To Kit*] Did he tell you he's Episcopalian, too? A Carolinian Episcopalian. [*Sings*] "Nothin' could be finer than to integrate a diner in the morn-o-orn-nin'!"

COLIN: [*To Kit*] Well, I was baptized one, but I'm really nothing.

MANNY: Just a zero? I didn't know you had such a low self-esteem.

KIT: What have you been smoking in the kitchen?

COLIN: It sho' ain't ham, honey!

MANNY: It's not behind your back, it's under your nose!

[*Manny produces a joint from his breast pocket, extends it to Kit. She pushes it away.*]

KIT: No thanks. My cup runneth under.

[*She goes to refill her glass.*]

MANNY: [*Offers the joint to Colin*] How 'bout you, suh?

COLIN: [*Holds up his glass of champagne*] Ah think ah'll jes' sip on mah bourbon and branch water.

MANNY: [*To Kit*] When you say you've stopped smoking—I thought you meant cigarettes.

KIT: I *did* mean cigarettes. I'm just not in the mood.

MANNY: What the matter, afraid it's gonna get you all hot and bothered? All reefer madness and sex-crazed?

KIT: [*With exhausted indulgence*] Yes, Manny, that's *just* what I was afraid of.

MANNY: [*Re: Kit and Colin*] Am I interrupting something here? I get the feeling I've just sorta stepped on my cock.

COLIN: [*Re: joint*] How much of that stuff have you had?

MANNY: [*Snapping mildly at Colin*] I am not getting paranoid, if that's what you're implying. What were you two discussing in here—The Life and Times of Manny Boy?

KIT: Incredible as it may seem, your name was never mentioned.

MANNY: Well, then maybe what you have to say to each other is not for my ears. Maybe I should just leave. Fold my petals and drop my tent.

COLIN: Just don't drop your pants.

KIT: [*To Colin, laughs*] Oh, you've caught that act, have you?

COLIN: [*Nods, to Kit*] Pretty, isn't it?

MANNY: *I'm not budging.*

KIT: [*To Colin*] Anyway, as I was saying . . .

MANNY: [*Mock huffily*] Before you were so rudely interrupted.

KIT: . . . we've got to do something about Josh. The first thing is that I want him to see some kind of therapist.

MANNY: Christ, I'm not even finished with analysis myself and my son is already starting!

KIT: I didn't know you were seeing a doctor.

MANNY: Off and on. I'm not that sick, you know. I mean, *you* may think I am . . . [*To Colin*] . . . and *you* may think I am, but I'm not!

KIT: I think it's great that you're seeing someone. I wish you'd done it years ago. I wish *I'd* done it years ago.

COLIN: I saw someone for a while, right after Jim died. It helped a lot.

KIT: I'm sure it would help Josh a lot, too. I hope you, agree, Manny.

MANNY: Oh, I'm all *for* it. I just don't want to *pay* for it, that's all. How do poor people pay for it?

COLIN: I don't know any poor people who are seeing analysts.

[*Colin takes the champagne bottle out of the bucket . . .*]

COLIN: [*To Kit*] A tad more?

KIT: [*Extends her glass cheerfully*] A tad, thank you. [*Moves to the foot of the stairs . . .* ] I should go up and get into a gown—not a dress, mind you, but a *gown*—something on the bias—after all, this *is* Hollywood—and make an entrance down the stairs and sweep over to the door and stand with the knob in the small of my back . . . [*Moves to stand with her back against the front door*] And sweep over to the fireplace and stand, staring soulfully into the fire . . . [*She glides to the fireplace, looking into an unlit pile of logs*] Of course, there should be a fire for me to stare soulfully into.

COLIN: [*Smiling, charmed*] That should be easy enough to arrange.

KIT: You mean ignite the tree or are these gas logs?

[*Manny jumps up and goes to the fireplace.*]

MANNY: *Don't touch that tree!* And those are not gas logs! Those are *real* logs. There is, however, a gas starter—just to make life a teensy-weensy bit easier than rubbing two sticks together—the way you do it way back east in the land of no bullshit!

KIT: [*Calmly*] I have a gas starter, way back east in the land of no bullshit. You're so defensive!

[*Manny has bent to turn on the gas starter which ignites the fire.*]

MANNY: [*Stands, to Kit*] You were completely born out of your generation, weren't you? You were really born to do *The Continental*, weren't you? You and Rogers and Astaire.

COLIN: Astaire and Rogers. Let's get the billing right.

MANNY: [*An eye-roll*] Oh, God, yes, let's!

[*Kit crosses to Colin at the bar.*]

KIT: Love, love, *love* Rogers and Astaire.

COLIN: Well, who doesn't?

KIT: [*Flatly*] *Manny* doesn't.

[*Kit holds out her empty glass and Colin refills it.*]

MANNY: See, I told you you'd like each other. I knew you'd have all that old shit in common.

KIT: [*Entre nous, to Colin*] Don't mind *him*.

COLIN: [*Refilling his glass*] Oh, I don't mind him at all.

KIT: [*To Colin, enthusiastically*] I saw a marquee once—honest to God—that said, "Fred and Ginger in Irving's *Top Hat*"—!!!

COLIN: N-ooo!

KIT: I swear!

COLIN: How wonderful!

KIT: I think that about says it, don't you?

COLIN: I think that about does!

[*They both break up.*]

MANNY: [*Grimly*] *About says what?!*

[*Kit and Colin stop laughing, turn to look at him blankly.*]

MANNY: I hate all that old crap! I hate wallowing in nostalgia. I hate anything that's "avec schmaltz"!

COLIN: You're afraid of feeling, Manny. You're afraid of sentiment. You confuse it with sentimentality.

MANNY: [*Snakily*] I didn't know you'd be interested in coming on with my wife.

COLIN: [*Calmly*] Not even with your *ex*-wife. And one more remark like that and I'll hit you with this jeroboam right in your big, expensive teeth!

KIT: Now, this is no way for best friends to act on the last day of the year!

COLIN: Oh, we're not going to fight. Manny doesn't like confrontations.

KIT: No, but he likes to provoke them.

COLIN: Yeah, then tuck his tail and run. Actually, Manny doesn't know too much about friendship, so we're hardly best anything. He never calls unless he wants something. He never really talks to me unless it's about himself.

MANNY: What are friends for?

COLIN: You don't know the meaning of give and take. All you know is take. When somebody else is in trouble you are nowhere to be found.

MANNY: I wish I were nowhere to be found right this minute!

COLIN: Sorry, but this time, I'm the one who's going to walk. [*Drains glass, turns to Kit; softly*] I don't know what to say to you. I . . .

KIT: [*Gently*] It's all right. Good night, Colin, and thank you.

MANNY: [*Interrupting*] I know what you're talking about.

COLIN: What?

MANNY: You're talking about the night Jim died.

COLIN: Jim and I were real, true friends, Manny. Not just lovers—best friends. It happens when you hang in with each other long enough, surviving what life has in store for you. And the night he died is the night I needed another friend—and I thought it was you. I thought that's what we called ourselves. I thought that's why I listened to your story hours on end, days on end, months . . .

[*Manny is not only silent, he's almost catatonic. He doesn't move, just sits and stares into space.*]

COLIN: You're not a friend, Manny. You're not someone I could call in the middle of the night if I needed help—because I don't know if you'd be there for me. I don't think you would be.

[*Manny doesn't affirm or deny the statement, just remains totally still. Kit is completely aware of this, dividing her attention between what Colin is saying and its effect on Manny.*]

COLIN: I needed you once—the night Jim died and you weren't there for me. It wasn't in the middle of the night when I called—it was just about this time—and I was drunk. Oh, I was *very* drunk. Sloppy, maudlin, full of self-pity and *desperate*. It was clear from the moment I arrived. You were distant and cold—rude, almost, because I had called on the phone, drunk, *begging* to come over and talk to you. Here it was, the test of our friendship. I needed you and you weren't there. I thought I'd never forgive you for that, but I have. Because in spite of everything I think about you, I think there's something to you.

[*A long moment, then Manny slowly gets up.*]

MANNY: You wanted something else and you won't admit it.

[*Manny crosses to the front door, goes out, closing it behind him. After a moment, Colin turns to Kit.*]

COLIN: Would you like to come to the party with me?

KIT: I honestly don't like parties. And tonight of all nights, I don't want to be pretending I'm having a good time when I'm not.

COLIN: How about if I try to book a table somewhere? It's late in the day, but there're a few head waiters that know me.

KIT: [*Thinks for a moment*] Okay. We can't leave before the pizza comes. And you'll have to wait while I change and say goodnight to the kids.

COLIN: I'd be delighted to wait as long as you like.

KIT: Have another glass of your gorgeous champagne. You look a bit white-lipped and I don't wonder.

COLIN: [*Re champagne*] I think I'll do that very thing.

[*They look at each other a moment.*]

KIT: [*Simply*] Are you in love with Manny?

COLIN: I thought I was once. And for the longest time, I kidded myself into thinking something was possible. As someone once said, "When the wrong man comes along, I'll know him." Besides everything else, Manny is hopelessly straight.

KIT: [*Nods*] You don't have to tell *me*. But enough about Manny, it's *you* who concerns me.

COLIN: [*Nods sardonically*] Because we have something in common. [*Directly*] Well, it's nice to know I now have a friend who understands.

KIT: [*Smiles*] Thank you, Colin. I feel the same way.

COLIN: Manny was right about what I really wanted from him the night my friend died. I wanted physical love. But I had wanted it on so many nights that I now wonder if my friend's death made the need that night any more special than any other night—or if I was just drunk and dramatizing, using Jim's death to try to get what I really wanted. Because, after all, it was Manny I loved.

KIT: I don't suppose you'll ever know.

COLIN: At any rate, it was clear that if it wasn't going to happen that night—then it was never going to happen. I think, for me, that realization was the end of our friendship in a special, idiosyncratic, no-holds-barred way, and the start of something ordinary. Something true and perfectly honorable—just nothing unique.

KIT: I think you underestimate true, honorable friendship. I think it *is* unique and not ordinary, at all.

[*Colin relishes Kit's sympathetic response*]

—Maybe Manny's just not who or what you need him to be, Colin. Maybe he's not what you thought he was or even what he allowed you to believe.

COLIN: You're probably right.

KIT: Creative people are so narcissistic that attention in any form is so welcome, they take it from anyone and anywhere they can get it. Adoration, recognition, validation . . . well! . . . they beg for it like dogs at a table. They wag their tails. They whine. They flirt for it. Outrageously. With anyone.

COLIN: Yeah. Trouble is, they just take and take and take and then they just walk away.

KIT: [*After a moment*] Colin . . . why do you want something you can't have?

COLIN: Kit . . . why do you want something you don't want?

[*A slight pause.*]

KIT: [*Smiles faintly*] It won't take me a minute to change.

[*Kit turns and goes out the terrace doors. Colin goes to the wine bucket, refills his glass, goes to the telephone, picks it up, starts to call the restaurant.*]

*The CURTAIN doesn't not come down, but the SOUND of CHEERING comes over the house speakers as the light cross fade to . . .*

## SCENE 2

*Shortly after midnight. The lighting is somewhat softer and moodier than before. A few lamps have been turned off and the embers in the hearth cast a warm, cozy glow ever the room.*

*Josh, dressed in pajamas and a robe, is sitting on his knees in front of the TV with the volume turned up. An announcers's voice is reporting the events of the New Year's celebration, straining above the revelers.*

*One of the terrace doors is opened and Manny comes inside. He sees Josh, stops. Josh turns to see him, quickly turns off the news report and gets up.*

MANNY: You don't have to turn it off.

JOSH: I already saw what I wanted to see.

MANNY: What was that?

JOSH: The countdown.

MANNY: Five, four, three, two, one . . . Haaappp!–peenooyeer!

JOSH: [*Tentatively*] It's really exciting—time running out . . . tick, tick, tick, going, going, gone . . . and bammo, it's a whole 'nother year.

MANNY: [*Without expression*] Yeah, tick, tick, tick . . . bammo.

JOSH: I was just writing the new date on a piece of paper and it looks so weird. I can't explain it.

MANNY: I know what you mean. It's always March before I put the right date on a check.

JOSH: That happens to me in school, too.

MANNY: [*Feeble attempt*] You write checks in school?

[*Josh laughs cautiously, releasing a bit of nervous tension.*]

MANNY: I'm surprised to find you up. I didn't see any lights over the garage. I thought everybody was asleep.

JOSH: The trip and all that swimming really knocked Nell out.

MANNY: What about you?

JOSH: I still couldn't sleep.

[*Brief pause. Manny glances upstairs.*]

JOSH: Mom went out with your friend.

MANNY: Oh.

JOSH: She got all dressed up and he took her someplace fancy.

MANNY: Probably the party he was invited to.

JOSH: You know Mom doesn't like parties. They went to a restaurant. [*Josh goes to the phone, picks up a pad, crosses to hand it to Manny.*] She left the number like she always does—in case someone breaks their neck. Ever heard of this place?

MANNY: Ohh, yes. You're right—very fancy.

JOSH: Fancy-schmancy?

MANNY: Yeah, you need a blood test to get in.

[*Brief pause.*]

JOSH: Where'd *you* go? To a party?

MANNY: No, no, I . . . just went for a drive.

JOSH: By yourself?

MANNY: Yeah.

JOSH: [*Looks at balloons*] Where'd the balloons come from?

MANNY: Nick sent them.

JOSH: [*After a moment*] You and Mom had a fight, didn't you?

MANNY: No, we didn't have a fight.

JOSH: I thought maybe you did. I mean, it's pretty weird to come all the way to California for New Year's and you go for a drive and she goes out with a stranger.

MANNY: I guess it is pretty weird. I guess I'm a pretty weird dad.

JOSH: Not as crazy as some.

MANNY: Thanks.

JOSH: Some of my friends have really sick parents. You're nowhere near that sick.

MANNY: Thanks. How . . . how sick am I? I mean, as a dad . . . as a parent? In your opinion.

JOSH: [*Reluctantly*] Ohh, I don't know . . .

MANNY: I mean, tell me about *me*. I want to hear—I'd *like* to hear.

JOSH: I don't know . . . I . . . I . . . [*Turns away*] I don't want to talk about it, okay? I'm going to bed.

[*Josh starts toward the terrace doors.*]

MANNY: [*Quickly*] Oh, Josh, don't go to bed yet. Stay here for a moment. Please? Stay here and talk to me?

[*Josh hesitates, doesn't turn back, doesn't look at Manny.*]

MANNY: How's . . . how's your friend?

[*Josh folds his arms, doesn't speak for a moment . . .*]

JOSH: What friend?

MANNY: The one who was in the accident with you.

[*Josh slowly unfolds his arms, turns to Manny.*]

JOSH: Mom told you about that?

MANNY: [*Nods*] She was very worried. She *is* very worried.

JOSH: [*Puts hands in pockets, looks at floor*] I figured she'd tell you, but I didn't know if she had or not because you never said anything. But then, that's just your way.

MANNY: [*Directly*] What do you mean, "my way"—?

JOSH: [*Weakly*] The way you are.

MANNY: [*Pressing him*] How do you mean?

[*Josh doesn't answer.*]

MANNY: Can you kinda fill me in on that?

[*No answer.*]

MANNY: You mean my . . . you mean . . .

[*Josh turns away. Silence.*]

MANNY: You mean the way I do what you're doing right now?

[*Still no answer. Josh moves over by the TV.*]

MANNY: Oh, Josh . . . you remind me so much of me. And for your sake, I'm truly sorry. I really don't want you to grow up with my bad qualities. I . . .

[*Josh turns on the television. The announcer's VOICE comes on . . .*]

MANNY: . . . I . . . I'm really sorry for what . . .

[*Josh turns up the volume. The sound of the hysterical mob becomes louder . . .*]

MANNY: . . . I know I haven't always been there for you. And I regret that. I deeply regret it and I hope it's not too late to make up for . . .

[*Josh turns the volume louder . . .*]

MANNY: . . . When you were little, I don't know if you remember something you said. Something you said about me. You said, "Who is that man who lives with us?"

[*Josh turns the volume all the way up. The sound is deafening.*]

MANNY: [*Over the noise*] Who is that man who lives with us?! And now *I'd* like to know, if it's not too late, who my own son is?!! Who is this son I'm living with?!

[*Josh kicks the TV off button with his foot. The sound ceases.*]

JOSH: [*Angrily*] You don't live with me! You never have! And I don't mean just under one roof. Even when we lived together you weren't there. *You were never there!*

MANNY: I know. I know. And I'm sorry. I want to be there. I want to be there for you. Even if you live in the east and I live in the west—I want you to know I'm there for you. Always. In spite of distance, in spite of anything. And I want us to try to talk to each other . . . to try to communicate.

[*Manny has come over to Josh, reaches out, puts his hand on the boy's shoulder. Suddenly, Josh wheels around and starts violently beating Manny on the chest and arms. Manny's hands go up defensively, but he allows Josh to play this out, to exhaust himself until he stops and collapses in tears. Manny puts his arms about Josh and hold him as he continues to sob.*]

[*A moment, and Josh pulls himself together and steps back from Manny.*]

JOSH: Goodnight.

MANNY: Goodnight, son.

JOSH: I hope . . . I hope we have a happy new year.

MANNY: I'm going to try to make it that way. I'm gonna try to do my best.

JOSH: [*Quietly*] Me, too.

[*Josh goes to the terrace doors and exits. Manny watches him. After a moment, he begins to whistle the tune to "Let's Face The Music And Dance."*]

MANNY: [*Speaks/sings*]
> *Before the fiddlers have fled,*
> *Before they ask us to pay the bill*
> *And while we still have the chance,*
> *Let's face the musice and dance.*

[*Manny looks at his hands. They are trembling.*]

[*The front door is opened and Kit enters. She looks ravishing. She's dressed in a chic, short black dress with a skirt that "moves," showing, for the first time, her beautiful legs and feet in high heel pumps. The only jewelry she has on are Nick's diamond earrings.*]

[*Kit doesn't see Manny. She closes the door and starts to go up the stairs . . .*]

MANNY: You didn't call to cancel.

[*Kit stops halfway up the stairs, turns to look down at Manny.*]

KIT: We didn't have a date, to my recollection.

MANNY: You didn't call to find out if we did have one, and if we did, to cancel. It just isn't done. I'm extremely hurt.

KIT: Oh, Manny, it's too late in the evening—too early in the year, to start up with your . . .

[*She breaks off, continues up a few steps. Manny comes to the bottom of the stairs.*]

MANNY: *You are staying in my house. You are my houseguest.* And I think it's a pretty rude and inconsiderate thing for a houseguest to do.

KIT: [*Stops, turns, slowly descends the stairs*] I think it's a pretty rude and inconsiderate thing for a host to do—behave like a brat and walk out, leave his guest and his houseguest high and dry.

MANNY: [*Crosses center*] Even after the floor had been thoroughly wiped up with the host?

KIT: You asked for it.

MANNY: I left you high, but hardly dry.

[*Kit goes to take a cigarette from the box on coffee table, looks at the brand . . .*]

KIT: Pardon me, while I read your cigarettes.

MANNY: [*Seriously*] I *am* hurt, damn it! By him and by you.

KIT: [*Passes him, crossing to bar*] Are you going to sulk?

[*She investigates the cigarette box on the bar for another make.*]

MANNY: If I want to! Where's your escort?

KIT: My escort escorted me to the door and then escorted himself home.

MANNY: Where'd he take you—some gay bar?

KIT: [*Finds a cigarette*] Ah, my brand! [*Suddenly, she puts the cigarette back, shuts lid firmly*] Nope, Katie is going to be strong this year.

MANNY: He kissed you goodnight, of course. Kissy-wissy, cheeky-weeky.

KIT: No, Manny, we kissed *each other* goodnight. And not in the air and not on the cheeks and not, as you would so attractively put it—a big wet toilet plunger. Just a very dear, sincere kiss. [*A moment, then almost to herself:*] Lovely man.

MANNY: Oh, yes, splendid chap, sterling fellow—most loyal and devoted friend any shit like me ever cared to let down. I knew the two of you would like each other. I just didn't know you'd like each other so much.

KIT: Yeah . . . well . . . we liked each other a lot.

MANNY: What is it with you and him?! I've never seen you respond to anyone like that right off the bat—even *me*! It was a month before I could get you to look me in the eye, let alone the rest of it.

KIT: *Wrong*, Manny! I was in bed with you long before I ever looked you in the eye!

MANNY: He waltzed in and whammo!—instant eye contact and ten minutes later you're doing the foreplay two-step, Fred-and-Ginger style! Did I get the billing right?

KIT: [*Incredulous realization*] You're *jealous*!

[*Kit laughs to herself . . .*]

MANNY: [*Looking at his watch*] Do you know what time it is?

KIT: [*Picks up a balloon which has sagged to the floor*] Sometime after midnight. I know that because I had champagne at midnight.

[*She gives the balloon a little deliberate kick and it bounces away.*]

MANNY: You had champagne *before* midnight, too!

KIT: [*Crosses to bar*] Not much. Oh, look, there's some left. How about a tad?

MANNY: No, thank you.

KIT: [*Pouring herself a glass*] You know, I really quite like this stuff. I mean, for a person who doesn't like to drink, really.

MANNY: [*Looking at her*] For a person who doesn't like to dress, really—doesn't like to go on in public—doesn't like parties, loves their precious privacy, you certainly *have* changed. And I don't mean just your clothes!

KIT: [*Draining her glass, pouring another*] I'm a late bloomer. And when at last I bloom, *watch out!*

[*Kit belches. Quickly covers her mouth, giggles.*]

MANNY: I feel like I don't know who the fuck you are, anymore!

KIT: [*Confronting him*] When did you ever?! I *always* liked pretty clothes. And I always like putting them on when there was something to put them on for. Or *someone*. And I like taking them off, too. When there was something or someone to take them off for!

MANNY: You're pissed!

KIT: [*Coolly*] Not really. Oh, I probably shouldn't operate any heavy machinery.

MANNY: You've had too much Christmas!

KIT: [*She has another sip*] I'll have a non-stop, coast-to-coast headache tomorrow, but what the hell! I've always relished the special occasion, have I not?

MANNY: And this, I take it, is some special, special occasion?

KIT: You got it! You *so* got it! It isn't the way I thought it was going to be. It isn't why I packed this dress in so many reams of tissue paper I had to pay air freight! But tonight *is* an occasion! This *marks* something. This puts a period to a period of my life, if you catch my drift.

MANNY: Sounds like you didn't have a very good time.

KIT: That's what you'd like to think, I know! I know you, Manny—you have a shitty evening, so you want everyone else to, as well.

MANNY: You mean I didn't manage to ruin things after all?

KIT: Not in the least! In fact, you caused me to have one of the most pleasurable evenings I've had in a long, long, *very* long time! And, by the way, I still hate parties! *Hate 'em like rat remover!*

MANNY: Just the ones *I* took you to.

KIT: But as long as I can be in the middle of the melee with one person I really like, having a party all our own. Then it's fun!

[*She has picked up a noisemaker out of the silver top hot and blows it. It rolls out, extending almost to the tip of Manny's nose, makes a noise and rolls back.*]

MANNY: You're all wound-up tonight, aren't you? Wound-up like a goddamn Rolex!

KIT: Yeah, a gold Rolex, a *solid gold* Rolex in your particular case, which I happened to notice! And also in your particular case—a solid leather Gucci case with your initials on it—I also happened to notice a Louis Cartier tank watch.

MANNY: Go on, say it! Gone Rodeo Drive! Status Symbol Sam, that's me! That's what I clang together to make beautiful music to make beautiful money to pay your beautiful bills! My gold symbols and my gold balls!

KIT: *Solid* gold balls, if you please! Solid *monogrammed* gold balls! I rather liked the tank watch.

MANNY: [*Heatedly*] I love 'em all! And I love the Springs—that's *Palm* Springs to you, although you probably thought I meant the bed springs, which I happen to love, too! And I play tennis now and try to keep a tan so I'm no longer that attractive shade of bleu cheese I used to be in New York! And I watch my diet and work out in a gym . . .

KIT: Christ, you really know you're in Hollywood when you see Jews with muscles!

[*Manny picks up the shocking pink Christmas tree and hurls it across the room. It hits the wall, shattering the few pink ornaments.*]

KIT: That was too good for it!

MANNY: [*Heatedly*] You think you can reach me but you can't! You think *you* like privacy! HA! All you know how to do is crawl into a hole. I know how to crawl into myself. You know how to hide out, I know how to *deaden* out! So I never have to feel that awful feeling of what it is to be alive!

KIT: [*Calmly*] For a person who doesn't like confrontaions, you certainly have changed, too.

MANNY: Yeah, and my hands are shaking and my head is pounding and I feel like my hair's on fire!

KIT: *You, you, you!* Do you ever read a book or a newspaper? Do you know what's going on in the world except what's going on with *you*?! Do you ever discuss anything? And I don't mean talk about yourself! You are, without a doubt, the most selfish, self-involved, self-absorbed son-of-a-bitch I have ever known. It's a wonder you aren't cross-eyed from contemplating your navel!

MANNY: And you! Giving of your perfect self to the point of treachery! It's impossible to live with a goddamn saint!

KIT: [*Lightly*] I think it's time to swim ashore.

[*Kit starts for the stairs. Manny stops her.*]

MANNY: You set standards no one can live up to! You guarantee it that you're going to be let down, betrayed. It's built-in from the start. Somebody's got to fall short of the mark sometime and when they do, *look out!* You're just sitting there, primed to be devasted—to take it personally!

KIT: I don't know where I got the idea that if you don't allow someone to shit all over you, you're being rude.

[*Kit goes up the stairs . . .*]

MANNY: Where're you going?

KIT: To bed. Alone. And you, Manny, *quo vadis?*

MANNY: [*After a moment*] I'm circlin' the drain. Without you, I'm going nowhere.

KIT: [*Continuing*] Well, I'm traveling light. I'm going back to the back woods of Connecticut—back where I belong.

MANNY: [*Runs to the railing*] Oh, Kit, come back to *me!* You don't have to leave tomorrow . . . wait . . . stay . . . stay with *me!* Live with me! Marry me again!

[*Kit stops, turns back to Manny.*]

MANNY: I'll die if we don't get back together. Without you, I'll wither up and blow away.

KIT: You might think you will, but you won't. That's how I always felt when the Wall-Of-Silence got built—panicked that I was going to fall apart if I wasn't able to pull you back. But I survived. And you will, too. You'll get through.

[*She turns and goes up a few stairs, but he grabs her hand over the railing.*]

MANNY: But I've *changed*, Kit! And I want to change more! The only thing that *hasn't* changed is that I still love you.

KIT: [*Sincerely*] And I still love you, Manny. And I always will. But sometimes love just isn't enough.

[*Manny releases her hand.*]

KIT: I have to try too hard with you. There ought to be some little something that just naturally comes from loving someone—some gentle, effortless benefit—something that innately, ineffably enriches—that is graciously given on its own. It shouldn't have to be such hard work *all* the time. So relentlessly uphill. So patently unrewarding. Something must be shared—a thought, a laugh, half the weary load. I've changed, too, Manny. And not just my clothes.

MANNY: [*A bit stunned*] Oh, I can see that. I can *really* see that. But, Kit, some things about you I hope will never change.

KIT: Like?

MANNY: Like the way you watch me—when I'm talking to another woman, or when I'm kissing the children goodnight. There's that split second glance that let's me know there's something special that goes on with no one else but the two of us. I treasure that conspiracy.

KIT: [*Softly*] I treasure it, too.

MANNY: Would someone else ever understand that?

KIT: Not *our* secret. But with someone else, perhaps we'd have a new and special secret with them.

MANNY: Yeah, but it wouldn't be as terrific as ours.

KIT: Who can say? I would hope so. The Other Woman and The Other Man are not necessarily out of the question. And they're not necessarily just jerks or fools.

MANNY: Wendy is no fool but she's out of the question! And Nick *is* a jerk and he's *absolutely* out of the question!

KIT: And you and I are out of the question. And no two jerks have acted more foolishly than we have, and there's no question that we love each other—it's just an unworkable love. And we both have to face it.

[*Kit starts to go, but Manny immediately speaks, stopping her one more time . . .*]

MANNY: I talked to Josh.

KIT: [*Quietly*] Thank you. I'm proud of you. I really am, Manny. I know it wasn't easy for you.

[*Manny nods modestly, pleased that he has pleased her . . .*]

MANNY: [*Earnestly*] Come on, now, Kit, gimme a "Y," gimme an "E," gimme an "S-Oh-S"! Oh, Kit, I'll be there for you! With *balloons,* if you like. With a *band!* with *bells!* Ring-ring-ring!!

[*The doorbell begins to RING. . .*]

MANNY: [*Non-plussed*] Who the hell is *that?*

KIT: Well, it's about a year too early for Santa.

MANNY: [*Fuming, crosses to door*] Well, if it's fucking Father Time, his timing is shit, too! I know who it is! Mr. Half-The-Weary-Load!!

KIT: You mean, Colin???

[*Manny tears open the front door to reveal Nick . . .*]

NICK: Kit!

KIT: *Nick*!!!

MANNY: Oh, my God, it's "Good Goods"!!! [*Hysterically*] Go-back-go-back-go-back!!!

[*Manny immediately ties to slam the door but Nick steps in and is half caught with Manny wildly pushing it against him. Nick starts to yell and force the door back . . .*]

KIT: [*Racing down the stairs*] Manny, stop! You're hurting him!

MANNY: *I'm trying to KILL him!*

[*Kit runs to tug at Manny long enough for Nick to recover and push the door back forcefully, sending both Kit and Manny to the floor. Nick rushes to Kit . . .*]

NICK: [*Realizes what he's done*] Ohh, Kit, I'm sorry! Are you hurt?!

[*Nick helps her up. Manny is scrambling to his feet . . .*]

KIT: What are you doing here? I just got balloons from you!

[*Manny fiercely grabs the huge bouquet of balloons, hopelessly tangling himself in the strings as he smashes them, kicks them, stomps them . . .*]

MANNY: *Yeah, here, take these fucking things and go round the world in them!!!*

NICK: [*Re: Manny*] *I knew he was going to do something tricky so I knew I had to do something tricky, too!!!*

MANNY: *GET-OUT-GET-OUT-GET-OUT!!!*

[*Manny, tangled in the balloons, comes at Nick again, tackles him and they tumbles into the "bouquet," popping the balloons like firecrackers with their weight . . .*]

KIT: *Oh, Manny, stop it!!! Both of you, stop it!!!*

[*Kit now helps Nick to his feet while Manny remains more ensnarled than ever . . .*]

NICK: Kit, come with me! I've got a taxi waiting outside!

MANNY: [*Condescendingly*] A *taxi*?! How very "old money" of you!

NICK: [*To Kit*] Please, darling!

KIT: Oh, Nick, I can't. Besides, there's not a flight till morning. The kids and I are already booked on it!

NICK: I've chartered a plane to take us all to Palm Springs!

MANNY: Oh, so you like the Springs, too!

NICK: [*To Kit, intensely*] We can be married there. We can have our honeymoon there. Start the New Year there. Our new life together!

KIT: Oh, Nick, I can't! Can't you see I can't?

NICK: I'll wait outside till you pack. Till you and the kids get ready!

KIT: [*After a moment, simply*] I can't because I don't love you.

[*Silence. Manny watches them breathlessly . . .*]

NICK: [*Crestfallen*] Well, that *does* make a difference. It doesn't make it impossible, it just makes a difference.

KIT: Oh, Nick, you don't want *me*. You'll meet someone else. You've had so many wives, I know you can find one more.

NICK: What are you *talking* about?! I've been married *once*!

KIT: But you were engaged to those others.

NICK: *Others*? I've been engaged twice. Once to the woman I married and once to you!

MANNY: Well, that's *plural*! So that's *others*!

*[Kit takes off the diamond earrings . . .]*

KIT: Nick, you're a wonderful person. Better than all of us. My mother loves you.

MANNY: Yeah, so why don't you marry her mother?

NICK: *[Directly to Manny]* Because I don't love her mother!

MANNY: Well, neither do I.

KIT: And neither do I. Well, I love her and I hate her, if you know what I mean.

MANNY: *[To Nick, shrugs]* Yeah, the usual.

KIT: *[Sincerely, to Nick]* You have no idea how truly sorry I am that this couldn't work out . . . but it would be a mistake. It would be a lie.

NICK: A lie?

KIT: *[Nods]* Well, I know I'd be lying to myself. And I don't ever want to lie to *you*— *[Quickly]* or to myself, if I can help it. *[Puts the earrings in his hand]* I hope this new year holds for you . . . all the things you deserve. But I know I'm not one of them.

NICK: Do you love Manny?

*[Kit looks at Manny. He returns her look expectantly.]*

KIT: Yes. I always have and I always will. But it was a mistake to marry him, too, and I'll never, ever make that mistake again.

*[Manny 's face sags.]*

MANNY: *[Swallows dryly]* I'm dehydrated.

NICK: I'm not surprised. All that foaming at the mouth.

*[Nick looks at Kit a long moment, turns and silently goes out. Kit slowly closes the door. Manny quickly goes to the bar, quickly pours himself a glass of champagne, chug-a-lugs it.]*

*[Kit crosses to the stairs and begins to ascend them again . . .]*

MANNY: *[Turning]* Kit, wait! Listen to me!! I'll try to open up and you try to be less perfect. Now I ask you, what could beat that combination?

KIT: *[Stops; sweetly and directly]* Nothing.

MANNY: Yeah, *nothing!*

KIT: But let's be honest. Even at that, do you know what hell it would be?

MANNY: I'm afraid I do.

KIT: I'm afraid I do, too. Goodnight, Manny. And, once more with feeling . . . goodbye.

[*Kit smiles at him, turns and goes up the rest of the stairs and OFF.*]

[*Manny watches her until she is gone. He turns away from the stairs, facing the audience, trying to think what to do. Suddenly, he goes to the phone, punches a number, and while it's ringing, he consults a telephone book.*]

MANNY: [*Into phone*] Music Express? Charlie? Yeah, hi, it's Manny, happy New Year! Listen, I want to cancel a limo I booked for tomorrow morning to take my family to the airport. No, they're not going. Decided they like it here so much they're gonna stay. Yeah, how about that! Yeah, thanks a lot.— [*Hangs up. Referring to number in phone book, punching it into phone:*] Hello, American Airlines? I want to cancel a reservation for three on your eight a.m. flight to New York. Sure, I'll hold on. You never talked to anybody who'd be so thrilled to hold on.

[*Manny smiles to himself . . .*]


CURTAIN

# FOR REASONS THAT REMAIN UNCLEAR

For
**Millie and Toby Rowland**
on the occasion of their
fiftieth wedding anniversary—
without whose instigation,
encouragement, and love . . .

*For Reasons That Remain Unclear* was first presented on November 9, 1993, at the Olney Theatre, Olney, Md., James A. Petosa and Bill Graham Jr., producing directors. The scenery was designed by James Wolk, the lighting was by Howard Werner, and the play was directed by John Going.

The original cast was:

| | |
|---|---|
| PATRICK | *Philip Anglim* |
| CONRAD | *Ken Ruta* |
| WAITER | *Fred Iacova* |

*At rise, the stage is dark and uninhabited. Through a floor-length window center right, the intense violet light of a dying summer day—poised between late afternoon and early evening—slowly fades up to "half" to partially reveal a light wood-paneled bed/sitting room in the Hassler Hotel in Rome.*

*Brocade portieres with sheer center curtains cover the tall glass doors which open onto a shallow balcony overlooking the Piazza Di Spagna. The exterior shutters are folded back, admitting the refracted iridescence. The glass doors are slightly open, and a gentle breeze stirs the gauzy fabric, casting soft patterns across the heavily shadowed interior.*

*Upstage left on a wide raised platform, there is a double bed with its covers and linen sheets neatly turned down. The headboard and dust ruffle are of the same brocade as the draperies. On either side of the bed, there are built-in night tables above which there are brass "extension" wall lamps in mirrored panels, presently not illuminated. On the stage-right table there is a bottle of mineral water and a tumbler on a tray. On the stage-left table there is a panel of service buttons.*

*Along the left wall is a chest of drawers with a Venetian-style mirror above it. On top of the chest, there is a handsome toiletry case and various smart toilet articles in evidence—cologne, talcum, a comb and brush. A door center left leads to a marble-walled bath. Luxurious towels, featuring the name and logo of the hotel, can be seen folded over a brass warming rack.*

*Downstage of the bathroom door, against the wall, there is a luggage stand with an expensive suitcase on it. Out from the wall, almost at the curtain line, there is a low drumlike upholstered dressing stool.*

*Within wood-paneled arches, supported by slender marble columns, in the up-center-right and stage-right walls of the sitting area, there are unlit Venetian-style glass sconces with half shades. Standing away from the walls, there is a brocade settee facing front, a brocade lounge chair angled stage right of it, and a low drinks/coffee table before them.*

*All the wooden pieces of furniture are reproductions of traditional Italian designs of the eighteenth century. The upholstered ones are of the fascist period.*

*A man's pale gray linen suit on a Hassler clothes hanger is neatly folded over the back of a chair. In a flat wicker basket on the seat of the settee, there are some stacks of colorful shirts and some white silk boxer-style undershorts which have been returned from the hotel laundry. The basket is covered with a piece of paper on top of which sits a pair of freshly shined Italian loafers.*

*The door to the public corridor is upstage center. After a moment, it is unlocked from the outside. It is a bolt of the European variety, which requires several revolutions of the key. Presently, two male figures enter, silhouetted to the audience by the light spill from the hallway. Even in the chiaroscuro, it is apparent that the first man is in dark apparel, the second in light-colored clothing, and that both are wearing sunglasses. The second is laden with shopping bags from smart stores on the Via Condotti.*

*It is just after six p.m., and a nearby church bell is ringing the Angelus.*

FIRST MAN: [*Crossing to balcony, with enthusiasm*] Dio mio, as they say, just look at that view! Oh, I was hoping your room would be on the front of the hotel and have a view of the steps and piazza!

[*He parts the sheers, widens the doors, and scans the view. A long shaft of cool, purplish light bisects the room. Street sounds rush in. The bells louden. The second man closes the entry and goes through the shadows to deposit the shopping bags on the bed*]

Magnificent! Is that the dome of St. Peter's in the distance? What am I saying—of course it is! [*Pointing*] I'm staying just to the right of it. My God, that's a heavenly sight!

[*The second man stands silently observing the first man for a moment before snapping on the lamp on the night table, introducing a small pool of warm, rosy light to the area surrounding him. In spite of his dark glasses, he is revealed to be in his early forties, trim and average-looking, but well-groomed in a creased ecru linen suit and soft white shirt without a tie*]

SECOND MAN: Yes. And magic hour, to boot. Very picture-postcard, don't you think?

[*The first man, at the balcony window, observing the view [through his sunglasses], turns inside to reveal that he is in his late fifties, dressed in the black garb and Roman collar of a priest*]

FIRST MAN: Oh, if only I could stamp and mail this moment! [*Turns back to react to bells tolling*] And just listen, Patrick . . . the Angelus, so *near you* can almost touch it!

PATRICK: [SECOND MAN] Mmm. Almost, but not quite.

FIRST MAN: Is it coming from Trinità dei Monti next door?

PATRICK: Too far away for that, Father.

FIRST MAN: [*Faces Patrick again*] Now, please, do call me Conrad. Father sounds so . . .

PATRICK: Paternal?

CONRAD: [FIRST MAN] *Respectful!*

PATRICK: [*Putting room key in side jacket pocket*] You must take off your sunglasses so you can really get the full-tilt "schmear."

CONRAD: [*Re: sunglasses*] Ohh! Had them on so long I completely forgot! Wear them all the time in California. I really don't like the sun much.

PATRICK: Well, then, you live in the wrong place if you don't like to be sun-kissed.

CONRAD: Maybe it's something I inherited from my mother. She never liked the sun. Said she couldn't see for the light! [*Picking up from before*] The full-tilt *what?*

PATRICK: Schmear. The whole deal.

CONRAD: [*Comprehending*] Oh. That's not Italian, is it?

PATRICK: Yiddish.

CONRAD: Oh. [*Removes his glasses, turns back to luxuriate in the view*] Oh, oh, oh, oh, *ohhhhh!*—Well, yes, that *does* make a difference! Now I can really see what's going on! [*Turns back to Patrick, who now slowly takes off his glasses*]

PATRICK: And now we can see each other too. [*Dryly*] And not through rose-colored glasses.

CONRAD: [*Laughs*] Yes, finally! I couldn't make out your eyes behind your shades at lunch. From here they look blue. Very, very blue.

PATRICK: They're green. It's the light playing tricks. [*Looks away*] And *your* eyes are . . .

CONRAD: Bloodshot, probably, after all that wonderful wine!

PATRICK: [*Staring off*] Brown. Dark, dark brown.

CONRAD: It's the black Irish in me. I must say, you have better sight than I do. [*Re bells*] Ahh, just listen to that! Such a clean sound. [*Turns out, listens; after a moment*] Where do you think it's coming from, San Silvestro? Or one of the churches in the Piazza del Popolo?

PATRICK: Who knows? In this town church bells ring like telephones.

[*Patrick moves around to the other side of the bed as Conrad steps back into the room. Patrick begins to empty the shopping bags and put the contents away (Armani trousers, Gucci agenda boxes, brand-name cologne bags, and a Cartier watch case)*]

CONRAD: Such a treat, isn't it?—coming from Los Angeles, where you never hear church bells at all!

PATRICK: [*Aside*] Mmm. The lost Angelus of Los Angeles.

CONRAD: [*Chuckles*] Isn't that odd?

PATRICK: [*Wryly*] One more odd thing.

CONRAD: You mean about L.A.? Or our both *being* from L.A.?

PATRICK: That too.

CONRAD: Absolutely incredible! Imagine, meeting each other halfway round the world! [*Turns to the open window, listens*] Such a reassuring sound! We're really cheated in L.A. It's so spread-out, we can't even experience one of the most reassuring things in the world.

PATRICK: For me, one of the most reassuring things in the world is a plate of pasta.

CONRAD: [*Hesitates, then laughs*] Well, then, you're in the *right* place!

PATRICK: And so are you if it's ding-donging that you find reassuring.

[*Conrad becomes aware that Patrick is staring at him, turns toward him as they both listen to the bells for a moment*]

CONRAD: There's that faraway look of yours again. What are you thinking, if I may ask? You seem lost.

PATRICK: [*Focusing*] Forgive me. [*After a moment, agreeably*] I must admit, I too love to hear bells tolling. But for some reason the sound always makes me sad.

CONRAD: Sad?

PATRICK: It's a melancholy sound. But, at least, a bell is something civilized man has made when he's made so many terrible things.

CONRAD: The call of angels.

PATRICK: A bell is an elegant . . . noble creation—as admirable as the quaint little rituals man's invented for ringing his brainchild.

CONRAD: [*Amused*] You mean a "quaint little ritual" like the Angelus.

PATRICK: That too. The Angelus, the time of day, New Year's. All ring-out-the-news occasions are all the same to me, no matter what. And no matter how joyous—even if it were the end of a war—I don't know, it's a plaintive sound.

CONRAD: Funny—I think just the opposite. Even a bell tolling at a funeral is a joyous sound to me. I remember that, when my mother died, thinking that she was so much better off.

PATRICK: Well, I do find a death knell joyous! *You* think it's just the beginning of something. *I* think it's joyous because it's the end. *Finally! Over! Hallelujah!*—I *hope!*

CONRAD: Now, don't tell me you don't believe in the hereafter.

PATRICK: Let's just say, I believe in the *future*.

CONRAD: And when we die?

PATRICK: I can't conceive of what might be in store, but I hope that when this is over, *that's it.* I don't want any more. Bad or good. And how good can it get? I can't think of anything more maddening than an eternal orgasm.

[*Conrad chuckles a bit self-consciously. Patrick snaps on the left bedside lamp, widening the warm circle of light*]

CONRAD: Nice little room you have here!

PATRICK: It's majestic. But I call it home. [*The Angelus ceases as Patrick comes around the bed and crosses to the panel in the upstage wall, right of the corridor door . . . Indicates*] Please . . . sit anywhere you like.

CONRAD: Thank you.

PATRICK: [*Re suit and basket on the settee*] That is, anywhere you can find a seat. Here, let me get the laundry out of the way.

CONRAD: It must cost a fortune to stay here.

[*Conrad crosses from the window toward the settee . . .*]

PATRICK: Well, I'm not paying for it, the brothers Warner are. And, *yes* . . . it costs a *fortune* to stay here. [*Conrad laughs as Patrick snaps on a wall switch, illuminating the sconces, which infuse the stage right sitting area with the same rosy glow as stage left. Crossing down behind settee*] Sorry things are messy.

[*Conrad has reached the chair first, picks up the hanger with the pale linen suit . . .*]

CONRAD: Such beautiful clothes.

PATRICK: As you've probably heard—they make the man.

[*Patrick leans over the settee to pick up the wicker basket of laundry with the shoes on top and takes the hanger from Conrad*]

CONRAD: Such beautiful shoes.

PATRICK: If the shoe fits, charge it!

[*Patrick goes to the bed, puts down the wicker basket, picks up the shoes and takes them to the upholstered dressing stool, drops them on top of it, and takes the suit of clothes into the bathroom*]

CONRAD: [*During the above*] You should see *my* room!—Like the inside of a crashed plane! Compared to me, you're the very soul of immaculacy.

PATRICK: [*Offstage*] "The soul of immaculacy!" That sounds so Catholic—when all I am is anal-compulsive. Anyway, it's all show. Inside, I'm . . . well . . .

CONRAD: What?

PATRICK: [*Offstage*] Like the inside of a crashed plane. You say you're staying on the right side of St. Peter's?

[*Conrad settles on the left arm of the settee*]

CONRAD: Well, I always try to stay on the right side. [*Chuckles*] A big old palazzo which is a convent now. The nuns are away for the summer. Of course, my room is nothing grand like this.

[*Patrick reenters, goes to pick up the pair of loafers on top of the dressing stool, and sits down on it. He starts to take off his shoes and put on the loafers*]

PATRICK: The first time I came to Rome I stayed in a place laughingly called the Grande Hotel—not the famous, fancy one near the Piazza della Repùbblica—a little dump in Trastevere. It was so awful, in fact, that I stumbled home pissed-out-of-my-mind one night, took a Magic Marker, and in front of the name, I printed the words "Not Very." The *padrona* wasn't at all thrilled I'd rechristened his establishment the "Not Very Grande Hotel."

[*Conrad laughs. Patrick finishes changing shoes*]

PATRICK: [*Re loafers*] Ouu, does that feel better! *My* mother always used to say there's nothing that relaxes you like changing your shoes. Would you like a pair of slippers? I just charged some very smart velour ones the other day. We look to be about the same size.

CONRAD: [*Hesitantly*] Oh, no, I don't think . . .

PATRICK: [*Gets up*] Please. Get comfortable and stay awhile.

CONRAD: [*Relenting*] Well, I have been on my feet since dawn. You walk much more in Rome than in New York even. And, of course, in L.A. you never walk anywhere at all.

[*Patrick exits into the bath, taking his original pair of shoes with him as Conrad crosses to the dressing stool . . .*]

CONRAD: If you've been here three months and the movie studio is paying for it, why haven't you rented a place?

[*Patrick returns with a pair of black velour slippers. Conrad starts to take the slippers from Patrick, but Patrick puts his hand on Conrad's shoulder and gently pushes him down on the stool, then kneels before him and begins to unlace his shoes . . .*]

PATRICK: [*During the above*] I'm a hotel boy. Love hotels. Lived in the Algonquin for four years.

CONRAD: The Algonquin? Oh, yes. The place with the famous table.

[*Patrick removes Conrad's shoes and puts the slippers on his feet*]

PATRICK: Checked in one night when a play of mine was in rehearsal. The play closed, but I stayed on. And on and on. Till the money ran out. To me, being in a hotel is like being in a wonderful hospital where all the doctors and nurses are dressed up in disguise as waiters and maids. Room service is my idea of therapy!

CONRAD: [*Re Patrick's action*] You make a pretty good valet!

PATRICK: [*Wryly*] You're a servant of the Lord, and I'm a servant of the servant of the Lord. [*Finishing*] There now. Isn't that better?

CONRAD: Ohh my, yes!

PATRICK: Good.

CONRAD: [*Re: slippers but also glancing at Patrick*] Very handsome, indeed.

PATRICK: Yes, I liked them so much I took them in every color, but the black seems to suit you. And speaking of room service—what can I offer you?

[*Patrick takes Conrad's shoes, stands, and crosses to place them neatly beneath the luggage rack. Conrad rises and walks around in a circle, getting the feel of the slippers, ending up down right*]

CONRAD: I really shouldn't have any more.

PATRICK: Not even a coffee?

CONRAD: Well, I wouldn't say no to a coffee before I go.

PATRICK: I never say no to a coffee when I'm in Italy. It never tastes the same anywhere else in the world, I don't know why.

CONRAD: Well, you're a connoisseur. Man about several towns.

PATRICK: I'm just a country boy. Shucks, what do I know?

CONRAD: Some country boy! You like your Italian coffee in Italy, your French fries in France . . .

PATRICK: [*A droll sigh*] My Turkish baths in Turkey.

CONRAD: You say that so wearily.

PATRICK: I say that nostalgically. [*Changing subject*] Now, about that coffee.

CONRAD: [*Looks at his watch*] You're sure you have the time?

PATRICK: I have nothing but time. That's why I invited you back. You said you like Sambuca?

CONRAD: [*Relenting*] Yes, I do. I probably shouldn't have any more, but— well, yes, an espresso will send me on my way. And a *liquore*. Is that how you say it?

[*Patrick starts to cross to the panel of service buttons on the stage left bedside table*]

PATRICK: [*En route*] Sounds good to me. I'll ring for the floor waiter.

CONRAD: In a moment, if that's all right. [*Patrick stops, looks at Conrad. Conrad moves back to the window. Re: view*] I'd just like to take all this in a bit longer.

PATRICK: No rush. We'll just go *piano-piano*.

CONRAD: Did you learn to speak Italian just by being here?

PATRICK: Oh, I don't speak it. Even after years of coming here.

CONRAD: You did very well at lunch.

PATRICK: Menu Italian, that's all. I have no talent for languages. I put the sin in syntax.

CONRAD: [*Smiles*] But it's obvious you have a talent for living. Thanks again for the extravagant meal! I like eating late. So long and leisurely. And for the drinks on the way back at the Caffè Greco.

PATRICK: Meals are included in the deal.

CONRAD: Lunch was on the brothers Warner?

PATRICK: [*Nods*] Mmmm. And it cost them a *fortune!*

CONRAD: [*Chuckles*] Well, I thank you anyway. You're very gracious and hospitable. You spare no expense.

PATRICK: It's almost impossible for me to do anything cheap. Almost. Especially with other people's money.

CONRAD: [*Laughs*] God bless that expense account!

PATRICK: [*Grimly*] Believe me, Father, it's small compensation for what one is put through.

CONRAD: Please. Call me Conrad. [*Patrick doesn 't respond. Expansively*] Seriously, this has all been such a treat! And all in Rome. As close as you can get to heaven! The Holy City, the holiday, the high life!

PATRICK: A real summer cruise.

CONRAD: Oh, and am I dreading when the boat docks. I'll never forget this trip. It's made such an impression on me.

PATRICK: Funny how some things make an impression and others make no impression at all—like, do you remember where you were when Reagan was shot?

CONRAD: I must admit, I get excited by all these luxuries which seem to exhaust you.

PATRICK: Please, don't misunderstand. It's writing to the dictates of a committee that gets me down. It's the traditional, time-honored, fraudulent, formulaic bullshit of Hollywood that wears me out. Not what it can pay for.

CONRAD: [*Chuckles*] No respect for writers or the written word?

PATRICK: Hollywood: nothing but brilliantly packaged lies.

CONRAD: Hollywood must package what it packages for a reason.

PATRICK: Lies sell tickets. Shit sells.

CONRAD: If it upsets you, why do you stay in such a profession?

PATRICK: [*Gestures about the room*] I make a very good living selling shit.

CONRAD: You sound bitter.

PATRICK: [*Wryly*] As bitter as that Campari you had before lunch. [*After a moment*] Funny how everything you place your trust in turns around and dumps on you.

CONRAD: I hope you don't believe that's always the case.

PATRICK: Sorry if it sounds a tad self-pitying, but I think it's been the case for me.

CONRAD: I'd say it sounds more cynical.

PATRICK: I'm not ashamed of being cynical. I think being cynical is just being realistic. [*Sits on the edge of the bed platform; with a heaviness*] I must say, I'm bone-tired of the grind-of-it-all. Exhausted by the last go-round with this script. Believe me, it takes a velour slipper now and then to keep one's spirits up.

CONRAD: Of course, I don't know anything about how true show business is—but from the outside, it always *looks* and *sounds* glamorous.

PATRICK: I suppose it can be, but most of the time it's just like anything else—very hard work. People in the entertainment business work hard at putting on a show for those who've worked hard all day and need to be entertained. And them that totes the weary load see a show and look at all the so-called glamorous entertainers having what looks like a lot of fun. And these glum folks with their noses pressed against the glass think they're missing out on something—when all they're missing out on is the very thing they're sick and tired of—hard work. In the end it's a joke all the way round. Everyone working hard and, most of the time, not having much fun. And everyone fed up and longing for something that doesn't exist. That's show business, and that's life.

CONRAD: You *are* cynical. But life can be wonderful. This day has been wonderful for me. And I wish it had been for you too. After all, we have a lot in common.

PATRICK: Such as?

CONRAD: When the weary come to me, I don't entertain them, but I try to send them off refreshed . . . and not with lies, of course, but with the truth.

PATRICK: There's a market for everything. You sell your brand of shit, and I'll sell mine.

[*Silence. After a moment, Conrad stands . . .*]

CONRAD: May I indulge in my little vice?

PATRICK: What?

[*Conrad takes a pack of cigarettes from a side pocket of his jacket . . .*]

CONRAD: May I smoke in here?

PATRICK: Of course.

[*Patrick gets up off the bed platform, goes to pick up an ashtray from the chest of drawers and crosses to Conrad, placing it on the low table*]

CONRAD: [*Re ashtray*] Smoking in the restaurant—well, in that little enclosure of hedges on the street—that was one thing, but in your bedroom . . .

PATRICK: Oh, I don't care. When in Rome . . .

[*Conrad laughs. Patrick takes a matchbook from the ashtray, lights Conrad's cigarette*]

CONRAD: [*Re the light*] Thank you.

PATRICK: Living in L.A., I think it really would be hypocritical of me to get all bent out of shape about the quality of *air*.

CONRAD: Oh, but you know how people can be about secondary smoke. Actually, we're back where we started—fifty years ago we had to go behind the barn to do it, and that's where we have to go again!

[*Patrick goes to the bed to remove the paper from the wicker basket and gather up a few shirts. He crosses down left to open the top of the suitcase on the luggage rack and begins to pack them. Conrad takes a long drag on his cigarette*]

PATRICK: Do sit down and make yourself comfortable. I'm sorry, but did you tell me why you're in town?

CONRAD: In town? You mean the *Vatican*?

PATRICK: And environs.

CONRAD: You know, there were times at lunch when I believe I completely lost your attention.

PATRICK: I apologize if I drifted off. Staring into space is one of my favorite things.

CONRAD: No need to apologize, you weren't rude at all. I just had the impression that sometimes we weren't really connecting.

PATRICK: Actually, my thoughts never left you for a moment—even when I got lost in them.

CONRAD: I hope you don't mind my saying so, you struck me the same way when I approached you on the street and spoke to you. You seemed to be just standing there in your own world.

PATRICK: [*After a moment*] Yes, you sort of woke me up—I couldn't have written a better scene.

CONRAD: It *was* a bit like a movie, wasn't it?

PATRICK: Mmm. A real meet-cute.

CONRAD: A *what*?

PATRICK: Meet-cute. I suppose the classic example is when Claudette Colbert meets Gary Cooper shopping for pajamas. She only sleeps in the tops, and he only sleeps in the bottoms, so they buy one pair and split them. They meet-cute. And, it goes without saying, live happily ever after.

CONRAD: Ohh. And *our* scenario?

PATRICK: Let's see. Ohh, American religious, lost in the Holy City, looking for God or whatever—and along comes Godless American, lost in his head, looking for God knows what.

CONRAD: [*Chuckles*] I see. We met-cute.

PATRICK: Well, close but no pajamas. And who knows where the story goes from there.

CONRAD: Well, I, for one, hope we know each other happily ever after. Imagine! The first person I stop in that maze of little alleyways to ask directions was another American from Los Angeles who knows his way around like a native! What are the chances of that?

PATRICK: Slim.

CONRAD: Just imagine!

PATRICK: But the *world* is just a maze of little alleyways, isn't it? We might have bumped into each other anywhere.

CONRAD: Or we might not have.

PATRICK: Or we might not have.

CONRAD: Now that I've met you, Patrick, I do hate to think of that.

PATRICK: Who can fight fate? Now, remind me why you're here.

CONRAD: Well, actually I'm here on business, but it's been a lifelong dream to see this city. St. Peter's city—the rock upon which the church is built. But no harm in mixing a little business with pleasure.

PATRICK: Oh, yes, pleasure. I was focused for that part. And the business?

CONRAD: I'm attending a conference.

PATRICK: [*Groans*] Ohh, conferences. I must have been staring into space for that part.

[*Patrick turns his attention to the laundry on the bed, goes to it*]

CONRAD: A series of lectures, actually.

PATRICK: Contraception, women priests, gay rights, that sort of thing?

CONRAD: [*Laughs*] Well, not quite. Not yet!

PATRICK: Maybe on your next trip.

CONRAD: If I ever come back.

PATRICK: Maybe by then celibacy will be out and priests will be married. If that's their bent.

CONRAD: I must admit I'm more for tradition. I'm one of those who even wish it were all still in Latin.

PATRICK: Well, lots of luck and *Dominus Vobiscum*.

CONRAD: In my opinion, celibacy isn't going to go so easily. Because in many ways, I think it is a good thing.

PATRICK: Name one.

CONRAD: Well . . . it keeps a man from having to think about so many things that have nothing to do with his vocation.

PATRICK: Oh, come on, Father. Celibacy never stopped one human being from thinking about things he shouldn't be thinking about.

[*Conrad gets up, stubs out his cigarette in the ashtray on the low table and crosses toward Patrick. Patrick takes part of the stack of shirts and moves away from the right side of the bed before Conrad reaches him. Conrad studies the contents of the wicker basket. Patrick crosses from the suitcase back to the left side of the bed, standing opposite Conrad, and scoops up the rest of the shirts*]

CONRAD: Beautiful shirts. Like so many Easter eggs.

PATRICK: I try to get a little color in my life.

CONRAD: Beautifully finished.

PATRICK: They're brilliant at washing and ironing in this country. It's still done the old-fashioned way with such care and thoughtfulness, it's almost like forgiveness!

CONRAD: Extraordinary undershorts.

PATRICK: [*Smiles, crosses back to suitcase*] They're lavish.

CONRAD: Silk?

PATRICK: Mmm, pure silk. *Seta pura.*

CONRAD: Italian, of course.

PATRICK: [*Nods*] Local threads.

[*Patrick takes a handful of the silk shorts and goes back to the suitcase. Conrad comes closer to the bed and extends a hand to finger the edges of a remaining pair of silk shorts*]

CONRAD: Custom-made?

PATRICK: Just the shirts. The shorts are from the shirtmaker's marvelous little haberdashery. Wonderful robes and scarves—*slippers,* of course, and . . . oh, I don't know, odd things.

CONRAD: Beautiful.

[*Conrad withdraws his hand as Patrick returns and collects the rest of the shorts and transfers them to the suitcase. Conrad turns and begins to slowly circle the sitting area of the suite, up right behind the settee. Patrick closes the suitcase and goes to take the empty wicker basket off the bed and put it on the top of the chest of drawers. He looks up into the mirror to watch Conrad as he takes out his pack of cigarettes, removes one, and lights it, stopping at the window to blow out the match and toss it over the balcony. He puts the pack in his inside breast pocket*]

CONRAD (CONT'D): The Italians really know how to do it, don't they?

PATRICK: They do, indeed.

CONRAD: Wonderful style in everything.

PATRICK: They're really with-it about the general *presentation* of life. Which is *love,* I suppose.

CONRAD: [*Looks out at the city*] Yes, it seems to be in the air here.

PATRICK: Sort of secondary, you might say. You just breathe it. Good for every organ.

[*Conrad laughs, turns back, and goes to the ashtray on the lower table*]

CONRAD: [*Crushing his cigarette*] Enough of this self-pollution! I think I'll just get used to inhaling *amore*.

PATRICK: Ah, yes, *amore*. I suck up as much as I can.

CONRAD: That restaurant really did it with love. You could breathe that. It was palpable.

PATRICK: It was the garlic. A little too much garlic, actually. That restaurant really used to be much better. It's changed over the years. Like everything.

CONRAD: [*Jovially but a bit sadly*] And everyone.

PATRICK: [*Looking at Conrad*] Exactly. [*Turns to look at himself in a mirror*] Getting old is the worst.

CONRAD: You're not old. *I'm* old.

PATRICK: [*Turns away from mirror*] The truth is, I've always felt like I was never young.

CONRAD: Really? Why?

PATRICK: Ohh, my childhood was sort of short-circuited by . . . circumstances. [*Turns back to mirror*] But now I can actually see myself falling to bits. It's the visual-of-it-all that's so disconcerting.

[*Patrick now turns from the mirror as if he cannot bear to look at himself. A pause. Conrad goes to the window again and looks out*]

CONRAD: Things can be beautiful *because* of their age. Just look at this city.

PATRICK: When *I'm* three thousand years old, *I* should look so good! I heard an Englishwoman on the street the other day, looking up at the Villa Medici and saying quite forlornly, "It wants a coat of paint."

[*Conrad laughs pleasantly, looks at Patrick, who again looks at himself in the mirror*]

PATRICK: *I* could use a coat of paint.

CONRAD: Are you talking about covering up the truth?

PATRICK: What's the point? Not worth it.

[*Conrad turns to study the view out the balcony window*]

CONRAD: [*Turns to Patrick*] I really don't know what I'd have done if you hadn't come along this afternoon.

PATRICK: [*To Conrad, thoughtfully*] I don't know what I'd have done if *you* hadn't come along. Just carried on with my life in the same old way, I guess.

CONRAD: You didn't have any plans?

PATRICK: Still don't.

[*Conrad crosses to the armchair but does not sit*]

CONRAD: Surely you must have many friends here. Surely, you're not . . . well, you're not lonely. Are you?

PATRICK: Lonely?

CONRAD: For companionship.

[*Conrad takes a step toward the dressing stool. Then takes another. Patrick immediately gets up and crosses in a slow straight line across the stage, up behind the settee, until he reaches the balcony . . .*]

PATRICK: [*On the move*] I'm never lonely when I'm in this city. Even when I'm alone. Even when I'm lost in a labyrinth of streets. This is one of my favorite places on Earth. I've always felt secure here. Solo, but surrounded by love. I never feel more whole than when I'm in Rome.

CONRAD: I'm afraid there's a lot of the tourist in me. My first days here— whenever I was out alone and I heard someone speaking English, I'd always say hello.

PATRICK: I usually run for the nearest exit when I hear anyone speaking English.

[*Patrick turns from the window and crosses to the back of the settee, sits on it, one leg hiked up, facing Conrad . . .*]

CONRAD: But you didn't run when *I* spoke to you.

PATRICK: [*After a moment, directly*] You interest me.

CONRAD: You're an intriguing fellow yourself, Patrick.

PATRICK: [*Flatly*] I'm strange. And I know it.

CONRAD: [*Chuckles*] I think all of us are stranger than we let on.

PATRICK: I'm stranger than you'd think, Father.

CONRAD: You'd never know it to look at you.

PATRICK: Or to look at *you*. [*Conrad laughs uncomfortably*] I told you, what you see is what you *don't* get. It's all just show. If I were turned inside out, *you'd* run for the nearest exit.

CONRAD: [*Sits on the arm of the armchair*] Now, that's hard for me to believe.

PATRICK: I'm as creepy as the creepiest person you ever saw on a street and wouldn't dare ask directions even though you were hopelessly lost.

CONRAD: Why do you usually run from people when you hear them speaking English?

PATRICK: Don't like familiarity, I suppose.

CONRAD: You hear so much about fear of intimacy these days. Self-help books, TV talk shows, the Internet.

PATRICK: [*Dryly*] Everything but semaphore. [*Conrad laughs. Patrick moves to the window, looks out*] Solitude not only makes me content, in some strange way it exhilarates me. [*After a moment*] Even in the American cities I've lived in, I'd sometimes get in a taxi or get in my car and go to parts of town that were foreign, so to speak. Unfamiliar territory. And when I finally traveled to real foreign towns in real foreign countries, I felt that familiar, safe freedom of being a stranger in a strange place. I *wanted* to be lost. I didn't *want* to understand what was going on. And whenever I'd learn the language a little, I'd move on. To other countries with more difficult, more *arcane* languages which I could not possibly pick up. I tried that in Finland, once. Forget it.

CONRAD: Maybe that's why you've never learned the language in this country.

PATRICK: Yes, I don't want to spoil it for myself. I don't want to be disappointed by the banality of it all. I prefer the mystery. In my hometown, there were these wild Sicilians I adored but whose lingo I resolutely refused to pick up. A widow and her three children who became sort of my surrogate family. Of course, I always felt like a fifth wheel, but it didn't matter. They were so full of life—just a great big cliché, really—lots of loud and passionate squabbling, lots of tears, lots of love . . . and, of course, lots of *pasta*.

CONRAD: Which was reassuring.

PATRICK: Exactly.

CONRAD: It's a wonder you don't prefer Palermo to Rome.

PATRICK: [*Dryly*] Palermo is *too* Sicilian! Palermo is meshuga! [*Conrad looks blankly at Patrick*] *Pazzo!* Crazy!

CONRAD: Why were the Sicilians your surrogate family? Your parents were there for you, weren't they?

PATRICK: Well, they weren't there for each *other,* so, yeah, they were all over *me* like the mange.

CONRAD: What do you mean? I don't mean to pry.

PATRICK: [*Wave of the hand*] *Fa niente.* I just mean, divorce was out because of the Church, so I was a kind of excuse to keep their unhappy marriage together. I was coddled and coached and clocked to be a success, because my success would be *their* success. Of course, the stakes were so high, I was like something let out of a burning barn! I guess I would have flipped out for good if it hadn't been for the Sicilians and for . . .

CONRAD: Someone special who got you through? A teacher?

PATRICK: No, not a teacher—the movies. That bright ray of light from a projection machine very definitely dazzled me. It offered hope . . . and a way out.

[*Silence. A slight pause*]

CONRAD: I felt that way about the priesthood.

PATRICK: It offered a way out?

CONRAD: I think so.

PATRICK: A way out of what?

CONRAD: Ohh, life. As I knew it. My family life, I suppose. That, and I wanted to be in touch with man's suffering. I wanted to make a difference. When I was in school and a priest passed through the playground, there were no more fights, no more resentments. The face of the nastiest kid became angelic, everything changed. At least, for me. Oh, there are so many reasons why I became a priest.

PATRICK: Personally, I'd have only done it for the robes.

CONRAD: [*Incredulous*] The vestments?

PATRICK: I used to be crazy about dressing up as an altar boy—all that lace! It made me feel above the congregation.

CONRAD: Ritual is a powerful thing.

PATRICK: And it gives power.

CONRAD: Yes . . . but, when I was young I felt . . .

PATRICK: What? Powerless?

CONRAD: Well . . . incomplete. Fragmented. Not whole. The love of God and some contact with Him seemed to be the one thing that gave me strength. I remember when *I* was an altar boy . . . one morning no one showed up for six o'clock mass, and when the priest gave me communion— just to me and no one else—I never felt so special. I felt so . . .

PATRICK: What? Powerful?

CONRAD: Well, I found something that gave me the strength to pull myself together and have hope. It almost made me sick with joy to know that devotion afforded a way out.

PATRICK: Was your family religious?

CONRAD: My father died before I knew him. But my sister was, although she was quite a bit older; I never knew her much until I had to move in with her while I finished high school. Just before I went into the seminary.

PATRICK: Why did you have to move in with her? Did your mother die too?

CONRAD: Oh, no. I just couldn't live with her anymore. Things were just too . . . tense . . . and, well, unhappy.

PATRICK: Your mother wasn't a religious person?

CONRAD: Yes and no. She was like anybody else, I suppose—you know, commit . . . transgressions . . . and then go to confession, get absolution, and do her penance. She always said going to confession made her feel like a brand-new human being. Of course, as soon as she got home she would start all over again.

[*Conrad takes a handkerchief out of his outside breastpocket and starts to wipe his hands*]

PATRICK: What's the matter?

CONRAD: Oh, nothing. My mouth is just dry.

PATRICK: [*Looking at Conrad's action*] And your hands are wet.

CONRAD: [*Laughs, chagrined*] Yes! So they are!

PATRICK: Are you ready for the *caffè?*

CONRAD: Oh, my, yes! And maybe a little *acqua minerale.*

PATRICK: There's some beside the bed. Help yourself.

CONRAD: *Grazie.*

[*Patrick goes to press the service panel on the night table stage left of the bed. Lightly*]

CONRAD (CONT'D): Maybe we should have doubles! I must be putting you to sleep.

[*Conrad puts the handkerchief back in his breastpocket*]

PATRICK: On the contrary. I'm riveted.

[*Conrad goes to the night table stage right of the bed and pours some mineral water into a glass, drinks it, and replaces it on the tray. Patrick closes the suitcase, snaps it secure*]

CONRAD: Are you packing to leave?

PATRICK: In the morning.

CONRAD: [*Surprised*] *Really?!* I don't know why, I got the impression your work on the movie was going to keep you here much longer. I thought that's why you "drifted off" in the restaurant—I thought you were thinking about your work.

PATRICK: No, my work, such as it is, is finished. [*Looks at Conrad*] Give or take a loose end or two. And you're here just till the end of the week? Then it's back to Los Angeles and to teaching?

CONRAD: Why? Do I look like a teacher?

PATRICK: Yes, you do.

CONRAD: Well, I did teach once, but I don't anymore. Now I'm . . .

PATRICK: Why is that?

CONRAD: [*Evasively*] Oh . . . it's a long story.

PATRICK: Do you miss it? Teaching?

[*Patrick settles on the dressing stool*]

CONRAD: I do. I always got a great deal of satisfaction out of it. Seeing them learn and grow up and go out in the world. It made me feel I'd touched their lives.

PATRICK: It must have filled you with a great deal of pride.

CONRAD: Oh, it did. Because I was crazy about it—doing what I really wanted to do. And it went beyond the classroom. I had a nice car, and I'd pick up the kids and we'd drive to the country, take hikes, swim, have pillow fights, and I'd let them stay up as late as they'd like. There was nothing like helping those boys to believe in themselves, because a lot of them were from troubled backgrounds and really didn't know . . .

PATRICK: Love?

CONRAD: [*Nods*] They really didn't know what it was to have anyone take an interest in them. Oh, we had some terrific times!

PATRICK: They must have worshiped you.

CONRAD: Oh, it was so rewarding. For them. For me. [*Adds, lightly*] Of course, I'd always let them win!

PATRICK: You sound like you were just a big kid yourself.

CONRAD: Maybe so. Sometimes I got into trouble with my superiors because I was rather lax with the paperwork.

PATRICK: The grown-up stuff.

CONRAD: Yes, you might say that. Kids never give a damn about paperwork.

PATRICK: You don't deal with them at all anymore?

CONRAD: No.

PATRICK: That must be very hard on you.

CONRAD: Now I'm chaplain in a hospital. For a while I was in school administration—picking out textbooks, that sort of thing. Then I did a short stint as an adviser to Catholic charities. Then when parish work didn't pan out, I became a chaplain.

PATRICK: What hospital?

CONRAD: Oh, I move around a lot within L.A. Go where the job is. [*Lightly*] Kinda like being in show business, I would imagine.

PATRICK: [*Not responding*] You must deal with a lot of AIDS.

CONRAD: What?

PATRICK: People with AIDS.

CONRAD: Oh, well, naturally. [*Changes subject*] Anyway, the only thing I was really good at was teaching. I enjoyed it. [*Thoughtfully*] Yes, I enjoyed it so much. [*Slight pause*] And you? Back to L.A.? Or is it New York?

PATRICK: Both, eventually. First, I'm going to stop in London and have a meeting with a producer. I have a play in mind, and he's offered to put it on if I can just write it.

CONRAD: If you can just write it?

PATRICK: Yes, I've had this play in mind for years, but I can't seem to get at it.

CONRAD: Not enough time?

PATRICK: Oh, no, not that. The famous writer's block.

CONRAD: The creative process! It's always fascinated me.

PATRICK: And eluded me.

CONRAD: Do you have any idea as to why you're blocked?

PATRICK: Well, I know I'm only blocked when it comes to writing something personal. Something of my own. So that's why I'm in Hollywood selling shit.

CONRAD: What a pity that you can't get in touch with your true feelings.

PATRICK: It's hard, don't you think, getting in touch with your true self?

CONRAD: Maybe I'm blessed, but I don't know that I've ever had that problem.

PATRICK: Oh, well, then you *are* blessed.

CONRAD: Oh, I may have had a crisis—a spiritual crisis in my time, but I've always managed to pull through. I think prayer saved me. I'm very devoted to the Blessed Mother. What a pity you can't . . .

PATRICK: Ask Her to get me out of the fix I'm in? Place my faith in God?

CONRAD: I think you already have faith, Patrick, no matter what you say.

PATRICK: [*Shrugs*] Faith is personal and easily misunderstood.

CONRAD: God understands.

PATRICK: [*Sardonically*] You can swear to that on a stack of Bibles?

CONRAD: There are so many issues on which the Church seems adamant, but . . . well . . . I mean, there is an official position, of course, and these days particularly I have to take that position in the pulpit, but there can be mitigating circumstances.

PATRICK: You can bend the rules to stay in the club?

CONRAD: Well, no, but for instance, in the context of one couple to one counselor regarding, say, contraception . . . we can . . .

PATRICK: Do lunch.

CONRAD: Well, there is always the official versus the unofficial.

PATRICK: Just a tad hypocritical around the edges, isn't it?

CONRAD: [*Defensively*] Well, life is not black-and-white! Life, I'm afraid, is endless shades in between!

PATRICK: [*Controlled*] You're talking out of both sides of your mouth!

CONRAD: [*Mounting ire*] Talk about hypocrisy after what you've said about your profession as a writer!

PATRICK: I don't defend *my* profession!

CONRAD: It's the same in all institutions, religious and secular!

PATRICK: [*Drolly*] Yeah, who's ever heard of a politician who's even masturbated.

[*Conrad is somewhat embarrassed, and the moment is defused*]

CONRAD: [*Covering his discomfort*] If I had your quick wit, just imagine the sermons I could write!

PATRICK: Would you practice what you preached?

CONRAD: [*Getting back to the original subject*] At lunch you told me you've written very personal work in the past.

PATRICK: Oh, yes, I've bared my soul, so to speak. All fired up with ambition and productivity. And I don't understand how I did it one bit. I think if I can ever rediscover my imagination, I'll find myself.

CONRAD: Imagination can be more revealing than the truth.

PATRICK: Exactly. I once had an analyst in Beverly Hills who never wanted to hear the mundane particulars of my daily life. She'd say, "Just bring me a big, fat, juicy dream." [*Conrad laughs*] Anyway, I have an idea for a play— I know how it starts now, how it progresses up to a point—it's kind of a dream.

CONRAD: A big, fat, juicy one?

PATRICK: Mmmmmm. Quite tasty.

CONRAD: But you don't know how the dream comes out yet? Is that it?

PATRICK: Well . . . it's getting there.

CONRAD: What's it about?

PATRICK: [*Avoiding the question*] You know, when I was a child I could draw picture after picture and never get tired or bored or exhaust my imagination. At Christmas I could wrap gift after gift—each different, more charming, more original. And when I started to write, I was tireless at writing sketches and playlets and, finally, plays one after another. But I cannot write plays anymore. Not even the one floating around in my head. Why can't plays come out of me like pictures and presents?

CONRAD: In my own way, I know what you mean. In the hospital, I find it very difficult to counsel grieving families. It's one thing to console the dying but quite another to know what to say to the living! Because when someone dies, those left behind feel . . . responsible. How do you give them hope and strength to go on? I'm afraid that's something not in my power. What are you thinking?

PATRICK: I hope we both find our way.

CONRAD: We'll find a way. I know we will. If we just go *piano-piano*.

PATRICK: From your mouth to God's whatever, Father.

CONRAD: Conrad. Your friend.

PATRICK: Conrad.

[*Silence, for a moment, which is broken by the room service waiter unlocking the door with his keys. He enters. He is about Patrick's age*]

WAITER: [*Entering*] *Permesso.*

PATRICK: *Si, avanti.*

WAITER: *Prego, signori?*

PATRICK: [*To Conrad*] Coffee and a *liquore?*

CONRAD: That would be very nice.

PATRICK: Do you want Sambuca, or would you like to try something else?

CONRAD: You mean like grappa?

PATRICK: [*To waiter*] Do you have any Genepy?

[*Note: Pronounced in English and Italian GEN-a-pee*]

WAITER: I will ask the barman downstairs.

PATRICK: If so, we'll have that. And two coffees.

WAITER: *Due* Genepy. *Due caffè.*

PATRICK: *Solo uno* Genepy *e due caffè, perfavore.*

WAITER: *Grazie.*

[*Patrick goes to retrieve the laundry basket and hands it to the waiter*]

WAITER: Everything was nice and clean?

PATRICK: *Sì, sì. Era limpida come la pipi di un' bambino.*

[*The waiter laughs wickedly and goes out*]

CONRAD: I couldn't understand that, but from the way he laughed, it must have been something dirty.

PATRICK: Not really. Just an expression. I said everything was as clear as baby piss.

CONRAD: [*Chuckles*] What is Genepy?

PATRICK: Something from the Dolomites. Made from juniper berries. Rome's a little far south to have it.

CONRAD: I'm sure a hotel like this has everything. But even I understand enough Italian to know you didn't order one for yourself. You said, "*Solo uno . . .*"

PATRICK: I don't drink. That is, I don't drink *anymore*.

CONRAD: When you refused the wine this afternoon, I thought maybe you just didn't imbibe at lunchtime.

PATRICK: I used to imbibe at lunchtime, cocktail time, dinnertime, and stay up all night and sing 'em all! Now . . . I don't *drink* at all. Or, rather, I struggle not to. I'm an alcoholic. An alcoholic blocked writer—how's that for original?

CONRAD: An *ex*-alcoholic.

PATRICK: Well, I'm what we call in the program a "recovering" alcoholic.

[*Conrad stands, takes his pack of cigarettes from his side pocket, and lights one. Conrad moves to look out the window*]

CONRAD: If you ever had a serious drinking problem, I think you must be some kind of miracle.

PATRICK: There you go getting religious again.

CONRAD: But these twelve-step programs are all *about* spirituality.

PATRICK: Yes, and that's not to be confused with religion. Religion is what people get when they're afraid of going to hell. Spirituality is what they get when they're on their way back from there.

[*Conrad laughs*]

CONRAD: Are you on your way back?

PATRICK: I'm in transit.

CONRAD: If you're . . . agnostic, what do you make your Higher Power?

PATRICK: The group.

CONRAD: The power of the collective.

PATRICK: For me it's the humanity of the group. There's something very poignant about the *humanity*. And very compelling. Something about the frailty of a group of vulnerable human beings, struggling valiantly against their darker instincts.

CONRAD: I wouldn't have any problem whatsoever turning myself over to God. I never have— And you wouldn't either, if you saw what I see in a hospital. Yes, you were right . . . I see so many who die of AIDS.

PATRICK: I thought you must, but you didn't seem to want to talk about it.

CONRAD: I don't know why I didn't before. [*After a moment*] Anyway, there was one young man whose family rejected him. He was near the end, and I came by to give him what I still call Extreme Unction and was shocked to find him in the best spirits I'd ever seen! He said it was because, at last, his friends had come to say good-bye. The room was empty, and he was blind, so I asked, rather carefully, who was there. "Don't you see—there's Violetta and Lucia and Mimi." Well, I don't know the first thing about opera, but he introduced me to the three of them and said, "You know, I'm blind, but I can really see them, so this must be a miracle." And I said yes, it sure is, and took it as a sign that it was time to give him the last rites. When, suddenly, he sat bolt upright and gasped some strange word—"*Ree-na-chee!*"—and then fell back on the bed as dead as dead can be. Well, after all *that*, I didn't need a drink—I needed the comfort of God. And I went to the chapel, and I prayed. Prayed for that young fella's soul. The whole *idea* of a power higher than myself was very comforting to me.

PATRICK: *Rinasce.*

CONRAD: I didn't know what the hell he was talking about.

PATRICK: Violetta's last line in *La Traviata*. She's Italian, so naturally she goes on a bit longer. "*In me rinasce,* yadada, yadada, yadada, *oh, gioia!*" It means, "In me, there is rebirth. Oh, joy!"

[*Pause*]

CONRAD: I suppose you know a lot about opera?

PATRICK: No, I don't. What I know a lot about are those long, long intermissions. I always enjoyed them so much more than I did the opera itself. It was my favorite time to get shit-faced on champagne. And I didn't even *like* champagne! I much preferred the comfortable haze of the first dry martini.

CONRAD: You only went to the opera to drink between the acts?

PATRICK: To get drunk, really.

CONRAD: Well, there must have been a less expensive way.

PATRICK: Well, yes, but as you put it about praying to God in the chapel— the whole *idea* was comforting to me, the romance-of-it-all, the glitz, the glamour—long-stem glasses and more than a bit of the bubbly in a splendid crush bar or some dead-assed Founders' Circle— That and a lot of *posing*, no doubt. *Heavenly.* Except when it turned hellish.

CONRAD: [*With private interest*] It could turn on you?

PATRICK: Could, and finally did. I once flew to Paris with a friend for *La Bohème* on Christmas Eve. Well, now, the very *idea* of an opera taking place on Christmas Eve and seeing it that very same night, and *Paris,* and *Puccini,* and the *interminable* intervals, and all the chilled champagne in the whole of France was too much for me! I drank so excessively after the first act that I passed out and snored all through the Café Momus scene in the second. Then woke up and threw up. Ruined my new dinner jacket. My friend had to get me up the aisle and out. By this time, I was singing along. Needless to say, I was not a hit at the Paris Opera. And my friend hasn't forgiven me to this day.

CONRAD: Talk about "bottoming out" in style!

PATRICK: Oh, so you know about bottoming out, do you?

CONRAD: [*Quickly*] Well, I know what's meant by it. [*Moving on*] I envy you. In your own way you've redeemed yourself. In the end, I hope I'm redeemed. And delivered.

PATRICK: Are you guilty of something?

CONRAD: Who among us is not?

PATRICK: Is that why you've come to Rome?

CONRAD: Of course not. But it is inspiring here. I feel . . . *cleansed* here.

PATRICK: [*With an edge*] Purged?

CONRAD: That's a good word.

PATRICK: [*Heating*] Absolved? Pure as silk? Clear as baby piss?!

CONRAD: [*Evenly, but with an effort*] You penetrate with words, Patrick. It's obvious you're a writer.

PATRICK: And an ex-Catholic. Guilt is an old friend of mine. As the joke goes—the Jews may have invented guilt, but the Catholics perfected it.

CONRAD: [*Testily*] You're not an ex-Catholic, you're a fallen-away Catholic.

PATRICK: [*Adamantly contrary*] Maybe I should say, a *recovering* Catholic.

CONRAD: [*Not conceding*] But once you are baptized, you are *always* a Catholic! [*Flippantly*] Something like being an alcoholic, isn't it?

PATRICK: [*Sarcastically*] Once a Catholic, always a Catholic. Once a priest, always . . . safe.

CONRAD: [*Testily*] I'm not ashamed to say God keeps me safe—that the priesthood is, for me, like a haven.

PATRICK: [*Tauntingly*] Like a cover?

CONRAD: [*Thrown*] A cover? [*Forced lightly*] You mean like a security blanket or like . . .

PATRICK: [*Bluntly*] I mean like a *mask*. Like something safe to *hide* behind.

CONRAD: [*Heatedly*] Now, just one minute, my son.

PATRICK: [*Snidely*] I am not your son, Father.

CONRAD: [*Angered*] But I am still a priest!

PATRICK: And a priest is still a human being! He's still a man, and the Church is no haven, no "safe house" in which a man can hide out from temptation.

CONRAD: [*Pointedly*] No, and in order to resist the more insidious temptations of this world, most human beings place their faith in God! In the end you'll believe in God. Mark my words, you'll call out for Him, and it's going to be such a powerful epiphany, your tongue is going to rot in your mouth!

PATRICK: [*Bitterly*] In the end, this fugitive from the premises of God only prays he has the courage to meet the unknown and die without screaming for a priest!

CONRAD: [*Violently*] Enough of this!

PATRICK: OK! *Basta.* [*Slight pause. Silence. Deliberately*] I once heard someone say in a meeting that the three requisites for being alcoholic were, one—being an orphan, two—being a survivor of child abuse, or three—being a Catholic. I thought they had a point. I qualify on two of those counts. I'm not an orphan.

[*Conrad is silent. The sound of a key enters the lock. The door opens, and the floor waiter enters*]

WAITER: *Ecco, signori!*

PATRICK: [*Re liquore*] Ah, you *do* have Genepy!

WAITER: I have brought you the whole bottle!

PATRICK: *Bravo!*

WAITER: *Salute!*

[*The waiter sets the tray on the low table*]

CONRAD: [*Crossing*] May I have a look at the label?

[*Patrick picks up the bottle of liqueur and hands it to Conrad, who studies it as Patrick takes the bill from the waiter*]

CONRAD: What a color! As green as your eyes, Patrick.

PATRICK: Help yourself.

CONRAD: Thank you. I do want to try it.

[*Conrad opens the bottle and begins to pour himself a pony of Genepy as Patrick signs the bill*]

PATRICK: Among its other powers, it's great as a *digestivo*.

CONRAD: Then it's heaven-sent.

PATRICK: [*To waiter, handing him the bill*] Grazie.

WAITER: *Prego, signor. Grazie a lei. Buona sera.* [*Deferentially*] *E buona sera, Padre.*

CONRAD: [*Nods pleasantly*] *Buona sera.*

[*The waiter goes out. Patrick follows him to the door as Conrad tastes the Genepy. Re liquore*]

CONRAD (CONT'D): Oh, my, that *is* delicious. [*Aspirates*] But strong! My God!

PATRICK: [*Rolls his r's in mock exaggeration*] Forte! Forte! [*Suggestively*] It'll put starch in your collar, Padre.

[*Conrad is a bit thrown by the vulgarity of the remark but laughs feebly*]

PATRICK (CONT'D): Just put on a Roman collar and people automatically have respect for you, don't they?

CONRAD: Or contempt.

PATRICK: Does that happen in America the way it does here? I mean that little tacit courtesy?

CONRAD: Sometimes.

PATRICK: Anyone could dress up in that costume and get respect, couldn't they?

CONRAD: Or contempt.

PATRICK: Sometimes contempt can be more exciting than respect. Too much respect can be paralyzing. [*Patrick has picked up the espresso pot and poured two cups*] Sugar?

CONRAD: Just black, please. [*Patrick hands Conrad a demitasse*] Thank you.

[*Conrad takes his cup and sits on the left end cushion of the settee. Patrick goes to sit on the right end cushion, then hesitates a moment before deciding, instead, to turn and settle into the armchair. Re espresso*]

CONRAD: I need this. [*After a moment*] I really shouldn't drink, either. One or two's my limit—three tops.

PATRICK: Just to put the stopper on, so to speak?

CONRAD: Well, I will admit I used to be able to handle it better. I just have to exercise a little more control these days.

PATRICK: Control's always a good thing to exercise. Control and one's abdominals.

CONRAD: [*Smiles, pats his stomach*] Oh, no dinner for me tonight! Just very early to bed. [*Re Genepy*] I'll be ready after this. Delicious.

PATRICK: [*Re Genepy*] Yes, I have fond memories of it.

CONRAD: It's not a problem if I drink this in front of you?

PATRICK: You could swing from the chandelier if we had one, and it wouldn't faze me.

CONRAD: You mean you never even think of it anymore?

PATRICK: Oh, it's always on my mind—like death.

CONRAD: [*Laughs, sips Genepy. After a moment*] Do you know why you drank?

PATRICK: To get some feeling going. And to stop any feeling.

CONRAD: Can you run that by me again?

PATRICK: It all boiled down to that—to fill one's system with *anything*—anything just to stop *feeling* something—or anything to *feel* something.

CONRAD: [*Reflectively*] I see you've given this some thought.

PATRICK: Sometimes I wanted to feel as bad as I could and would smoke or snort or swallow anything to make me feel just as rotten as possible because, at least, I *felt something*. To feel *bad* is, at least, to *feel*.

CONRAD: I grew up with a family of drinkers. Working-class people from Ireland. Both my parents were big, big drinkers. My father used to say he didn't trust a man who didn't drink. You've heard that one.

PATRICK: [*Dryly*] Yes, and from no one I admire.

CONRAD: My father was banned from every pub in Galway, no mean achievement. So he came to America and started all over.

PATRICK: Do you know what an Irish queer is? A fellow who prefers women to drink.

[*Conrad laugh hollowly. There's a slight pause*]

CONRAD: My father died of cirrhosis when I was just a boy, and although my mother died years later of heart failure, it all was brought on by years of drinking too. Slow drinking. I somehow wish she'd have gone first. It would have spared me so much . . . so many . . . [*Breaks off*] It's one reason I think I went in the priesthood as soon as I could.

PATRICK: What is?

[*Slight pause*]

CONRAD: [*Rationalizing*] She was a good person, basically. But, like anybody—human. With human flaws. [*Directly*] Forgive me, for rattling on. I don't know what got me started.

PATRICK: Tell me more. Dump the cargo and fly low.

[*Conrad smiles, takes a deep sip of Genepy*]

CONRAD: It's something I never talk about—my family. My mother.

PATRICK: Why's that?

CONRAD: [*Forced lightly*] I suppose you might say I'm blocked.

PATRICK: It's not easy being numb.

[*Silence. Conrad takes another sip of Genepy*]

CONRAD: [*After a moment*] Let's just say my parents weren't happy people.

PATRICK: That's something we have in common.

[*Conrad is silent, takes an even bigger swig of Genepy*]

CONRAD: [*Motioning to Genepy*] May I? [*As Patrick nods*] It's really and truly funny to think of us both as blocked.

PATRICK: Well, not *too* hilarious.

CONRAD: You're a bit of all right.

PATRICK: Am I?

CONRAD: You're a "cozy" person—like the dark snug of a pub. I feel I've known you forever.

PATRICK: Maybe it's my Southern charm.

CONRAD: You're from the South?!

PATRICK: Is the Pope celibate?

CONRAD: But you don't have an accent.

PATRICK: I had one once that you could cut with a sugar cane machete.

CONRAD: Sugar cane . . . let's see—Louisiana?

PATRICK: Mississippi.

CONRAD: [*Stunned*] *Mississippi?!* You're *joking!* You didn't tell me that at lunch!

PATRICK: I was too busy impressing you with all the celebrities I've known.

CONRAD: But I assumed you were from New York!

PATRICK: No.

CONRAD: Where in Mississippi?

PATRICK: Oh, just a little cow track.

CONRAD: Well, that *is* interesting.

PATRICK: [*After a moment*] Is it? Why?

CONRAD: Well . . . for one thing, you certainly don't sound it. I'd never have guessed. How did you get rid of your accent?

PATRICK: I was a speech and drama major in college—and I took lessons to get rid of it.

CONRAD: Whatever for?! Southern accents are so charming.

PATRICK: I thought a regional twang made one sound like a hick. Appear stupid. Of course, that's just what I was—a stupid hick. But I didn't want to *sound* like one! [*Pensively*] Also . . .

CONRAD: Yes?

PATRICK: I saw it as a kind of failure. Something imposed on me without my consent. One *more* thing, I should say. [*Deliberately*] I once felt that way about my homosexuality.

[*Slight pause. Conrad tries not to appear thrown by Patrick's remark. Conrad reaches for the Genepy bottle and pours himself another drink*]

CONRAD: [*A bit uncomfortably*] You didn't tell me that, either.

PATRICK: I didn't think I had to.

CONRAD: [*Lightly*] If you'd drunk as much of that Pino Grigio as I did, Patrick, I'd say it was the vino talking now. But, then, all you had was mineral water.

PATRICK: So maybe it's just the gas talking.

CONRAD: [*Laughs nervously*] *Con gas!* That's about all the Italian I've picked up. *Acqua minerale. Con gas o senza gas!*

[*Conrad chuckles feebly at his own joke. Patrick doesn't. Silence. Conrad rummages nervously through his pockets . . .*]

PATRICK: Have you lost something?

CONRAD: I . . . I . . . [*Quickly*] I don't know what I did with my cigarettes. [*Gives up search*] It doesn't matter. Better if I don't find them, anyway.

PATRICK: They're in your left side pocket.

CONRAD: You'd make a good detective. [*Conrad takes out the pack of cigarettes as Patrick picks up the matches and strikes one. Conrad puts a cigarette in his mouth, and Patrick gets up and lights it for him*] Thank you.

PATRICK: [*After a moment*] Didn't it cross your mind?

CONRAD: [*Quickly*] What? No. It didn't.

PATRICK: Really?

CONRAD: [*After a moment, lightly offhanded*] You certainly are very candid.

PATRICK: There's no point in being anything else. It takes too much effort to lie. All that keeping track of the "official" story. Not worth it. Unless, of course, I get paid for it.

CONRAD: Well, telling the truth is indeed a great virtue. [*Patrick is silent. Conrad takes another long swig of Genepy, then becomes more serious*] You say you considered your . . . sexual proclivity . . . some kind of failure?

PATRICK: I guess I did. I tried to get rid of that too.

CONRAD: And you didn't succeed?

PATRICK: Well, let's just say, the attempt was less successful than with my accent. I knew I was gay from the time I was six, and I wasn't very happy about it. But I no longer feel that way.

CONRAD: If *I* may be candid—exactly how did you try to go about getting rid of it? Your . . . homosexuality. Therapy of *another* sort?

PATRICK: Exactly.

CONRAD: The psychiatrist in Beverly Hills?

PATRICK: [*Turns to Conrad*] Psychoanalyst. She was one of several. All women. Most all of whom were of some note. Maybe I should have dropped their names at lunch too.

CONRAD: You do everything first-rate.

PATRICK: As I said, it's almost impossible for me to do anything cheap. *Almost.*

CONRAD: [*Expansively*] Of that, I'm convinced!

PATRICK: So far I've simply chosen to tell you one side of the story. The safe side. The cozy, snug side. I don't think you'd want to hear about my nostalgia for the gutter. The cheap side. However, in its way, that was always first-rate too, inasmuch as you couldn't get any lower.

CONRAD: I doubt that I'd be shocked. I've heard a lot in my time.

PATRICK: In confession?

CONRAD: Well, yes, of course. But I *am* a man of a certain age. I may have been born yesterday, but I wasn't born *late* yesterday.

PATRICK: [*Laughs*] I like that. I think the Genepy has knocked the edges off.

CONRAD: [*Raises his glass of Genepy*] Cheers!—and *buona notte!*

[*Patrick doesn't laugh, just looks at Conrad. Slight pause*]

I know a priest who works with homosexuals.

PATRICK: "Works with"? That sounds arduous. Like it might even smart.

CONRAD: There are some, Patrick, who would like to reconcile themselves with the Church.

PATRICK: And what if they just can't pretend they're something they aren't?

CONRAD: Well, off the record, and admittedly it's becoming more difficult, but I suppose if there's a consensual, nurturing, monogamous relationship . . .

PATRICK: You can work out a deal. Forgive me for saying the obvious, but who wants to be a member of that cockamamy club? *Cockamamy*—that's Yiddish too.

CONRAD: [*Chuckles*] Why do you keep using Jewish words? You're not Jewish.

PATRICK: I might as well be—show business and psychoanalysis are my life!

CONRAD: Of course, Jesus was Jewish.

PATRICK: No, He wasn't. He was Irish.

CONRAD: What?

PATRICK: Consider the facts—on the last night of His life, He went out drinking with the boys. He thought His mother was a virgin, and she thought that He was God.

CONRAD: [*Laughs, holds up glass*] What's the name of this?

PATRICK: Genepy.

CONRAD: Genepy. Great stuff. I wouldn't have missed it for mass! [*Looks heavenward*] Just kidding, Lord! [*Another slight uncomfortable pause. Conrad gets up, goes to the balcony window, looks out, and sips his Genepy thoughtfully.*

CONRAD (CONT'D): . . . *After a moment*] Whoever said "small world" really knew what he was talking about!

PATRICK: What do you mean?

CONRAD: [*After a moment*] I once taught school in Mississippi.

PATRICK: Now, that's something you didn't tell *me*.

CONRAD: I'm telling you now.

PATRICK: Why didn't you mention it before? When I said I was from Mississippi.

CONRAD: [*Evasively*] Well . . .

PATRICK: Well, what?

CONRAD: [*Uncomfortably*] Well, suffice it to say I *did* teach there. Isn't that another unbelievable coincidence?

PATRICK: [*Casually*] Small world. Enormous fate, I guess.

CONRAD: Amazing!

PATRICK: Life *is* . . . *amazing* sometimes.

CONRAD: Yes, imagine! Each of us now living in the same random American city, never knowing the other existed within that city or state or space— and having also existed within another state and space at the same time, sometime in our pasts. And now, our paths cross in a distant, foreign place! What are the chances of that?!

PATRICK: Slim.

CONRAD: Of course, I'm not from L.A. originally. I'm from . . .

PATRICK: [*Evenly*] Boston would be my guess.

CONRAD: [*Dumbstruck*] You do have a sharp ear for accents! And I never even said, "I pahked the cahr in Hahvahd yahd!"

[*Conrad laughs at his own joke. Patrick does not*]

—Actually, I'm from South Boston. I'm a "southie." Went into the seminary outside Brookline and taught for a while in Beverly, Mass. Then I was sent to one of our schools in Mississippi.

PATRICK: And how did you wind up in L.A.?

CONRAD: [*Evasively*] I was . . . unhappy . . . in Mississippi . . . in that small town, so I asked to be transferred to a city. Any city anywhere that needed someone. I needed to be . . . swallowed up. [*Re Genepy*] May I?

PATRICK: But of course.

[*Conrad refills his glass, takes a long sip. Pause. conrad takes another sip, looks to see Patrick staring at him*]

CONRAD: You're so silent. You're not falling asleep, are you?

PATRICK: I'm not even staring into space.

CONRAD: What are you thinking? [*Patrick looks at Conrad a moment longer, doesn't answer, gets up, and goes to the window to look out*] Something you don't want to say?

[*Patrick is silent. After a moment, Conrad gets up and crosses to stand beside him. Silence. Some street noises. Someone somewhere is singing and whistling a snatch of "Non Dimenticar." Pause. Looking out*]

CONRAD: Ah, *bella Roma!* The Eternal City.

PATRICK: [*Looking out*] Maternal, paternal, eternal.

CONRAD: What a fantastic night. I've always preferred the night. The night always exaggerates things—there's a kind of heightened reality, isn't there?

PATRICK: Yes, it's like drink or a drug. I was a night person too, all my life. I used to feel alive *only* at night. Now I quite appreciate the day. There's nothing more beautiful than light—and what it does to things. Light and shadow are something to consider. I envy painters.

[*Conrad puts his hand on Patrick's shoulder and looks out at the city . . .*]

CONRAD: This has all been so extraordinary, I shall never forget it. Meeting you. Becoming friends. Imagine—just hours ago we were two strangers in a foreign country.

PATRICK: I have always been a stranger in a foreign country—always. There and then as a child in the South—and here and now in this Holy City. Excuse me.

[*Patrick gently slips out from Conrad's grasp, moves away, crossing to the back of the settee, where he sits, his back to the audience. Conrad doesn't leave the window, but turns from it to face Patrick*]

CONRAD: What's the matter, Patrick? Don't like being nostalgic?

PATRICK: I'm a person who dwells on yesterday to the point of pathology.

CONRAD: In some cases I think it's better to forget and move on.

PATRICK: The past, for me, is not a darkened stage whose players have vanished and are forgotten.

CONRAD: [*Almost as if he's seeking advice*] Do you really think you can resolve the troublesome things of the past?

PATRICK: Some things. But it's hard to confront the big time.

CONRAD: [*Re the Genepy*] You know, it's really *Kelly* green!

PATRICK: [*Drolly*] You mean it's user-friendly.

CONRAD: [*Warily*] Did you go to a Catholic school in Mississippi?

PATRICK: Mmm. I wonder if you can guess which one.

CONRAD: Well, there are so many! Isn't it amazing how many Catholic schools there are in a hard–core Baptist state? [*Picking up the Genepy bottle*] May I have a tiny drop more?

PATRICK: Be my thirsty guest. I not only went to Catholic grade school and high school but even a Catholic university. My father was rather cracked on the subject of religion.

CONRAD: And your mother?

PATRICK: Oh, she converted just to keep peace. She only went to church on Sunday to show off her fur coat.

[*Patrick gets up, moves away to the chest of drawers. He starts to place the toilet articles—cologne and talcum—into the zipper case lying on the top of the chest*]

CONRAD: [*Settles into the armchair*] The older I get, the more I find myself doing things just the way my mother did.

PATRICK: Such as?

CONRAD: Ohh, little things like . . . tucking my handkerchief in the sleeve of my cassock or checking things several times before I can go out—the light in my room, the front door, the back door. Sometimes I lock and unlock and relock the doors three or four times before I can leave.

PATRICK: Just as she did.

CONRAD: Yes. [*Hesitantly*] And in the last couple of years I've noticed something else—something I hated as a child—something I never thought I'd be doing.

PATRICK: Like?

CONRAD: Like . . . taking to bed in the middle of the afternoon when I've always been so on-the-go, so active. I've always hated lying around. But sometimes I get depressed—just like she used to get depressed.

PATRICK: What about?

CONRAD: Things I thought I'd left behind so many years ago in South Boston.

PATRICK: And why did you leave? Mississippi, I mean. Not Massachu-setts.

CONRAD: [*Carefully*] As I say, I was transferred.

PATRICK: You said you *asked* to be transferred.

CONRAD: Yes, that's right. [*Lightly*] Are you taking this down?

PATRICK: I'm a good listener, Father.

CONRAD: You certainly are.

PATRICK: And an even better scopophiliac.

CONRAD: What's that?

PATRICK: The morbid urge to observe. You were saying?

CONRAD: I came to love the South, but . . . well, it got to be too . . .

PATRICK: What? [*Playfully*] Too humid? Too hot?

CONRAD: [*Seriously*] Too painful . . . for me to stay there. [*With a certain difficulty*] I had a bad experience—got myself into a . . . troublesome situation there, so it was somewhat of a relief to get out.

PATRICK: Then it *did* get too hot for you?

CONRAD: [*Tonelessly*] Well, you might say that.

PATRICK: And sticky?

CONRAD: [*Grimly*] Yes. I guess you might say . . .

PATRICK: The heat was on?

CONRAD: Believe me, it was no joking matter.

PATRICK: I believe you.

[*Pause. Conrad puts down the coffee cup on the low table, picks up the pony of Genepy, and drains it. He pours himself another, settles back in the armchair. After a moment*]

PATRICK (CONT'D): What's the matter, Conrad? Are *you* nostalgic now?

CONRAD: [*Evasively*] Just very mellow. This Genepy is making me very, very sleepy. I must get up and stretch. [*Stands, yawns*] Ohh, my, your bed looks so inviting.

[*Patrick looks at Conrad reflected in the mirror. He doesn't turn to face him. Conrad puts down the empty Genepy glass on the low table and comes up to the left head of the bed*]

CONRAD (CONT'D): The sheets! Real linen, are they?

PATRICK: Mmm. I love that about good hotels in Europe.

CONRAD: [*Extends his hand*] May I?

PATRICK: Go ahead. Give it a feel.

CONRAD: [*Touches the pillow*] Soft and smooth— [*Conrad then sits carefully on the bed. Reacting to the comfort*] Oh, my! How luxurious. I'd better not go any further or I could curl up and spend the night!

PATRICK: Could you?

[*Conrad slightly bounces up and down on the mattress*]

CONRAD: I could indeed.

[*There is the sound of a key in the door as the floor waiter returns*]

WAITER: [*Entering*] Permesso.

PATRICK: Sí, avanti.

[*Conrad immediately gets off the bed . . .*]

WAITER: Are you finished with the tray?

PATRICK: We're finished with the coffee.

[*The waiter crosses to the low table*]

WAITER: I will leave the Genepy.

PATRICK: Thank you.

WAITER: *Mi scusi*, Padre, you like the Genepy? [*Picks up bottle, looks at contents*] Oh, I see you like it very much.

CONRAD: Yes, it's very soothing.

WAITER: It is good in the wintertime—for "After-ski."

CONRAD: Well, you might say I've been going downhill all afternoon!

[*The waiter doesn't really understand but smiles enigmatically and refills Conrad's glass. He sets the bottle on the low table and picks up the tray with the coffeepot and used cups and starts to go*]

CONRAD: *Grazie.*

WAITER: *Grazie, a lei, Padre. Buona sera.*

CONRAD: *Buona sera.*

WAITER: [*To Patrick*] *Buona sera, signor.*

PATRICK: [*Pointedly*] *Grazie et buona notte.*

[*The waiter goes to the door. Conrad goes back to the low table and picks up the drink as Patrick comes around the bed and follows the waiter out. Patrick casually locks the door [three revolutions] and puts the key in his side jacket pocket. Conrad's back is to Patrick, but he hears the sound of the door being locked. Whether he thinks anything of it or not, he doesn't react or comment on it. Patrick doesn't move from the door. Conrad goes to the window. Some car horns are heard from below and a few indistinct exchanges in Italian. A Vespa goes by. Pause. Conrad turns to face Patrick, who is looking at him*]

CONRAD: [*After a moment*] What are you thinking?

PATRICK: I'm thinking about your sitting on my bed.

CONRAD: Oh, I hope you don't mind, it just looked so . . .

PATRICK: There was a time—not so very long ago, Conrad—that I'd have taken that as a come-on—if someone had come up to my room and patted my pillow and asked to give it a feel.

CONRAD: [*Lightly*] Now, really, Patrick, are you trying to shock me?!

PATRICK: I'm not saying what was on *your* mind. I'm just telling you what was going through *mine*.

CONRAD: I just meant that . . . well . . . what I *mean* is, I'll definitely take a little nap as soon as I get back to my room. [*Looks at his watch*] —and I really have to think about going.

PATRICK: [*Looking at the bed*] The difference between then and now is that I'd have been drinking like you've been drinking this afternoon. Half-pissed and horny, I'd have picked up someone in a bar or off the street or in a pissoir and probably paid them. That would have been the first-rate gutter side of me. But not anymore. Those days are over. I'm too sober. [*Grimly*] And the world's too sober today too. The leaves are knee-deep in the pissoirs in the Borghese Gardens now. Sign of the times.

CONRAD: You know, Patrick, sometimes you go a bit too far.

PATRICK: It could have been an afternoon like this afternoon, Conrad. After all, I did sort of pick you up on the street too, didn't I? And brought you back here with me?

CONRAD: [*Admiringly intrigued*] You just don't care what you say, do you?

PATRICK: I just don't think there's any point in pretending. [*Shrugs*] Not worth it.

CONRAD: Actually, I wish I were like that. I admire people who say what they think. People who have that power.

PATRICK: You mean it's tough for you to let down your hair. Expose yourself?

CONRAD: I don't think anything would shock you.

PATRICK: It'd take some doing. Try me.

CONRAD: You mentioned something earlier that made me think of something in my past. It's been on my mind ever since.

PATRICK: What has?

CONRAD: I don't know what telling you would accomplish. I've never spoken to anyone about it— [*Waves his glass*] What is this, anyway?

PATRICK: Jet fuel.

CONRAD: [*Lightly*] You're going to have to roll me out the door and point me in the direction of the Tiber! And even then, I'm still bound to get lost.

CONRAD (CONT'D): [*Re Genepy*] What *is* it, anyway?! I know you say it's made from juniper, but it's like . . .

PATRICK: Truth serum! In juniper veritas!

CONRAD: [*Sits on the settee*] I believe you may be right. [*After a moment*] You've made me think of things that really have always been just out of mind. [*After a moment*] Funny, I feel so light-headed.

PATRICK: Take a few deep breaths and just go *piano-piano*.

CONRAD: [*Chuckles*] Yes. That might help.

PATRICK: It helps *me*.

[*Conrad is silent. A slight pause . . . Patrick sits on the foot of the bed. Conrad sits next to him*]

CONRAD: [*Breathing heavily*] As I say, I've never talked to anyone about this, and I don't know if I'm prepared even to tell you. I'd like to.

PATRICK: [*Carefully*] Would it help if you thought of me as your, well—as your . . . father confessor?

CONRAD: Are you being . . .

PATRICK: Tongue-in-cheek? No, for once.

CONRAD: [*Tentatively, re liquore*] I think this . . . this Genepy has loosened my tongue.

PATRICK: Do you always have to drink to loosen up?

CONRAD: Well, it always helps.

PATRICK: And are you relaxed now? Are you comfortable with me?

CONRAD: Yes. You certainly know how to put a man at ease.

PATRICK: Thank you.

CONRAD: You have that power.

PATRICK: Thank you, again.

CONRAD: Power must be the most intoxicating thing in the world. Far more heady than alcohol.

PATRICK: Maybe there's just something about me that encourages you to be intimate.

[*A loaded pause*]

CONRAD: [*Anxiously moves away*] I don't think I can. Speak of it. I'm sorry. Been bottled up in me too long.

[*Silence. A pause. Conrad silently sips the Genepy. Patrick gets off the bed*]

PATRICK: [*Flatly*] I doubt if you could tell the truth about yourself to anyone.

CONRAD: [*Somewhat startled*] What?

PATRICK: You have done nothing but pretend to me since I met you. Pretend to be chaste, pretend to be celibate. And yet you sit on my bed and make seductive remarks. You can be had, Conrad.

CONRAD: What did you say?

PATRICK: Too intimate for you?

CONRAD: I don't know what you mean!

PATRICK: And you're a drunk! That's one's choice, of course, but you lie about that too—pretending "one or two's my limit—three tops!" You have no limit. There is no top. Boundaries are a problem for you, Conrad.

[*Conrad is unsettled, knocks over the glass of Genepy on the low table, and looks up with apprehension*]

CONRAD: [*Flatly*] Patrick, you're way out of line!

PATRICK: [*Drawing nearer, quietly*] You're a failure at everything you set out to be—a teacher, a shaper of young minds, the bearer of the word of your God. With your lies you have betrayed the integrity of a tradition centuries old. You're a flop as a priest. You're a flop as a person. Conrad, you are a *flop*.

CONRAD: And you are something evil!

PATRICK: If I am, I am your creation, dear Father!

CONRAD: What are you talking about?!

PATRICK: [*After a moment, directly*] I have a confession to make concerning that play that I can't seem to get at. It's about a betrayal of trust. Emotional betrayal. Sexual betrayal.

CONRAD: [*Standing, anxiously*] *Give me my shoes!!*

PATRICK: What's the matter, don't you like being in mine?!

CONRAD: I'm leaving!

PATRICK: I'm not finished telling you about the play.

CONRAD: I don't think I'm interested!

PATRICK: It's about a teacher who sexually abuses a nine-year-old student.

[*Pause. Conrad stands silently aghast, staring wide-eyed at Patrick*]

CONRAD: [*Hisses weakly*] Who are you?!

PATRICK: [*Calmly*] Don't you know? I loved you once.

CONRAD: What?

PATRICK: I said, *I loved you once.*

[*Conrad's jaw sags with recognition*]

CONRAD: [*After a long moment*] It's not possible!

PATRICK: Apparently, it is. *Very* small world department!

CONRAD: [*Quickly*] His name wasn't Patrick!

PATRICK: Yes, it was! His middle name was Patrick, but you called him by his first name. You called me . . .

CONRAD: [*A hushed gasp*] Ned!

PATRICK: Yes. You called me Ned. Ned for Edward, which is my first name. Just like my father. You remember my father, of course.

CONRAD: Your father?

PATRICK: Your friend, *Eddie!*

CONRAD: [*Remembers*] Of course, I remember your father. Dear, kind Eddie. How . . . how is Eddie?

PATRICK: Dead. So he's just fine.

CONRAD: [*Compassionately*] I am sorry to hear that. We were great friends. I liked Eddie so much.

PATRICK: And he was impressed with you. Bright young Irish-American priest. What he probably always wanted to be himself.

CONRAD: Eddie probably did think he missed his calling. Yes, I suppose he did look up to me.

PATRICK: He'd do anything for you. Give you anything. Anything you wanted. And you *wanted* the things my father could give you. You loved the perks. The cigarettes. The liquor. The good wine. The gifts of money. The car. The Christmas-of-it-all!

CONRAD: I didn't ask for those things!

PATRICK: You didn't have to. My father was generous, and in that small town he thought you were special. Educated, cultivated, and *holy!* A man of God. Good for his boy. And how did you pay him back? By molesting his son!

[*Conrad runs to grab his shoes from under the luggage rack. Patrick races after Conrad and snatches his shoes from him and hurls them across the room. Conrad is suddenly terrified of Patrick's unbridled wrath, collapses back onto the top of the closed suitcase on the luggage rack*]

CONRAD: [*Hysterically*] Why have you come back?! To get even?

PATRICK: [*Hovering*] Ask your all-knowing God that! Ask Him why, after all these years, He's permitted this curious little collision in the mad mix-up of streets in this ancient holy town!

CONRAD: Let me go! Let me out of here!

[*Conrad starts to get up, and Patrick shoves him back onto the suitcase*]

PATRICK: And while you're at it, ask Him why He permitted you to sit beside me at my desk in the middle of a room of prepubescent students and put your arm around me and slip your hand down the sides of my overalls to fondle my . . .

CONRAD: Stop it! Stop it!

PATRICK: Why He allowed you to slip my hand into your cassock where your trousers were unzipped.

CONRAD: [*Covering his ears*] Stop! Don't do this!

PATRICK: Why He let you take me to your room after class to kiss me and suck me and have me kiss and suck you.

CONRAD: Please, for God's sake!

[*Conrad pushes past Patrick, races for the door. Patrick doesn't move. Conrad begins to tear at the knob . . .*]

PATRICK: [*Calmly*] It's locked. Didn't you see me lock it when the waiter left? [*Removes key from his pocket, holds it up*] Here's the key.

CONRAD: [*Rushing back to Patrick*] Give it to me!

PATRICK: [*Calmly puts the key back in his pocket*] No.

CONRAD: [*Pathetically*] Give it to me. Please.

[*Conrad breathes hard, backs away from Patrick, stumbles on the raised platform, and falls onto it [downstage of the foot of the bed], panting. Patrick looks at Conrad contemptuously*]

PATRICK: [*Icily*] You look a bit green around the gills. As green as that Genepy you've been lapping up. As green as my eyes. [*Calmly*] I remember a day, a day of dread and anxiety the likes of which I have never known again—although at nine years of age I didn't know what the unnamed thing in me was. I wonder if you remember that day?

CONRAD: [*Breathing hard*] What day? What are you talking about?

PATRICK: [*Without affect*] A cold day one winter when you were colder than the day outside. I knew something was wrong the moment I saw your face that morning. The moment you looked away from me and never looked at me again. I thought I had done something. I thought something was *my* fault. I couldn't eat at the lunchtime recess—the smell of sausage in the cafeteria made me ill. I couldn't play in the playground. I couldn't even see clearly, even though there wasn't any bright sunlight—just a canopy of gray, that chilly, dull noon. All I could do was wonder and worry and wait for the bell to come back to class . . . when you finally spoke to me. Without looking at me you told me to stay after school—that you had something to talk to me about. What had I done? What had I caused to make you so cold?

CONRAD: You didn't understand.

PATRICK: The hours dragged by like days that day of dread until, at last, at three o'clock on that cold dreadful afternoon, the school bell rang again and the rest of the students left, leaving me alone with you. And you locked the door.

CONRAD: Please, I want to forget—

PATRICK: You remember there was a mesh grating over the windows in that room—

CONRAD: Yes . . . yes, I remember.

PATRICK: And I remember how that day the mesh seemed like a cage to me. The moment you started talking, I wanted to get out of that room. I

PATRICK (CONT'D): was going to suffocate. I asked you to unlock the door, and you said, "No, I have to talk to you."

[*Patrick crosses to bed platform, stands over Conrad, and addresses him directly. Conrad avoids Patrick's gaze*]

PATRICK: You didn't sit beside me at my desk this time—you sat on the one in front of me—you didn't touch me, you kept your distance. You couldn't look at me when you finally said, "What we have been doing has to stop. What we have been doing is wrong. What we have been doing is a sin."— Do you remember?

CONRAD: [*After a moment*] Yes. Yes, of course. How could I forget?

PATRICK: You unlocked the door and let me go. And I've never felt free again. After that—the hours, the days left in that year—the interminable anxiety of having to be near you in the classroom, hearing your voice day after day. Seeing you in the schoolyard at recess, playing with the other children—running into you on the stairs, in the corridors, never having our eyes meet again, never knowing what was going on in your mind. Then, coming back after the summer and suddenly finding out you were gone. Disappeared. They said you'd been transferred. I never knew where, never knew what happened to you, never heard of you again. Until this day.

CONRAD: I can't believe this day!

PATRICK: Believe it. You're good at putting your faith in things which stretch credulity far more than this day. Such is life and show business in a bewildering world.

[*Patrick moves away, crossing unsteadily to lean against the back of the settee. Conrad slowly gets up off the platform, begins a slow semicircle downstage around Patrick, edging right to search for his shoes. The next exchanges are rapid-fire*]

CONRAD: [*Moving*] How long have you been following me?!

PATRICK: I haven't been following you!

CONRAD: You followed me here to Rome, didn't you?

PATRICK: No. I didn't.

CONRAD: You tracked me down, haven't you?!

PATRICK: Running into you was just what it was—an accident. A sort of *divine* accident!

CONRAD: You planned this!

PATRICK: I had no plan! But I do now.

[*Conrad has edged his way down left. He finds his shoes, picks them up, goes to sit in the armchair, takes off the slippers. Patrick slowly comes around the settee, up to the armchair to loom over Conrad, who finishes pulling on his shoes, leaving them unlaced. Conrad panics and runs to the balcony as a Vespa grinds past on the street below, making a racket. Patrick doesn't move from the door. The sound of the Vespa loudens . . .*]

CONRAD: [*Yelling outside, over the noise*] Help!—*HELP!!!*

PATRICK: [*Without passion*] The word in Italian is *aiuto! Aiuto!* It means "help." [*After a moment*] What's the matter? Can't you say it?

[*Conrad is frozen with fear, unable to utter a syllable. We hear the rasp of the Vespa fade in the distance. Patrick calmly crosses to the balcony, steps around Conrad, and closes the exterior shutters, then the glass doors, shutting out the exterior noises. He then draws the brocade portieres. Conrad stumbles dizzily back to center stage, starts to moan and contract his arms about his midsection. He collapses on the floor.*]

PATRICK: [*Turning, tonelessly*] Get up.

CONRAD: [*Moaning*] I can't.

[*Patrick calmly crosses to stand above Conrad but does not touch him*]

PATRICK: I said, *get up!*

[*Conrad starts to gasp and crawl across the floor toward the bathroom door*]

CONRAD: I'm sick!

PATRICK: What's the matter? Choke on your rosary?

[*Conrad moans loudly, grabs his stomach with one hand, and covers his mouth with the other, as if he is about to vomit. He gets to his feet and stumbles the rest of the way across the stage into the bathroom*]

CONRAD: I'm going to be sick!!

[*We hear him retch offstage. Patrick slowly approaches the open bathroom door, looks in. After a moment, he speaks . . .*]

PATRICK: [*With mild contempt*] Pity. All that expensive expense-account lunch down the toilet.

[*The sound of the toilet being flushed can be heard offstage . . . Patrick steps across the threshold to the bath, where he can still be seen by the audience, whips*] *a towel off the warming rack, and hurls it off to where Conrad would be. Patrick steps back over the threshold, into the room. The sound of running water is heard offstage . . . Suddenly, Patrick pulls the bathroom door shut and collapses against it, hyperventilating. He stands there gasping a few seconds, then forcefully pushes himself away from the door, propelling himself around, stumbles to center stage, where he stops, frozen for a moment, before he begins to shake violently . . .]*

PATRICK: [*Desperately, to himself*] Pat, Pat, Pat, Pat, Pat, Paddy, Paddy, Paddy . . . [*He gasps for breath*] Neddy, Neddy, Neddy, Ned, Ned, Ned, take a few deep breaths . . . take a few deep breaths . . . Hold on . . . Hold on . . . Hold on . . . *Piano-piano . . .*

*[A pause. He calms. And straightens. And smooths his hair . . . The sound of the running water in the bathroom is turned off. After a moment, the door to the bathroom is thrown open and Conrad staggers out, looking ghostly pale. He has taken his suit jacket off and clutches it in his hand. His hair is wet, and a towel is around his neck . . . Conrad moves unsteadily to hold on to the chest of drawers. He looks up at himself [and at Patrick] in the mirror. Patrick becomes aware of the eye contact, turns away to look straight out front . . . After a moment]*

PATRICK: Do you recognize me?

*[Conrad does not turn around—continues to look at Patrick in the mirror]*

CONRAD: I didn't at first. You're older, of course . . . But now . . . [*Turns to face Patrick*] Well, yes, you are unmistakably you—

*[Conrad turns back to the mirror, takes the towel from around his neck and wipes his face, picks up Patrick's comb and smooths his hair. He puts down the comb and the towel on top of the chest]*

PATRICK: [*Turns to face Conrad*] Even before I saw you, I knew. I heard your voice when you spoke to me, and I knew. Then I looked at you, and even behind dark glasses, I knew—

CONRAD: I'm older too. My hair . . . it's all salt-and-pepper.

PATRICK: Not to worry. There's still more pepper than salt. [*Out front, simply*] I've seen your face in so many people through the years. Someone will look up and see me staring at them—on a plane or in a restaurant or a theater, and they'll never know that I wasn't looking at them at all. I was seeing you.

CONRAD: [*Not looking at Patrick*] Even though you're a grown man now, you still have the same sweet face, Neddy.

PATRICK: Don't call me that!!

CONRAD: That's who you are.

PATRICK: No. That's who you want.

CONRAD: [*Weakly*] I've got to lie down.

PATRICK: [*Coolly*] You've been wanting to get in my bed since you got here, haven't you?

[*Conrad stumbles to platform, steps up on it, and falls onto the bed . . . Patrick goes to his suitcase, flings the top open, and scoops up all his pairs of silk boxer shorts. He crosses to the bed, mounts the platform, and stands over Conrad, pelting him with the undergarments . . .*]

PATRICK: Here. You've been wanting these too. Hold them. Feel them. Smell them.

CONRAD: [*Shrieks at Patrick*] You can't even it out! For God's sake, Ned!

PATRICK: I said, *Don't call me that!!*

CONRAD: All we can do is repent for the unthinkable monstrosity of what happened . . .

PATRICK: [*Lashes out*] Of *what you did!* Not *what happened.* There is nothing even in what happened! We're talking about the unspeakable monstrosity of *what you did!*

CONRAD: Do you blame me for everything that's gone wrong with your life?

PATRICK: Do you have any idea how you changed my life?! And I don't mean you made me homosexual. I mean, do you know how you fucked with my mind?! [*Conrad doesn't respond. Patrick turns to him. Directly*] Well, *do you?!!!*

CONRAD: I have paid for what I did!

PATRICK: You've *never* paid for what you did!

CONRAD: [*Directly*] How would *you* know! You don't know me. You don't know the way I've had to live my life. [*Hysterically*] *You don't know the secrets of my heart!*

PATRICK: *Then SHOW me your heart if you have one!*

CONRAD: [*Lashes out*] What do you want me to do?! I've confessed, I've been absolved, I've done my penance. I've begged God over and over and *over* for forgiveness!

PATRICK: [*Confronting Conrad*] *I* am the only one who can forgive you! *I* am the child you violated!

CONRAD: [*Looking up at Patrick, terrified*] What are you going to do?! *What?* Hurt me?!

PATRICK: [*Calmly but steely*] Sorry, no bamboo shoots under the fingernails!

CONRAD: [*Stoically*] Are you going to kill me?

[*Patrick straightens, very controlled, turns, and moves a little way left of Conrad*]

PATRICK: Hold a linen-covered pillow over your face until you suffocate? Push you off the balcony and have you splatter your guts all over the Spanish Steps? Too predictable. No, this scene will not be written by the dictates of a committee. This scene will be of my own invention.

[*Conrad gets up and runs for the door and begins frantically twisting the knob. patrick crosses to him, catches him by the back of his collar, and swings him round. Conrad swings round and drops to his knees, center stage, sobbing*]

PATRICK: *Listen to me!*

CONRAD: [*Covers his ears*] No!!

PATRICK: [*Takes him by the lapels, shakes him*] I said, listen to me, goddamnit!!!

[*Conrad tries to crawl away from Patrick's grip. Patrick jerks him around so forcefully that Patrick himself is brought to his knees. Conrad screams. Now they are both kneeling, face-to-face, Conrad down on both knees, cowering—Patrick on one knee only, slightly higher and above Conrad, in the stronger position with more physical advantage. Conrad sobs as Patrick tightens his grip on Conrad's jacket lapels . . .*]

CONRAD: Patrick, I'm an old man!!

PATRICK: A *dirty* old man! A filthy old pervert in a costume!

CONRAD: I'm a man of God!

PATRICK: Then ask your God why He permitted you to be the first person to teach me what I thought was love?! *Love!* For the first time in my life! And for the last time in my life!

CONRAD: What are you saying? You didn't want me to end it?

PATRICK: You should never have begun it! What has love meant to me ever since? Humiliation and betrayal. I can have sex with strangers, but I can't make love with anyone who could love me or for whom I could feel one authentic emotion. And for that, I have you to thank.

CONRAD: I had to end it! It was wrong!

PATRICK: At the moment you *told* me it was wrong—that it was what you called a sin—at that moment you taught me the meaning of guilt.

CONRAD: Mother of God, I never meant to hurt you!

[*Conrad struggles with Patrick. Patrick stands and violently pulls Conrad to his feet and hurls him across the room onto the bed, pinning Conrad down*]

PATRICK: You wrecked me inside forever! I was left with nothing but apathy, indifference, a detachment toward everything that is given any emotional credence in this world. The thought of a human being about whom I might genuinely care makes me ill. It makes *me* want to vomit. And left with that numbing emptiness, I fill it with a pathological commitment to luxury, a life of living beyond my means, an obsession for expensive, inanimate possessions of quality which cannot betray me. That is why I want nothing more than for my life to end. Certainly I want nothing after it is over. I despise life. I do not believe in anything beyond it. I have nothing but contempt for the idea of your God. I want you to live with that knowledge. I want you to live knowing that you are responsible for the *death of a soul of a human being.*

[*Patrick releases Conrad, steps off the platform, and walks away to center. A pause. Conrad weakly lifts himself up on his hands on the bed, looks at Patrick*]

CONRAD: [*After a moment*] I often wondered if you'd even remember.

PATRICK: *Remember!*

CONRAD: I thought it might be something so shameful that you'd force yourself to block it out forever.

PATRICK: It doesn't work that way!

CONRAD: [*After a moment looks at Patrick*] Did you tell your father?

PATRICK: I told my mother.

[*Slight pause*]

CONRAD: [*After a moment*] What did she do?

PATRICK: Nothing. I think she was afraid to tell my father. But she didn't go to anyone else—your superior, for instance. She did nothing. All she said was "That dirty old son of a bitch. I always knew he was freaky."

CONRAD: I thought about getting some treatment. I knew it was something dark for which I needed help, but it seemed easier to bury it. We should never do anything with the hope of forgetting. [*After a long moment*] The irony is, it happened to me. That's what I wanted to speak of but couldn't. What was so difficult to admit a few minutes ago now seems like nothing. I was abused. All my young life—by my mother.

[*Patrick looks at Conrad*]

—After my father died, she made me share the same bed with her until I finally took it upon myself to get out and go live with my sister. I couldn't endure the . . . tension of it anymore, the cat and mouse of it . . . the unspoken *fact* of it. In the winter months we'd sleep spoon fashion, and I remember one night when I was twelve years old, lying there I felt the warm satin of her nightgown pressed up against me, rubbing me. I began to get excited, and I got an erection. At first, I didn't know whether she was asleep or not, but after a while . . . after she let me almost reach the point of ejaculation, she reached behind herself and pushed me away—I knew she knew. I turned over . . . facing away from her . . . and I . . . This went on time after time, year after year, nothing was ever said—even though the sheets would be circled and slightly discolored the next morning. It explains something, I suppose. Not enough. But something. But so what? Is that supposed to make what you did to me all right? It hasn't made me do it. It hasn't made me even think about doing it.

CONRAD: I never did it again either. If you can believe it—never with another child after you. Ever!

PATRICK: I don't know that I *can* believe it.

CONRAD: There've been adults.

PATRICK: Teenagers?

CONRAD: Consenting *adults!*

PATRICK: In California, the age of consent is *eighteen.*

CONRAD: You were the only child! The only one!

PATRICK: If that is true, it's a privilege I could have lived without.

CONRAD: I know that doesn't make it any less wrong—any less my fault!

PATRICK: No, it doesn't. Because *you* were an adult. I was a child.

CONRAD: Yes. A bright child. A seductive child. Alluring and dangerous. You were like a little spark of divinity, tinged with a shadowed side, some inner sadness, a melancholy I recognized and wanted to fix by touching you, holding you, making it all right. I could never get over how long you could sustain eye contact with me. You were never shy. You never looked away. You were bold.

PATRICK: Oh, I see. So *I* was the source of temptation! All children are seductive, but they are *children.* They are not the ones in control!

CONRAD: Yes. Yes, I know. I know better than anyone that children are helpless.

PATRICK: What did you think about what you were doing?

CONRAD: I knew it was risky. I knew it was against the laws of God and man, but at the time I must not have considered anything except . . . the excitement.

PATRICK: You didn't consider the consequences?

CONRAD: They made me sick with fear.

PATRICK: The consequences to *you.*

CONRAD: And to *you.* I never told anyone about it, except some unknown priest in a confessional. I finally got up the nerve and drove to New Orleans—no one would know me there. I didn't tell him that I was a priest, only that I was a teacher. He said he would grant me absolution only if the sin were never, ever repeated.

PATRICK: [*Snidely*] And you felt like a brand-new human being.

CONRAD: I can still hear his voice. He said the sin was mortal—that if I continued, I would be excommunicated, denied the sacraments, forbidden all contact with Holy Mother Church. He asked me if I thought I was fit to be a teacher and suggested I find another profession—remove myself from the near occasion of sin—the company of children. I promised I would, and he absolved me. On the drive back I was in a stupor, but I knew I had to speak to you the next day and somehow get through the rest of that term. Leaving abruptly would've caused a scandal. When that year was finally over I asked to be transferred and prayed that would be the end of it.

PATRICK: [*Sarcastically*] A simple moral failure, according to the club. Something calling for penance and plain old willpower. So it's five *Hail* Marys and out the door for ten *Bloody* Marys! It would have been far worse if you'd have slept with a woman. That would have meant you'd broken your *vow!*

[*Conrad, in an attitude of exhaustion, slowly, heavily swings his feet to the floor but doesn't seem to have the strength to get off the bed. Looking off right*]

PATRICK: You were a decent man, Conrad. Do you know why you did it?

CONRAD: [*Looking off left*] I have no idea. The whole thing is something I've never understood. Why I did what I did to you—why I did what I did to myself. Teaching was my calling . . . and I ruined it. Now I am a minister to the comatose—giving sacraments to people who don't know if they're in this world or the next, let alone that I'm standing there, praying for their salvation. It's an empty task to say empty homilies over and over and over to a congregation that's long since stopped listening. Now, I'm surrounded by death. And when I think of my own death approaching, I don't even have my faith to comfort me.

PATRICK: All I want is to resolve the past so that I can go on, go on to God knows what. It's a joke, but some mysterious part of me wants to love and be loved—wants it in the mildest, most removed but most insistent way. In the end, none of it makes sense. Nothing tracks.

CONRAD: Like our having met the way we did after all these years. It's all a mystery.

PATRICK: Exactly. *Pazzo*. Meshuga.

CONRAD: What I did is something I'll never forget or get over or comprehend.

PATRICK: You can try, and all you'll get is a giant explosion, like the first blast of the universe. Something you simply cannot explain. In the end, whatever you figure out, whatever you really *crack*, just reassembles into a question mark as soon as you turn your head.

[*Silence. A pause. Patrick goes upstage center, takes the key out of his pocket and unlocks the door [three revolutions] and leaves the key dangling in the latch. Conrad slowly gets off the bed. Patrick slowly moves downstage right, facing away from Conrad as he goes to the door and stops . . .*]

CONRAD: [*At the door, after a moment*] I want to ask something of you.

PATRICK: [*Not turning, facing out*] What is it?

CONRAD: Would you please . . . put your arms around me? Hold me for a moment?

PATRICK: [*Not looking at Conrad, after a moment*] I wouldn't be at all interested in that.

CONRAD: [*Resigned*] I understand. [*Conrad opens the door. Patrick hears the sound of the latch opening but still does not turn. Conrad opens the door, starts to go, stops, shuts the door and turns back . . .*] Will you . . . [*Patrick's body reacts to Conrad's voice, having assumed that the sound of the door closing meant Conrad had departed . . . Begs*] . . . Will you please forgive me?

PATRICK: [*After a moment*] I don't know.

[*Conrad slowly comes beside Patrick and kneels down beside him . . .*]

CONRAD: [*Quietly, begging*] I want to atone for my sin. I want to be good— to be clean. Forgive me. Only you can make me clean. Make me—after all these years—pure. Restore me. Make me whole. I beg you.

[*Patrick doesn't respond. Conrad takes Patrick's hand, presses it against his forehead . . .*]

CONRAD: I confess to Almighty God and to you, my son, that I have sinned against you. Forgive me, Patrick. Forgive me, Ned. I beg you to forgive me.

[*A church bell begins to toll somewhere in the distance . . . The sound is faint, as the doors to the balcony are shut*]

PATRICK: [*After a long moment*] I . . . . . . . . I . . . . . . . . forgive you. [*After another moment, absently*] Go in peace.

CONRAD: God bless you. [*Conrad kisses Patrick's hand. Patrick does not pull away. Conrad lets go of his hand, gets off his knees, and goes to the door. Patrick does not look at Conrad as he opens the door and leaves, closing the door softly behind him. A beat, as the church bell continues to toll. Patrick turns toward the muffled sound, goes to the window, and with his two hands whips the portieres apart and pulls open the balcony doors. Suddenly, a surreal blaze of white light incandesces the room from outside as a strong wind blasts inside, billowing the sheers out, ruffling Patrick's hair and suit jacket and trousers. Simultaneous with the blinding light and the blast of wind, the sound of the church bells louden to an earsplitting pitch. A beat . . . Black out*]

THE END

# THE MEN FROM THE BOYS

## A SEQUEL PLAY

For
Tricia Guild and Richard Polo

From their Best Man

*The Men From the Boys* had its world premiere at The New Conservatory Theatre Center, San Francisco, [Ed Decker, Artistic Director] on October 26, 2002. The scene design was by Eric Sinkkonen, the music by Larry Grossman, and the stage manager was Phillip Lienau. The play was produced and directed by Ed Decker.

The cast was:

| | |
|---|---|
| DONALD: | PETER CARLSTROM |
| MICHAEL: | RUSS DUFFY |
| EMORY: | MICHAEL PATRICK GAFFNEY |
| SCOTT | OLEN CHRISTIAN HOLM |
| HAROLD: | WILL HUDDLESTON |
| HANK | TERRY LAMB |
| RICK | RAJIV SHAH |
| BERNARD: | LEWIS SIMS |
| JASON | OWEN THOMAS |

Special thanks to:

Andrew Nance [Actor, Conservatory Director]
*and*
Buddy Thomas [playwright, agent who brought TMFTB to TNCTC]

Keri Fitch [costumes], Melissa Kalstrom [wigs, hair, and makeup], Victoria Kirby [publicity], Nancy Mancias [properties], Jonathan Retsky [lighting], and Steve Romanko [sound design].

TNCTC and the author wish to acknowledge

Mr. Steven Buss
*and also*
Mr. Arnold Stiefel of Stiefel Entertainment

for their individual support and generosity.

# Act I

*THE SET: A deliberate reproduction of the concept for an East 50s Manhattan duplex [bedroom upstairs], designed by Peter Harvey for* The Boys in the Band: *a black-and-white photo blowup collage of chic rooms [as seen in interior decor magazines], which completely covers all wall surfaces. Abstract and stylish.*

*In the original production there were only "Deco" black Naugahyde chrome tube chairs, a settee, and a couple of chrome and glass side tables. That was it. In any case, the effect should be deliberately minimal, monochromatic, and clean-lined, without a single unnecessary item of dressing. Dramatic and anal. And, of course, it should positively scream "taste."*

*From a state of complete darkness the lights suddenly illuminate full-tilt to reveal a stage occupied by five characters from* The Boys in the Band, *now thirty years older but still pulled together. Their ages [and the state of their hair] are: MICHAEL, fifty-nine, thin-ish or a meticulous, studied comb-over; EMORY, sixty-two, dyed auburn; BERNARD, fifty-seven, salt and pepper; DONALD, fifty-seven, blond/silver; and HANK, sixty-one, distinguished gray temples. HAROLD, sixty-one, with receding curly black hair, will enter eventually.*

*This quintet is positioned formally at various interesting levels: standing with hands in pockets or arms folded; seated on a chair or a stool or the stairs. They all look directly at the audience, completely poker-faced [Sad? Dazed? Imperious?], as if caught in an artfully composed still of the early Avedon/Stern school. All wear suits or jackets and ties: EMORY in a Charvet bow cravat and black velour suit [minus the jacket]; MICHAEL in a charcoal-gray flannel two-piece Armani and solid charcoal tie. DONALD, alone, has loosened his striped rep, unfastened his button-down collar, and removed his navy Brooks Brothers blazer to sling it over his shoulder.*

*The "men" of the title are lit in hotter pools of light than the three new "boys," who face upstage with their backs to the audience. They are SCOTT, twenty-six, JASON, thirty-something, both Caucasian; and RICK, twenty-four, an Asian-American.*

*They are all dressed in more relaxed, up-to-the-minute styles, from slacks and pullovers to jeans and jackets with T-shirts. They are scattered among the originals, posed in more casual attitudes: draped against the stairs, lolling on the back of the sofa, or lying on the floor, propped on an arm. Their facial attitudes are concealed, but their body language varies from studied casual to subtly provocative.*

*After the "shock illumination" of the frieze, there is what seems to be an interminable pause. We hear only the SOUND of heavy rain and* EMORY's *delicately pulling a needle and yarn through a small, unfinished, petit point pattern. The dimmer circles of light sneak to the level of the hotter ones. No one moves or speaks. The older characters continue to stare straight forward, enigmatic; the younger ones remain turned away, their attitudes unknown. Then, just as the audience is about to break with restless nervousness, in reaction to the prolonged silence, stillness, and scrutiny,* EMORY *starts to cough uncontrollably. Everyone else slowly, deliberately turns his head without moving his body to glare at EMORY [Disapprovingly? Sympathetically? Affectlessly?] and hold until* EMORY *calms, heavily clears his throat.*

*Finally, EMORY sheepishly scans the sea of attention, chagrined at everyone looking at him . . .*

EMORY: [*Tongue-in-cheek*] It must be the excitement. We're having too much fun here.

*[No one cracks a smile. Not a titter. They all continue to look at Emory a moment longer [Contempt? Compassion? Indifference?], then Donald breaks the mood, flings his blazer aside, goes to a bar cart, and pours a crystal tumbler of water from a pitcher]*

MICHAEL: [*Sardonically*] Excitement, indeed! Some "celebration of life!" It's so fucking quiet in here, you could hear boll weevils pissing on cotton!

DONALD: [*Palm to ear*] Listen! I think I hear them! No, it's just pissing with rain.

MICHAEL: Let's have some music, Bernard. Liven up this taffy-pull.

BERNARD: [*Facetiously*] Sure. I'll just put on a little gangsta rap.

*[Bernard goes to an étagère, begins to shuffle through some CDs]*

MICHAEL: [*Dryly, offhand*] You do and there's gonna be some strange fruit hangin' from the poplar trees.

*[Emory, with an arched "Ahem!" clears his throat at Michael's "wit." Rick, the exotically attractive Asian-American, speaks up]*

RICK: [*To Michael*] Is that a racist remark?

BERNARD: [*Weary, tongue-in-cheek*] Well, Michael's not exactly out in a cornfield at midnight, burning crosses. His ambivalent generation of so-called Southern liberals has just got to die out. [*Dryly*] It shouldn't be long now.

[*Meanwhile, Donald has crossed to Emory, hands him a tumbler*]

DONALD: Here, Emory, drink some water.

EMORY: Is it bottled or just from the tap?

MICHAEL: [*Quickly, an edge*] It's from the toilet. It's toilet water. Every morning I submerge an empty Evian bottle in the toilet. It's multipurpose eau de toilette—you can either drink it or put it behind your ears.

[*Emory shoots Michael a withering look, takes a sip from the tumbler, returns it to Donald*]

EMORY: [*Sweetly*] Thanks, Donald. You're a real "sis."

[*This remark is met with some audible groans from Jason, Bernard, and Donald. Note: There is an open bottle of Dom Perignon in a wine cooler on the cart and Hank and Rick take a sip champagne from flutes already in their hands.*]

[*Everyone begins to shift, get up, and move about. All except Scott, the loner with the knockout good looks, who noticeably remains apart from the group—perhaps leaning on the far side of the stairs, hands in pockets, staring into space*]

BERNARD: [*Generally, re Emory*] Wouldn't you know she only drinks designer water.

EMORY: Don't say "she"! You, of all people, know that's *not* politically correct! [*Big flirty smile to Jason*] Is it, Jason?

BERNARD: [*Quickly, to Emory*] Calling people "sis" is not exactly *enlightened*.

[*Jason, proletariat activist, gym-body, sexy in an obvious way, turns at the mention of his name . . .*]

JASON: It's all right, Emory. We make allowances for those who have gone before.

EMORY: [*Drawing himself up*] Do I detect the remotest innuendo that I am slightly older than you?

JASON: [*To Emory*] You planted the redwoods, didn't you?

[*Some scattered laughter. Emory makes a quick decision to take the high road . . .*]

EMORY: [*To Jason, mock-insulted*] Oh, you're *terrible*! [*Coy, a beat*] But I like you.

*[Jason looks indifferent, turns away. Emory recovers with a certain practiced [and practical] dignity, joins Bernard at the étagère to select CDs]*

DONALD: Did you know the UN declared this "The Year of the Older Person"?

JASON: I'm glad they declared *something*.

MICHAEL: *[Still on earlier thought]* I *am* the most liberal Confederate who ever lived! Why, when I was sixteen my father gave me a convertible, and do you know my best friend was a black gay boy. Oh, he'd have to sit in the back seat, of course, so no one would say anything. It was the acceptable, hypocritical, *idiotic* way things were done.

BERNARD: If you'd had any guts, you'd have made him sit up front.

MICHAEL: Then he'd have looked like the chauffeur.

BERNARD: In the *passenger* seat *beside* you!

MICHAEL: Funny thing, Bernard, dear. Neither of us wanted our balls between a split rail. We were smart. *We played the system.*

JASON: Somebody has to put their balls on the line sometime.

MICHAEL: *[Re empty flutes]* Jason, why don't you *act up* like the old days and freshen everyone's drinks? You're so good at it.

JASON: That's why I'm a bartender *these* days!

MICHAEL: Oh, well, if you're offended and going to picket or protest this solemn occasion, then . . .

*[Jason ignores Michael, goes to the bar cart as Rick . . .]*

RICK: *[To Emory]* You're the first real interior decorator I've ever been around.

EMORY: Designer. We prefer interior *"designer."* Like flight attendants prefer "flight attendant" instead of "stewardess."

JASON: Or "steward," if you happen to be a man.

EMORY: *[Quick and pointed]* So few are.

BERNARD: *[To Jason]* You've had more careers than anybody I know.

JASON: *[Refills his flute]* Mmm, I've careered from career to career, to quote somebody, and guess what?

MICHAEL: You're still queer.

JASON: I'm still a major fuck-up.

DONALD: [*Crosses to Jason*] I thought I held that title.

BERNARD: Why *not* go into politics? Being a fuck-up seems to be a pre-requisite.

JASON: I'm too old for that. Haven't got a law degree and haven't got the money to get one. Had to drop out, as it was. [*To Donald*] What can I do for you, sir?

DONALD: [*Bit too flirtatious*] Beer. No, a glass of white wine. No an extra dry Bombay martini on the rocks, please.

EMORY: Beer! Wine! Booze! Make up your mind! It's readiness that makes a woman!

[*He is ignored by everyone*]

JASON: More champagne, Hank?

HANK: No, thanks.

JASON: [*Re empty bucket*] We need ice.

MICHAEL: There's no ice? I thought . . .

DONALD: [*Picks up bucket*] I'll get it.

SCOTT: *I'll* get it. Sorry.

[*Donald stops. Everyone reacts to Scott having spoken. He goes to Donald, takes the silver ice bucket*]

DONALD: [*To Scott*] You don't mind doing it?

SCOTT: [*For Michael's benefit*] I'll do anything if I'm not humiliated.

MICHAEL: [*To Scott, calmly, seriously*] Did I humiliate you? Have I *ever* humiliated you? [*No answer*] Well? [*Scott exits off left to kitchen*] I guess that was a rhetorical question.

EMORY: [*CDs in hand*] So, what are we going to do, kids? Put on some music and dance our tits off?

DONALD: [*Moving away*] I'd rather be in a ditch.

EMORY: [*Ever the fun one*] Well, then, I just heard about this marvelous new party game! Everyone takes his clothes off and forms two parallel lines, facing each other. And then, when someone yells "Go!" the two lines make a mad stampede toward each other . . . and the first one that gets in gets a kiss!

[*He breaks himself up, laughing. Nobody else cracks a smile, they all just glare at him again*]

EMORY: [*Trying to save the moment*] I forgot to say condoms are passed out first. Does that make it funnier? [*Silence*] Okay, why don't we all just pull on our wet suits and grovel around on top of each other?

MICHAEL: [*Grimly, calmly*] There will be no dancing. There will be no games played. And for the duration of this event, no one is allowed to take off so much as a necktie. For that, you'll have to see some *serious* gay theater. All-male nude Chekhov, that sort of thing.

BERNARD: [*To Emory*] No nudity tonight. Not with *this* crowd. [*Looks at Jason*] Well, not with *most* of this crowd.

RICK: [*Re earlier thought*] I'm glad we're not gonna play that game!

EMORY: [*To Rick, sympathetically*] Me, too, actually. Because of a few unwanted kilos. But, I'll soon have a new bod. I now have a personal trainer, and he's marvelous. He said to me, "First we lose the weight, then we sculpt."

BERNARD: That ought to be as simple as chopping a fifth face on Mount Rushmore.

EMORY: I've lost four pounds! Can't you tell?

DONALD: Not from this angle.

BERNARD: [*Re music*] Whatta you want, Michael? [*Quickly*] Ella-Mabel-Judy-Peggy-Barbra—or Bobby?

MICHAEL: You know I don't own any Streisand.

EMORY: [*Holding up a CD*] Yes, you do, right here, the one that's got "When in Rome" on it.

MICHAEL: That belongs to Harold.

JASON: Is there anything that was written in the last forty years?

[*Michael gives Jason a look as Scott enters with the filled bucket. Bernard puts on something like Chet Baker's recording of "Tenderly."*]

JASON: [*To Scott, taking bucket*] Thanks, Scott. What'll it be?

SCOTT: [*Dryly*] I'll have some of that toilet water. With a twist.

[*Jason puts some ice in the martini he has made, hands it to Donald*]

JASON: Donald.

DONALD: Thanks.

[*Jason pours Scott an Evian. Scott returns to the outer limits by the stairs*]

DONALD: [*Sips drink, reacts*] Oh, yeah, Jason, that's good.

JASON: [*Smiles noncommitally*] Thank you, sir.

[*Jason walks away from the bar cart with a can of Diet Coke just as Emory says . . .*]

EMORY: I'd like some coffee.

[*Jason pops the top of the Diet Coke can and drinks. Emory forces a stiff smile at being ignored. Rick puts down his drink, picks up a silver coffeepot and cup and saucer from the bar cart*]

RICK: [*Pleasantly, to Emory re coffee*] How do you like it?

EMORY: [*Campily sultry*] Like I like my men.

BERNARD: [*To Emory, re Rick*] Sorry, he ain't got no gay coffee!

EMORY: [*Snaps*] I meant hot and café au lait!

BERNARD: He knows what you meant. And he still doesn't give a shit.

[*Emory sucks a tooth, nose in the air. Rick picks up the silver coffeepot, looks at it appreciatively*]

RICK: [*Ingenuously, not a trace of chichi*] What a nice coffeepot. Nice and simple, you know.

[*Rick pours Emory a cup . . .*]

EMORY: And a lovely ice bucket too. Really too lovely for ice. [*To Michael*] You ought to float a pansy in it.

MICHAEL: [*"Menacingly"*] I might just do that. Facedown.

[*Rick hands the coffee to Emory . . .*]

RICK: [*Pleasantly*] There you go, Emory.

EMORY: [*Taking the cup, with flirty charm*] *Merci, mille fois.*

RICK: [*Innocently*] Oh, you speak French?

EMORY: No, I was just . . . Well, it's hard to explain exactly. It's what used to be called *charm.* Of course, that was a while back. [*A look to Jason*] Only those who've "gone before" might remember.

RICK: [*Back a beat, to Emory*] I just thought with a name like Em-or-ee . . . . and cafe au lait . . . [*re Michael*] . . . and him saying the thing about Evian . . . and . . .

[*French pronunciation of Evian: Aye-vee-anh*]

MICHAEL: [*Tolerantly*] I have a name too, and it's not *him*, it's Michael.

RICK: [*Conciliatory*] Sorry. [*Continuing, to Emory*] And Michael here, saying the thing about . . . well, I don't know, I just thought you might be French or something. 'Cause *I* speak French.

[*Emory is silent, thinking this over*]

MICHAEL: [*To Emory*] Did you follow that? Or were you knocked senseless by *The Great Language Barrier Reef of Time?*

EMORY: [*To Rick, simply*] Emory was my mother's family name, and she wasn't French. At least if she was she never told *me.*

RICK: My mother *was* French. Well, French-Vietnamese.

MICHAEL: [*To Rick, slightly grand*] I don't believe we've been formally introduced.

RICK: [*Extends his hand*] Oh, I should have introduced myself.

MICHAEL: I mean, you *look* familiar, but . . .

RICK: [*Shakes hands with Michael*] I'm out of uniform.

[*Michael reacts oddly, takes this in*]

HANK: [*To Rick*] Well, *I* know you. I remember you nights—mostly nights.

RICK: [*To Michael*] Yeah, the graveyard shift. I'm a practical nurse. Part-time.

MICHAEL: Oh, of course you are!

RICK: [*Tentatively*] When Larry couldn't sleep, we'd talk—or I'd just hold his hand. We . . . became quite close. He gave me some of his artwork . . . stuff he had in his room. And some books. [*To Hank*] I hope you don't mind.

HANK: Why should I? They were his things.

RICK: [*To Michael*] I know I wasn't exactly invited, but I thought it was kind of an open house . . .

MICHAEL: [*Chagrined*] Oh, it *is*. Why, you're *very, very* welcome, Rick. I just don't remember you. I wasn't there much in the evening, but then, Larry tended to keep people in his life rather compartmentalized.

JASON: It's kind of a gay thing, don't you think?

SCOTT: [*Involuntarily*] Yeah. Friends, anyway.

MICHAEL: ["*Graciously*"] Well, now, Rick . . . what do you do when you're not *nursing*?

RICK: I'm an art student. Part-time. Larry encouraged me to enroll in Parsons. He said if I'd go he'd pay for my tuition.

MICHAEL: I see.

[*Hank reacts with mild surprise. Bernard looks to Hank. Michael looks to Scott, who turns away, then to Donald*]

MICHAEL: [*Remembers; generally*] Oh, uh, there are some hot hors d'oeuvres! I don't know where my mind is.

DONALD: [*Re Scott*] I do.

[*Michael shoots Donald a look*]

EMORY: [*To Rick; French pronunciation for "design"*] Michael had Cuisine "Duhzine" do the food! I love their takeout! They make the best vol-au-vent.

[*Rick stares at him blankly. NOTE: the name of the caterer is "Cuisine Design, but pronounced, as if, in French.*]

BERNARD: Do real men eat vol-au-vent?

EMORY: [*Getting up, sighs*] Well, if no one else is going to do it . . . So what else is nouvelle?

MICHAEL: *Don't* use the microwave.

EMORY: [*Very American accent*] *Jamais, cheri.* It dries 'em out.

[*Emory exits to the kitchen*]

BERNARD: [*To Michael*] Is Larry's mother coming?

MICHAEL: [*Shakes his head*] Had to get back to Philadelphia.

HANK: The older brother never liked me. He "disapproved." I called him when Larry got so sick, but it was the same old story. I'm not surprised he didn't show. But Larry's mother and stepfather managed to get here before he died. They stayed with us . . . I mean, with me.

[*Bernard comes over to Hank, puts his arm around him, and comforts him. The group watches stoically*]

HANK: [*Quietly appreciative*] Thanks, Bernard. This may sound strange, but you know, even after all these years I can't say I really knew Larry all that well. Do you find that some sort of demented statement?

BERNARD: No.

SCOTT: [*To no one in particular*] Who ever knows anybody? You never know what's really going on with someone.

HANK: [*Absently*] Yeah.

[*Michael takes note of Scott's remark*]

BERNARD: I think we always keep some part of ourselves *to* ourselves.

HANK: Larry had his secrets, of course. But that, in its way, had its allure. He was always a little bit of a mystery to me. And, I think, to a degree, to himself too.

BERNARD: I sure don't think I know myself.

JASON: Does anyone, really?

BERNARD: I mean . . . I don't think I can *explain* myself.

HANK: I know that even at my age I'm still finding out things about myself.

RICK: Me too. Now that it's over, I feel relief. And that's the truth. I feel so *relieved* that the nightmare is finally fucking over.

[*A moment of silence. Emory enters with a silver tray of canapés. All heads swivel to him, a repeat of the opening tableau when he coughed. The room is hushed. All heads follow Emory as he crosses to Hank*]

EMORY: [*To Hank*] Doughnut, soldier? Sorry, *finger* food?

HANK: [*Has to laugh*] No, thanks, Emory.

[*Emory passes among the group*]

EMORY: Cheese puffs? Meatballs? Rumaki? If that dates me, how about: cellulars, nicotine patches, sex toys?

RICK: [*Re tray of food*] Very artistic, Emory. The presentation.

EMORY: I'm a born stylist.

[*There are reactions of "Mmmm." Some take a canapé and a paper napkin from him, some do not. He comes to Michael, who does not take anything, just stares icily at him . . .*]

MICHAEL: You used the microwave, didn't you?

EMORY: No, I didn't.

MICHAEL: *Liar.*

HANK: [*Picking up thought*] The time had long since past when we were physical with each other, but emotionally, we couldn't have been closer. He wanted to die. And he wanted me to *help* him die.

RICK: [*To Hank*] And did you?

HANK: I would never be able to go on living with myself if I'd actually fed him the pills. That's funny, because I think I'm capable of *anything*—even killing someone. Anyway, I agreed to be with him—stay with him up to the point where he would swallow them—but I told him I wanted to leave before he did.

JASON: You have to be so careful of the fucking law.

HANK: I said I'd give him a scrambled egg so there'd be a little something in his stomach—give him a Dramamine so that he wouldn't vomit and strangle. But he'd have to actually *do* it himself. Swallow the pills alone. But in the end he didn't.

MICHAEL: [*Looks at his watch*] Oh, where the hell is Harold?!

JASON: He must be caught in the rain.

EMORY: Oh, rain or shine, Harold'll be late for his *own* memorial.

BERNARD: I saw him at the service. Didn't you see him, Donald?

DONALD: [*Nods*] With something very blond. Well, from the neck up.

[*The front door buzzer sounds . . .*]

MICHAEL: Speak of the devil.

[MICHAEL *goes to the panel beside the front door down right, presses a release button, tears opens the door, and goes out into the hallway*]

HANK: [*To no one in particular*] Larry conned every doctor in town out of pills. He made sure he had a stash. He never told anybody, and he never took them. Not a single one. But he made sure he had them . . . and yet, he wouldn't take them. Explain that.

EMORY: I'd have had Kevorkian on the speed dial.

[*Michael returns*]

EMORY: Is it Hallie?

MICHAEL: No, it's the super. Scott, did you chain your bike in the entry?

SCOTT: Yeah, to the radiator. Why, is it in the way?

MICHAEL: He wants to mop up the rainwater or something. Bring it up here.

[*Scott puts his glass on the stair rung, crosses, and goes out. Michael shuts the door*]

HANK: [*Weeps*] Forgive me, I seem to be the only one wallowing in this.

DONALD: Don't be ridiculous, Hank.

[*Bernard helps sit Hank down, takes Hank's handkerchief out of his jacket pocket, and dries his eyes for him*]

HANK: [*Re his tears*] I'm sorry, I really am. This is supposed to be a celebration of life.

EMORY: Frankly, if I never attend another "celebration of life" as long as I live, it'll be too fucking soon! And *if* I receive another invitation to a "celebration of life," I *hope* there's a scratch–and–sniff cyanide capsule enclosed! These postfuneral "cocktail huddles" only make you wonder who's next!

BERNARD: How can you say such a thing!

EMORY: I'm just saying for *me*, all these things have begun to blur. I know it sounds polit . . .

MICHAEL: If you say "politically incorrect," I'm going to rip out your tongue and slice it for sandwiches.

[*The sound of a key in the lock in the front door is heard. The door is opened by Scott, who rolls his bike inside and recloses it. He leans the bike against the wall. Jason crosses to the bike, stoops to "investigate" it.*]

JASON: [*Re Scott's bike*] There's not a mark on it. Looks just like it did the night I sold it to you. From the way you were talking, I thought . . .

SCOTT: It's just the idea that it was stolen out of my apartment that made me feel so . . .

JASON: Maybe one of your friends was just a playing a trick on you. After all, it was returned to you.

SCOTT: I found it in the foyer of my building. Lying under the stairs, like it'd been dumped.

[*Scott looks to see Michael is staring at him and so are Jason and Rick. Scott moves away from Jason and remains apart from the group as Emory bites loudly into a celery stalk. Everyone turns to stare at him*]

HANK: [*Continuing*] Larry loved his students, and by God, he would go to class when he really didn't have the strength to even stand up. He taught when he was in such pain most of us would have . . .

DONALD: Begged for a morphine drip . . .

BERNARD: But Larry was clean and sober. Like Michael and me. We all wound up in different "rooms."

MICHAEL: [*Almost to himself*] Ah, those rooms. Some dead, some dying.

BERNARD: [*Upbeat*] But some saved.

HANK: [*Smiles to himself*] My son said we needed God in the bullpen, but He was out of town with another team.

MICHAEL: What I don't understand about Christian Science is that you can have a million face-lifts, but you won't go to a doctor.

BERNARD: Larry never had a face-lift! Some people just look that good.

HANK: And he wasn't a Christian Scientist. He was a Scientologist.

DONALD: He *was*?

HANK: Well, for about five minutes.

BERNARD: He liked to try everything. I'm all for that.

EMORY: Remember when he was in EST? Once upon a time. [*To Jason*] I know you weren't born yet, so just cut me in half and count the rings.

BERNARD: [*Re drugs and booze*] And he *Just Said No* up until he had to be taken to the hospital and then other people—doctors—started making the decisions.

RICK: [*Reflectively*] I only met him after he was first hospitalized.

JASON: Did he ever come to terms with it?

BERNARD: Come to terms with what?

JASON: Being ashamed of what he had?

HANK: Ashamed?

[*A slight pause . . .*]

BERNARD: Larry didn't die of AIDS.

JASON: Well, I know that's the official story.

BERNARD: That's the *true* story! He died of *cancer*.

MICHAEL: Cancer without the "quotes." The respectable kind. The *esteemed* kind. The kind you get where it doesn't show.

EMORY: Pancreatic.

RICK: Yeah, that's what was on his chart.

JASON: I thought it was . . .

MICHAEL: We know what you thought! Gay men *do* die of other things! They do die of prostate tumors and heart attacks and get blown up on planes and all the rest of those good things, just like real people!

EMORY: Or they're *murdered*.

MICHAEL: Or—they just die of old age. Their medical profiles are impeccable, but they're so old that when they pee sand comes out.

DONALD: [*Absently*] The thing about a real good heart attack is that it's fast.

EMORY: The good thing about Alzheimer's is that you get to hide your own Easter eggs.

BERNARD: What's good about *that*?

EMORY: Forget it. [*Realizes*] Sorry!

HANK: What's good about cancer?

BERNARD: Nothing, except it's possible to beat it, and that's good.

EMORY: [*Generally*] You can get over a heart attack. Michael did.

JASON: [*Sarcastically*] You can't get over a *fatal* one. [*To Emory*] Are you sure Michael had a heart attack? Maybe it was just a pain down in his arm from the weight of his Rolex.

MICHAEL: You'll be happy to know I can't afford a Rolex and disappointed to hear I *do* have a heart.

JASON: It's only disappointing that you have such a *strong* one. You know, Michael, you may be the most cynical person I've ever encountered.

MICHAEL: Then they oughta let you out more often!

BERNARD: *Please.* Could we just . . .

MICHAEL: I see no reason for "*Forced Family Fun.*" Must we *pretend* to be gay—and by that I mean in the linguistically traditional sense of the word "gay"?!

JASON: That is the one thing you'll never have to pretend, in any sense.

EMORY: [*Privately amused, to Jason, coyly*] Oh, you're *terrible*! But I like you.

JASON: [*Heated*] I'm sick of self-centered retros like you, who wouldn't get their Guccis stepped on, fighting for what they believe are—

HANK: [*Rises, the peacemaker*] Now, wait a minute, fellas! This is not why we're here.

MICHAEL: I'm beginning to wonder why some of us *are* here.

RICK: You mean me.

MICHAEL: [*Bluntly, tolerantly*] I *said* you were welcome!

JASON: [*To Rick*] He means me. He's never liked me and never liked the fact that Larry liked me.

MICHAEL: [*Testily*] Doesn't anyone of this enlightened generation know how rude it is to refer to someone in the third person who happens to be standing in his presence?

JASON: You hate me and you hated my relationship with Larry—which was none of your goddamn business.

MICHAEL: You didn't even know what he died of! What *relationship*?!

JASON: We were friends. Sometimes *loving* friends. At one time Larry and I happened to be what he called "occasional regulars."

[*Hank looks away*]

RICK: Does that mean what I think it means?

JASON: It means what it means. I mostly bumped into him at Fire Island.

EMORY: Are people still going there?

JASON: You can't kill human nature. You can *die* of it, but you can't kill it.

EMORY: [*Placating Jason*] I see nothing wrong with patrolling the lush, dark, tedious Pines—if you play safe . . .

BERNARD: [*To Emory, bluntly*] You have hookers. That's hardly safe!

EMORY: I do not!

BERNARD: Bullshit. You don't know whether they're going to infect you or cut your fucking throat.

JASON: When I saw him in the hospital, I was blown away. He'd been so hot . . . for an older guy. [*To Michael*] So I made a mistake about what he died of! So, sue me!

MICHAEL: It's the city *you* ought to sue—for those legs.

JASON: What?

MICHAEL: You've got "sue the city legs." You ought to sue the city for building the sidewalk so close to your ass!

DONALD: [*To Michael*] You ought to keep your personality on a leash.

MICHAEL: You thought he'd been punished by God for his way of life!

JASON: That sounds more like something *you'd* think. I'm just sorry I jumped to a conclusion.

EMORY: If you're going to jump, you may as well dive. It gives a better line.

JASON: [*To Hank*] I went to Larry's funeral *because* of the feeling I had for him. [*To Michael*] And I'm *here* because of it. Throw me out if you want to! *You're* not my friend! Larry was! I'm here for *him*. And for myself.

BERNARD: If this is going to turn into something other than what it's meant to be, I'm going home. I've learned my lesson in this living room.

MICHAEL: Yeah, here we are back in the same old living room.

BERNARD: [*Moving to leave*] With the same old queens!

DONALD: Wait, Bernard . . . we're *all* upset.

EMORY: And you're all acting like kids!

HANK: [*After a moment*] Well, the grown-ups are acting like kids. The kids are acting quite grown-up. Rick has barely opened his mouth. And Scott hasn't said a word at all.

[*Scott shifts uncomfortably, crosses to the bar cart to pick up a Diet Coke and go behind the stairs, his back to the group*]

HANK: [*Calmly*] Look . . . we're here to share our sorrow, and we're free to act as angry and frustrated and scared and sad and depressed as we feel.

MICHAEL: [*Musically, "great star" largesse; lovely smile*] And as "happy." [*For Jason's benefit*] Or we're free to feel just as sad as if he *had* died of AIDS.

DONALD: [*To Michael*] Why don't you have a double Shirley Temple and cool it.

[*Michael bristles at Donald's remark. The door buzzes*]

EMORY: Well, final*ment*!

[*Emory sits on the floor, behind the coffee table, leaning against the sofa. Michael goes to press the door release button, opens the front door, goes out into the hallway*]

HANK: Is it Harold?

MICHAEL: [*Offstage*] No. Flowers, I think.

JASON: Who needs a refill?

[*Jason goes to the bar cart, takes the Dom Perignon out of its cooler and goes to refill glasses—Hank's, Emory's, Rick's. Michael returns with a beautiful, elegantly arranged, home-grown cut flowers in a vase*]

EMORY: [*Impressed*] Oh, my, who sent that?!

MICHAEL: Do I know? They're for Hank.

EMORY: I can live without food, but I can't live without flowers.

BERNARD: Then you better lay off the chocolate-covered nasturtiums.

[*Hank opens the card*]

HANK: [*Reads card*] They're from Patsy and Jessica.

EMORY: The butch dykes who run the animal clinic? [*Quickly corrects*] The rather male-identified professional women in the country . . . ?

RICK: [*To Michael re flowers*] Where're you going to put them?

EMORY: Well, Lady Astor always said, "Build a garden under a lamp." *And she oughta know.*

[*Michael gives Emory a look and plunks the bouquet in the middle of the coffee table, completely covering Emory from view*]

JASON: [*To Emory*] Don't you have any consciousness at all?

EMORY: [*Rising into view*] I'm kidding, for Christ's sake!! That was a joke, you serious, solemn sex machine! *Although,* I must tell you, dykes do not eat egg salad sandwiches, and they don't pack their clothes in tissue paper. *That* is a *vérité.*

[*Bernard looks away. Jason shakes his head*]

HANK: [*Ignoring everyone*] I haven't been to the country for weeks, and Patsy and Jessica have been so good about the dogs and the plants and the pipes— they've really taken care of the place for us. Well, for me, now.

JASON: I don't know that gay men are going to be as supportive. Can you see us marching for breast cancer?

DONALD: Yeah, we're not really interested in their culture—I mean, we don't read lesbian novels or see the latest lesbian film, when it's almost a supposition that they support gay men's art.

MICHAEL: Gay guys are so much more self-involved. They'll just continue in their me-me-me, gym-gym-gym, sex-sex-sex, business-as-usual way.

HANK: [*Continuing*] Larry was only sixty. That's too young to die.

RICK: With all due respect, that's old to me. He seemed so much younger.

JASON: [*To Hank*] Was he really sixty?

HANK: He knocked a few years off, but he was sixty. It was hard for him to get old. He was the kind of guy who was meant to be young and handsome forever.

MICHAEL: There's no such thing as fair—there's just luck. If I had to be born at all, I'd rather have been born male than female, rich rather than poor, straight instead of gay. It would have made life much easier *not* to have been gay. [*Looks at Bernard*] And some of us got a double whammy, right, Bernard?

BERNARD: I'm surprised you didn't say, "Some of us got it in spades." If you want to hate, there's always something to hate about everybody.

MICHAEL: I'd rather be white instead of black, brown, yellow, or red. And that's just the way I feel. I'd rather be gentile than Jewish, Protestant rather than Catholic. Actually I'd rather have been religion-free . . . [*Rick, Donald react*] It's *easier* that way.

DONALD: What's so great about the easy way out?

MICHAEL: Only a fool would want the *hard* way out. I'd rather be good-looking instead of plain—why couldn't we all truly have been created equal? It would have been just as easy, but, oh, no, that's not life. Some of us had to be born "interesting." And some of us, *not* so interesting. Some of us flat-out ugly. Some of us started out okay and wound up like toads. I want it easy! I want it all aces. I want something not so uphill as . . . life, *grinding, luckless life*!

JASON: You need help, Michael. Professional help. Your mind is like a bad neighborhood. You shouldn't go in there alone.

EMORY: [*To Jason, re Michael*] He's here, he's veneer, get used to it.

RICK: [*Crosses to the terrace doors, looks out*] It's stopped raining.

DONALD: Yeah, why don't we all move outside on the terrace?

SCOTT: Good idea, it's getting pretty stale in here.

DONALD: Michael has sucked all the oxygen out of the air. That's about all he's permitted to do these days.

[*Michael ignores Donald as Jason opens the doors*]

MICHAEL: Emory just blew a fucking fortune fluffing it up for the summer.

EMORY: [*Gets up*] I want to see if that hunky guy from the nursery did just what I told him to do with the pots of geraniums.

JASON: I'd kill for a cigarette.

BERNARD: Me, too, but my wife and I finally gave it up. Booze first, then tobacco.

JASON: Your wife?

HANK: [*Offhandedly*] Things change.

BERNARD: She was my first sponsor.

JASON: You met her in a twelve-step program?

BERNARD: [*Nods*] It was a slow process. We'd both been hurt—and dealt with it the wrong way. So . . . we talked a long time, and then lived together a long time, and then . . . I'm sorry she couldn't be here. She's in Detroit with my mother, who's not well.

JASON: [*Curiously*] She knows you're . . . well, whatever it is you are?

BERNARD: [*Smiles, nods*] We know all about each other. She was married to a very nice, ordinary guy, but she says he treated her in a way that was . . . well, like what you might call "sexual bigotry"—although he didn't have a clue. He just behaved that way as a matter of course. With me, she says she feels like an equal. We have fun together. [*With meaning*] All kinds of fun.

JASON: Are you happy?

BERNARD: [*Drolly*] You mean, in spite of my flying in the face of being gay and "going hetero"?

JASON: I'm just trying to understand.

BERNARD: Well, then . . . I guess I've come to think happiness is habit. And so, yeah. And, yeah, we love each other but, more important, we're each other's best friend. I used to not like sleeping with my friends—the people I laughed with and told everything to. But now, she's the only person I actually trust. And, oh, yeah, "the other" sometimes goes through my mind, but I've been there. And it didn't work out. I guess something could happen again, but I'm not planning on it.

EMORY: [*Quietly*] But *I'm* your best friend.

BERNARD: [*Calmly, sincerely*] No, I'm *your* best friend. You're my best *male* friend. [*To Jason*] I have to admit—it all scares the shit out of me.

JASON: Well, whatever works. Whatever does it for you. Whatever . . . *satisfies*.

EMORY: [*Sighs*] Yeah. Like finding your own shade of rouge.

[*Jason removes a pack of cigarettes and goes outside*]

RICK: I could stay in this room forever. This must be what they call *soignée*.

BERNARD: I think this child has been seduced by decor.

EMORY: [*With meaning*] It wouldn't be the first time.

[*Bernard gives Emory a look as Emory exits to terrace. Rick wanders the room, studying things. The phone rings*]

MICHAEL: [*Into phone*] Hello? Yeah . . . oh, *hi!* Yeah, he's fine.

HANK: I bet that's my son.

[*Rick stops, looks up*]

MICHAEL: [*Into phone*] We'll see that he gets home. You both looked great too. Sorry you can't drop by, but I understand. Let me know when the big day arrives. Promise? Right. Bye. [*Hangs up and says to Hank*] It's too uncomfortable for Kate to get around till the baby comes.

DONALD: When's it due?

HANK: Any minute.

BERNARD: Hank's second grandchild!

[*Bernard crosses to check on Hank as Rick watches, curiously. Jason takes out a cigarette, puts it between his lips, and exits to the terrace, searching his pockets for matches. Hank drops his head and turns away*]

EMORY: [*Loudly, offstage*] That goddamn dumb, muscle-bound son-of-a-bitch from the nursery!! I told him no fucking vulgar Puerto Rican pink geraniums!! I said I only wanted pale Martha Washington colors!! But what did *he* know about *subtlety*!!

[*Hank dries his eyes, hands the handkerchief to Bernard . . .*]

HANK: [*Re handkerchief*] Thanks, Bernard.

BERNARD: That's yours, baby.

[*Bernard takes the handkerchief and tucks it in Hank's suit breast pocket*]

HANK: [*Nods*] Oh, yeah, so it is. Thanks.

EMORY: [*Enters, almost in tears*] This celebration of life is ruined! Just ruined!

[*Emory whips back outside. Hank looks to see Rick staring at him. They exchange a smile*]

DONALD: [*To Rick, flirting*] I thought you wanted some air.

RICK: [*Forces a smile*] I do. How about you?

DONALD: [*With a twinkle*] Yeah, I'd love to come up for air.

[*Michael takes stock of Donald as he goes outside, buzzing in Rick's ear*]

EMORY: [*Offstage, outraged*] I . . . DON'T . . . FUCKING . . . BELIEVE
IT!!!

[*Michael has crossed to the stairs and Scott*]

MICHAEL: Champagne?

SCOTT: No, thank you.

MICHAEL: Not even for your birthday?

SCOTT: My birthday was two weeks ago.

MICHAEL: I know very well when your birthday was. Since we haven't
spoken, I was wondering how it went.

SCOTT: As you might expect, thanks to my father.

MICHAEL: And how *is* your father?

SCOTT: The same. After he asked me what I wanted for my birthday and I
told him, he didn't give me anything. Just blustered into my place drunk;
didn't even shake my hand.

MICHAEL: It seems that all you can really count on with him is for him to
let you down.

[*Michael puts his hand on Scott's shoulder as Donald enters from the terrace. Scott
sees Donald, shrugs off Michael's hand. Michael looks at Donald*]

MICHAEL: [*To Donald, re Rick*] How are you, shall we say, making out?

DONALD: [*Re Scott's shrug*] I'd say about the same as you. The chairs are wet.

MICHAEL: [*With an edge*] I'd say get some towels and dry them off.

DONALD: Right. [*Finishes his drink*] First things first.

[*Donald goes to the bar cart and freshens his martini for Michael's benefit. Michael
makes a disapproving face as Emory flies inside*]

EMORY: [*Petulantly*] What are we having to eat? I'm absolutely rav!

MICHAEL: Just some chicken hash and a little endive and watercress salad.

[*Rick reenters*]

EMORY: [*Flirty, to Rick*] Richarr, shall you and I heat up the Cuisine Duhzine?

RICK: Why don't I just wipe off the chairs. I'm better at cleaning up.

[*Crestfallen, Emory exits to the kitchen. Donald crosses to the stairs, drink in hand*]

DONALD: [*To Michael, with disgusted awe*] Caterers and decorators.

MICHAEL: [*Defensively*] I just got a job!

DONALD: And you're already spending what you haven't made yet.

MICHAEL: [*Dismissive*] Yeah, yeah, yeah.

DONALD: I thought you told me you had to dip into your pension fund because you hadn't worked in so long.

MICHAEL: I did. Anyone who doesn't live beyond his means suffers from a lack of imagination!

[*Donald gives Scott a look, goes upstairs and into the bath*]

SCOTT: [*Re Donald*] He's jealous of me, isn't he?

MICHAEL: He's jealous *of me*. He just resents *you*.

SCOTT: Well, he doesn't have to feel threatened by *me*.

[*Michael is silent. Scott finishes his Diet Coke. Michael turns to the group . . .*]

MICHAEL: [*Graciously, but swallowing dryly*] How're everybody's drinks?

HANK: [*Holds up empty flute*] Mind if I get a beer?

MICHAEL: Of course not. There's some in the fridge.

[*Hank exits to the kitchen*]

MICHAEL: [*Sotto voce, to Scott*] I was genuinely happy that you called this morning and suggested we go to the service together. I wanted to see you before I left for California.

SCOTT: Is it a good job?

MICHAEL: Just a TV rewrite.

SCOTT: How long will you be gone?

MICHAEL: A month or so.

SCOTT: [*After a moment*] I'm so confused about our so-called friendship.

MICHAEL: Scott, I really don't think this is the proper time to get into all that.

SCOTT: Do I have to make an appointment?!

[*Bernard and Rick look up. Michael turns to them, smiles awkwardly. Bernard takes a soft drink, opens it. Michael turns away*]

MICHAEL: No. You don't have to make an appointment. [*After a moment*] Why don't you go up to the bedroom, and I'll come up in a minute.

SCOTT: I think I'd just better leave.

MICHAEL: No, Scott, please, don't.

SCOTT: [*After a moment*] I'm sorry I forgot to put the ice out.

[*Donald comes downstairs to hear Michael's plea. They exchange an uneasy look*]

DONALD: [*Hands over towels*] Here, Rick, start on the chairs, I'll get the cushions.

[*Rick exits to the terrace with the towels*]

MICHAEL: [*Sotto voce, to Scott*] Please? Go on. I'll be up in a minute.

[*Scott crushes his Diet Coke can, passes Donald on the stairs, goes up, tearing off his T-shirt, continuing off into the bathroom. The bedroom light fades*]

DONALD: [*Re Scott*] It'll never work.

MICHAEL: Why?

DONALD: Because he doesn't make you laugh.

MICHAEL: [*Shaken, edgy*] Something you read in a book? Or has the booze finally reached what's left of your wet brain?

[*Michael glares at Donald, as Emory exits the kitchen with a stack of ceramic plates*]

EMORY: [*Singsong*] Behind you!

[*Michael moves aside to let Emory pass as Jason enters from the terrace, exhaling from a discarded cigarette. He waves his hand to disperse the smoke*]

JASON: It's nice out.

EMORY: [*Whizzing past*] Then *leave* it out!

[*Emory exits to the terrace. In the bedroom Scott paces, sits on the bed, then quickly gets up, smoothes the cover. Downstairs, Donald replenishes his drink*]

MICHAEL: [*Not to Donald*] Will somebody roll the bar outside and get the wine while I see about the food?

JASON: If you'll cease fire, I'll do the bar. I'm good at it, remember?

MICHAEL: [*Lightly, but unrelenting*] You're sure you don't have a date on a float somewhere? [*Sighs, to Jason*] Okay . . . time out. [*Indicates up right wall*] The corkscrew and wine buckets are in the cabinet. The wine's in the fridge.

[*Jason goes up right to an "invisible" cabinet: doors seamlessly cut into the photo blowup wall. He throws them open to reveal glass shelves that light up and contain a stupefying supply of liquor and glasses*]

BERNARD: [*Reacts with anxious dismay*] Good Christ, Michael!

[*Michael remains completely cool . . .*]

MICHAEL: [*Sardonically*] A fully stocked bar is a happy bar. Besides, these days you never know when there's going to be another celebration of life!

[*Hank enters from the kitchen with a bottle of beer in hand . . .*]

BERNARD: [*Unnerved, re bar*] The sight of that is *staggering*—in the classic sense of the word!

MICHAEL: [*Facetiously*] A sip is not a slip. Is it, Bernard?

BERNARD: [*Angrily*] You're not serious!!

MICHAEL: Of course I'm not serious!

BERNARD: Who knows with you?

MICHAEL: [*Irritated*] What do you mean by that?

BERNARD: I mean you still go to bars with people.

MICHAEL: I *accompany* people to bars. I happen to like the way bars smell.

BERNARD: And you drink nonalcoholic beer!

MICHAEL: It's less than five percent—less than what's in *orange juice*!

BERNARD: [*Re stocked hidden bar*] And you keep this . . . this *speakeasy* behind closed doors!

MICHAEL: *Speakeasy!* You're dating yourself! I'm just not a zealot! And I should hardly think *you* would be!

BERNARD: After what we've been through?! It's like keeping a loaded gun in the apartment, just waiting for the baby to find it!

MICHAEL: Who the hell got you in the program in the first place, I'd like to know!

BERNARD: Well, now it looks like it's *my* turn! How much time have you got?

MICHAEL: *Nine* years!

BERNARD: Well, I slipped at *seven*! You're playing with fucking dynamite, man!

MICHAEL: Oh, Bernard, there's something comforting about having liquor on the premises. Like having prescription drugs. You just know they're there. I'd panic if there weren't any anesthetics in the house.

BERNARD: You sound like Harold.

HANK: Or Larry.

BERNARD: Fucking dynamite, man! Everything you say or do!

MICHAEL: I know, and I'm sorry! Did I upset you that much?

DONALD: Of course you upset him that much!

MICHAEL: Well, I apologize!

BERNARD: [*Levelly*] It's all right to hate, Michael. It's just not all right to act in a hateful way.

[*Bernard exits to the terrace, fuming*]

MICHAEL: [*Re Bernard's reaction*] Christ of the Andes! Where did *that* come from?

DONALD: It wasn't funny.

MICHAEL: What about *you*! Still knocking them back as if time had stood still! [*Re Bernard*] Why doesn't he say something to *you*?

DONALD: I *want* to drink, Michael.

MICHAEL: Well, so do I, but I can't because I'm a drunk!

DONALD: And so am *I* and so *what*?! [*Drains his glass*] Larry would have understood this conversation is out of bounds—why can't you?!

[*Michael restrains himself. Jason, having found the corkscrew and a wine bucket, exits to kitchen. Donald goes up right center to another "invisible door," opens it, and removes some new, smartly upholstered exterior chair cushions*]

BERNARD: [*Offstage*] Hey, Rick, my man, you really *do* know how to mop up!

RICK: [*Offstage*] Well, I've cleaned enough toilets in my time.

BERNARD: [*Offstage*] Yeah, what's one more or less, huh?

[*Michael stiffens and exchanges a look with Donald, who closes the cabinet doors and exits to the terrace with the seat cushions.*

*Hank has gone to the étagère and put on a CD—something like Ella Fitzgerald's "Skylark" begins to play. Jason enters with several bottles of white wine, which he puts on the bar cart, then starts to roll it outside. Emory enters from the terrace as Jason starts to lift the bar cart over the threshold . . .*]

EMORY: [*To Jason*] Need a hand, big boy?

JASON: Thanks.

EMORY: I take it that you work out.

JASON: Yeah, American Fitness.

EMORY: [*Nods, knowingly, play-on-words*] "Oh-Mary-Can-Ya-Lift-This"? The fit American goes to American Fitness. That's why Eighth Avenue between Fourteenth and Twenty-third looks like an open call for Spartacus, the Musical.

[*They lift the bar cart over the jamb and exit to the terrace. Michael sees Hank has picked up a photograph in a silver frame on the étagère and is looking at it. Michael comes over to Hank . . .*]

HANK: [*Re Scott's photo*] He's a handsome kid, Michael.

MICHAEL: Scott's aunt took that of us.

HANK: He introduced you to his family?

MICHAEL: He just wanted me to meet his aunt. She's all he cares about—the only one who's ever been the least bit kind to him. We took her to lunch. I loaned Scott my dark blue cashmere blazer, and he looked so elegant. His aunt was so proud of him. She held his hand on the top of the table for a long time after the plates had been cleared away, and he didn't seem uncomfortable at all.

HANK: Is he uncomfortable at a show of affection?

MICHAEL: From some people, I guess.

HANK: He looks *very* proud of you, Michael.

[*Michael smiles, takes the picture of Scott from Hank, turns, and goes up the stairs.*

*Hank now picks up a photograph of Larry and studies it a moment. Donald and Rick come inside. Rick watches Hank*]

DONALD: [*To Hank*] Nice shot of Larry.

HANK: I think so. Brazil was great. We had a good time there.

[*Hank replaces the photograph and exits to the terrace. Rick goes to the étagère, picks up the framed photograph of Larry. Suddenly, Rick dissolves into tears. Donald goes to him, puts his arm around him*]

RICK: [*Distraught*] Oh, God, Donald, what am I going to do?!

DONALD: What you can't do is let Hank see you break down.

RICK: [*Sobbing*] I loved him.

DONALD: I know you did. Sort of like the hostage-captor syndrome in reverse, I guess.

RICK: Please, don't joke! I helped him die. He begged me to turn up the drip till he was gone, then turn it down before I called the doctor. I *couldn't*. I . . . I . . . put some morphine suppositories on his bedside table, then I left the room. When I came back, I took the empty foil wrappers and flushed them down the toilet so no one would know. Then, I did what he told me. I called the doctor.

[*Rick falls against Donald and sobs. Donald puts his arms about Rick, kisses him on his cheek, forehead, and, finally, sweetly on the mouth. Rick responds passionately. Jason enters with the empty ice bucket, stops on a dime, watches them. Rick's head goes limp on Donald's shoulder*]

RICK: I wonder who else knows I loved him?

DONALD: I don't think anyone *here* knows . . . [*Looks up at Jason*] Well . . .

JASON: I don't know a thing. Not a thing.

RICK: [*Recovering*] There's nothing to know, really, except that I . . . felt about Larry the way I do. I think he just liked the idea that I was crazy about him. [*To Donald*] You never told Michael, did you?

DONALD: Of course not.

[*Jason turns and exits to the kitchen*]

RICK: [*Looks at photo of Larry*] He was so much fun. When he was in remission, after his classes, we had kind of a standing date. Nothing much, really—Starbuck's, the movies, my place. He was so loving. [*Through tears*] But I knew it could never lead to anything. [*Rick puts the photo back on the shelf*] Hank never knew. He hardly remembers me. I'm sorry about this . . . acting like this . . .

DONALD: I understand.

RICK: Thanks, Donald. I hope you don't get the wrong idea.

DONALD: What's a little kiss between friends?

[*They get a grip. Jason enters, the ice bucket refilled*]

RICK: Have you seen my guitar case?

JASON: [*Nods*] In the kitchen. You gonna sing us that song?

RICK: I'm gonna sing somebody that song.

[*Rick exits to the kitchen*]

JASON: So, Bernard says you live in the Hamptons. I'm house-sitting for a friend out there.

DONALD: Well, you ought to give me a call. We could have a picnic on the beach . . .

JASON: It's still a little chilly for that, isn't it?

DONALD: I could make a thermos of martinis.

JASON: I'm in the program.

DONALD: Not you too! You're like the pod people!

JASON: [*Laughs*] There's only Michael and Bernard and me left. Three out of nine—that's not such a frightening average. And I'm a bartender!

DONALD: Keep up the good work!

JASON: I feel like such an enabler. You know, what's wrong with this picture?!

DONALD: I'll give you my phone number anyway.

[*Donald and Jason go outside onto the terrace in conversation. Lights begin to fade as Rick exits the kitchen with his guitar. He strums a few chords, goes onto the terrace.*

*Lights fade out downstairs, come up in the bedroom as Scott exits the bath, pulling on one of Michael's solid cashmere sweaters. He sees Michael put down the photograph of them*]

SCOTT: My T-shirt was damp. Mind if I borrow this? [*Michael shakes his head*] You cleaned out the medicine cabinet.

MICHAEL: I didn't. Maybe the maid did. Looking for something?

SCOTT: I kinda got a headache. [*After an awkward pause . . .*] Listen, I quit school.

MICHAEL: I know. I was wondering if you were going to tell me.

SCOTT: How do you know? Did one of those old bastards . . .

MICHAEL: No, I went to meet you after class last week. I thought we ought to have a chat and clear the air. You weren't there.

SCOTT: NYU was a mistake. I was in over my head. I couldn't cut it.

MICHAEL: It's my fault for insisting.

SCOTT: No, it's not. I like it that you cared. It's more than my own father ever did. I think I need to work outdoors. Landscape gardening. Or maybe I could be a vet. Maybe you could introduce me to those friends of Hank's in the Hamptons.

MICHAEL: Sure. Anything. But, Scott, *study something*. You've got a good mind.

SCOTT: Listen, I think I'm going to slip out now. You know, parties—well, whatever you call this—are just not my thing. [*Michael nods*] Now I suppose you're going to drop the bomb.

MICHAEL: [*After a moment*] I'm simply going to try to tell you how I feel. Unless there is some physical contact, some show of . . . affection . . . between us . . . I can't . . .

SCOTT: Here it comes.

MICHAEL: What does "drop the bomb" really mean?

SCOTT: What do you think?

MICHAEL: Well . . . I think you think that it means you will be emotionally betrayed. *Abandoned*—which seems to be the major theme of your life.

SCOTT: Michael, just say what's on your mind and I'll go.

MICHAEL: I've said it.

SCOTT: [*Sheepishly*] You want me to go now?

MICHAEL: [*Sharply*] Scott, *make sense!* You knew from the start how I felt about you!

SCOTT: Knew what *you* wanted, you mean!

MICHAEL: Yes! I've never tried to hide what I wanted. And in spite of the "threat" to you, you allowed things to progress.

SCOTT: Threat?

MICHAEL: [*Impatiently*] You heard me. *Threat*. A show of those feelings from me, a negative response from you, and my reaction—which, to you, meant that I would go away and leave you.

[*Scott goes to sit on the bed, but the moment he does he gets up and moves to a chair*]

SCOTT: I don't want any emotional involvement with anyone! Or physical, either! I like you as a friend. Why can't we leave it at that?

MICHAEL: Scott, I don't want to continue in what is a painful and unhappy situation for me. But you don't want to hear that. Because you want all the advantages and none of the responsibilities. In short, you want me to be a checkbook and an ear. Well, what's in this for *me*?!

[*Scott gets up, picks up the picture, looks at it*]

SCOTT: I don't want things to change. In any way. I've told you that my aversion to being touched is not just with you, it's with everybody.

MICHAEL: That's not good enough! Scott, we were like lovers without the sex.

SCOTT: My body is my own.

MICHAEL: [*Coolly*] Well, yes. It is. Yours to keep or to give to whomever you want. And if you don't want to give yourself to me, you must try to understand what that does to me!

SCOTT: Do I have to try in front of all these old farts?!

MICHAEL: I suppose you mean my contemporaries. And of course, I'm folklore.

SCOTT: I'm sorry. I actually like them. Well, *two* of them. Well . . . *one* of them.

MICHAEL: Chronologically, I am aware that I could be your father. In some climates, possibly your grandfather.

SCOTT: Age has nothing to do with it. *Really.* [*Frustrated*] Oh, forget it. Goodbye.

[*Scott makes a move toward the stairs, Michael doesn't try to stop him. Scott stops, says emphatically . . .*]

SCOTT: I said, *goodbye.*

MICHAEL: [*As if he's just heard him. Casually*] Sorry. Goodbye.

[*Scott is silent, sinks to the floor, starts to weep. Michael looks at him for a moment, then goes to lower himself to the floor beside him*]

SCOTT: It has nothing to do with *you,* I've told you that. It's with anybody. *I don't want to be touched!*

MICHAEL: [*Touches Scott's knee*] Are you really that damaged? [*Scott recoils*] Or am I repulsive to you? Tell me. I can take it. It would be such a relief to know what's really going on in your head.

SCOTT: [*Turns away, sobs uncontrollably*] I can't fight the things that have been done to me.

MICHAEL: Listen, my roots were, I think, uglier than your own—an emotional torment I don't know how I survived.

SCOTT: [*Weeping*] How'd you do it?

MICHAEL: I met people who were smarter and wiser than I was, and I learned from them. Like I've tried to pass on things to you. [*Directly*] Like believing in yourself. Your *self:* that thing you feel when you go through a revolving door—that post, that center, that something *unshakable* . . . around which everything else spins!

[*Scott turns to Michael, keeping his distance . . .*]

SCOTT: [*Through tears*] I had always hoped . . . dreamed that one day I would somehow cross paths with a person like you—someone who'd see something in me. Don't you think I know you've spent a lot of money on me—all the restaurants and clothes and the classes you've paid for? And don't you know I can't help feeling, in some way, undeserving of all this? [*Scott starts to dry his eyes, gets to his feet . . .*] But I know it'll payoff, though I could never pay you back.

[*Michael stands up next to Scott*]

MICHAEL: [*With meaning*] Yes, you could.

[*Michael turns back, embraces Scott awkwardly. Scott is thrown, flustered*]

SCOTT[*Jokey, laughing nervously*] Quick! Fast-forward this! Michael hangs on to him steadfastly . . .

MICHAEL: [*Intense whisper*] Be *real*!

[*Scott violently disentangles himself, stumbles backward awkwardly, flailing his arms, panicked. He almost falls over a chair, almost upsets the bedside table. Michael doesn't move, straightens with a regained dignity. Scott recovers, stumbles downstairs, stops in the middle of the room, leans against the sofa, gasping for air. Michael slowly descends the stairs*]

MICHAEL: [*Looks at Scott*] Breathe! You always stop breathing the moment there's any inference of emotion or sexual demand . . .

SCOTT: [*Hyperventilating*] I can't!

MICHAEL: Take a breath, goddamn it!

SCOTT: [*Gets up, gets his breath*] I can't help it if I feel like . . . like I'm suffocating.

MICHAEL: Well, I wanted many things—but never to *asphyxiate* you. I want you to be able to feel something authentic for someone. If not me, then someone else. Even if you have to abandon *me*.

SCOTT: [*Not looking at Michael*] When I was seventeen I was already getting into bars with a fake ID . . . this guy came on to me—but the more he did, the more I was obnoxious. I don't know when he left the bar, but I stayed till it closed and started walking home. At a traffic light a car pulled up beside me. It was the guy. He offered me a ride. I knew it was stupid, but I got in. He pulled a gun and drove me all the way to his place in Jersey.

MICHAEL: [*Quietly*] Oh, Christ.

SCOTT: [*Takes a breath*] He ordered me into his house and handcuffed me at gunpoint. He made me take my clothes off, then he shot me up on drugs and loaded a pistol. Then he blindfolded me and fucked me with the barrel. [*Turns to Michael*] I was so drugged, so scared that it became a sort of "out of body" experience. When it was over, he uncuffed me and handed me the gun and told me to shoot him for what he'd done.

MICHAEL: Well, I certainly hope you *did*.

SCOTT: [*Shakes his head*] He tried to make me take money to make up for it. And I refused. Finally, he offered me drugs. And even though I really wanted them, I refused. I pulled on my clothes the best I could and staggered out and just kept trying to put one foot in front of the other. [*After a moment*] Did you know that Emory is working on some very "rah-sha-sha" needlepoint pillow that says "Elegance Is Refusal"?

MICHAEL: [*Nods sardonically at the "in" joke, re "recherche"*] Yes, *very* "rah-sha-sha."

[*They both break-up laughing*]

SCOTT: [*Comes closer to Michael, reflectively*] I was the way I am before that ever happened. I'd had sex before then. I just never liked it all that much. It was never possible for me to combine being physical with someone who I'd let into my confidence.

MICHAEL: Are you trying to tell me that's why I have the rare privilege of your body *language* rather than your *body*?

SCOTT: [*Comes closer*] It's the way I am. I'm as queer as I can be and have no problem with that, but I don't like to be touched. I don't like to be stared at. I won't even shower at the gym after my workout.

MICHAEL: Why, is it too cruisy?

SCOTT: [*Tough*] *Life* is cruisy!

MICHAEL: [*After a moment*] I love you.

SCOTT: [*After a moment*] And I love you too.

[*Scott is silent, gets his bicycle, rolls it to the front door . . .*]

MICHAEL: You think Jason had a point? You think maybe it was one of your friends who took your bike?

422    THE MEN FROM THE BOYS

I never have anyone over. You know that. I must have just left my door unlocked by mistake. [*Starts to move, stops . . .*] Uh, I hate to ask you this, but can I borrow twenty dollars?

[*Michael takes his wallet out of his pocket without hesitation, gives it to him*]

MICHAEL: Here—take forty. Or sixty. Take whatever you want.

SCOTT: Forty's enough. [*He hands the wallet back to Michael, who returns it to his pocket*] Thanks. [*Unyielding eye contact*] I'll never forget what you've gone through with me, and I'm going to try to make sure the effort wasn't for nothing.

MICHAEL: [*Simply*] Thanks.

SCOTT: I'm sad that I haven't turned out to be what you'd hoped I'd be for you. I'm sad that I still don't know how to love or be loved.

MICHAEL: I hope you find out before you're my age.

[*Scott opens the front door, rolls the bike out, and closes the door. Michael doesn't move. Hank has entered in time to see Scott exit, but Scott does not see him. Michael turns*]

HANK: Doesn't Scott want anything to eat before he goes?

MICHAEL: [*After a moment*] It's not going to work out, Hank. I think he's gone for good.

HANK: Did he tell you that?

MICHAEL: He didn't have to.

HANK: Are you okay?

MICHAEL: Let's see . . . what am I? Crushed. Depressed. Suicidal. No, not that. I've always looked for love in inappropriate places. So, yeah, I'm okay. I'm fine. I won't drink over this, if that's what you mean.

HANK: That's what I mean.

MICHAEL: To be honest, I want to, but if I did I might as well put a gun to my head. Not that that wouldn't be a welcome relief. Anyway, I don't want that. Not *yet,* anyway. So . . . not to worry. Hank, I'm that dreaded word . . . *survivor.*

HANK: Michael—the love of another person is a discipline not easily won or maintained.

MICHAEL: But you think it's worth the risk.

HANK: It took a long time for Larry and me to get to that point. Well, that is, it took *me* a long time. But I finally understood what he was driving at. It's so simple. You be you. I'll be me. *But . . .* we'll be together.

[*The doorbell rings three times. Michael looks at Hank expectantly, goes to the door, and opens it. HAROLD is standing there, not having aged a great deal; still thin, still with kinky black hair. He has on sunglasses and a rain cape and carries a dripping umbrella*]

MICHAEL: Well, if it isn't the antichrist!

HAROLD: I take it you were expecting someone else. I rang thrice so you wouldn't think it was the postman and get all wet and coozy.

MICHAEL: How'd you get in?

HAROLD: Your divine super was mopping up downstairs. Feisty little bugger. I told him I was here for the Yale reunion. He directed me to your apartment.

[*He hands his umbrella to Michael, slips out of his rain cape, and hands that to Michael too, as if he were an attendant*]

BERNARD: [*Enters from terrace*] What've you been doing with that blond, Harold?

HAROLD: [*Kissing Bernard*] Petal!

BERNARD: You're so tanned!

HAROLD: I've been in St. Bart's—playing Dorothy Dandridge in *Island in the Sun.*

MICHAEL: Everybody else came directly from the service! That was an hour ago, at the very least! [*Dumps umbrella and cape*] There's been time for a deluge! Foyers have been flooded! Arks have been built!

HAROLD: [*Entering*] Surely you know by now I have absolutely no sense of time.

MICHAEL: If that is true, then why are you never an hour *early*?!

BERNARD: Maybe your watch stopped.

HAROLD: [*Looks at his watch*] I don't think so. It was running perfectly when my man put it on me this morning. [*Reacting to light*] Oh, my *God,* this is real straight-boy lighting! What *is* this, the open-heart surgery room?!

MICHAEL: You're stoned!

[*Emory pops in from the kitchen with a silver casserole in chafing frame*]

HAROLD: Hello, d'yah. [*NOTE: That's "dear" very, very clipped*]

EMORY: You're just in time for food, Hallie.

HAROLD: Oh-I-can't-eat-a-thing-what-are-you-having?

EMORY: Lean and mean "Cuisine Duhzine."

HAROLD: [*For Michael's benefit*] Ohh, minced pig's nipples on toast points. From that trendy frog gonif on Second Avenue?

[*Emory hoots, whips outside as Donald enters. Harold passes Donald en route to Hank*]

HAROLD: [*Not looking at him and not stopping*] Donald, good to see you.

DONALD: [*With resignation*] As always, Harold.

[*Donald goes to the wall bar, removes a stack of Italian ceramic plates. Harold comes up to Hank, takes his hands*]

HAROLD: [*With great feeling*] Hank. How are you, bubelah?

HANK: [*Hugs Harold*] Thanks for everything, Harold. I couldn't have arranged it without your help.

HAROLD: What can I tell you, some of my best friends are morticians. [*Sincerely*] I wish I could say I know just how you feel. I have no idea how you feel. That was a terrific little mention in the *Post* on Larry's work.

HANK: I thought so.

EMORY: [*Enters, empty-handed*] Oh, I didn't see it, and I read the *Post* every day.

HAROLD: It was in the Lifestyle section. We're never news—we're always lifestyles.

[*Outside, Rick begins to strum his guitar*]

EMORY: Oh, Rick's about to sing! I'd better get my act together.

[*Emory runs up the stairs and into the bath, closing the door. Meanwhile, Harold goes to the terrace door, looks outside*]

HAROLD: [*Re: group on terrace*] Jesus! It looks like the United Colors of Benetton out there! [*To Michael*] Have you got Sitting Bull stashed in the closet?

HANK: Some of Larry's younger friends.

HAROLD: And a fine looking lot they are too. The white one's a serial killer, at the very least. And I thoroughly approve of him.

MICHAEL: Who was the bottle blond you were with at the service?

HAROLD: An actor-singer-dancer-waiter. Well, he's not really a dancer, but he moves. In fact he's moving into my apartment this very minute.

MICHAEL: What?!!

HAROLD: Just temporarily till he finds a place. I'm only trying to do my bit for the arts. He sent his regrets.

MICHAEL: I'm *distraught* that he couldn't come.

HAROLD: I knew you would be. He and I are making dinner at home tonight so I dare not eat a thing. In fact, I've got to lose twenty pounds by seven-thirty. He's cute as a mouse's ear, dontcha think? [*Exits to terrace, expansively*] Hello, boys, here's your Aunt Harold! Come cheer me up!

[*He glides outside, humming. Those left in his wake exchange looks. Rick can be heard singing "Que Reste-il De Nos Amours? What's Left of Our Love?" French lyrics and music by Charles Trenet. NOTE: The English version is called "I Wish You Love," and the lyrics, like the title, by Albert A. Beach are original, not an adapted translation of Trenet. The stage lights begin to fade . . .*]

RICK: [*Offstage; sings*]
*Ce soir, le vent qui frappe a ma porte*
*Me parle des amours morts*
*Devant le feu qui s'éteint.*

*Ce soir, c'est une chanson d'automne*
*Dans la maison qui frissonne*
*Où je pense aux jours lointains . . .*

[*Michael is left alone, moves toward the bar cabinet. He opens it. In the fading light, it seems even brighter, more sparkling, more seductive than before. Rick's voice continues outside . . .*]

RICK: [*Offstage, singing*]
*Que reste-il de nos amours?*
*Que reste-il de ces beaux jours?*
*Une photo, une vielle photo*
*De ma jeunesse. . . .*

[*The lights fade, with only the bar light intensifying. Another moment . . .*]


BLACKOUT

END OF ACT I

# Act II

*As the house lights fade, Rick's voice can be heard singing, accompanying himself on the guitar . . .*

RICK: [*Offstage, singing*]
  *Les mots, les mots tendres qu'on murmure*
  *Les caresses les plus pures*
  *Les sermons au fond d'un tiroir*

  *Les fleurs, qu'on retrouve dans un livre*
  *Dont le parfum vous enivre / Se sont envoles, pourquoi?*

  *Que reste-il des billets doux*
  *Du mots d'Avril, des rendezvous*
  *Un souvenir que me poursuit*
  *Sans cesse.*

[*As the lights come up on stage, Michael closes the bar cabinet, shutting off its light. Outside, on the terrace, Rick finishes up* Que Reste-il De Nos Amours]

RICK: [*Offstage, singing*]
  *Bonheur fane*
  *Cheveux au vent*
  *Baisers voles*
  *Rêves émouvants*
  *Que reste-il de tout cela?*
  *Dites-le moi.*

  *Un p'tit village, un viêux clocher*
  *Un paysage si bien caché*
  *Et dans un nuage le cher visage*
  *De mon passe.*

[*Applause from all. Michael slowly crosses to the terrace door*]

HAROLD: [*Offstage*] Fabulous, Rickola! Or, should I say, "Fah-boo-*luzz*"! Now, let's hear a *Yankee* song! For us *Yanks*!

MICHAEL: [*At terrace door*] That *was* a Yankee song, Harold! For us Yanks from New Orleans.

[*Thunder. Groans all around from everyone outside*]

HAROLD: [*Offstage, in comic Southern accent*] Well, ah declare, y'all, ah do believe we are about to have a spring *squall!*

BERNARD: [*Offstage, in comic Southern accent*] Sugah, you know a real good squallin' generally follows a heat wave—'specially a *French* one!

[*There is a clap of thunder. Audible reactions from the group outside, followed by the sound of a sudden downpour*]

MICHAEL: Just leave everything on the table under the awning and cover the casserole!

[*Much hooting as everyone dashes inside, most carrying their drinks, plates of food, and smart cotton napkins, which they use to blot the raindrops. Rick hangs on to his guitar but waves an empty stem glass . . .*]

RICK: Did anyone grab that champagne?

DONALD: [*Holding up Bombay bottle*] I grabbed the champagne of bottled gins. First things first!

MICHAEL: [*To Donald, disapprovingly*] You *could* just start the day with a gin enema. Why fuck around and wait for things to take effect? [*To Rick, re champagne*] There's a bottle of Cristal in the fridge. [*Re rainstorm*] Somebody close the doors till it slackens a bit!

HAROLD: [*Blotting his brow*] Maybe we ought to ask the super to come up and mop us off.

[*Jason slides the terrace doors shut. Rick goes to put his guitar back in its case*]

JASON: [*To Rick*] Rick, what's that song mean in plain English?

BERNARD: Yeah, what about us dumb bastards who didn't go to Le Rosey?

[*Rick strums the intro again and speaks the song in a loose translation of the original French, not the Albert A. Beach English lyrics of "I Wish You Love." Rick accompanies his oral recitation [delivered more briskly than the singing] with the appropriate chords . . .*]

RICK: [*Speaking, not singing*]
   *Tonight, the wind that beats on my door*
   *Speaks to me of love that's lost*
   *And I think of times gone by . . .*

*What is there left of our love?*
*What is there left of happy days?*
*A photograph, an old photo*
*Of my youth . . .*

*Of faded bliss,*
*Of wind-blown hair?*
*A stolen kiss,*
*A dream we share—*
*What's left of this?*
*Can you tell me?*
*A memory.*

*Letters you wrote that I still keep*
*Lines I can quote that make me weep*
*The rest is gone. Why is it gone?*
Pourquoi?

[*More enthusiastic applause than before*]

MICHAEL: [*To Bernard*] You *do* comprehend *"pourquoi,"* don't you?

BERNARD: Yeah, it means *"fuck you,"* doesn't it?

[*Hank crosses to Rick*]

HANK: [*Calmly, sincerely*] That was terrific, Rick. Really. Larry told you he liked that song?

RICK: [*Carefully*] Yeah. [*Deeply appreciative*] I'm glad *you* liked it, Hank. I hoped you would.

HANK: I did. Very, very much. Thank you.

[*Rick smiles at Hank, turns to go put his guitar in its case*]

BERNARD: [*Looking about*] Where the hell is Emory?

HAROLD: Who's next on the bill and what language is it in?

[*The bathroom door opens, Emory quickly emerges and strikes a pose at the top of the stairs*]

EMORY: [*Theatrically*] *I'm* next! And it's in the mother tongue! For all you mothers!

[*Everyone looks up as a kind of vision descends the stairs. Emory is completely, and wonderfully, made up: bright, glossy red lipstick, shaded cheekbones, dramatic eye shadow, and thick false lashes. No wig, however, and no women's clothes. He has only put on the jacket to his black velour suit, turned up the lapels, and buttoned it to the throat. Around his neck are several strands of sparkling rhinestones. Brilliant drops dangle from his ears, and on his wrists and fingers are dazzling bracelets and rings. He is carrying a cassette and a small camera.*]

[*Instant applause, hoots, and whistles*]

[*Emory goes to pop the cassette into the tape deck and deposit his camera on the étagère. There is a round of applause as everyone settles into chairs, on the stairs, or on the floor*]

EMORY: [*A seasoned pro from the school of yesteryear*] Thank you. Thank you, ladies and gentlemen—and you among you know who's who. This next little ditty does not come from Paris, or Pa*ree*, whichever you prefer. Personally, I prefer New York! Yes, make mine Manhattan, and make my day! [*Imperiously, to Michael*] Michael, my *lights*! My *lights*!

[*Michael goes to a wall switch as the intro on the tape begins. A hush falls over the, room, Michael hits the wall switch, and Emory stands in a lone pool of strategically focused light*]

[*The next exchanges are rapid volleys . . .*]

HAROLD: Oh, the Marlene keylight! Why didn't I have that for my entrance?!

EMORY: Check the cheekbones!

BERNARD: Did you say chicken bones?

EMORY: [*Re Bernard*] Oh, *kill her*! *Cheek*bones! How're my cheekbones?

JASON: They look like Carlsbad Caverns!

EMORY: [*Playfully*] Well, that's not because of the light. That's because I had all my wisdom teeth extracted this afternoon!

[*He sucks in his cheeks. Mild laughter*]

EMORY: [*Campily sultry*] I come before you without wisdom. [*French pronunciation*] But with "cou*rage.*"

HAROLD: Yeah, first comes "cou*rage,*" then comes regret.

EMORY: [*American accent*] *Je ne regrette rien, cheri!*

[*Bernard sits on the stairs, gives a grandstand razz . . .*]

BERNARD: [*Through cupped hands*] I hope your song's better'n your material!

EMORY: [*To Bernard*] Oh, you're *terrible*!

BERNARD: But you're fucking nuts about me!

DONALD: [*To Bernard*] Quiet in the bleachers!

JASON: Yeah, come on, guys, settle down! Shhh . . .

[*Everyone quiets. Emory stands perfectly still in his "spotlight," sparkling with command*]

EMORY: [*Over accompaniment*] Larry always spoke up for freedom. Freedom to be yourself, with no need to lie or pretend. This song is for Larry.

[*The taped intro ends, and the accompaniment begins. Emory sings/speaks a song entitled "I'm Not the Man I Planned." NOTE: What follows is a suggestion of what the "flavor" ought to be— particularly its bawdy music hall/burlesque house tone*]

EMORY: [*Sings/speaks*]
 *I'm not the man I planned:*
 *A life I'd founded on fam'ly aesthetics,*
 *A wife surrounded with kids and athletics.*
 *Instead I astounded the town with cosmetics.*
 *My structure faltered—*
 *My foundation altered—*
 *An' I'm not the man I planned.*

 *I'm not the guy I dreamed.*
 *The square in conventional coats and ties.*
 *Though I still wear suits, now I mesmerize*
 *Simply because I accessorize.*
[*He whips a red ostrich fan from under his jacket, snaps it open, and fans himself*]
 *With plumage I pepped up*
 *With high high heels I schlepped up*
 *And I'm not the guy I dreamed!*

 *Now it's a cinch,*
 *I'm gay as a finch!*
 *And I tell you without much ado—*
 *I'm such a queer bird*
 *That maybe you've heard*
 *I'd never love a dove*
 *But I'd kiss a cockatoo!*

EMORY (CONT'D): [*Singing*]
   *I'm no longer boring and bland,*
   *A dead-on-arrival fashion victim*
   *Now I'm archival, and this is my dictum:*
   *Provincial drag is an outmoded mess.*
   *Come to New York 'n' cross-dress for success*
   *I divested in transis.*
   *Got arrested in Kansas . . .*
   *But I shout "Eureka and encore!*
   *I'm not in Topeka anymore!"*
   *And thank God not the clod I planned.*

[*Applause and whistles. Emory bows graciously, a geisha shielding half his face behind his fan. The noise dies down . . .*]

MICHAEL: How many musical interludes are there going to be?

HAROLD: Well, I hope it's not like what they used to say about films from India: "If it's serious, there are only *ten* numbers." Just kidding, Em, you were heaven!

EMORY: [*To Harold*] That was the second and *last* number, thank you very much! I always close the bill! The musical portion, anyhow.

MICHAEL: [*To the group*] Now, anybody who has something to say can say it.

[*There is some low mumbling among the group, but no one stands immediately . . .*]

EMORY: [*Low hiss*] Bernard! Bernard! Say something!

[*Emory crosses to the étagère to put away his fan and get his camera. Bernard stands, clears his throat as Emory goes to sit on the stairs unobtrusively*]

BERNARD: [*To the group*] The last time I went to see Larry in the hospital he said a funny thing to me—because no matter what spiritual fad he was into, he really thought organized religion was destructive and just caused trouble between people. So I was surprised when he said, "After I'm gone, will you do me a favor? Will you go in a church and light a candle for me?" And of course, I didn't question him, I just said I would. But then in typical Larry fashion he added: "Not just *any* old church but someplace like that one you see across the street when you come out of the 50th Street side door of Sak's 5th Avenue." That was Larry.

[*Applause. Bernard sits down as Harold goes to the étagère and picks up the photograph of Larry . . .*]

HAROLD: Has everybody seen this wonderful picture of Lair? Hank took it on the beach in Brazil.

[*Harold hands it to the person nearest him and it is passed hand-to-hand in a circle until it is seen by all and returned to him. Meanwhile . . .*]

HAROLD: [*To Hank*] How long ago?

HANK: I swear I can't remember.

JASON: [*Coolly*] It'll be three years this summer.

RICK: That's a great straw hat. He had style.

EMORY: In fact, sometimes he was style-*heavy*. Remember the summer when he bought fish bowls from Pier 1 for wine glasses?

DONALD: [*Nostalgically*] And we never had to get up to freshen our drinks.

BERNARD: And when we *had* to get up, we *couldn't!*

[*Laughter from the old-timers, especially Donald. Rick and Jason don't find it funny, and Bernard's smile fades with realization . . .*]

BERNARD: Gives me the shakes just thinking about it.

MICHAEL: [*Absently*] Me too.

EMORY: [*To Rick*] That was back when we smoked and drank and there were no gyms and restaurants cooked with grease.

HAROLD: Yeah, and the baths were great for emergency love.

MICHAEL: Yeah, and I hated myself for being gay. Then I came out, and *other* people hated me.

JASON: The dark ages.

[*Laughter*]

EMORY: Yeah. Now the world's enlightened and in a holding pattern. I'm in a holding pattern. Well, I know my *looks* are in a holding pattern. Now, who's gonna say something?

[*There is a moment of mumbling as everyone wonders who's going to be the next person to speak. Jason stands and the group quiets as Harold replaces the picture on the étagère . . .*]

JASON: [*To the group*] It was not in Larry's nature to be somber or self-pitying, so I'm going to do my best to be like him. We, in this room, are

Larry's "family." Each of us was sort of a different relative, with a different sort of relationship. Each of us may know something about him the others do not, but each of us knows what the other has lost. I think it's his honesty I'll remember most—more than his wit or his charm or his ageless good looks.

[*A round of applause*]

JASON: [*Shifting gears*] Larry loved life and lived it by his own code. There was an edge to everything he believed or said, whether it was smart-ass or serious. He had his own standards and refused to live by . . .

MICHAEL: Where's this going?

JASON: Larry believed that men with men—and women with women—are a completely different human dynamic from men with women and women with men.

MICHAEL: [*Overlapping*] Are you coming to the point?

BERNARD: [*Calmly*] Michael, let Jason say what he wants to say.

EMORY: Yeah.

JASON: [*Pressing on*] For Larry, the fight for legalized gay marriage was about protection: tax exemptions, benefits, inheritances . . .

MICHAEL: *Now, wait just a minute!*

DONALD: *Michael!*

JASON: [*Accelerating, overlapping*] Basically being fed up with gays getting screwed out of what any spouse who had a piece of paper would be entitled to!

MICHAEL: [*Interrupting*] Listen, *poster boy,* this is not a pep rally, nor a protest! You are *not* on a platform *nor* a soapbox, you are in *my* living room, and I will not have you haranguing or handcuffing yourself to the Biedermeier!

[*Hank stands*]

HANK: [*With authority*] That's really enough out of the two of you! [*The room immediately quiets. Coolly*] Jason, you're right about Larry, but you *are* a bit off track. And Michael, as usual, you're just *out of line.*

MICHAEL: [*Thinks, sighs*] Of course I am. I apologize.

JASON: So do I.

HAROLD: [*After a moment*] Thanks, Hank. I was hoping someone would kick them *both* in the nuts!

MICHAEL: [*Sarcastically*] What do you want to be when *you* grow up, Harold?

HAROLD: [*To Michael, deadly*] Broad-minded.

HANK: [*After a moment*] Yes. Broad-minded. Larry greatly appreciated the "differentness" of being gay. So he didn't want to ape heterosexual conventions—particularly marital ones. Larry knew that a real bond between us had nothing to do with a piece of paper—that it was only important that he and I be married in our minds. He knew being wed had nothing to do with legality—only to do with the personal, private, unique contract between two consenting grown-ups. And the ground rules you make yourself. And they can't be the same for all. Maybe it's only now that I can say something to him . . . to *myself:* That through it all—faithfulness, fear, infidelity, forgiveness—our *marriage* was never threatened. We were together a long time on our own terms.

JASON: Hear, hear!

MICHAEL: [*To Jason*] Will you shut the fuck up?!

DONALD: Michael, please!

MICHAEL: Oh, all right! Cut my throat. See if *I* care.

EMORY: Let's all raise our glasses in a final toast.

[*Everyone stands, raises his glass, no matter what it contains, wine or water or soda*]

EMORY: [*Rises*] To Larry. Peaceful at last.

[*Everyone drinks. Hank goes over to Jason and puts his arms around him to hug him for a long moment. Rick watches closely*]

EMORY: [*Waving his camera*] Photo op! Photo op!

HAROLD: [*Covers his face with Emory's fan*] No pictures, *please!*

MICHAEL: [*With disgust*] Snapshots?! Ugh!!

EMORY: Hush! Both of you! [*Corralling the group*] Now, don't everybody break up! Move in! Move in!

BERNARD: Come on, Michael! Come on, you guys! Bunch up!

DONALD: Orgy time!

HAROLD: [*To Jason*] If only.

[*The group starts to assemble opposite the stairs*]

RICK: [*To Emory*] You're the one that ought to be in the picture!

EMORY: Don't worry!

[*He snaps a timing button, sets the camera on an eye-level rung of the stairs and rushes toward the center of the group. He lunges into a rope of interwoven arms and is bounced back to his feet, like a dazed, bejeweled prizefighter. He grabs Rick and Jason around their necks and holds on as the group lets out a raucous "Whooaahhh!"*]

HAROLD: [*Quickly*] Might know you'd take center stage!

EMORY: [*Quickly*] Shut up and lick your lips!

BERNARD: *Hold* it, everybody!

EMORY: And say, "Lesbian!"

THE ENTIRE GROUP: [*In unison, producing frozen smiles*] *LESBIAN!!*

[*The flash goes off! A cheer goes up! Emory rushes back to the camera, the group disperses. Rick slides open the terrace doors, goes outside*]

BERNARD: [*To Michael*] What happened to Scott?

MICHAEL: [*Coolly*] He had to go. He asked me to say his goodbyes.

HAROLD: I never even got a chance to say *hello!*

EMORY: And I'm sure you're heartbroken.

HAROLD: [*Feigning naïveté*] Why, whatever do you mean?

[*Rick enters from the terrace with the bottle of champagne*]

JASON: Yeah, what *do* you mean, Harold?

EMORY: Hallie doesn't care for the boy.

HAROLD: Scott is an acquired taste—which I have somehow failed to acquire. [*Bluntly, to Emory*] No, I don't. And you don't either.

EMORY: And neither does Bernard.

BERNARD: I've never said a word against Scott!

EMORY: [*To Bernard*] But you don't like him. I can tell. Larry liked him, I guess.

HAROLD: Larry just liked to *look* at him.

HANK: [*Correcting simply*] No, Larry *liked* him. He thought someone would be good for Michael.

[*A pause. Rick pours himself a flute of champagne, listens with interest*]

JASON: Scott's really kind of crazy. I mean, like, nuts. Really.

EMORY: Well, who isn't a little? [*Gestures with one hand*] *I'm* schizophrenic. [*Gestures with the other*] And so am *I*!

JASON: [*Continuing*] I found that out when I sold him my bike.

[*Michael eyes Jason suspiciously*]

HAROLD: [*Bluntly, to Jason, for Michael's benefit*] Scott's a crawler. And an opportunist.

MICHAEL: Don't hold back, Harold.

JASON: It's the crystal that makes him crazy.

MICHAEL: [*Seething*] How would you know that?!

JASON: When he came to our apartment to pick up the bike, his eyelids were on the ceiling. He sat on the floor for four hours playing a video game and didn't blink once. My boyfriend knows his dealer.

BERNARD: I thought he was clean.

JASON: That's *his* story.

MICHAEL: [*Snaps*] Scott does not lie!

JASON: [*To Michael, flatly*] Scott's the kind of guy who steals your drugs and then helps you look for them!

[*Donald freshens his drink with gin*]

DONALD: [*To Michael*] You don't know when he's lying and when he isn't.

RICK: He must tell the truth sometime.

HAROLD: Only when his imagination flags.

MICHAEL: [*To all, seriously facetious*] Scott is just a welcome antidote to heartiness.

[*Rick takes his guitar case upstairs*]

DONALD: He uses you, Michael. He plays you like a violin.

EMORY: He couldn't. Michael had all his old violins made into shoe trees.

HAROLD: Scott has made *Michael* into a shoe tree. It's one thing to get fucked. It's another to get fucked *over*.

MICHAEL: [*For Donald's benefit*] None of us ever likes any of our so-called "other" friends.

HANK: I like everybody and everybody's friends. Everybody here, I mean. *My* friends and their friends.

MICHAEL: That's because you're not a cunt, Hank.

DONALD: We all get rattled when we show up with a new trick, or a twinkie.

MICHAEL: Scott is neither a trick nor a twinkie, thank you very much!

EMORY: I guess you struck a nerve, Donald.

HAROLD: I think it was Jason who did the root canal.

RICK: [*Coming downstairs*] Is that how you think of us? That we're nothing but cheap tricks?

JASON: [*To Rick*] Speak for yourself.

RICK: I am speaking for myself. [*To group*] But, God, how could anybody's younger friends stand up next to you guys?

JASON: [*Drolly*] You mean for honesty and loyalty and charity?

RICK: I mean for *longevity*.

EMORY: Longevity?! You're not talking about old fucking redwoods again, are you?!

RICK: Longevity of friendship.

EMORY: I'll have you know I'm still in my deep forties.

BERNARD: If you're fortysomething, this must be your second time on earth!

DONALD: [*To Rick*] It's been a longer run for some of us than for others.

BERNARD: We do resent our "other friends." For once, you're absolutely right, Michael. We're proprietary as hell about each other. We're a closed corporation. We don't like anybody else. How could we, when we can barely stand each other?

EMORY: Don't be sil, we adore each other.

JASON: [*Sardonically*] Oh, yeah, sure you do!

BERNARD: We do! We just don't like outsiders. And not just you. [*To Emory*] How do you *really* feel about my wife?

EMORY: I adore your wife! How can you ask such a question? Women are not threats to gay men. "Other women." I don't know why. It's strange, but any guy I was ever interested in could have had all the girlfriends he wanted—just not boyfriends. We just get nervous to a degree when one of us shows up with a twinkie. [*Sees Michael glaring*] Eh . . . a recruit.

BERNARD: You wouldn't know what a real recruit was if you fell over one. I doubt if you know what the words "military service" mean.

EMORY: For your information, I've fallen over my share of recruits and serviced the military quite patriotically! Oh, Mary, don't ask and *don't tell*!

JASON: Do you have a patent on camp?

EMORY: [*To Jason, cuttingly*] Yeah, it's in *black* patent, sweetie! Some of us were more outrageous before Stonewall! Some of us were just as in-your-face as *you* ever hoped to be!

JASON: Flaming with resentment?

EMORY: [*With an edge*] We were funny, dear. [*Looks over the group; pointedly*] Now there're not so many of us left.

JASON: [*Re Emory's kind*] Mmm, you're an endangered species!

EMORY: [*Tough*] Listen, kiddo, before there were marches, there was a band.

JASON: [*To Emory*] And you were in the front line, were you? Well, congratu-lations.

EMORY: You don't have to get all Dorothy Darling with me now. I just happened to be walking by, minding my own business. Wearing a dress, of course, but minding my own business.

MICHAEL: Just out for the evening, trawling for love.

EMORY: We weren't just lifestyles *that* night, we were *news*!

MICHAEL: [*Aside, to Jason*] Stay off those floats! It's bad PR! [*Considering Jason*] A parade with three hundred thousand people in attendance, and the TV news has to focus on ten people in leather and chains and three of the ugliest drags known to man!

EMORY: Well, Stonewall changed my life. In fact, it brought me *to* life. It brought my hidden talents into a follow spot. I used to have to pay to get out of jail for doing what I *get paid* to do now!

RICK: I admire what you did. It took guts.

JASON: You may not be into leather or drag, Michael. You may not approve. But, like it or not, it's part of the real world.

DONALD: The public wants *theater*! Not dentists in their double-knit suits.

JASON: Yeah, if you want the boy next door, go next door.

EMORY: Didn't Joan Crawford say that?

MICHAEL: No, she said, "Just who is kidding *whom*."

[*Some mild laughter. Suddenly, Rick speaks . . .*]

RICK: I lie too. About who I am and what I am.

MICHAEL: What are you talking about?

RICK: Well . . . I'm not Vietnamese-American. My father wasn't an officer in the military. My mother didn't speak French. I just took a course at the Alliance. I'm Filipino.

HAROLD: So?

RICK: [*Calmly*] So I've lied about who I am all my adult life.

HANK: Why?

RICK: I always wanted to be *beyond* Polynesian, I wanted to be more "high born." More aristocratic. Do you know what the second largest population in Hong Kong is—after Americans? Filipino workers. Filipino *domestic* workers.

BERNARD: When it comes to domestic workers, what do you think about *my* people?

EMORY: You've never denied your background, Bernard.

BERNARD: I guess we all wonder just how honest we've been with ourselves. How much we've denied. I wish I could be more like Larry in that department. More up-front, no matter what. [*Reflectively*] When I was a kid in Grosse Pointe, there used to be a Chinese couple—who worked for the same family my mother did, the Dahlbecks. And their oldest kid, the

BERNARD (CONT'D): son, used to refer to them behind their backs as "the Slits." And when he did, I used to laugh. God only knows what he said behind *my* back about *me*. [*Laughs bitterly at thought*] I wonder if he used to laugh that way about the little colored hypocrite who had a crush on him? [*After a moment*] I went home last Christmas to see my mother. While I was there, I stopped by to say hello to him. He sold the big house and now lives alone in a big condo but still has two servants who live in.

JASON: *Two* servants! How can two people have a full-time job, working for just one guy? What's there to do?

BERNARD: Dust. Answer the phone. Take the abuse.

RICK: [*Sardonically*] Oh, well, *that's* always a full-time job.

BERNARD: Yeah, in some people's lives that's a *career*! Peter's a bitter and difficult old man now.

HANK: You think he's gay?

BERNARD: No, not at all.

EMORY: He couldn't be. Bernard described his furniture.

RICK: [*Reflectively*] There's even discrimination within the gay community; a bouncer just assumed my cock wasn't big enough to get into a leather bar. So he didn't let me in. God only knows what *he* was.

HAROLD: A bastard, for starters.

RICK: I've thought about plastic surgery—you know, "Westernize" my eyes.

HAROLD: I'd trade places with you just as you are. Oh, to have your skin. Oh, just to be your age—with your skin! I understand the contempt this country feels for the old. Getting old is the greatest sin in America. Worse than dying poor. [*Looks at Jason*] And why not, as long as Calvin Klein continues to make us feel awful about ourselves? But since we're no longer in hiding and it appears that we're going to live, what are we going to *do* with ourselves?

EMORY: It's not easy when you're asked to leave the dance floor. Why was it that with Larry, his age didn't seem to matter?

HAROLD: It did sometimes. And when it did, it hurt. It just didn't matter to everyone. [*Smiles at Hank; to Emory*] Larry was handsome, and you are not. Nor is Michael. Nor am I.

MICHAEL: Harold, you have an *obsession* with beauty. You always have.

JASON: [*Tauntingly*] You got something against beauty, Michael?

HAROLD: [*Coolly*] Thanks, Jason, but I can bridge this gap for myself. One, Michael, I'm an American. And, two, I'm human. And, three, I don't lie about such things. People don't want anything ugly. Clothes or cars or whatever. Of course, they may choose something that's fucking hideous or tacky or tasteless to others, but to them, you can bet it's beautiful. It's sexy! It sings! It *sells*! [*Reflectively*] The beauties of the world can never know us. And we can never know them. Because they never, ever have to deal with the nature of our agony in coming to grips with our baggage. Every day we are banking the fires. They live a life sustained in an oblivious, effortless, cozy glow—being worshiped, and adored, and catered to. Being . . . *wanted*.

RICK: [*"In-the-know" non sequitur*] Older gay men want younger men—just like older straight men want younger women.

BERNARD: And older women want good-looking young guys.

HAROLD: Well, love is one thing. Getting your pulse jump-started is another.

RICK: Yeah.

HAROLD: [*After a moment*] My outside has never reflected what's inside my brain, my aesthetic sense of myself. When I look in the mirror I do not see what I see in my mind s eye. I have never liked anything that fails to please me visually—including my own looks. I don't want to *have* Brad Pitt—I want to *look like* Brad Pitt. Anybody who says exteriors don't matter is full of shit. And you can quote me. Fulsomely.

JASON: [*Looking outside*] The rain has stopped.

EMORY: [*Generally*] *En voiture!*

[*Everyone starts to shift, stretch, make noise . . .*]

HANK: Could I say one quick thing before we break up?

BERNARD: Hang on, everyone!

[*The room quiets . . .*]

HANK: We'll go out of here, and all of this will be forgotten. But no matter, this was *done* for him. And for us. What we take away from here—the difference in the way we feel . . . and aren't even yet aware of—that's what this was about. Thank you all for being here. And thank you for not having asked all the wrong questions.

[*A final round of applause as Jason slides open the terrace doors*]

RICK: [*Re weather*] It's gonna be a nice day after all!

[*Everyone begins to break up and move*]

[*Harold goes to Jason, says a silent goodbye. Rick shakes hands with Hank . . .*]

BERNARD: [*To Emory*] You're not walking out of here with me looking like the eleventh-best-dressed woman!

EMORY: This is *not* my daytime look.

BERNARD: Well, get on your daytime *traveling* look and hurry up about it!

EMORY: I won't be a minute! Don't get in a tiz! I've just gotta tissue off my base and find my petit point.

[*Emory turns for the stairs. Harold and Jason finish their silent goodbye, Jason reaches for his cigarettes, takes out one, lights up, and goes outside. Michael furiously fans the smoke in his wake. Harold stops Emory at the base of the stairs . . .*]

HAROLD: [*To Michael*] I hate to dine and dash, but I've got to get back to my blond house-guest.

MICHAEL: [*Still fanning smoke*] Why rush?! You might be on *time*!

EMORY: Now, now, you two. We've already had dinner and a show.

HAROLD: [*To Emory*] Gimme a kiss, puppy.

EMORY: [*Kisses Harold on cheek, hurries up the stairs*] I wanna hear how it works out. All the lurid details.

HAROLD: [*To Emory*] I'll call you and give you a blow-by-blow account— oh, catch me, Dr. Freud, I'm slipping!

[*Harold hugs Hank, turns away. He picks up his rain cape and umbrella. Emory runs upstairs and peels off his eyelashes as he enters the bathroom*]

BERNARD: Bye, Hallie.

HAROLD: [*To Bernard*] Bye, love. Now, I don't want you cheating on your wife while she's out of town on an errand of mercy. [*Dryly*] Donald. We've got to stop meeting like this.

DONALD: Yeah, Harold, ain't it the truth.

HAROLD: You think I'm kidding!

[*Donald shakes his head, moves away. Jason turns to Bernard*]

JASON: [*To Bernard*] Will you help me bring in the bar cart?

BERNARD: Yeah, and it won't even send me into the well-known "downward spiral."

[*Bernard follows Jason; they exit to the terrace*]

RICK: Nice to see you, Harold.

HAROLD: *Sayonara*, Ricky. Sorry I can't say it in Tagalog. We should visit your homeland together—I'm mad to do the Pacific Rim. If you're ever in the Village, I'm in the book.

RICK: Don't be surprised if you hear from me.

HAROLD: Young man, nothing surprises *me*.

RICK: Michael, what'd you do with the rest of the raincoats?

MICHAEL: Hung 'em on the shower door.

[*Rick goes upstairs*]

HAROLD: [*To Michael*] Let's talk sometime within the next eighteen-hour window.

MICHAEL: Get out of here!

[*They air-kiss on both cheeks*]

HAROLD: Constant touch. Missing you already!

[*Harold whips on his cape with a great flourish and is out the door. Jason and Bernard lift the bar cart over the terrace door jamb. Hank puts on his coat. Rick lingers at the top of the stairs, looking down at Hank*]

BERNARD: [*To Hank*] How are you getting home?

HANK: Subway, I guess.

BERNARD: We'll share a cab and drop you off.

HANK: Thanks, but I'm way out of your way. Besides, I really want to be by myself.

[*Bernard nods*]

DONALD: So long, Hank . . .

HANK: Donald.

[*They hug. Donald turns back to the bar cart, takes the silver casserole chafing dish off the cart and into the kitchen*]

BERNARD: [*Loudly toward upstairs*] Let's GO, Emory! Thanks, Michael. I apologize if I lost it there for a moment.

MICHAEL: Amends are not necessary, Bernard. You know I appreciate your concern. By the way, are *you* still in therapy?

BERNARD: Just low-maintenance. Ciao, baby! Don't say it *ain't* been!

[*They kiss on the cheek. Bernard turns to Hank, and they silently and fondly hug each other. Emory comes out of the bathroom, heads downstairs carrying his small makeup case, his face clean. Rick enters the bathroom, closes the door*]

EMORY: [*To Michael*] Listen, *cheri*, it's been seamless. Absolutely seamless. When I go, I'd like to have a celebration exactly like this one.

MICHAEL: We have next Thursday open.

EMORY: Oh, that hurt worse than a slap with a suede glove!

[*Emory crosses to kiss Hank on the cheek*]

EMORY: [*Blows Michael a kiss*] Bye, dear. Stay pretty.

[*Bernard shakes his head, as he and Emory are out the front door*]

HANK: Some assortment, this group!

MICHAEL: Like a cheap box of chocolates. Some dark, some white. Even an exotic honey-dipped confection.

HANK: [*Reflectively*] Some soft, some brittle.

MICHAEL: [*Pleasantly*] And all either too sweet or too *bittersweet*. And that includes this old bonbon.

HANK: But we change whether we like it or not.

MICHAEL: You mean we get *older* whether we like it or not.

HANK: No, I mean we change. Change *is* possible. Growth *is* possible. I believe that, Michael.

MICHAEL: Some people change. Some people never change. Some just sit on the fence. I don't think we ever quite shake off whatever it is we settle on being somewhere around the age of three. It's all over by then. *I* believe that.

HANK: [*Salutes Michael with his stem glass*] Theorize, and drink champagne.

[*Hank drains his glass*]

MICHAEL: Listen, you don't think I've had *too much* analysis, do you? Or took a step too far? Like, *thirteen*. You know how I always overdo everything.

HANK: Well, none of it did you any harm. It couldn't have. It was either that or die.

MICHAEL: Hank, I've never told you how much I admire the way you dealt with Larry's extracurricular activities.

HANK: It may have been a marriage of now and then untrue bodies, but it was one of constantly true minds. Messy. Like life. [*Changes subject*] Listen, there isn't any possible way to say . . .

MICHAEL: [*Cuts him off, quietly*] No. Don't. Please.

HANK: I'm not. Not *now*. I'm going to try to write my feelings down and send them to you—and I know that's risky with a writer, but it's what I want to do.

MICHAEL: Oh, Hank . . . have no fear. I want to thank *you*. I won't forget this afternoon. For so many reasons.

[*Michael and Hank embrace and part. Michael opens the door for Hank, who goes out. Michael closes the door as Jason enters from the terrace*]

JASON: Everybody gone?

MICHAEL: Well, the tide's not *completely* out.

JASON: Why do you dislike me so? I don't think it's my politics. I actually think we're on the same side.

MICHAEL: The only thing we share is our anger.

JASON: You know, you might be useful if you were going in the right direction.

MICHAEL: Don't patronize me.

JASON: Hardly. Your contentment, your complacency may have allowed you to survive, but they won't get me through. I've got to do something about the way things are.

MICHAEL: You dismiss us—me and my kind—and worse yet, you make us responsible for everything you take for granted! How do you think you got it?

JASON: Well, you and your cronies have sadly outlived your purpose.

MICHAEL: So you'd be just as glad if we didn't exist. We're in your way.

JASON: That's right. You're expendable.

MICHAEL: Listen, Jason, if it weren't for boys like us, there wouldn't be men like you.

JASON: Now who's being patronizing?

MICHAEL: [*Bluntly*] You're the one who stole Scott's bike, aren't you?

JASON: What?

MICHAEL: You did drugs with him, and he passed out, and you took his bike, probably thinking it was still yours.

JASON: Michael, I don't do drugs, and I'm not a thief. I take an oath on my life—on my partner's life!

MICHAEL: If I didn't like you before, now I really have no use for you.

JASON: Well, if you won't listen to reason—

[*Jason starts to leave*]

MICHAEL: [*Softer tone*] Wait! I *will* listen to reason.

JASON: [*Stops and turns*] I sold him my old bike, which, I assume, was paid for with your money. He came by to look at it, said he'd think it over, and left. Half an hour later he called and said he'd take it. When I took it by his place, he asked if I'd like to do some "K" with him and go dancing, but I said no. I left the bike with him and left him alone. I'm not lying.

[*Donald enters from the kitchen*]

DONALD: [*To Jason*] Are you staying in the city or going back to the Hamptons?

JASON: I'm going back. [*Puts on raincoat*] But I have to stop and pick up the mail and get a sweater. It's colder on the island than I thought. Why—you want to get the Jitney together? Or take a train?

DONALD: I drove into town. My car's in a garage between First and Second. I don't mind waiting, if you don't mind driving. I've had a little more to drink than I thought.

JASON: I don't mind at all!

DONALD: You ought to come over to my place. I have a fire almost every evening. And I have lots of sweaters you're welcome to. Not as many as Michael, of course.

JASON: I wouldn't want to go in Michael's sweater closet for fear of being killed by falling Missonis.

[*Donald laughs a little drunkenly. Michael is slightly disturbed by Donald's condition*]

DONALD: [*To Michael, drolly*] I washed the stemware by hand.

MICHAEL: You don't still do windows, do you?

DONALD: Thanks . . . for the memories.

MICHAEL: Say no more.

DONALD: Where's *my* coat?

[*Donald stumbles on a rung of the stairs*]

MICHAEL: [*Sotto voce to Jason, caringly*] Will you . . . uh . . . will you be sure that he . . .

JASON: [*Nods; sotto voce*] Yeah, yeah, sure.

DONALD: [*Turns to them with dignity*] Surely, I'm not the first person you've ever seen fall *up* the stairs.

MICHAEL: Donald, I don't think you *had* a coat. Take one of mine if you like. [*Dryly*] And there's no danger of avalanche. You don't have to hazard the Missoni section for the rain gear.

DONALD: *I had a blazer.* I know I could find it if it had hair around it.

JASON: [*Picks up Donald's blazer*] Here it is.

[*Donald crosses to Jason, who helps him on with his jacket*]

DONALD: Thank you, dear boy.

JASON: So you're in real estate? [*Donald nods*] You think a good bar and deli would go out there?

DONALD: [*Friendly*] We'll do some pub crawling and see what's on its last legs. I know them all. I've long considered writing a book: *The Alcoholic's Guide to the Hamptons.* Not only furnish a complete listing of the best bars, but also have a vital statistics page with all the bar *obits,* that is, *celebrations* of bars that've died during the year.

JASON: Sounds great. I've been a flight attendant, a host in a restaurant, and, of course, a bartender. I think I could make a go of it with a place of my own. I'm good with the public.

DONALD: I can see why—you have charm. Not an easy thing to come by.

JASON: [*Smiles*] It's still raining pretty hard. Why don't you give me the ticket for your car and wait here. I'll be right back for you.

DONALD: [*Hands over ticket*] With the greatest of pleasure. No need to come up, just buzz and I'll go down.

JASON: And maybe have a cup of coffee in the meantime. [*For Michael's benefit*] There's plenty left in that nice, simple pot.

[*Donald laughs at Michael's annoyance. Jason goes out the front door*]

MICHAEL: [*To Donald*] Well, that's the last you'll see of him or that vulgar Lincoln Continental.

DONALD: [*Crosses to Michael*] Tell me the truth, Michael. You miss it, don't you?

MICHAEL: On occasion, yes. On a nice occasion—like today or a birthday or New Year's—something clear and chilled to perfection doesn't seem half bad. Yes, Donald, I miss that fine, cozy, boozy feeling when it was at its best. But it's not possible. I'm a drunk, and I can't drink. Ever, ever again.

DONALD: Pity. [*Smiles*] It was a very nice afternoon, Michael. And we got through it without ever using the word "dysfunctional." It was just what Larry would have liked. Done just the way he would have liked it, with just the people he liked.

MICHAEL: [*Tongue-in-cheek, re his expensive wristwatch*] You know, I like my Cartier watch better than any of those people I invited this afternoon. And I *don't* have a Rolex, no matter what your new boyfriend says.

DONALD: Didn't you hear Jason? He already has a lover.

MICHAEL: [*Looks at his Cartier*] Yeah, they ought to be halfway to Key West by now.

DONALD: [*Lightly*] Michael, I trust him. [*Laughs feebly*] Once upon a time I'd have had a chance with someone like Jason. But these days, I hardly stack up to Larry. But . . . I must have something he's interested in.

MICHAEL: I don't think it's your mind—*or* your body.

DONALD: Well, if he thinks I'm rich, he's in for an epiphany. I'm just cozy. And I can be helpful to him. And who knows, maybe he does *like* older guys. He liked Larry. [*With meaning*] Some other young men did too.

MICHAEL: [*Oblivious*] I guess I was just always so goddamned jealous of Larry. Of his looks. Of his body. How he seemed to be blessed. How even his toes were beautiful. Of how he seemed to get every guy he ever wanted. Of how he and Hank seem to beat the odds and stay together.

DONALD: You know, if you read Christopher Isherwood's diaries, you really wake up to find out nothing for nobody is ever easy in life.

MICHAEL: You know, Donald, you're not the only one who can recite the alphabet! Isherwood and Don Bachardy, were always my ideal couple. But I was stunned to learn their relationship wasn't what I thought it was. Not what I thought I'd *missed*. You must think it absurd that I was shocked to find out . . .

DONALD: To find out that they were human too?

MICHAEL: Yeah, I guess so.

DONALD: Nobody has it all, Michael. Each of us has a lot to survive. Nobody escapes.

MICHAEL: Yeah. Not even beautiful Larry. It's a shame to never have made a success of love with someone. But it just doesn't work for me. It can work for others. In fact, for others, it's essential. But it just can't work for me. It never has. For me, it's always been better to travel hopefully than to ever arrive.

[*The downstairs door buzzes*]

DONALD: [*Facetiously*] That would be my car and driver. Or should I say, my *designated* driver.

MICHAEL: You worry me, Donald. Be careful.

DONALD: You've mellowed, Michael. And that's to your credit. But don't ever lose your anger. Without that, you're a living dead man. Not a vampire. Something worse.

MICHAEL: I know. I know. Now, listen, keep your hands to yourself on the L.I.E. I don't want you dead in a car crash—even when you're not driving.

DONALD: Yessir. [*Lightly*] To be continued.

[*They hug, and Donald exits silently. Michael closes the door as Rick comes out of the bathroom and down the stairs*]

RICK: I hope you don't mind, I opened one of those little bars of soap, Michael. Like, I couldn't resist the label.

MICHAEL: That's what they're there for.

RICK: Thanks. Nice hand towels too. French?

MICHAEL: Italian. Thank *you* for the song. Maybe you ought to consider a really sensible career move, like show business.

RICK: I've got other ideas   all thanks to Larry.

MICHAEL: Good on you, as the Australians say.

[*Rick goes to the door, turns to Michael*]

RICK: By the way, I couldn't help overhearing . . . Jason was telling you the truth. He didn't take Scott's bike—*I* did.

MICHAEL: *You?*

RICK: It was my first time to do crystal, and I never want to do it again. Honestly. That's definitely not my scene. But I just couldn't resist the temptation, the curiosity. So we went to his place.

MICHAEL: Why did you take his bike?

RICK: I can't explain it. It was crazy. I was speeding—and in a hurry on top of it. Scott was in the shower, and the bike was by the door, and I just took it. But I took it *back*! I didn't *want* it! I didn't even remember where he lived. I had to ask Larry.

MICHAEL: Did you have sex with Scott too?

RICK: I wasn't interested.

MICHAEL: You knew Scott before today? You met him at the hospital at night?

[*Rick nods*]

MICHAEL: [*Shocked*] He never told me he went there without me.

RICK: Maybe like Larry, he kept his friends compartmentalized too.

MICHAEL: I guess he *did*.

RICK: At first, I thought that he was Larry's lover, but then I began to see Hank and found out the story.

MICHAEL: Funny, I'd never even considered it—Scott and Larry.

RICK: I don't really know if they'd ever had a thing or not. I doubt it. Scott never said so.

MICHAEL: The two of you talked about it?

RICK: [*Nods*] The night we did drugs. The night I "borrowed" his bike.

MICHAEL: [*Incredulous*] But you didn't even say hello to each other today.

RICK: I said "Hi" to him outside. He didn't want you to know we knew each other—or why.

MICHAEL: Scott still isn't aware you're the one?

RICK: [*Shakes his head*] I never had a chance to explain.

MICHAEL: You don't think Larry and Scott had a thing, do you?

RICK: [*Shakes his head*] I just think Larry was a soft touch.

MICHAEL: Scott asked him for money?

RICK: He just told him what a hard time he was having making it through school, and Larry felt sorry for him. Frankly, I think Scott just wanted it to buy drugs.

[*Suddenly, the door buzzes. Michael goes to the wall panel, pushes the door release button*]

MICHAEL: Goodbye, Rick.

RICK: I hope we see each other again sometime.

MICHAEL: Yes . . . yes, of course.

[*Rick pulls on his coat. The apartment bell rings*]

MICHAEL: *Now what?* [*Michael opens the door*] [*Surprised*] Hank! What's wrong?

HANK: Nothing. The flowers—

MICHAEL: Oh, I can bring them over in the morning—you don't have to bother with them now.

HANK: No, no, you keep them. I just want Patsy and Jessica's note. It was very beautiful. They must have put a lot of thought into it. I guess I'd forget my head if it wasn't . . .

[*Rick picks up the envelope, hands it to Hank*]

HANK: Thanks, Rick.

RICK: I'll walk you to the subway. I go your way.

HANK: Okay. Good night, Michael.

RICK: Yes, and thanks again.

MICHAEL: You're welcome, Rick. And *bon chance.*

[*Hank smiles at Rick, puts his hand on Rick's shoulder, and they go out. Michael turns to survey the damage [which isn't all that bad], and exits the terrace doors. For a moment, the stage is empty, then the doorbell rings. Michael enters from the terrace with a stack of plates and takes them into the kitchen. The bell rings again. Michael enters, turns the lights down low, crosses to the door to open it*]

MICHAEL: [*Crestfallen*] Ohh, *you* again! How'd you get in this time?!

HAROLD: Hank and Rick were just leaving together. Interesting.

MICHAEL: [*Deliberately*] *The . . . party . . . is . . . over.*

[*Harold "casually" enters. Michael steps into the corridor, looks about*]

HAROLD: Now it's so dark in here, you need night-vision glasses. I take it you were expecting someone other than myself just now.

[*Michael comes back into the room, closes the door, flips on the lights, turns to Harold . . .*]

MICHAEL: [*Ignores the remark*] I thought I'd gotten rid of you.

HAROLD: [*Puts on dark glasses*] I guess so. When you opened the door, your face sank like a lost cause.

MICHAEL: [*Matter-of-fact*] I thought it might be Scott.

HAROLD: Don't fret, he'll be back. He's not through with you yet.

[*Michael is annoyed, tries not to show it*]

MICHAEL: [*Reasonably*] I love him, Harold.

HAROLD: But he doesn't love you. He never has, and he never will, no matter how much you invest in him. And that's the plain and simple truth. If you want someone, go after someone you can get.

MICHAEL: I don't *want* anyone I can get!

HAROLD: [*Offhandedly*] Who'd Jason leave with?

MICHAEL: Donald.

HAROLD: *Not* so interesting. But interesting.

MICHAEL: God, Jason's so common, I bet he smokes in the shower.

HAROLD: Listen, every time I look in Scott's face I think of Easter Island.

MICHAEL: [*Testily*] When I met Scott, I knew instantly he had intelligence and potential.

HAROLD: Well, he *had* seen a movie with subtitles.

MICHAEL: I thought you were so eager to get home to that blond who was with you at the service!

HAROLD: I am. He's almost *obscenely* sexy, dontcha think?

MICHAEL: [*Magnanimously*] I'm not being judgmental about your choice of companions, Harold. You know I don't give a good goddamn about morals, but *taste* is everything!

[*Harold sucks a tooth*]

What're you going to do with that boy? Tonight, I mean. When you *finally* get home.

HAROLD: We *may* pull a condom over the entire apartment and have safe sex, or I *may* just take my 800-milligram Xanax with a tall beverage and isolate.

MICHAEL: Well, I hope you're careful. After all, who knows about his status?

HAROLD: I know his status, and he knows mine. But maybe I'll just have to settle for chinning myself on his nipple rings.

MICHAEL: And you gave that trash the key to your apartment?

HAROLD: Scott has the key to yours, doesn't he?

MICHAEL: You can spare me any character analysis of Scott.

HAROLD: That oughta be like a dial tone.

MICHAEL: You disapprove, like Donald.

HAROLD: I don't do *anything* like Donald! It would be too easy to call Scott a cock-teaser. It would also be unfair, because I think he has *some* consideration for you in his own mixed-up, sorry way.

MICHAEL: You just think I'm a fool.

HAROLD: All you need are bells and a scepter.

MICHAEL: [*Tongue-in-cheek bravura*] I like a *challenge*! [*Grimly*] He let me down about school. Again.

HAROLD: He'll let you down again and again and again. And you'll forgive him again and again and again. I think that's what love is all about.

MICHAEL: You've never let me down, Harold.

HAROLD: You never tried to put me through college.

MICHAEL: [*Short*] What did you come back for?! Are you still *stoned*!?

HAROLD: I wish I were, but I didn't want to blur the edges before I returned. I wanted to be completely . . . well, as you always put it—I wanted my faculties functioning at their maximum natural capacity.

[*There is a more awkward pause, a silence, between them as Harold looks directly at Michael*]

HAROLD: [*After a moment*] I've got AIDS. It's still with us, you know—despite the dancing in the streets. [*Reacts to Michael's expression*] Now, don't go and get all . . .

MICHAEL: [*Interrupting sharply*] I'm not going to go and get all anything!

[*Contrary to what he says, Michael seems dazed*]

HAROLD: Well, for God's sake, don't cry.

MICHAEL: You know I never cry in a *real* crisis.

HAROLD: [*Indirectly*] It's the lies we tell ourselves that really matter.

MICHAEL: [*Ignores this*] What about all the new medications?

HAROLD: It's probably a tad too late for the cocktail hour. Besides, who knows if I'm one of those who can tolerate the mix.

MICHAEL: [*Stupefied*] How long have you known?

HAROLD: Two months.

MICHAEL: *Two months!*

HAROLD: Yeah, I'm a tricky little thing.

MICHAEL: How do you feel? Do you *know* how you feel?

HAROLD: [*Removes dark glasses*] In an odd way, like Hank said, I feel relieved. I've spent a lifetime thinking about death. One thing I know I'm going to try to do: be a better Jew. And by that I don't mean run to temple every time I have an anxiety attack. What I mean is—try to practice some of the things I really believe in.

MICHAEL: Are you gonna get religion now so you can go to heaven?

HAROLD: Not at all. Catholics are worried about what comes after—you know, carry your cross today, and go to the party later. Jews are more focused on the here and now—business, family, food. All that kosher stuff is based on living well. I'm going to try to live well in the here and now and let tomorrow take care of itself.

MICHAEL: I'm all for that. You mean you knew when you went to St. Bart's?!

HAROLD: I didn't go to St. Bart's in the West Indies. I went to St. Vincent's in the West Village. Well, the paramedics had to haul me away. I had Pneumocystis. I had to stay for the full twenty-one days. Then home for another . . .

MICHAEL: Why in the world didn't you tell me?! Why didn't you call me?

HAROLD: I did call you.

MICHAEL: From the *hospital*?! I thought you were calling from . . .

HAROLD: That's what I *wanted* you to think. I certainly didn't want to see anybody, and I didn't want anybody to see me. I was too sick. But tonight, well, I wanted you to know.

MICHAEL: [*Blankly*] No one else knows?

HAROLD: Naturally, my doctor knows. And the odd divine, tawny attendant. Actually, I don't care who knows I have AIDS, I just don't want anyone to know I'm gay.

[*He turns toward the front door*]

MICHAEL: Where're you going?!

HAROLD: Home to that heavenly creature.

MICHAEL: Wait a minute.

HAROLD: [*Turns back*] Why?

MICHAEL: [*Heatedly serious*] Oh, Harold, you can't be that glib about mortality!

HAROLD: [*Eyeball to eyeball*] I can.

[*A pause. They continue to look at each other directly . . .*]

MICHAEL: [*Heartfelt, quietly*] I'll be there for you, you know that.

HAROLD: [*Seriously*] It never crossed my mind that you wouldn't be. [*A beat*] That is, if you don't perish in a private plane crash on your next junket to the Cote D'Azur. [*After a moment, with meaning*] I know you'll do whatever I want. Whatever it takes—fight City Hall, face the dawn with arms linked, ride a *float* even.

MICHAEL: [*Without rancor*] Harold, I'm serious.

HAROLD: I know you are, and that's why I can't be.

MICHAEL: [*After a moment*] We'll get through this together.

[*Harold is both touched and made somewhat anxious by the genuine declaration of love for him*]

HAROLD: [*Turns to leave*] I really do have to go now, and I'm not just trying to get out of here—although I'm trying like hell to get out of here. [*Old brand of wryness*] I don't want blondie to break the Lalique samovar.

[*Goes, stops, turns, says genuinely*]

HAROLD: I had such spilkus I just couldn't *not* not tell you any longer. I know that's a triple negative, but fuck it. When I heard you speak at the memorial this afternoon, I knew I had to come clean. I liked what you said about Larry. I hope you'll say a few words about me . . .

MICHAEL: Harold.

HAROLD: Something like, "He was a smart-ass with heart. A Scorpio with vulnerability."

[*Michael nods, refusing to give in to the moment . . .*]

MICHAEL: I'll think of something. [*Then, sincerely*] I do wish you would have told me earlier.

HAROLD: I didn't want anybody there!

MICHAEL: [*Incredulously*] You didn't want *me* there?! *Me,* of *all* people?!

HAROLD: Yes, you of *all* people!

MICHAEL: How can you say a thing like that about me?!

HAROLD: Now you sound like my mother!

MICHAEL: [*Sardonically*] By the way, tell me, is your mother still dead?

HAROLD: [*Half incensed, half amused*] She is presently deceased, yes. But when I'm around you, I'm not so sure! [*Hating what he's about to say*] You know, nobody, *nobody* can get to me the way you and my mother can! [*Corrects himself*] Could! [*Quickly*] Can! [*Tries again*] Could . . . and can!

MICHAEL: Calm down.

HAROLD: Oh, eat shit and die!

MICHAEL: You have every right to be angry.

HAROLD: You know, I think I liked you better when you were drunk!

MICHAEL: You know what? I liked *you* better when I was drunk too!

HAROLD: [*Quickly, with "dignity"*] I also think with whatever time I have left, I oughtta start hanging out with a better class of losers!

MICHAEL: [*Matching him*] Well, you can start tonight in your own bed!

HAROLD: [*Matching him*] At least, there's somebody *in my bed tonight*!

MICHAEL: [*"Grandly"*] I hate you when you get like this.

HAROLD: [*"Philosophically"*] Well, you *are* what you *hate*.

MICHAEL: [*Wearily*] Oh, Harold, let's *not*!

HAROLD: [*Fiercely vulgar*] No, goddamn it, *let's*!

MICHAEL: [*Evenly*]: We're too old for this game!!

HAROLD: [*Facetiously*] Too analyzed, too grown up, too mature?!

MICHAEL: *Yes!* And too *old*!

HAROLD: *I'm* the one who's analyzed, grown up, and mature! *You're* just old! You peaked at eighteen, and it's been downhill ever since. And you are now fifty-nine and counting!

MICHAEL: Thank you and fuck you!!

[*Michael quickly picks up Harold's rain cape and umbrella and tosses them to him*]

MICHAEL: *GETOUTTAHERE!*

HAROLD: [*Exiting apartment*] *CALLYATOMORROW!!!*

[*Michael slams the front door. After a moment, Michael turns, slowly goes to open the bar. He stands, looking at all the colored bottles and sparkling glasses. As Michael stands staring at the tempting display . . .  [will he or won't he?] . . . slowly, all lights fade to black*]


END OF ACT II

END OF PLAY

Dominick Dunne

# About the Author

Mart Crowley was born in Vicksburg, Mississippi. After graduating from the Drama Department of The Catholic University of America in Washington D.C., he was Production Assistant to the acclaimed director Elia Kazan. Besides his plays for the theatre, he adapted and produced William Friedkin's film version of *The Boys in the Band*, produced the long-running ABC television series *Hart to Hart*, and co-authored Kay Thompson's *Eloise Takes a Bawth*. He lives in New York City.